American Structuralism

JANUA
LINGUARUM   Series Maior 102

Studia Memoriae
Nicolai van Wijk Dedicata

edenda curat

C. H. van Schooneveld

Indiana University

American Structuralism

Dell Hymes and John Fought

Mouton Publishers
The Hague · Paris · New York

Main body of text originally published in
Current Trends in Linguistics, Vol. 13, part 2
© 1975 Mouton, The Hague

ISBN: 90-279-3228 X (Clothbound)
        90-279-3428 2 (Paperback)
© 1981, Mouton Publishers, The Hague, The Netherlands
Printed in Germany

CONTENTS

0. INTRODUCTION

This article must be something of a prolegomenon to the work it should describe. So far as American structuralism is concerned, serious historiography has barely begun. To be sure, there exists writing that has historical flavor, and even writing that makes claims to historical adequacy, but little of it is based on scholarship, if by scholarship one means the seeking out of evidence and the testing of interpretations against it.

The explanation for this lies in the recency of the period which most linguists would associate with the term, 'American structuralism'. One might almost say that those interested in it remember it, and those too young to remember it are not interested. For both groups, 'American structuralism' does not seem a historical problem, but a known quantity. For most younger linguists, it denotes a period just before the advent of Chomsky's version of transformational grammar, when linguistics limited itself to surface structure and ignored or positively opposed the study of meaning and the investigation of universals. Its faults are to be explained by the dominance of a perverse behaviorist, antimentalist ideology, or, more charitably, by the field work context in which it first arose. In any case, there is little motivation to serious historiography; the period is over, it was wrong-headed, and its significant characteristics are both known and explained.

This widely repeated portrait of 'American structuralism' is mistaken, almost ludicrously so. Enough is already available to show that American structuralism has had a complex development, extending from the first years of the century, and that Chomskyan linguistics, as contrasted with, say, Prague structuralism, has continued some fundamental traits of its predecessor, recovered others, and unwittingly rediscovered still others. The study of meaning and the investigation of universals, for instance, were vital to leading figures of the earlier period. The analysis of underlying relationships, semantically significant, was pursued by leading linguists of the 1930s (cf. Hymes 1971a:236, n. 10 on Sapir, and 1971a:236, n. 9, 1963:95 on Whorf).

The image that most scholars today hold of 'American structuralism' is a construction out of elements in the work of a few men dominant in a short period of time. These men, the 'Bloomfieldians', who held the center of the stage for ten or fifteen years (about 1942 to 1957) were the immediate target for Chomsky's intellectual attack and bid for academic power. But to form one's understanding of a period from the accounts of its successors is no better than to form one's understanding of Chomsky's work from accounts by those whom he displaced. Either way, it is rather like characterizing the United States or the Soviet Union relying only on the press of the other country.

Such cases are all too common in the history of ideas. Despite its varied debts to classical writing and scholarship, the early Christian church rejected classical antiquity as an age of idolatry preceding the advent of the true faith. The Enlightenment stamped the Christian middle ages with the image of a dark period of idolatry and repression, discovering precedent for its own concerns in classical antiquity. The Romantic movement stamped the Enlightenment with the image of a period of ideology and superficial optimism, discovering support for its own concerns in medieval times. Today we realize that the middle ages were not without science and invention, as the Enlightenment image might have it, and that the Enlightenment was not without history and realism, as the Romantic movement might have it. The pattern of the slaying of fathers, and the rediscovery of grandfathers, continues nevertheless. The rejection of traditional grammar by a generation of structuralists, and its revaluation by Chomsky, is a case in point. The rejection of a generation of structuralism by Chomsky is one half of another, with hints of revaluation now appearing. One liberating effect of historiography may be to save us from eternally repeating this pattern.

In this article we shall be sometimes in the position of seeming to advocate a revaluation of pre-Chomskyan structuralism. In large part this is inescapable. A cardinal tenet of historiography is that one understand an approach in its own terms, understand its answers in terms of the questions it itself asked (Collingwood 1939), and understand the questions in terms of the times. This requirement often puts one in the position of defending a feature of the past against misinterpretation of it in the present. Such defense is not necessarily advocacy.

It would, however, be disingenuous not to admit that both of us have roots in the body of work whose historiography is our main concern. Both have followed the career of the 'Chomskyan revolution' or 'Chomskyan paradigm' (Koerner 1972b) without being able to experience conversion. Perhaps these personal histories qualify us for our task, in that we meet one of the desiderata for the historian of linguistics set by Malkiel (1969:532 — an invaluable essay). Moreover, one of us (Hymes) resisted the preceding 'paradigm', that of the Bloomfieldians, as well, finding spiritual sustenance as a graduate student in rediscovering a variant tradition in Boas and Sapir; the other (Fought) was trained in a late version of the Bloomfieldian approach to which the figures of both Sapir and Chomsky stand symbolically in opposition. If our roots give us sympathies with the subject of our account, they are not identical sympathies, and we hope that our joint view of the materials considered here is the more balanced for that.[1]

Jakobson has cogently said (1964:1136–7) of the sequence 'traditional grammar', 'structuralism', 'Chomskyan transformational grammar':

> Yesterday linguistics, said to be structural, stood defiantly opposed to the traditional doctrine. If today we hear slogans calling for the rehabilitation of 'traditional grammar', this is neither retreat nor eclecticism. In Hegel's terms, one might say that the antithesis of the traditional tenet yielded to a negation of negation, i.e. to a synthesis between the immediate and the remote past. This rehabilitation of the latter . . . must not be mistaken for an imitation or actual restoration of the past invoked. The ancestors would hardly recognize their descendants, even though the latter claim that their 'roots are firmly in traditional linguistics'.

The same holds, mutatis mutandis, for any rehabilitation of the tradition of earlier structuralism here. Our views of theoretical issues and directions find nourishment in the past, but not a home there.

Our purpose, then, is to justify, not structuralism, but its study: to have the history of American structuralism taken as something complex, uncertainly known, and in need of research, so that an article such as this, if written ten or twenty years from now, may have a wealth of basic research to draw on. We attack a received image of the earlier period because it is false, but also because it cuts off inquiry. We think inquiry into the actual history desirable and rewarding, because of the intrinsic interest of the material, and because of the interests of linguists themselves.

Developments in linguistics have a personal and social dimension, as well as an intellectual one, and occur as they do partly because of those dimensions. It would be of considerable intrinsic interest, then, to trace such matters as the dramatic changes in personal intellectual outlook of Sapir and of Bloomfield between the second and fourth decades of the century; the causes of Yale's invitations to Sapir and Bloomfield successively to Sterling Professorships at a time when linguistics hardly existed as a profession; the causes of the University of Chicago allowing Sapir and Bloomfield successively to leave for Yale; the role of a declined Sterling Professorship in founding the Survey of California Indian Languages; the effect of the social atmosphere of Yale, including anti-Semitism, on the personal lives of Sapir and of Bloomfield; the role of joint government service in New York City during the Second World War on the formation of the inner circle of Bloomfieldians; the causes of the dispersion of Sapir's inner circle, geographically and in terms

---

[1] A participant in one of the varieties of post-war structuralism assessed Hymes (1970) as follows (F. Trager 1972:96): 'Hymes . . . traces the history of language and culture studies, but in so doing he undermines the work of those he cites . . .'

of influence, in the years following his death in 1939 (put otherwise, one might try to imagine the shape of American structural linguistics in the 1940s had Sapir lived and been active until age 65 (1949)); the role of the European emigré community in New York in the formation of the Linguistic Circle of New York and the founding of the journal *Word*; the antagonistic response of some Bloomfieldians to the most distinguished linguist among the European emigrés, Roman Jakobson, in contrast to the welcome provided by Boas (who took him into his house); the role of defense funds for research and scholarships in forming the linguistic profession in the United States and in supporting the successive paradigmatic communities of Bloomfieldians and Chomskyans; the reflection of conflicts among linguistic groups in government and foundation funding agencies; the role of missionary enterprise in providing a base and constraint in Pike's development of tagmemics; the professional and linguistic interplay between the Summer Institute of Linguistics and the American Bible Society; the consequences of the election of Eisenhower for the circle around Trager (Smith, Birdwhistell, Hall, and others), which was based in the Foreign Service Institute of the State Department until 1952; the consequences to linguistics in anthropology of the inability of Swadesh to obtain a job in the United States during the McCarthy period; the role of the Society of Fellows at Harvard in the development of linguistics in the Cambridge area; the means by which the journal *Word* was lost to the circle around Weinreich in New York; the curious absence of a major center of Chomskyan grammar at any Ivy League institution; etc.

It can be urged on general grounds, in the interests of linguists, that the self-awareness to which historiography contributes ought to be part of the sciences of man (cf. Scholte 1973). This is of course to call for scientists to transcend the effects hitherto of what Kuhn (1962) calls a 'paradigm', a characteristic of which is inability of the adherents of one paradigm to understand the adherents of another. This call would be in keeping with the conception held by the great figures in the founding of the American discipline, e.g. Bloomfield (1914:325): '. . . linguistic science is a step in the self-realization of man.'

One can argue for historiography on specific grounds as well. An appeal to scholarly standards, or to justice to misrepresented predecessors, may move some linguists to research in the subject. Others may be moved by consideration of the present situation in linguistics. Current images of the history of American structuralism serve boundary maintenance, legitimating some concerns and contributions, and excluding others. In a time of renewed diversity some may wish to change the boundaries of legitimate ancestry as part of a change of the boundaries of the acceptable present. Indeed, the cultivation of new directions seems always to require some reassessment of the contributions and limitations of predecessors for its own orientation. These considerations apply especially to current interest in discourse, conversational analysis, pragmatics, semiotics, analysis of language in context and interaction, variability, and the social relevance and use of linguistic work in education and other areas. At the very least there is instructive precedent in the complex history of American structuralism in this century, but the opportunity to benefit from it is lost so long as the prevailing image of the history of American linguistics treats the period before 1957 as already known, and the developments before and after as purely intellectual affairs. The philosopher Alfred North Whitehead once said something to the effect that a science which hesitates to forget its past is lost, but a science cut off from its past is an orphan, and, in a field like linguistics, likely to illustrate a maxim of Santayana, that those who do not know the past are condemned to repeat it (cf. Thorne 1965:75, Lyons 1968:3, Hockett 1968:81–2, Maher 1973:47). It is likely largely to ape progress, by reinventing what it has forgotten.

These remarks are addressed to linguists because control of linguistics is necessary to the historiography, and because historians of linguistics have so far been drawn almost entirely from the ranks of linguists. Yet it should be acknowledged that other kinds of competence are required as well. Linguistic knowledge can provide for the internal history of work and ideas, but, like a purely internal approach to the history of a language, it can not offer much in the way of causal explanation. It can identify the materials, problems, and possibilities of a period intellectually, but the outcome of a period lies in the interaction of the possibilities of its internal development with personal, institutional, national, and even international factors (accounts of American structuralism almost never mention the depression, the Second World War, and the repression of Marxist orientations in the 1950s). These kinds of evidence are more usually controlled by biographers, social historians, sociologists of knowledge, and the like. An historical explanation of the development of linguistics should not of course be limited to any one discipline, but should embrace the institutionalization and development of academic disciplines generally, together with the climates of opinion that affect them all. There may be much in the development of linguistics to interest the historian and the sociologist of science, and it is to be hoped that such scholars will contribute to research in the field, or at least to the training of those who do the research. (It may be easier for linguists to acquire this training than for nonlinguists to acquire the necessary linguistics.) It may be that the closest allies of historiographically oriented linguists, so far as American structuralism is concerned, will be in the field of American civilization, whose scholars may provide contextual understanding of 'lives and times', while linguists provide analysis of 'works'. There are already signs of this (cf. Rollins 1971). In any case, linguists must build ties with other historically oriented disciplines if linguistics is to have the history it deserves.

As said at the outset, this article must be something of a prolegomenon to the work it should describe. In the absence of a coherent body of scholarship, the scope of the subject is problematic, and must be discussed first. After this general discussion (1), we consider the kinds of materials that are available as contributions to the historiography of the subject (2), partly from a methodological standpoint.

We then consider the various materials more closely in terms of a series of substantive aspects of the subject. In historiography of American structuralism two explanatory themes have been introduced so often as to amount to clichés: behaviorism and antagonism to meaning, on the one hand, and anthropological field work, on the other. The first often seems a harsher, the second a more charitable explanation, but the two are also often combined. We will assess both these explanations, but let us point out here that there is much more to be explained than these themes address. There is the very emergence of a discipline of linguistics, amid others concerned with language (3); the careers and characteristics of such major figures as Boas, Sapir, Whorf, and Bloomfield (4); the formation of 'paradigmatic' communities around successive approaches to synchronic structure (5); and the treatment of preceding approaches, and crucial examples, in quasi-historical technical literature (6). All of these subjects arise in the literature; we will consider each in the order indicated — it is roughly chronological, and reflects something of the foci of successive concern of linguists themselves.

Our presentation includes some exposition of the history itself. This has been necessary, because of the pervasiveness of inadequate or mistaken notions. There does not appear to exist a general knowledge of the subject, such that one could simply appeal to a reader's sense of it. We have had to present something of an account and interpretation of the history, so that our criticisms would not appear to be arbitrary assertions.

Let us note here that Hymes is initially responsible for sections (1) and (7), Fought for section (6). The rest of the text has been drafted primarily by Hymes with the aid of memoranda prepared by Fought. Both authors have discussed and reviewed the several parts and the whole.

1. SCOPE OF THE SUBJECT

The scope of our topic in space and time cannot be taken for granted. We will delimit it broadly here, and take up aspects of its internal organization in the following sections, especially (4).

1.1 *'American'*

The notion of 'American structuralism' is taken here as equivalent to 'structuralism in the United States'. To do so requires an immediate apology to the rest of the Americas for the offense that this equation may give.[2] Clearly the history of 'American structuralism' properly includes the history of structuralism in Canada

---

[2] It would be desirable to avoid as much as possible, at least in titles, the use of 'America' and 'American' found in Joos 1957, Teeter 1964, and Levin 1965.

time of their dominance, adherents of this approach commonly called it 'descriptive linguistics' (e.g. Gleason 1955, Joos 1957), as has an analyst of its historical fortunes (Wells 1963). Nida (1949) used the phrase 'descriptive analysis' in his title. Moreover, an expositor of European approaches (Martinet 1953) tended to agree with such adherents that their approach should be called descriptive and not 'structural', although what for them (e.g. Joos 1957:9) was a virtue was for him a criticism. One sensitive observer (Bolinger 1968) has sorted out a sequence of 'descriptive' linguistics (assigning to it Boas and Sapir, and missionary linguists), 'structural' linguistics (equivalent to 'Bloomfieldian'), and 'formal' linguistics (transformational generative grammar). There is some justice to this, since the goal of synchronic description, based on a framework in need of (non-traditional) justification), was indeed launched, as something with a cumulative history in the United States, by Boas, and marvelously developed by Sapir; fixed models of linguistic structure as a base of inferences concerning the empirical properties of languages come later and are prominently identified with Bloomfield and his followers, although Sapir also played a crucial role. It is with Chomsky and his followers that logic and mathematics thoroughly replace postulates and procedures, although forms of mathematics and logic were already on the scene as overt sources of models in the work of Harris, Hiż, Hockett, and Greenberg (for Chomsky's criticisms of the work of the latter two, see 1957a:18–23, 1957b, 1959), and one had been assumed by Bloomfield (cf. Silverstein). Yet such a chronological partitioning does injustice to the actual history. Let us consider briefly here the appropriate uses of the terms 'descriptive', 'structural', and 'formal' as applied to linguistics.

Certainly the great figures, Sapir and Bloomfield, considered languages as structures, as the contents of their books, Language, each show,[4] and so did other

---

fieldian' as applying to one who regarded Bloomfield as founder of the tradition in which he or she worked. But then the natural immediate constituent division (into (post) and Bloomfieldian)) applies to Chomskyan transformational grammar (as against a division into (post Bloomfield) and (ian)).

The term 'Neo-Bloomfieldian' is used by Joos 1958:284, Voegelin 1959:117, and Langendoen (1969), and it captures nicely the sense of a group which based itself on what it took to be the spirit of Bloomfield's work, while being conscious of fresh developments of its own. We shall sometimes use this term, when it seems most appropriate to a context. Generally we shall use 'Bloomfieldian', in the sense of work taking Bloomfield as its point of departure. Lyons (1970, ch. 3) has introduced 'Bloomfieldians' in this sense, and the term has the virtue of avoiding controversy over prefix altogether, while capturing the intent of the other terms in a simple form.
[4] Both Sapir and Bloomfield use 'structure' significantly for the general character of a language or sector of language ("Types of linguistic structure", ch. 6 in Sapir (1921); "Phonetic structure", ch. 8 in Bloomfield (1933 – cf. esp. pp. 128-130, and also p. 264)). But 'structure' is far from exclusively, or even centrally, used. Both Sapir and Bloomfield employ 'system' (Sapir 1921:10, 17, 57-8 et al., Bloomfield 1933:103, 109), and both use 'configuration' and 'pattern', especially the latter. Bloomfield uses 'configuration' in a limited sense (1933:128), whereas the term takes on a prominent role in work following Sapir – cf. Harris 1944a on Newman's Yokuts; Sapir's use of 'pattern' is well known from the title of Sapir (1925); cf. also the index to his *Language* (1921). Bloomfield's 1933 index makes much use of 'phonetic pattern', even though the term itself is not

and Latin America (but now see Malkiel 1972). Obviously, the same holds true for the history of American linguistics generally. We very much regret that we cannot cite comparative or general studies of linguistics or structural linguistics in the New World. This gap is one of the most serious to which our survey points.

If historiography is to rise above chronicle to explanation, then comparative, cross-cultural studies are essential. Even if one is concerned with forces that are specific, in character or configuration, to a single country, it is a comparative perspective that can demonstrate their specificity. In this connection, the differential acceptance of structural linguistics in different forms in various parts of the New World is especially significant. The success of linguistics in the United States may be so taken for granted, that historical attention is focused only on individuals and ideas prominent in the success story. Comparative studies would illuminate the roles of other factors, such as cultural values and concerns, economic ups and downs, the degree of mobility within a social hierarchy, the social origins and aspirations of recruits to the new profession, the organization of learned disciplines and their relations to other institutions, including government, and so forth, all the matrix of opportunities and obstacles in a society.

We are also unable to cite studies of the diffusion of American structuralism in both the New and the Old Worlds. The significance of this diffusion has been noted (e.g. by Chatterji 1964: 283–4, 290–2), and it has doubtless been significant for linguistics in the United States as well. Opportunities for travel, lecturing, teaching, and research abroad, principally since the end of the Second World War, have helped to expand the base of the profession in the United States, and have probably influenced its composition and some of its work, but we know of no studies of these matters.

Despite these limitations, 'structuralism in the United States' can be defined positively. In the United States itself a line of development can be traced that is not only geographical, but that has a certain social and intellectual unity. At the same time, the phrase 'in the United States' reminds us of the diversity within the unity. With a discipline, as with a language, the understanding of change requires us to take the actual heterogeneity of the community into account.

1.2   *'Structuralism'*

The unity of American structuralism would be associated in the minds of most linguists today with the approach variously called 'post-Bloomfieldian', 'neo-Bloomfieldian', or simply, 'Bloomfieldian'.[3] There is a question here, since at the

---

[3]   The term 'post-Bloomfieldian' is used by Teeter 1964, Hockett 1968:17, 18, 21, Matthews 1972, and Derwing 1973, among others. This term has two unfortunate properties. One must remember to take 'Bloomfieldian' as applying to Bloomfield alone, as in Hockett (1968a:34), ... the Bloomfieldian and Sapirian view of language'; and the temporal scope implicit in the term is ambiguous. When one is referring to persons, rather than a view, it is almost impossible not to take 'Bloom-

later figures, even when working under the heading of 'descriptive linguistics' (cf. Nida 1949:4, 5). In fact, the two principal loadings of the term 'descriptive' were in opposition not to 'structural', but to 'historical' and 'prescriptive' (cf. Nida 1949: 1, 3, Chao 1968:5–6, and Hall 1969:194). The most widely used textbook of 'descriptive linguistics' gives this definition (Gleason 1961:iii): 'descriptive linguistics, the discipline which studies languages in terms of their internal structures'. And the major methodological statement of the period begins unequivocally (Harris 1951a:1): 'This volume presents methods of research used in descriptive, or, more exactly, structural, linguistics.'

Harris' book had indeed been initially entitled, *Methods in* DESCRIPTIVE *linguistics* (cf. *LSA Bulletin* 21 (1948):15, *Bull.* 22 (1949):13, and Hockett 1949, n. 8). Perhaps the change of title reflects what Hill (1964: 8) says of the 1947 Linguistic Institute:

This Institute also directed itself toward unifying the science of language, after the important new developments in the war years. It was, for instance, during this Institute that the term 'structural analysis' came to replace the previously generally used 'descriptive analysis'.

The term 'replace' is an overstatement, however, in the light of Bloch's course title at the 1950 Institute ('Descriptive Linguistics') and the titles of Gleason (1955, 1961) and Joos (1957). Indeed, Harris' book was still entitled 'Descriptive' in 1948, and praised as an important contribution to 'the methodology of descriptive linguistics' by the very Director of the 1947 Institute, Hans Kurath, who was also chairman of the LSA's Standing Committee on Research (see *Bull.* 22 (1949):13) that recommended publication of the book. And contrary to Hill, Joos (1957:96) had written that 'structural' was an *older* term for the new trend in linguistics, which 'descriptive' came to replace (in the United States in the early 1940s). It would appear that both terms could be used, rather interchangeably. Each had connotations of its own, but neither 'replaced' the other, across the discipline as a whole. Thus there would seem to be evidence of stylistic variation, not of contrastive classification, in the following passage, a report read by J. M. Cowan for Kurath (*LSA Bull.* 21 (1948):15):

Two manuscripts have been considered by the Committee; their publication under the auspices of the Linguistic Society of America has been recommended:
    1.   Robert A. Hall, Jr., Descriptive Italian Grammar

---

explicitly introduced in the text, nor always used on the pages cited. The use of 'pattern', as of 'configuration', owes something to the anthropological use of the period, but the latter did not necessarily have the same methodological basis (cf. Hymes 1970a:269, 277-8; for a current parallel, cf. Hymes 1971b:84, n.10). If a single term were to be chosen as most important, though, it might be 'form' ('linguistic form' (Sapir 1921:112), 'linguistic forms' (Bloomfield 1933:158) – form *in* language for Sapir, forms *of* language for Bloomfield. One gains the impression that 'structure' was taken pretty much for granted, as applicable to language, and that 'form', and to some extent 'pattern', were the more freighted, talismanic words. Close studies of usage would be interesting.

2. Zellig S. Harris, Methods in Descriptive Linguistics

Hall's manuscript is ready for the printer. Harris' manuscript should be carefully edited before it goes to press.

Both books are important. Hall's is the first detailed descriptive grammar of a well-known language prepared in accordance with the new descriptive technique. Harris' book represents the first consistent exposition of the technique (or one technique) of analyzing and describing languages from a structural point of view.

The term 'structural' has come more and more to the fore, perhaps influenced by Harris' final choice of adjective in his title, and by rapprochement in the 1950s with European approaches (Harris' 1951 bibliographic references themselves being notably trans-Atlantic), with 'descriptive' retaining something of a 'made in America' connotation. Yet all approaches to analysis of language retain a descriptive dimension, and the term itself is retained for a fundamental task of linguistics in Chomsky's conception of 'descriptive adequacy' (1965).

As has been indicated, formalism was an attribute of linguistics before Chomsky. In their own day pre-Chomsky formalisms were regarded by many as mystifyingly abstract. If the goal of formalism is understood as the precision of explicitness, then Chomsky himself has called attention to its presence and its merits in earlier work (1964a:91, 1966b:106, n. 105; cf. 1964a:996, where 'generative' and 'explicit' are equated).

In sum, each of the terms, 'descriptive', 'structural', 'formal', has senses, or connotations, in terms of which it can be opposed to the others, but it does not seem possible to treat the terms as mutually exclusive. It would be useful to trace the varied application of the terms in titles of articles and books and courses, and there is an obvious respect in which there has been a chronological pattern in linguistic activity itself: the proportion of 'describing' to 'formalizing' work has of course dramatically changed. But there seems no useful or ultimately valid way in which to treat 'structuralizing' as the property of a particular period or school. The object both of description and formalization is structure. If a reasonable sense of 'structural' is adopted, then, one must agree with Lepschy (1970:37) that the adjective should designate all 'those trends of linguistic thought in this century which deliberately and explicitly tried to gain insight into the systematic and structural character of language'. Such usage is in agreement with that of Lyons (1968:50), who terms the characteristic of all linguistics of the modern day 'the structural approach'; of Bierwisch, who writes (1971:44) that with Chomsky (1957), 'structural linguistics entered a new phase' (cf. Bierwisch 1966:104); perhaps of Lakoff (1971:267-8), who writes that 'early transformational grammar was a natural outgrowth of American structural linguistics'; and certainly of Matthews (1972:ix), who addresses 'my fellow structural linguists' in a work which contains extensive consideration of Chomskyan lines of analysis, but which also finds relevance in work from Sapir (1921) onward (cf. Matthews 1972:96, n. 1; and other notes passim).

Such usage is even suggested by Postal (1969:413). Having distinguished two types of linguistics, one concerned with the structural properties of sentences (SD Linguistics), and one concerned with the system which assigns structural properties (Rule Linguistics), Postal remarks that SD Linguistics is inherently limited, since most of the structure of language is necessarily ignored: 'It is ironic therefore that much of SD linguistics is associated with the term "structural linguistics".'

Major historiographic terms are not an appropriate subject for irony; the obvious solution is to generalize 'structural' to its proper scope. Postal himself implies as much later in his review (1969:422), referring to facts dealt with by Rule Linguistics (but not SD Linguistics) as structural properties. There is also abundant precedent for this in the major works of Chomsky. The title of his first book is of course *Syntactic structures*; he refers to its contribution as 'an entirely new conception of linguistic structure' (1957a:44). His major presentation of 1962 concludes with a statement of his goal as 'extending and deepening our understanding of linguistic structure' (1966b:975). In his other major work on linguistic theory, Chomsky continues to employ the term as a basic or elementary one (1965:27):

A theory of linguistic structure that aims for explanatory adequacy incorporates an account of linguistic universals, and it attributes tacit knowledge of these universals to the child.

Further, the index to the book references discussion of an essential tenet of Chomsky's approach under 'Structures, innate' (1965:251).

In short, there is a continuous story to the work in the United States in this century that has tried to gain an understanding of the systematic and structural character of language. No term other than 'structural' is adequate to designate it. At its proper level of contrast, 'structural' linguistics in the twentieth century stands in opposition to 'historical' linguistics in the nineteenth, as the designation of a distinctive, overriding emphasis and goal. The use of 'structural' for a single limited approach, the approach most distant from the leading characteristics of other twentieth-century structuralism (see, for example, Searle 1972) is a tendentious obstacle to understanding, and should be dropped. It is their common concern with structure that justifies comparing these approaches and claiming that they differ in merit. Indeed, why should transformationalists attend so closely to 'structural' approaches, if they are not competitive? Chomsky and his followers have not attacked etymologists, philologists, dialect geographers, or Indo-Europeanists. Instead, critical attention has been lavished on competing conceptions of the same activity, the analysis of linguistic structure.

1.3 *Termini and Topics*

Let us now consider the scope of structuralism in the United States a little further, as to (a) *terminus a quo*, (b) the relevant range of phenomena (institutional as well as intellectual), and (c) *terminus ad quem*.

1.3.1 *Terminus a quo*

Let us start again from the salient example of American structuralism, the school we shall henceforth call simply *Bloomfieldian*. Its doctrines did not spring full-blown from the mind of Leonard Bloomfield; indeed, their relationship to him is a particularly interesting problem. (If the real 'Bloomfieldian' of the standard image were to stand up, it might turn out to be George L. Trager — cf. now Stark 1972: 414–415.) The Bloomfieldian approach developed out of two generations or more of synchronic description of languages in the United States. Behind the years of the Bloomfieldians were both Bloomfield and Sapir, and behind them, as both acknowledged, was Franz Boas (Sapir 1922:8, and Bloomfield 1946a:5 — Bloomfield's tribute was originally longer, showing continuity with the attitudes and purposes of Boas even more clearly (Bloomfield 1972; cf. Stocking 1974; see also Bloomfield 1945:625 for admiration of Boas' character)). The continuity stemming from these three men, Boas, Sapir, and Bloomfield, has been recognized in most discussions of linguistics in the United States (cf. Bolinger 1968: 190–1, Greenberg 1968:63, Hockett 1952b, Hymes 1964:7–11, 1970:255, Ivić 1965:153, Robins 1967:207, Voegelin and Voegelin 1963:14–16, 22–25).

1.3.2 *Range of topics*

The development to be traced is one not only of ideas, and major figures, but also of careers, institutions, and climates of opinion in the formation of a professional discipline of linguistics in the United States. Enterprises for the organization and support of research, such as the Linguistic Society of America and the Linguistic Institute (cf. Voegelin and Voegelin 1963:16–20), and the Committee on Research in Native American Languages of the American Council of Learned Societies (cf. Hymes 1971a:236–9) are inseparable parts of the story. Boas, Bloomfield, and Sapir, as well as others, were involved in development of these as well as in development of methods and ideas.[5]

The scope of the historiography of structuralism in the United States, then, extends to all that has contributed to the formation of a discipline of linguistics in the United States. What we call 'structural linguistics' has been the intellectual arm,

---

[5] Thus the historian of linguistics, as of Marxism, is confronted with the problem of 'an analysis relevant both to the movement of thought and the actions of men' (Lichtheim 1961:xvii). Indeed, if 'structural linguistics' is substituted for 'Marxism' in Lichtheim's next two sentences, they provide an excellent description of our task: 'For it if it is true that we are dealing with a social transformation of which structural linguistics was both the theoretical reflection and the political agent, there is no point in confining the discussion to either the historical or the theoretical side. What is required rather is an effort to comprehend the manner in which both came together to bring about the situation now confronting us.' Between the two passages just quoted Lichtheim does remark, 'no distinction being drawn between what people thought and what they did'. Probably this means only to draw no absolute (arbitrary) distinction (cf. Öllman, 1971, Part I). To comprehend the manner in which the historical actions of linguists, as agents, and the thought of linguists, as theoretical reflection, have come together to bring about our present situation requires that we be able to distinguish between the two. In the light of the whole, Lichtheim's meaning no doubt is this: unity, not identity, of ideas and men.

so to speak, of a larger development, reshaping aspects of academic life. The ideas and the leading figures may catch our eye, but without the formation and institutionalization of linguistics as a discipline, there would have been little or no stage, as it were, little audience, for the ideas and leaders. The institutional substructure includes activities that appear trivial or tiresome, even to those whose incomes and budgets partly depend upon them. Nevertheless, to take one instance, governmental support for the teaching of English to speakers of other languages, and of major foreign languages to speakers of English, has been important to the development of linguistics, as has been support for the missionary and anthropological goals of translation into and from little-known languages. The disappearance of major governmental funding for machine translation has not entailed disappearance of the theoretical papers made possible by it. The field of applied linguistics generally has been (and remains) crucial to a history of linguistics in the United States as a history of persons, places, and opportunities. Important also is the role of professions and departments other than linguistics, as these have variously hindered or helped the building of institutional bases for linguistics, and as these have interacted with linguistics in patterns of differential intimacy that shift over time.

If the scope is broad, the focus can remain the emergence of linguistics itself. Here the point of greatest interest is the emergence of professional self-consciousness and self-definition. The formation of a new discipline, a new way of doing something already done (the description of languages), of course entails self-conscious separation from preexisting ways of doing and organizing things. (There is an obvious parallel to the problem of class-consciousness.) Indeed, our present sense of a paradigmatic status for linguistics in the United States, beginning with the Bloomfieldians, and succeeded (captured) by a new paradigmatic community around Chomsky, reflects the self-conscious aspirations and identifications of both.

Two relations appear to be vital here: that between the new discipline and the matrix of other disciplines and choices of career, and that between the emergence of the new discipline in one region (the United States) and corresponding developments in Europe. Both relations have usually been understood as matters of scientific ideas, but both have a sociological aspect as well.

Hymes (1972a:418–9) has noted the significance of such different disciplinary backgrounds as anthropology, dialectology, and traditional language and literature fields, and more especially, of conversion from and reaction against them in some cases. The significance of such affiliation, and nature of a diversified pattern of continuities of outlook, has been brought out by Malkiel (1969:549):

Students of language who originally were Orientalists, classicists, teachers of modern languages, archeologists, anthropologists, logicians, form different crews or clans, as it were, use diversified jargons, obey contrastable traffic rules for Academia, and believe in irreconcilably discrepant scales of values. Typically, each group so delimited also inherits a wealth of prejudices from its earlier affiliation; it is thus, to cite just one example, impossible to trace the tragic decline of Romance linguistics in this country without taking into account the barely mentioned fact that the founders of the LSA were, for the most part, professors of Greek, Latin, and German, who had small reason to rejoice at the prospect of any flowering of Romance studies; a stab in the back was, of course, concurrently dealt by those literary scholars in the Romance departments — they formed a solid majority — who saw little point in encouraging an emphasis rightly or wrongly associated with the predominance of German culture.

The intellectual distinctiveness of a specific tradition, and an explanation of its causes, is investigated by Malkiel (1964) in a pioneering paper that should be emulated. The role of a specific tradition in regard to structural models is also noted by Matthews (1972:105, n. 1):

Thus for Russian and other Slavonic languages, where a structuralist tradition had been established before IA [Item and Arrangement] . . . the continuity is not broken even in the United States . . . .

(To this should be compared the discontinuity signalled by Harris' IA restatement of Newman's exemplification of Sapir's processual model (Harris 1944), and Nida's IA redefinition of his own approach (1949:v).) Waterman (1963) is essentially a study of the Germanic tradition, but unfortunately it is not conscious of itself as such, and is instead presented as a general history. Notice the quite different and broader scope of contemporary work in Posner (1970), concerned with the place of the Romance tradition. Study of Finno-Ugric tradition in a similar vein is much to be desired.

This topic is linked to that of the possible influence of language type on general models of language structure. In the note cited just above, Matthews makes mention of it with regard to Slavonic languages, and his book discusses the point at length with regard to Classical Latin. One might study the impact of typological thinking about American Indian languages on the general linguistics of Boas and Sapir, well documented in Boas (1911) and Sapir (1921), or the influence of English on some initial features of transformational generative grammar, and hence, perhaps, the attractiveness of such grammars to users of English.

Turning from European languages to European linguistics, there is no doubt that European ideas were known and felt within the United States. Boas, Bloomfield, and Sapir were oriented toward international cultural and intellectual life, and took part in international activities. The long range interplay between linguistics in Europe and the United States, indeed, has been recently highlighted by discussion of William Dwight Whitney's influence on de Saussure, and de Saussure's on Bloomfield (cf. Godel 1966:480, Jakobson 1971, and now Koerner 1972b:302, 1973). Yet it is not possible to accede to Godel's proposal that there is 'no reason to contrast "Saussurean linguistics" with "American linguistics" '. Intellectual influence and common ground there certainly is, but there has also been conscious opposition. A contemporary observer (Whitehall 1944:675) referred to '. . . the depressing and sometimes hysterical conflict between the "Americanist" and "Prague" schools . . .'. A participant, reflecting historically, has commented (Voegelin and Voegelin 1963:20):

We do not know when the close knit membership of the LSA, inhospitable to European theory, began to realize that Bloomfield had given them a wholly American and wholly explicit linguistic theory. We do, however, know that they could talk about nothing else at the half-dozen Linguistic Institutes preceding World War II; and, more importantly, they could talk to Bloomfield, who was present at every one of these LI's. Having virtually no Ph.D. students himself, Bloomfield taught the postdoctoral representatives of the LSA who were teachers and visitors at the LI's. They admired Bloomfield above every living linguist.

The inhospitability to European theory has been commented upon by another participant-observer in economic terms (Hall 1969:194, n. 3):

... the strong anti-European feeling of many American linguists in the 1930's and 1940's had its main roots in often-times bitter personal experiences. Not a few young Americans saw, and frequently more than once, positions (for which they had been trained and were eminently qualified) snatched from under their noses and given to European refugees. Such a reaction, though by no means generous, was easily understandable in the days of the depression when any job at all was hard to come by, especially since American scholars, then as now, were not protected by citizenship-requirements of the kind prevailing in virtually all European university-systems. A frequent remark heard from our 'Group 1' [those to whom 'post-Bloomfieldians' has come to be applied, narrowly speaking, especially Bloch, Trager, Smith and (in the 1940's and early 1950's, Hall specifies), Hockett and Harris, all distinct from (2) Fries-Pike-Nida et al. (196, 198), and (3) a number of individual scholars, such as Swadesh (198)] was: 'We'll show those Europeans we have something they never dreamed of.'

Nor can de Saussure be put at the head of the American tradition because of his sympathetic reception by Bloomfield (Godel 1966:480; cf. Levin 1965:84–5), or, perhaps, because of the early date of the publication of his posthumous *Cours de linguistique générale* (1916). Joos (1957:v) asserts that de Saussure's contribution was used by Sapir, but there is no evidence, so far as either Levin (1965:84, n. 5) or we can ascertain (cf. Ivić 1965:153), that this was so.[6] Nor is it correct to say that a number of de Saussure's ideas 'remained' to be arrived at independently by American linguists, instancing as a historical puzzle that (Levin 1965:84):

Sapir, who of all American linguists might have been expected to be most sympathetic to many of de Saussure's views, does not seem to mention him.

The fact of the matter is that the Sapir, who had completed his Takelma grammar (1922) some time before February 20, 1911 (the date of its submission for publication as part of *Bulletin* 40, Part 2 — see the Letter of Transmittal on p. iii of the volume), had no need of a 1916 publication to stimulate him to the synchronic, analytic study of languages. Nor for that matter did the Boas who years before had launched the project which lay behind the *Handbook* volumes (1911, 1922, 1934).

---

[6] Holmes (1940:237) does write as follows, regarding the Genevan school of Saussure and Bally: 'I do not believe that many Americans – the late Edward Sapir being a prominent exception – have appreciated fully the linguistic theories of this group. No citation to work or words of Sapir is given.

By 1916, Sapir, indeed, had laid the basis for our knowledge of the structure of six languages (Takelma, Wishram, Yana, Southern Paiute, Nootka, and Chasta Costa). The Takelma study itself is one of the finest grammars of a previously undescribed language ever written, almost a miracle for its time.

In any case, de Saussure's effective role, as distinct from his symbolic role, is badly in need of close investigation. Joos marvelously confuses the two (1957:18). The social setting of the symbolic role is put into perspective by Malkiel (1969: 537):

> while Saussure's posthumous *Cours* (1916) invites and richly deserves assessment on the strength of its splendours and accomplishments, its instantaneous impact, especially outside Central Europe, cannot be properly measured without some allowance for the feelings of that time: The acceptance of the leadership of a French Swiss genius connoted for many Westerners then opposed to Germany a strongly desired, rationalized escape from the world of Brugmann, Leskien, Osthoff, and Paul.

Malkiel goes on to relate the delayed impact of Vossler's work of 1904 and 1905 in German Romance studies to the 'yearning for radical change, for rejuvenation after the loss of a war and the collapse of a regime' (1969:537).

Postwar linguistics in the United States was already possessed of a synchronic approach, and one, furthermore, richer than that of de Saussure, since it did not reject diachronic studies, but pursued them integrally with synchronic work (both Sapir and Bloomfield being notable examples of this); the postwar period, and its disillusionments, did not affect its continuity.[7] Something of the later shrinking of international interest, however, and the appeal of an assertively (as opposed to an inevitably) distinctive 'American' approach, and the appeal of the rejection of traditional views, including 'mentalism', may be due to the cumulative effect of the interwar climate of opinion.

Consciousness of an American variety of linguistics as something distinct does indeed seem to come with the generation after Sapir and Bloomfield, as the quotation from the Voegelins indicates, and to gain force at the time of the Second World War (cf. Joos 1957:108). New York City would seem to have been the setting. We can only guess as to the consequences of the concentration of a number of younger American linguists at 165 Broadway, working on language teaching materials for the United States Army, at the same time as the city became a home-in-exile to

---

[7] See discussion under Philology in (3.1). Boas' growing skepticism as to proofs of genetic relationship, as well as his disinterest in reconstruction or other pursuits of historical linguistics, do make him something of a counterpart to de Saussure in subordination of diachronic work. But Boas had a dynamic, rather than static, conception of synchronic study, and his neglect of comparative-historical research was superseded by the cultivation of it by his student, Sapir; Boas' opposition to the thrust of such work in the second decade of the century rather isolated him (cf. Hymes 1961a, Darnell 1969). Sapir's relation to Boas in this regard might be seen as parallel to the relation of Jakobson and others to de Saussure's legacy. Sapir's public integration of historical work (1916, 1917) indeed followed establishment of a synchronic descriptive focus under Boas by a dozen years or so, thus by about the same interval by which the 1929 Prague School theses integrating synchrony and diachrony followed publication of de Saussure's *Cours* in 1916.

European intellectuals. We would like very much to see a study of the founding of the journal *Word* toward the end of the war, and of the composition of its board of editors and its audience, in relation to the official (and then only) linguistic journal in the United States, *Language*, whose then recently appointed editor, Bernard Bloch, was a recruit from English and Germanic philology to Bloomfieldian linguistics, by way of the *Linguistic Atlas of New England*. A related matter equally deserving of study is the interplay between Roman Jakobson and the men most associated with the Bloomfieldian position. Jakobson's influence on such diverse developments as generative phonology, componential analysis, stylistics, the ethnography of speaking, and the acquisition of language, is a principal theme of our subject from the time of the Second World War. His role as an international leader in the field changed during that period, however, and it would be well to trace this particular thread of history while so many of its participants are still active. The adherence of some native and resident American scholars to a variety of European approaches (cf. Haugen 1951), the visits here to teach and lecture by Firth, Hjelmslev, and others, and the role of scholars of European origin who remained in linguistic and language programs, all require attention.

These points are meant to show the sense in which the topic of 'American structuralism' must be studied in terms of an evolving scholarly community, although neither mechanically (geographically) nor chauvinistically. The community has evolved always with internal diversity and various responsiveness to external influence, but its continuity and consciousness of continuity cannot be missed.

The question of distinctiveness and continuity is not limited to visible ideas and institutions, but involves other aspects of the culture (in an anthropological sense) of a discipline: modes of work, the characteristic practice of a group. A true history of linguistics, indeed, should not proceed as if linguistics were never done, but only stated and organized. The relevant ways of doing linguistics include the handling of data and of colleagues. One would want to know how these things were developed and transmitted, by whom to whom, and how they implemented or stimulated general orientations.

Such things influence what can become visible, both as intellectual and institutional force. De Saussure's *Cours* would have remained on a shelf with Croce's *Aesthetic*, if a practice had not been developed that treated the book as symbolic fount.

Genres of presentation are of interest here, and the roles of editors and advisors. In the United States certain modes of obtaining and presenting results were developed and communicated without being fully articulated as models, but through being implemented in relations between scholar and colleagues or students. The Boas 'model' for American Indian linguistics has attracted attention and analysis (Hockett 1952b:90, Voegelin 1952a, Stocking 1974); the existence of an early Sapir model of grammar has been noted (Hymes 1963:88–90), and a later Sapir model, exemplified in Newman's Yokuts, has been explicated (Harris 1944). The collecting of texts, the eliciting of supplementary forms, the organization and preparation of these, the care of notebooks, and later of wire and then tape recorders, all these have underlain the existence of a practice of linguistics. The persistence of habits of work is a major factor in the persistence of loyalty to theoretical goals. Some linguists trained in pencil and paper work never became comfortable with tape recorders; linguists trained only in the consultation of intuitions will doubtless cling to them long after being convinced of the need to study language in context.

The importance of this dimension of the development of linguistics can hardly be overstated; yet, evidence for its historiography can hardly be found. The Voegelins' account of Bloomfield's impact at Linguistic Institutes implies his role as a guide to a specific way of doing linguistic analysis in the context of courses in field methods (cf. Harris and Voegelin 1953). The impact of Sapir in such a context is indicated by Pike (1967). And Kroeber told of the decisive impact on his career of the discovery of pattern in analysis of Chinookan texts in Boas' home (Malkiel 1969:548).

To modes of presentation and acquisition of data may be added modes of argument and persuasion. All are linked to general notions, of course, but also to personalities, life styles, climates of opinion, and the like. Experience suggests that the linkages at a given time or for a given group, while perhaps appearing necessary, have in fact a component of the 'arbitrary', being due to historical circumstances as well as to inner connection. Historiography research is desperately needed. No major change in 'paradigm' can be considered a change only in what people say; obviously it is also a change in what people do, including what it is customary or easy, what unusual or difficult, to do. Explanation of changes, and resistances to change, can not be adequate without attention to habits and customs of practice.

In sum, writings about the history of the field have understandably concentrated on the theoretical aspects. Social groupings and affinities among linguists, and between linguists and others, have been noticed mostly as a projection of the theoretical issues. Institutional and professional circumstances affecting linguistics, and the practice of linguists in handling languages, and each other, have mostly been ignored, but must be included.

1.3.3 *Terminus ad quem*

The third boundary of our subject has to do with its *terminus ad quem*. Most linguists, pressed for a quick answer, would probably suggest 1957, give or take a few years, the date of publication of Chomsky's *Syntactic structures*. Certainly a major change came about at that time, as we all know, and as discussions such as those of Wells (1963) and Lounsbury (1960, 1962) illuminate. Yet the quick answer, which is also the considered answer of some scholars, reflects the way in which our historiography rests on premises, which, if unexamined, may confine us to surface appearances. Earlier we gave reasons (and cited precedent) for considering 'structural' the term to apply to the main direction of linguistics from early in the century to the present time. Let us now consider specific features which make a termination of our subject before the present difficult, if not impossible. Let us take up chronological, and then conceptual, factors.

Most would grant that the history of American structuralism, even when narrowly defined, must be extended past 1957, insofar as approaches existing then have continued to have adherents. It would be a grotesque history of structural linguistics in the United States that knew no work by Zellig S. Harris, Charles F. Hockett, Kenneth L. Pike, or George L. Trager later than 1957, to name scholars well known for their work with general models of language structure (including mathematical aspects in the case of Harris, Hockett, and Pike). There is of course also the work in the last decade or so of Bernard Bloch, William Diver, C. A. Ferguson, Paul Garvin, H. A. Gleason, Jr., J. H. Greenberg, A. A. Hill, Henry Hiż, Floyd Lounsbury, Stanley Newman, H. L. Smith, Edward Stankiewicz, and others. But there is more here than the persistence of established scholars in established ways of work. Despite paradigmatic revolution, a variety of supposedly eclipsed approaches have attracted new followers among younger scholars. It is not that the younger scholars do not read the scholarly equivalent of the newspapers. These exceptions to the 'rule' of paradigmatic succession indict any portrait of the history of linguistics which does not include or explain them, and suggest that the notion of 'paradigm' is not adequate to capture whatever generalization can be made about the history (cf. Hymes 1974b).

A cut-off point for American structuralism becomes all the more difficult to locate when we consider that Lamb's stratificational approach (more recently, relational network approach) was developed *after* 1957. One might of course distinguish between periods and stages, noting that Lamb's approach belongs chronologically to the same period as Chomsky's, but deciding that as a type, it belongs to a prior stage (cf. Postal 1964a). Such a decision of course presupposes a certain theoretical position, and becomes difficult to maintain. First, the history of tagmemics (Pike, Longacre, Elson, Waterhouse, Pickett, et al. (cf. Pike 1966)), and the history of stratificational grammar (Lamb, Gleason, and, for a time, Hockett (cf. Makkai 1972)) is unintelligible without reference to the climate of opinion shaped by Chomsky, and the response to it by these approaches. Second, the interaction, from a certain position at least, has been mutual. Chomsky's revisions of his initial system (cf. Chomsky 1957c, 1965), and the dissent from it of major followers under the heading of generative semantics, as well as the cognate approach of Wallace Chafe, have essential features to be found earlier in Lamb (particularly the recognition and place of a 'sememic' stratum). At the time of Chomsky's revision of his initial system, indeed, Lamb was openly cheered by what he saw as a convergence toward his own model (cf. Matthews 1972:141, n. 1, 143, n. 1, 200, n. 2; Makkai 1972:69, n. 12). A fair amount of the recent history of new issues within the Chomskyan framework appears to consist of the discovery of issues previously raised within other structuralist frameworks, and of attempts to deal with them more satisfactorily, or satisfactorily at all. Thus, some recent work on 'conspiracies' in phonology appears to discover the phenomena dealt with by Sapirian structuralists in such terms as 'canonical formulae', and even to rely for data on Sapirian descriptions. Some recent papers on language in context appear to rediscover or to repeat points made earlier outside the transformationalist community (one often can not be sure of the distinction, since sources outside the community are usually not credited). In other cases earlier concepts and structural schools are being reevaluated rather more positively (e.g. with regard to the concept of the phoneme (Schane 1971); or with regard to a school, in this case not in the United States (Langendoen 1969)).

Finally, if a cut-off point for structuralism in the United States is to be hazarded now, it is with Chomsky's own work that one seems to see its culmination and conclusion. On the one hand, a few years after Hockett has despaired of formal grammar, urging a return to the Bloomfield of a generation ago (1968b:153), we find some leading younger transformationalists also abandoning the goal of an integrated description, of the systematic unity of a single grammar, and advocating clear treatments of particular points. We have in mind the views of Fillmore and Lakoff, as we understand them as of Fall 1972.

If structuralism can be taken to imply a conception of language as an integrated structure, a system where *tout se tient* and can somehow be shown to do so, then Chomsky almost seems a defender of fundamental structuralist principle against its dissolution in particularist or atomist approaches. In this connection, it is significant that some psychologically oriented students of language see a need to treat grammatical features within a model of performance, or learning strategies, or the like, which renders an autonomous grammar redundant. Note also the suggestion that the actual organization of linguistic features in communities is in terms of repertoires of ways of speaking, or speech styles (Hymes 1972b, 1974a).

We do in fact think that if the fundamental premise of structuralism is seen as the study of language as an autonomous system, a system central to the understanding of the history and use of language, but to be analyzed independently of history and use first, then the ways in which Chomsky's work continues preceding structuralism and completes it seem more decisive than the ways in which it does not. Or, if we see in the history of structuralism a complex development, with specific complexities at any one time, and the autonomy of linguistic form as an initial impulse and goal gradually arrived at, then again the unfolding and deepening of that impulse and goal would seem to culminate, so far as we can now see, in Chomsky's work. All of the preceding steps in the exploration of autonomous linguistic form are given a place in a single system, and the autonomy of that system from history and use is rationalized, indeed, given the noblest significance possible, by interpreting it in terms of the human mind, of the distinctive powers of human nature.

This is a judgment not all may accept, yet a judgment of a kind that must be made, if one is not to define the scope of a part of the history of linguistics superficially. One must weigh continuities against discontinuities, conscious against unconscious directions, in relation to a time scale that extends beyond one's own focus of attention. In short, one must face a problem intrinsic to significant historiography, the problem of *periodization*. It is a notoriously difficult problem, even in sectors of history that have attracted many scholars (cf. Barraclough 1972); probably decisions as to periodization cannot be separated from valuative premises (cf. Levich 1962). For this reason, and because the work which brings the history of American structuralism into the present obviously continues, the ultimate terminus ad quem of our subject must be left open. Later historians will be better informed, and will likely have a different sense of the continuities and discontinuities that demarcate the subject and its parts.

The question might be put, of course, as to whether it will be possible to speak of an 'American' structuralism, or linguistics, given the pace of internationalization in the field. A focus on the distribution of ideas, and the participation of scholars from many places in common research and publication, might easily lead one to doubt that the United States would remain a relevant context. And many scholars, now as in the past, would insist in principle, and hope in practice, for the irrelevance of nation and geography to progress in science (e.g., Lyons 1965:88, 89–90). There is a danger, however, of imputing to the world a universalism that conceals one's own parochial interest and limited vision (cf. Fekete 1973:107, n. 198). It is one thing for a citizen of the United States to regard its northern border as irrelevant, and another for a Canadian. A focus on the social matrix of linguistic ideas and practice leads one to anticipate that a discipline would continue to manifest (if indirectly) distinctive traits, as long as it has experience of a distinctive social environment, indeed, *Lebenswelt*. Just relative weight of numbers, and the location of centers of gravity within networks of communication, help to distinguish national and regional communities.

Structural linguistics in the United States, in short, will continue to have a social history, and, one can anticipate, something of a specific intellectual history. There may, indeed, be no *terminus ad quem* in the strict sense. There has been none to comparative and historical linguistics, whose history in the United States begins in one respect in the late eighteenth century with attempts to classify American Indian languages by Barton, and continues through Jefferson, Gallatin, Brinton, Powell, Boas, and Sapir to the present day; in another respect, methodological bases, there is also a specifically American history to be traced, in connection with the problems posed by American Indian languages and the perennial link with ethnology. What has happened is not a termination, but a displacement. Problems which were important to central figures in the development of the subject (Whitney, Boas, Sapir, Bloomfield) are not important to the central figures of a succeeding generation, whose interest in language history is somewhat belated and devoted to its bearing on models of language structure, not to its bearing on the history of peoples. Work of the latter sort continues, work which recognizes its continuity with Bloomfield, Sapir, and others, but it is considered peripheral. It is part of the background, not sharing the center of the stage. If the rising interest in the study of variation, styles, ways of speaking and the like should displace synchronic analysis of grammar, conceived as an autonomous and hegemonic genre, work with problems and principles of phonology, morphophonemics, morphology, syntax, and formal models of these and their interrelations, will continue, but, like comparative and historical linguistics today, no longer at the center of the stage.

We must, then, distinguish clearly between the *existence* and the *centrality* of an interest or line of work. Indeed, to set the terminus a quo of our subject in the early years of this century is implicitly to recognize centrality, not merely existence. There were synchronic grammars by linguists, and of American Indian languages in fact, before Boas (e.g. Gatschet's Klamath, Riggs' Dakota), but Boas made the analysis of grammars central to the tasks and theoretical interests of a fledgling discipline. We may indeed, then, witness a *terminus ad quem* of 'American structuralism' in our lifetimes, in the sense of centrality.

2. MATERIALS AND METHODOLOGY

2.1   *Sources Used and Models Followed*

We can best consider the nature of the historiography that has been done against the background of the kinds of materials on which historiography may be based. Sources may be grouped together according to what they elucidate: (a) linguistic theory and method; (b) the practice of linguists in handling data and problems; (c) affinities and influences among linguists, and between them and others not linguists; (d) institutional, professional, and societal circumstances affecting support for linguists; (e) beliefs, values, attitudes (explicit and latent) of persons, groups, generations, affecting orientation of linguistics.[8] As noted in (1.3.2), linguists writing about the history of their field have understandably tended to concentrate on (a), interpreting (c) often as a projection of (a), and for the most part ignoring or imputing, rather than investigating, the rest. For the most part, the sources of historiographic writing and comment are published professional works.

This fact is not surprising. Most of the historiographic writing and comment is part of the ongoing debates and developments within linguistics. It is the work of linguists who are protagonists or antagonists. Such writing can seldom achieve detachment and perspective, or escape a considerable element of apologetic or polemic purpose. Malkiel (1969:533) observes:

---

[8]   This classification is closely analogous to Neustupný's identification of five components of 'metalinguistic systems': thought, enquiry, communicative idiom, application, and social system of the discipline. See his use of the distinctions with regard to the place of the work of Einar Haugen in the development of American linguistics (1975).

. . . most linguists — including those writing historical accounts — are youthful, idealistic, enthusiastic, and, by the same token, often both uncritical in their endorsements and unfair in their condemnations and, above all, in their — more fashionable and more deadly — tacit omissions.

Until very recently, much of this writing was compressed into reviews, prefaces, and obituaries, where the lack of space may help to excuse the oversimplification of influences, styles, and schools. Sometimes the writing owes its existence to a specific wish to honor, criticize, or otherwise define the place of a person, group, topic, or problem, but by and large a certain kind of context is assumed, or painted in rather broad strokes. This context, the implicit narrative that gives coherence to comments, is the *mainstream* model of development, in which competing approaches to linguistics are presented as deviations from a central trend, or approximations to it, and are treated briefly, deprived of antecedents and consequences of their own. An explicit expression of this preference is found in Schnelle (1969: 449), commenting on a truncated historical sketch by Bierwisch (1966):

Bierwisch's able survey of structuralism . . . is not only a survey; it contains the program of an extensive linguistics on the basis of a theory of generative grammar. This program constitutes Bierwisch's frame of reference for the placement of the various schools of structuralism, the Neo-grammarians, Saussure and his pupils, the Prague, Copenhagen and American schools. They are all considered forerunners of generative linguistics. It might be debated whether such a point of view allows an objective evaluation of different shades of structuralist intentions; but is not a constructive development of structuralist ideas preferable to a meticulous account of each of its contributions?

The historian's view of such a treatment of historical development was well expressed by Marx (quoted from "A contribution to the critique of political economy" Lévi-Strauss (1958:337):

The so-called historical development amounts in the last analysis to this, that the last form considers its predecessors as stages leading up to itself and perceives them always one-sidedly, since it is very seldom and only under certain conditions that it is capable of self-criticism.

It is not that there is no truth to a picture of the history of the field as a succession of dominant, or central, approaches. There is obviously considerable truth to such a picture, and the most important task of historiography could be said to describe and explain that succession. But to *describe* requires adequate treatment of textural detail, close reading, and control of many kinds of source material; to *explain* requires a grasp of underlying relations built upon adequate description and illuminated by notions of sociocultural change. The relation between dominant ideas and their social basis in linguistics is not in principle different from the problem of the relation between Protestantism and the emergence of capitalism, or between Puritanism and the transformation of England in the seventeenth century. Whatever one's conclusion in the given case, one cannot begin by assuming that the salient ideas and the effective change were necessarily connected, but must allow for a measure of the contingent (cf. Wells 1963) and the ideological. Householder (1969:886–890), having given a set of 8 propositions felt to be basic in Bloomfieldian linguistics, and critically evaluated a set of 6 felt to be equally essential in introductory textbooks and courses today, concludes (perhaps with tongue in cheek):

The old catalog of beliefs . . . included at least some which were totally irrelevant to anything the linguist did. An affirmation of belief, however, was necessary to insure acceptance in the community of linguists. Much the same thing appears to be true now of the new credo; very few portions of a linguist's research activity are likely to be affected by his private opinions (provided he keeps his mouth shut, of course) on points such as the six exemplified here from Langacker. But we certainly don't want our students to be ostracized from decent linguistic society . . ., so it is quite right that these dogmas should appear in our elementary textbooks and that our students should learn them by heart and publicly affirm belief.

Again, whatever one's conclusion in a given case, one cannot assume that the successful successor was inevitable, for its intellectual merits alone, at least not in a field such as linguistics. The point is seldom made in linguistic historiography, but note Klein (1971:7):

Nur ein sehr einfältiger Mensch kann glauben, die Interessen und Methoden die das Bild einer Wissenschaft zu einer gewissen Zeit bestimmen, verdankten dies vorwiegend der internen Entwicklung der Wissenschaft selbst. Den Erfolg etwa der Transformations-grammatik in den letzten Jahren auf dem Gebiet der theoretischen Linguistik allein aus ihrer höheren Adäquatheit oder grösseren Exaktheit erklären zu wollen, gleicht der Teleologie eines Fussballreporters, für den der Gewinner immer zu Recht mehr Tore geschossen hat.

Nor is to be assumed that a given succession is all gain and no loss, that in linguistics, unlike other spheres of human activity, there are benefits that carry no costs.

Published professional books and articles, being largely part of a self-conception of the field as engaged in unidirectional progress, feed historiography subject to a similar conception. In recent years the term 'paradigm' has been taken up and freely applied in attempts to define one or another line of work as the new center of attention and mainstream. Strictly speaking, such use of the term as a claim for the incipient significance of one among mutually competing and communicating approaches is incorrect, and the existence of rival candidates for the status of *the* paradigm is evidence, not of paradigmatic status for any of the claimants, but of what Kuhn called the pre-paradigmatic stage (cf. Bursill-Hall 1970b:207). A difference of paradigm is supposed to entail dramatic discontinuity of understanding; competing claimants today often understand very well what each other is doing, which is why many arguments can be technical, not merely rhetorical. In any case, the term and notion of 'paradigm' have been found subject to a number of difficulties within the history of science itself (cf. Lakatos and Musgrave 1970, Koerner 1972:258, and Ferguson 1973), and have been criticized with regard to use in linguistics as in effect an honorific substitute for 'cynosure' (Hymes 1974b).

Whether one uses 'paradigm' or not, and whether one intends by it dramatic discontinuity or uses it loosely, a single term can not suffice. The 'paradigm' notion becomes in effect a variant of mainstream models and terminology generally (cf. Koerner 1972b). A more complex and differentiated notion of the development of the general field of linguistics is needed, together with more precise terms for the interplay of tendencies, interests, and component lines of work (cf. 4.2). An adequate notion is not likely to gain prominence, except insofar as the inadequacy of the simpler mainstream paradigm notion is recognized, through confrontation of it with the rich range of materials actually forming the data to be explained, the facts and relationships actually to be accounted for in the history of our field.

Malkiel (1969) is one of the few to raise questions of historical methodology (cf. esp. pp. 534–540 on models of development) and of source materials. He lists some ten types of source material, with apt examples of each: autobiographic sketches and self-appraisals (published and unpublished, and not excluding the 'curriculum vitae'); memoirs and reminiscences; prefaces, introductions, and epilogues by authors, especially prefaces to radically revised editions; exchanges of letters; Festschriften and other collections geared to special events; prefaces to writings of others; congratulatory or commemorative articles (including occasions of change of editorship); certain classes of book review; summings-up at symposia; types of institutional records, including announcements, and corrections preserved on galleys. To these can be added newspapers and news magazines, whose coverage of recent developments in linguistics affects public conceptions, and hence perhaps professional activity (cf. Householder 1970:133; Indiana Daily Student March 26, 1968, p. 1).

It is a mark of serious historiography that it uses materials of these kinds, 'all there is to use' in principle, and particularly that it uses unpublished materials that go beyond the official public record. This last is, so to speak, only the 'surface structure' of the subject. Historiography limited to such materials is unable to attain descriptive adequacy, much less explanation.

The present historiography of linguistics in the United States is commonly limited in this way. By and large, scholarship has not provided materials that permit an understanding of personal and institutional contexts and dynamics. We do find instances of published recollections (e.g., Voegelin and Voegelin 1963, Voegelin 1973), published correspondence (Lowie 1965, Hockett 1970 passim), reconstruction of participant observation (Joos 1957 passim, Hockett 1968, Hall 1969), and of course there are obituaries (some for our subject are reprinted in Sebeok 1966). A volume, containing sketches of the history of linguistics at selected universities in the United States, would be valuable (Sebeok, now cancelled). But the historiography of the subject has not much used such materials, nor called them into being. Only one project in oral history, begun some years ago by Martin Joos, is known to us, and it apparently remains unfinished; but the personal knowledge and perspective of linguists who have experienced changes in the climate and orientation of the field are invaluable (cf. Neustupný 1975: on 'the growing importance of the oral medium'; memoranda, notes, and other indications of talks and conversations, become ever more important if explanation is to be possible). The records of journals, such as Bernard Bloch's editorial correspondence and early files of *Language*, are an especially rich source, but Bloch's papers have been used so far only by Miller (1970), and the files of *IJAL*, *Word*, and other journals have not, so far as we know, been used at all. College and university records would reveal much of the patterning of personal and departmental association and influences; correspondence related to the filling and occasional deliberate creation of vacancies would help document the emergence of centers of influence and prestige within the growing discipline, and their relations to client or colony departments. These remain untouched, and it is not at all clear that sufficient care is taken for the preservation of these or other invaluable materials. The one center for such preservation with regard to one aspect of the field is the Library of the American Philosophical Society, whose Franz Boas Collection contains administrative as well as scholarly correspondence. The Collection has been used to advantage by several scholars (e.g., Stocking 1974, Hymes 1971a), but needs to be complemented by centers concerned with other aspects of the general subject.

Materials of these sorts make available, and inescapable, the situated and intentional character of the activity that has created the history with which one is concerned. Such materials enable one to realize the initial motivation of Kuhn's concept of 'paradigm', which, it should be remembered, was to transcend the distorted conceptions of the history of their fields held by scientists themselves, in virtue of their participation in the world view of a current paradigm. The future of the historiography of structural linguistics in the United States depends upon the collection, preservation, and use of such materials.

2.2   *Existing Kinds of Historiographic Writing*

We must take historiographic writing and comment on American structuralism where we can find it. In the rest of this section we survey briefly the kinds of writing and comment that do exist, and characterize the orientation of the more substantial pieces.

Book length treatments do not exist. Of monographic treatments of specific topics there are only two that are published and that have sufficient historical perspective to shed light on the general development. One is primarily a methodological treatise on a grammatical problem (Matthews 1972), the other an anthology concerned with phonology (V. Makkai 1972). Both are excellent of their kind. Part II, "Models of inflectional morphology", is the most pertinent section of Matthews' study, but there are footnotes with valuable references in time perspective elsewhere. Makkai's book contains useful introductory notes and bibliographies; it is oriented toward stratificational phonology, to which it gives pride of place (the conclusion), but it represents and makes available much of the true diversity and interplay of the development of the subject. (A critique of the book's conception of the 'Bloomfieldian' period is given in connection with Sapir in (3.2) below.) Wells' monographic treatment of a topic central to structural linguistics was noted long ago (Bloch 1948, n. 14), but remains unpublished; a portion was presented to a 1962 conference and is to appear in revised form (Wells ms. [ca. 1948], 1974).

2.2.1 *Histories of linguistics*

Book length histories of linguistics as a whole, of course, give attention to American structuralism. These books are almost exclusively of European origin. So are a number of surveys of contemporary (twentieth century, or 'structuralist') linguistics itself. On the history of linguistics as a whole: Grauer and Wald (1961), Helbig (1970), Ivić (1965), Leroy (1967), Llorente Maldinado de Guevara (1967), Loja (1961), Malmberg (1964); on the present century, or structural linguistics, Apresjan (1966; cf. 1973), Bierwisch (1971), Arutjunova et al. (1964), Davis (1973), Guxman (1964), Guxman and Guxman (1964) (see review by Vachek 1967), Lepschy (1970), Posner (1970). The concentration of publication in the mid-1960s and the end of the 1960s is striking. We have not been able to consult all these works (and indeed, are indebted for notice of several of them to Koerner 1972a, 1974). We will discuss four European works available in English translation at the time of writing, and therefore most likely to influence linguistics in the English-speaking countries. (These works perhaps attest to an American marker, but not an American motivation, for such studies.) The four works are Ivić (1965), Lepschy (1970), Leroy (1967), and Malmberg (1964).

Ivić, originally in Serbo-Croatian, is sympathetic to our subject and provides many references. In a single chapter on structural linguistics (ch. 15), she devotes a section between the Prague School and Hjelmslev to "The schools of American linguistics", distinguishing "The pioneers: Boas, Sapir and Bloomfield" (152–9) from "The epoch of distributionalism" (159–63), "Anthropological linguistics" (163–9), and "Psycholinguistics" (170–3). (Note also "The anthropological approach to syntax", cited as exemplified by Trager and Smith 1951 (p. 208)!) A separate chapter is given to "Linguistic syntax and the generative approach" (17, pp. 203–11) (cf. review of the book by Hymes 1966, Malkiel and Langdon 1969: 557–9, 569–71, Bursill-Hall 1970b:237–9).

Lepschy (1970) is something of a survey and history both. He devotes separate chapters to Prague, Hjelmslev, Sapir and Bloomfield together (V), Jakobson and Martinet ('functional linguistics'), post-Bloomfieldian linguistics (VII), and transformational grammar (VIII), thus paralleling Ivić in distinctions and order of treatment of the Americans, and bringing Jakobson (and Martinet) implicitly into the American sequence. (See Malkiel and Langdon 1969:561–6 for informative and precise comments on the development and impact of Lepschy's treatments of the subject through the 1966 original; see Dinneen 1971 for a review of the revised 1970 book.)

Leroy (1967) has had great success in Europe in its original editions in French. Reviewers may find some qualities in its favor, but are forced to agree that its treatment of American linguistics is, to say the least, bizarre (Malkiel and Langdon 1969:554–7, 567–9; Lyons 1969; Bursill-Hall 1970b:235; Koerner 1973b; Robins 1973). Nothing serious about the organization or other aspects of the development of American linguistics can be gleaned (cf. Malkiel 1969:554–5). The book perhaps is an object lesson, however, to scholars in the United States who may attempt surveys of the development of linguistics in Europe with similar lack of sympathy and knowledge.

Malmberg (1964), originally in Swedish, gives more sustained and informed attention to "Modern American linguistics" (158–185) (no other national development is given separate treatment). Among the various treatments of American linguistics in single chapters, Malmberg is one of the few and best in representing the internal diversity. He notes two trends, one eliminating semantic criteria and the other using them, and includes Pike in his summaries of positions. (Cf. review by Malkiel and Langdon 1969:559–61, 571–2.)

Two histories of linguistics, published in the same year, but one incognito, provide well informed accounts within their limited space. Dinneen (1967) is the more extensive for the twentieth century, discussing Sapir, Bloomfield, and (after Firth and Hjelmslev) Chomsky in separate chapters. Robins (1967) balancing his treatment more evenly with regard to the past, has only a few sensible pages (206–12, 216–7, 262–233) (cf. reviews of Robins by Dinneen (1968) and Bursill-Hall 1970b, especially pp. 233–4). Finally, a somewhat earlier short historical sketch (Waterman 1963, 1970) does not rise above canonization of Bloomfield and Harris in the first edition, and is not substantially changed in this regard in the second. (Cf. reviews by Hymes 1965, Teeter 1965, and comment by Koerner 1972a:428.)

Most accounts of the history of American structuralism, outside of histories proper, are chapters, sections, and even paragraphs in works intended as textbooks, anthologies, or methodological contributions. We noted a methodological contribution, and an anthology, at the outset of this section out of regard for their merit. Here we can consider methodological contributions that require analysis.

2.2.2 *Methodological studies as textbooks*

Bierwisch (1966) has been commented upon above (2.1); the remarks apply as well to the 1971 book. Postal (1964) is a systematic account of a similar sort, although focused upon a particular topic and a limited body of work. It may seem odd to treat it as a contribution to the historiography of linguistics, but it, and works like it, does indeed define the sense of history held by many linguists. Since an adequate historiography is lacking, such expositions shape most of what we read and even can imagine the history to have been. The difficulty with such works has been recognized by Voegelin and Voegelin (1963:22):

It places models of their own making as constructs followed by their predecessors and thereby distorts history.

The point was recognized in a review of Postal (1964), early in the development of the present standard consciousness of history that the book has helped to shape. Thorne (1965) starts with what Kuhn (1962:136–7) says about the role of textbooks:

'Unless he has personally experienced a revolution in his own lifetime, the historical sense either of the working scientist or the lay reader of textbook literature extends only to the outcome of the most recent revolutions in the field.

Textbooks thus begin by truncating the scientist's sense of his discipline's history and then proceed to supply a substitute for what they have eliminated. . . . Yet the textbook-derived tradition in which scientists come to sense their participation is one that, in fact, never existed. For reasons that are both obvious and highly functional, science textbooks (and too many of the older histories of science) refer only to that part of the work of past scientists that can easily be viewed as contributions to the statement and solution of the texts' paradigm problems.'

Thorne comments (74):

Seen from this point of view Constituent Structures represents the first post-revolutionary example of a textbook that partly rewrites the history of linguistics.

Thorne finds the book indispensable as an aid to evaluation of the work of linguists who do not, as does he, share Postal's assumption, but he is able also to analyze the logic of the book in terms which apply to many accounts, and on which we cannot improve (75):

While Postal, in a series of penetrating analyses, is able to show that the models proposed by these linguists can be interpreted as implying their commitment to phrase-structure grammars, the fact remains that what is actually presented in their work is in every case very far from being a phrase-structure grammar in the sense in which he himself uses the term. But this is not the criticism that Postal wants to make of this work. For him the charge that a grammar is a phrase-structure grammar . . . is the strongest criticism that can be made of it. For this reason he is prepared to ignore all the very great differences in ideas concerning the methods and aims of linguistics that separate him from these linguists, and to interpret their work as if it was intended to fulfil exactly the conditions that he himself would prescribe for linguistic research, in order, so to speak, to set them up for this final knock-out blow. The result is a view of the last thirty years of American linguistics which makes it look as if linguists in this period were groping towards the (in fact, entirely original) position adopted by Chomsky in Syntactic Structures. It is hardly surprising, therefore, that, viewed from this standpoint the most striking characteristics of their work should appear to be its imprecision, inconsistency, and an amazing tolerance of anomalies.

While it is more or less inevitable that this version of recent linguistic history will be adopted, it is, obviously, a false one.

Thorne goes on to say that the differences between the paradigm accepted by Postal and that accepted by the linguists whose work he examines are of a very different order from those implicit in a commitment to phrase-structure rather than to transformational grammar. He finds the key in a shift of center of interest from language as organized data to the organizing power capable of organizing that data. There is more to the question of continuity and discontinuity, as between Chomsky's outlook and that of predecessors, than this (see (3.3) and (4)), but Thorne is clearly right in locating the problem in a more general context. We do not like to think that it will always be the case that false versions of linguistic history must prevail. Thorne was right in his specific prediction to a great extent, but experience of the outcome may be prophylactic. Linguists' understanding of their history need not be permanently an uncritical, 'folk' understanding.

It is not that there is no place for systematic explications of elements common to a series of works or approaches. Such explication may be historically revealing. It is a matter of getting the facts and contexts straight, and careful research is needed to establish then. Thus, Lamb (1966:540) states:

C-[lassical]phonemics should not be confused with the fictitious framework which Chomsky calls taxonomic phonemics (T-phonemics), a system apparently created by him to serve as the helpless victim of a dramatic onslaught.

Derwing (1973:170–87), in contrast, thinks that, despite coinage of partly pejorative terms, Chomsky's analysis does correspond to principles employed by many linguists, but that the attack comes down to one against only the strict 'separation of levels' approach (itself not wholly ill-conceived), and not a valid attack against all preceding structuralists or all preceding structuralist phonology (187). This disagreement is a matter worth resolution, as a contribution both to history and to the clarification of mutual implication (or lack of it) of various principles. It is all the more worthwhile a matter historically, when pursued, as by Derwing, with some attention to the motives and plausibility of various positions. Here indeed is the general issue.

Systematic explication may be revealing, but it remains merely that, formal analysis of implications and consequences, so long as the only data taken into account are the data of linguistic analyses and models. Nothing can legitimately be said of motives, latent possibilities, contextual constraints and rewards, and interrelations of any kind, linguistic, personal, and social, that are not examined, data which are not included in the frame of reference. The *common move*, the *common fallacy*, of much post-hoc writing on past linguistics is to interpret a formal explication in terms of motive and context. Often enough this takes place in the classroom rather than in the published paper, but it may turn up soon enough in capsule accounts of history in published work. The failure of past linguists, as judged by an explication in other terms, comes to be felt to require explanation, and explanation is offered, not through research into the past, but through extrapolation and speculation. In this pursuit, it is common to attribute a particular assumption to an entire approach, or period, as a whole (cf. V. Makkai 1972:vii on this point and Derwing 1973:172 for analysis of an example). Also common is the assumption that explicit conceptions and actual practice were equivalent, or the one the clear cause of the other. Plausibilities, plausibilities. But a living period of history, within or without linguistics, is characterized by diversity, contrariety, even contradiction, as between persons and approaches, and even within persons and approaches. It is impossible to capture the dynamics of a period, hence impossible to explain change, without recognition of this and without direct investigation.

Whereas Postal is an explication of pre-Chomskyan syntax, Derwing (1973) is an explication of Chomskyan phonology, prefaced by an account of pre-Chomskyan work. Derwing intends, not to build a general prespective on transformational grammar, as does Bierwisch, but to build a general perspective once again on empirical foundations. He describes himself as once a convert to Chomskyan per- spective, and both phases of his intellectual biography appear in his historiography. The body of the book contains some reasonable, sometimes shrewd observations on earlier methodology vis-à-vis that of Chomsky, and Derwing rests his own recom- mendations on the conclusion that Chomsky has deprived his theory of empirical significance (285–90). But in his introduction of the 'Chomskyan revolution', Derwing gives a critique of prior work that is based in important part on Chomsky's own attack on its empirical concerns. And whereas Derwing's analysis of the deficiencies in the development of Chomsky's approach is first-hand, so to speak, his portrait of the deficiences of prior work is second-hand, and unfortunately so.

To give one example: Harris is cited (37, n. 1) as if he were a typical example of a general acceptance of non-unique descriptions, whereas Harris of course is famous for his special quality of nondogmatic exploration of formal possibilities (to use a different evaluative language). Much that Derwing deplores about the acceptance of Chomskyan *obiter dicta* later in the book is traceable to the loss of this nondogmatic attitude in Harris' student. In this context Teeter (1964) is cited as authority for the reduction of justification in prior linguistics to specification of field procedures, without concern to justify the justification (36–7); but, as we shall see, this view is false, in both its parts. 'Discovery' procedures are discussed below, in connection with anthropology (3.1) and Bloomfieldian work (3.3). Suffice it to say here, concerning justification, that Derwing's pages on this point would make it impossible to understand the vigorous, if not sometimes vicious, argumentation that went on in the period, concerning correctness of procedures. His portrait of a laissez-faire climate must be based either on ignorance of the period, or an assump- tion of homogeneity in it, perhaps both.

In sum, Derwing contributes much valuable analysis of the internal development of the Chomskyan approach, including an interesting argument that Chomsky essentially opposed one branch of earlier structuralism (in morphophonemics) to another (in phonemics) (169–189), so that the general standing of earlier struc- turalism was not properly at issue. He concludes that Chomsky's argument against 'discovery' procedures is invalidated by the fact that Chomsky's own model of language acquisition is simply a discovery procedure model in form, transferred from linguist to child (60–2). His attention to recent trends in philosophy of science is admirable (ch. 1) — but, again, his acceptance of Feyerabend's proposal for a wide range of alternative hypotheses in a science would appear to be incompatible with his rejection in the next chapter (in a Chomskyan mood?) of Harris' 'permissiveness' (37, n. 1). As a contribution to historiography, then, the book is somewhat schizophrenic, first a Chomskyan textbook evaluation of Bloomfieldian linguistics, then a rather Bloomfieldian analytic evaluation of Chomskyan linguistics, ending with a call on the final page to take up the Bloomfieldian heritage (322):

We do not start in a complete vacuum. Some of our predecessors, particularly Bloomfield and his 'structuralist' followers, have provided the basic conceptual and empirical foundations upon which a science of language-processing [i.e., acquisition] might now be cautiously constructed.

So Derwing ends by advocating a development that will lead to a view of the history of linguistics in which the Chomskyan stage will appear as an aberration, just as the Bloomfieldian stage usually appears from a Chomskyan standpoint.

Bierwisch and Derwing are representatives of two opposed tendencies within historiographic thinking, the *cumulative* and the *interregnum* views. Both are to be found within the work of the same scholar sometimes, and their coloring can vary greatly. Both are implicit narratives, sometimes dramatic narratives, for organizing the past, and we will note them again in (4).

2.2.3 Textbooks

Some recent textbooks give a sketch of the history of the subject amounting to as much coverage as found in general histories of linguistics. Such are Bolinger (1968:184–217), Fries (1963:35–92), Gleason (1965:1–87), Greenberg (1968:53–100), Hughes (1962:34–72), Lyons (1968:38–52), Posner (1970:509–19, 519–30). Here can also be mentioned texts with extremely brief notice of our subject, such as Gleason (1961:485–6), Moulton (1969:67–80), and Robins (1964:378), and also books expositing a position that have historical chapters, notably Dixon (1967:23–104), Hockett (1968:9–37), and Lyons (1970, ch. 3, "The Bloomfieldians").

Of these last Dixon offers discussion of a number of linguists in his chapter 2, "Opinions about language", conceived as a survey of past ideas about language and their ultimate derivation, so as to avoid forcing language into a procrustean bed of traditionally handed down misconceptions (vii). Dixon no longer holds to the specific methodological approach advanced elsewhere in the book, but perhaps he would consider the purpose of ch. 2 on opinions still valid, in the spirit of the remarks by Bursill-Hall (1970a:150):

There are lessons to be learned from the history of linguistics; there are themes which recur, and the problem of data and theory orientation is perennial. But the most important lesson to be learned is in accord with Martinet's axiom (Martinet 1955:125–6):

'Il faut répéter, une fois de plus, que ce n'est pas à la langue de se conformer aux édits des linguistes, mais aux linguistes d'adapter leurs méthodes si elles ne rendent pleine justice à la langue étudiée.'

Hockett provides an informative discussion of "The background" to the current debate regarding Chomsky's views. It is indeed a little disconcerting to find the issues of the relation between language structure and language change, the design of grammar (as what lies 'beyond' phonology), and the relation of grammar to meaning, described as certain issues that had not so much been settled as swept under the rug. These issues would seem to come close to defining the central concerns of general linguistic theory, and to leave little for the reasonable working consensus that Hockett says had been achieved by 1950 west of the Atlantic (9–10). It is quite revealing, therefore, that two of the four major theoretical developments cited by Hockett as part of the consensus are essentially matters of the existence and scope of a discipline of linguistics itself (confluence of the historical-comparative and philosophical-descriptive traditions (cf. Bloomfield 1933: 19), and their integration into a single, respectable, reasonably autonomous discipline (cf. our discussion in (1.3(b))), and that the other two are the phonemic principle, and development of the rest of linguistic analysis in emulation. There seems to be much reason to accept Hockett's characterization — the very existence of a discipline of linguistics, and the phonemic principle as its badge of unique, original contribution, were closely linked, and in their time, themselves heady wine. Hockett is particularly valuable on the distinction between Bloomfield's views and those of scholars, such as Hockett, who followed his lead but not uncritically, and on the diversity in the period of the 'post-Bloomfieldians' itself. He sees transformations as largely a corrective to certain temporary extremisms of the 1940's, a reintroduction, with improvements and a new name, of useful features of the Bloomfieldian and Sapirian view of language that had been set aside. And he finds the source of some of Chomsky's views (some of those most salient in the 'worldview' associated with Chomsky) in reaction to the lack of any *theory* (as distinct from methodology) of language in the work of his mentor, Harris (35–6). (Cf. Robins 1967:230–1, who sees Chomsky's views as much less of a break with European than with immediately preceding American outlook.) Hockett's chapter is a notable account of the recent history of American structuralism as diverse both within and across groups, yet essentially cumulative. He sustains this perspective by setting aside ingredients of ideology and 'world-view', and focusing attention on the design of grammar (including meaning). (On the general value of the book for history of linguistic theory, see Householder 1970:130).

Lyons' excellent chapter has been discussed in some detail in Hymes (1972: 417–20). Of the more substantial discussions in textbooks proper, Lyons (1968) is unexceptionable. Certain points of Bolinger and Gleason will be taken up with regard to anthropology in (3.1), while the general orientation of Greenberg and Bolinger can be commented upon here. It is worth noting that both men have intellectual roots outside either main paradigmatic community that shaped the Bloomfieldian and Chomskyan periods, which may be a factor in their serious interest in historical explanation.

In a chapter on "Grammatical theory" (#4, 53–77), Greenberg gives a careful account of the Bloomfieldian approach, concluding (73): 'The attempt to found a scientific descriptive linguistics along these lines can now be seen to have failed in every major respect.' His next chapter ("Phonology", 79–100) also adopts a historical perspective, the main theme being that it proved impossible to treat phonology independently of grammatical considerations. Strangely enough, neither the critique of an approach to grammar without recourse to meaning, or to phonology without recourse to grammar, makes mention of Pike's vigorous critique on just these grounds during the period in question. Here is a manifestation of the weakness of Greenberg's account, so far as explanation is concerned. He adopts a 'mainstream' approach which, while temporally oriented and sophisticated, and more informal and textured than Postal's approach, comes to much the same thing. The added sophistication indeed may be all the more misleading. When one has referred to structuralism as plausibly one phase of a broader intellectual movement in Europe and the United States, and noted the leadership of Boas, and Sapir, as well as Bloomfield (62–3), to then depict 'American linguistic structuralism' as an approach that emerged mostly after the deaths of the first two men, and in terms that both have rejected (as did some of their followers at the time), is to feed a stereotype, if not to be contradictory as well. Like many others, Greenberg here takes the work that held the center of the stage immediately before the advent of Chomsky as outcome and type of the whole.

In a chapter on "The evolving approaches to language" (11, 184–217), Bolinger, like Greenberg, is sensitive to reasons for earlier work, and sees limitations of the currently dominant approach as well. Having distinguished a Boasian period, developed and augmented by Sapir, and a second stage associated with missionary linguistics, he, like Greenberg, treats as 'American structuralism' what turns out to be 'Bloomfieldian' (in the 'post-' or 'neo-' sense) phonemics and immediate constituent structure. Again like Greenberg, once the initial impetus of field work has been noted, the course of the discipline is treated only in scientific (not in social) terms. To failure of a model, Bolinger adds growth of a storehouse of observations as an explanation for dramatic change. This slogan is familiar, but would seem to have expressed rather a wish to be *free* of accumulated observations, not to master them. The utility of previous work was largely disparaged; universals were postulated freely on the basis of one or a few languages. Apart from a few languages analyzed by Sapir and his students, and favored for restatement, earlier work was not used but ignored on the grounds of inadequacy. (Hymes recalls a discussion with Chomsky in 1961 in which earlier work was judged, not more or less adequate, but false.) Further, Hockett, Greenberg, and others had taken up the subject of cross-language generalizations and universals; within the anthropological context familiar to these men, indeed, the issue of universals had come to the fore at the end of World War II, being raised by Murdock, Kluckhohn, and others. The interest and activity was not absent, but the inductive basis of it was to be dismissed, and the activity subsequently ignored. As an explanation, then, the notion of a fullness of facts crying out for stocktaking is inadequate on two counts. Stocktaking had begun, and the new dispensation dismissed both it and its facts.

Both Greenberg (75) and Bolinger (194ff.) single out the weakness of pre-transformational grammar in dealing with syntax as its Achilles heel (Greenberg with a shrewd comparison to the initial success of structuralism in phonology, which had been the weakest area of traditional linguistics). The point that Chomsky's views succeeded first in syntax (Chomsky 1957a) at a time when the general development of the field had reached syntax is important; but it can not be maintained that all of the views successfully advanced by Chomsky were a necessary part of a successful treatment of syntax. (On the packaging of disparate tenets in a single approach, cf. Wells 1963.) It may have been inherent in the development of the discipline that the inadequacies of an approach be recognized, and crucial questions asked (cf. Bolinger 200–1); indeed, this was happening around and even within the dominant approach. It was hardly inherent in the situation that the outcome be the transvaluation of values accomplished by Chomsky. Elements of personal creativity, force, and predilection, changed social composition of the discipline, a new generation, and appeal to changed climates of opinion, must be taken into account as well.

These chapters, like any attempted account, must suffer from lack of basic research on which to draw, and the criticism directed at their explanations would attach to many shorter accounts and comments. The same limitations affect other genres.

2.2.4 *Articles*

There are many articles which are part of the controversial literature. Their insights into preceding work are an invaluable contribution, and their mistakes a part of the history itself, but we must pass over them here. There are just a few articles that are explicitly intended as general historiography. Their temporal cluster is perhaps significant. Hall (1951–2), like the commentary in Joos (1957), reflects a consciousness of accomplishment. Voegelin and Voegelin (1963) and Wells (1963) show awareness of a displacement under way. Teeter (1964, 1966) and Levin (1965) write with a displacement accepted as reference point for reassessment. (Notice that this characterization applies also to the relevant sections in Bolinger (1968), Greenberg (1968), and Hymes (1970 — drafted in 1966)). We will comment on the orientation and methodological import of the four articles of the mid-sixties, and, at the end, on their symptomatic significance. (Other aspects of the substance of the articles is taken up in connection with specific topics in (3).)

Voegelin and Voegelin distinguish a controversial, an incremental, and an eclipsing stance among linguists in regard to predecessors. The essay contains valuable information and comment, and illustrates in several ways dangers of misleading terminology. Thus, Boas' practice is called 'monolevel structuralizing' (16), and Postal (1964) properly objects. He provides evidence that Boas utilized features and representations of more than one kind in dealing with phonology. But the Voegelins' term is explained (strangely enough) as meaning *absence* of levels (17), i.e., of strict, explicit distinction and interrelation of levels (as in Sapir, Bloomfield, and, for that matter, Postal). Boas' practice might be best described indeed as recognizing several *sectors* (not levels) — sounds, grammatical processes, grammatical categories, vocabulary — whose connection, or intersection on occasion, would reflect the language in question. 'Plurisectorial' would be an awkward but not inappropriate label. The Voegelins' own paragraph account of Boas' work indicates this character of it (16). Postal's criticism of their account fits the misleading label more than the account itself, which is consistent with Postal's own explication of Boas' ad hoc, sometimes inconsistent, practice. Postal praises Boas for *recognizing* certain phenomena; the Voegelins set Boas apart for preceding formal (explicit) attention to the problems of *establishing* the place of such phenomena in a model of language design. So in the last analysis does Postal (275), on the ground of lack of ordering in Boas, and of 'relatively rudimentary' (274, 275), indeed unstated, development of the distinction between phonetic and morphophonemic levels. (Postal suggests, quite likely correctly, that the absence of attention to the subject in Boas (1911) is because the use he made of 'euphonic laws' was traditional and taken for granted.)

Postal is right in calling attention to the affinity of recent theory with Boas' practice (272), but runs the risk of confusing precedence and achievement in using terms such as 'level' and 'representation' for Boas' work. These terms imply to a reader today a model within which they have definition. Boas' implicit and inconsistent practice, requiring post-hoc explication, is indeed, after all, 'pre-level' in the sense that structuralizing in the twentieth century entails some commitment to the consequences of conscious assumptions about levels and their relationships. Postal's suggestions for historical research (274, n. 24, and 275, n. 30) are of interest, but the truly fundamental question escapes his notice. This question is not one of precedence, affinity, and unrecognized merit, but of the acceptance of commitment to explicit models of language design. Postal is far from suggesting that Boasian practice would be satisfactory today, but he does not (as most do not) appreciate the linguistic version of the paradox of the fortunate fall: had not linguistics left the garden of inexplicit recognition of phenomena, present-day linguistics would have felt no need for salvation in models which could recapture some of the richness left behind.

The Voegelins' find themselves the first to point out that pre-Bloomfield descriptive linguistics, such as that of Sapir, was not unsystematic or untheoretical (16), as against views such as expressed by Hall (1950). This '*neo*-Bloomfieldian' conception, as one might call it, in order to distinguish self-conscious ideology from acceptance of influence, repeats itself in the Chomsky period, with Bloomfield added to the pre-theoretical period (see Teeter 1964). In such usage the term 'theory' clearly is used as an honorific, rather than analytical, term; to have 'theory' becomes tantamount to sharing the goals and aspirations, the claims to ultimate significance, of a particular group. The fact that two successive periods could find immediate predecessors devoid of theory should show us the fallacy involved. On general grounds, of course, it is hard to understand how any scientific activity could be without an ingredient of theory. It is especially hard to understand how 'mentalists' of the Chomskyan period, who regard all normal human beings as having a theory of language, could deny one to some linguists. Presumably at least an implicit theory is inevitable. In sum, to talk of 'theory' as something that can be absent is a bar, one might say a vicious bar (in the legal sense), to adequate historiography. Theory is a universal component of human activity, including that of linguists. The historical question is not its presence, but its place and orientation.

Wells reviews a set of assumptions characteristic of descriptive linguistics, examines their motivation and interdependence, and neglected implications. He does not seek to explain the advent of transformational grammar (as revision or replacement of descriptive linguistics), but its reception (48):

Each school of thought . . . was presented as a 'package'. Each was rather vague. . . . But a thoughtful analysis would disclose each to be a bundle, or braid, or tangle of strands, such that one could pick out and keep some of these strands while discarding the others. But until this intellectual analysis has been carried out, people must take or reject together things that could have been taken or rejected one by one.

Each package also included some hopes and ideals (norms or goals) which are neither true nor false, but do fit better or less well with a climate of opinion. The switch toward explanation is seen as having taken place rather earlier in some other fields, including philosophy of science. Regarding one norm as preferable, and the norm and the method as inseparable, the preference for the method follows.

Wells does not neglect reasons internal to linguistics for change, but his attention to 'Zeitgeist', or changing climate of opinion, as a factor is rare and salutary.

Teeter (1964) addresses himself to an evident crisis in American descriptive linguistics. He believes that work of Boas and Bloomfield (that of the former taken as developed and augmented by Sapir) is fundamental and indispensable. He argues that certain views of Boas and of Bloomfield, taken out of context, hardened into unconscious and pernicious dogmas. These are termed the 'post-Boasian fallacy' that there are no linguistic universals, and the 'post-Bloomfieldian fallacy' that the assumption of mind can be dropped, or at least reduced to the sum total of human input-output correlations. Teeter relates the two interpretations in a story of cumulative reduction of the foundations of linguistics to a point at which nothing is left of linguistics, in principle, but field methods, and no basis for distinguishing or locating language itself. The analysis is recapitulated in these terms (204):

First, practice is divorced from theory (the post-Boasian error);
Second, theory itself is discredited (the post-Bloomfield error);

Third, under the influence of a theoretical drive which seems to be part of the nature of man . . . theory is equated to practice.

Teeter is careful to qualify his narrative by treating the literal assumptions as extrapolations, never fully accepted or expressed. Notice, however, that the entire argument depends upon the equation of 'theory' with linguistic universals, and universals of perhaps a certain sort. The argument also takes far from the only possible view of the desirability of a unity between theory and practice. Details of the accounts of Boas, Sapir and Bloomfield will be taken up with those men (3.2). Here we will only observe that the assumptions, and the narrative and consequences said to follow from them, are falsely attributed. It is indeed difficult to understand the picture of the desperate straits to which linguistics was brought, on Teeter's account, if in fact no one recognized it at the time, and if in fact (205)

the post-Boasian and post-Bloomfieldian traditions have made enormous and important contributions to linguistics. They have entirely succeeded in their initial aims to increase the proportion of reliable fact by which theories need to be informed.

Traditions which in principle (according to Teeter) could not distinguish language from the rest of mind or world must have had uncanny luck, or else something going for them that is not captured in Teeter's account.

The general answer, of course, is that each period and group did have theoretical notions, forms of general linguistics, if forms different from those brought to the fore by Chomsky. A particular part of the general answer is that field procedures never played the part ascribed to them by Teeter. Contrary to his account (203–204), procedures were justified among the Bloomfieldians, and the goal of going invariantly from sounds to phonemes had both a practical motivation (cf. Derwing 1973:184) and a theoretical motivation. Bloch (1941) reached a natural and logical consequence of acceptance of the principal of separation of levels, given an acute analytic mind such as Bloch had. And acceptance of the strict separation of levels was not a consequence of field procedure (cf. Boas, Sapir, Swadesh, Pike), but of acceptance of a conception of the logic of science. It was a conception not accepted by all (like others, Teeter oversimplifies the period), and it has a kinship with Chomsky's acceptance of a conception of the logical foundations of the science. Bloch's requirement that one be able to go from sounds to phonemes is a formal procedure (misnamed 'discovery procedure', see (3.3)) not unlike Chomsky's requirement of a formal 'recovery' procedure, whereby one be able to go from later steps in a derivation back to their source: both are intended to make evaluation of an analysis possible. Bloch wrote in an idiom in which the desirability of determining properties of new dialects and languages was salient, just as Chomsky writes in an idiom in which the desirability of determining properties of mind is salient. But the heart of the position in both cases is a concern to avoid indeterminacy in relating levels, or steps, of analysis.

One may not share this concern with equal firmness, but it is hardly strange in attempts at explicitness. The 'theoretical drive that is part of the nature of man' seems to have a strong thirst for rigor and a distaste for loose ends. At least it is this way with the theoretical drive that moves leading figures in structural linguistics, whatever their general views. In other words, for adequacy of description and explanation, a recurrent tendency, a general form of explanation is wanted here, not a narrative of a logico-historical *cul de sac*.

Teeter (1966) argues that there is a balance to be redressed in the history of the field, namely, a restudy of the sources with special attention to the theoretical concerns of the past. He is quite right, of course, in calling attention to the defects of a standard picture of past linguistic theory as having little or no interest, and to be evaluated only in terms of its contribution (slight) to empirical knowledge. (Cf. the general comments of Bursill-Hall (1970a) in a review-article centered around Mounin (1967).) Teeter points out an interesting agreement between the picture of past linguistics painted by Bloomfield, and that painted by Gray (1939), in a work otherwise quite distinct from what was to become the 'Bloomfieldian' standpoint (92, n. 3).

Levin (1965) takes recent (Chomskyan) developments to have extended the perspective by which one can judge and evaluate the historical growth of linguistics in America. He cites instances of reassessment just preceding his own, and proceeds to trace American developments in the light of de Saussure's distinction between *langue* and *parole*. The greater part of the article focuses on Bloomfield and, to a lesser extent, on Sapir, with an epilogue on Chomsky. Levin concludes that the element of agreement between de Saussure's *langue* and Chomsky's competence, as mental functions (94),

makes it possible to view the shift in orientation from the 'mechanism' of Bloomfield to the 'mentalism' of Chomsky as a return, with expected modifications, to the position so strongly urged by Ferdinand de Saussure and independently prosecuted by Edward Sapir.

This sensible conclusion is preceded by some apt analysis of Bloomfield particularly, but not much analysis of the notion of *langue*. It is the 'speech': 'language' dimension, rather than the 'individual': 'social' dimension, that receives most attention (cf. Householder 1969 on this confusion in de Saussure). Recent work by Labov and others will of course further extend the perspective by which one can judge and evaluate the growth of linguistics in the light of de Saussure's notion (cf. Labov 1970). Finally, like others, Levin speculates inaccurately about the sources of the 'American preoccupation with speech' (91–2) in work with American Indian languages (see under "Anthropology" in (3.1)).

Hymes (1970a) traces the interrelations of linguistic and ethnographic method in the United States, discussing Boas, Sapir, the period of the years just before and after World War II, the subsequent upsurge of linguistics-inspired models in ethnography, and the eventual critique of linguistics itself from an ethnographic standpoint.

The paucity of general articles suggests that an immediate sense of general crisis or displacement may be needed to provoke them. Despite considerable mention of new 'paradigms' in recent years, the concern with generative semantics, variation, and sociolinguistics generally has not provoked a set of articles like those just reviewed, although there has been a fair amount of revaluation and comment in reviews and treatments of specific subjects. In the absence of a cadre of specialists in the modern history of linguistics, then, it may be that general historiographic articles are primarily a sign not of the beginnings of serious historiography, but of a backward glance. The substance of a scholarly subdiscipline is beginning to appear, however, not in general sketches, but in articles treating general models of structure and practice over part or all of the past half-century; three have recently appeared (Huddleston 1972, Stark 1972, Fought 1973). The distinction from 'textbook' accounts and controversialist literature *per se* is to be seen in attention to diversity of views within the group or period treated, and recognition of the working out of alternatives implicitly available (some not taken up) within a framework. In varying degree all three show, not an 'eclipsing', but an 'explicating' stance. It may be that it is distance in time, the failure of a successor to achieve hegemony, or both, that makes possible such studies now. (These articles are discussed in (3.2) as regards Sapir and Bloomfield, and noted also in (3.3).)

2.2.5   Anthologies

There are a number of anthologies that bear partly on our subject: Arens (1955, 1969 (see an extensive review by Koerner (1972)), Bolelli (1965), Loja (1968), Zvegincev (1960, 1964–5 (cf. review by Lunt 1963)); Salus (1969) does not extend into our period (but cf. Koerner 1972: 430, and Koerner's review (1970b)).

One can generalize the comment of Percival (1970b:56): 'difficulty in compiling a satisfactory reader in the history of linguistics is partly due to the unsatisfactory state of the field itself.' The difficulty is not overcome by restriction to a single period, such as that of our subject, and the knowledge of a participant in it, to judge by the partisan character of Joos (1957), intended, as its subtitle states, to represent 'The development of descriptive linguistics in America since 1925'. To speak of the 'essential irresponsibility of what has been called Sapir's "method" ' (25) is a remarkable bit of irresponsibility in the light of Harris (1944, 1951a). The barely marginal indication of work by Jakobson and Pike (in a collection closing with four pieces on Spanish semivowels) makes the volume seriously unreliable as a representation of the period it treats. Treating the course of linguistics in the period as the triumph of a single group, it is an unintended precedent to later treatments of the period as overall a *cul de sac* (cf. Hymes 1958, Lightner 1968, Pandit 1970:280).

A second volume of *Readings in Linguistics* (Hamp, Householder, Austerlitz 1966) is evidence of the acceptance of interdependence between American and European linguistics; the collection expressly covers work outside the scope of *Readings in Linguistics I*.

2.2.6 Surveys, trends, and stock-takings

Some surveys resemble anthologies in their endeavor to represent a body of work, with citation replacing reprinting, but comment often more significant. The comments include historical observations, and observations with historical import to a later perspective. Early examples for our subject are articles by Hoijer, Lounsbury, and Martinet in *Anthropology Today*, by A. L. Kroeber and others (1953); Pike and Pike (1960–67); and the articles by Hamp, Hoijer, and Moulton in Mohrmann, Sommerfelt, and Whatmough (1962) (reviewed by Householder 1963, Lyons 1965). The surveys of work in linguistics in the *Biennial Review of Anthropology* (1959–71), edited by B. J. Siegel and published by Stanford University Press, are a valuable source; note especially (although not exclusively) Lounsbury (1960, 1962). The successor by the same publisher, *Annual Review of Anthropology* (1972–), promises to become of equal or greater worth; the currency of coverage of work in syntax by Silverstein (1972) is a fine example of the current trends genre.

Less catholic, but usefully bibliographic, are historically oriented articles which define an interest and position. The notable American author in this genre is Hall, with three successive surveys (1951–52, 1965, 1969a). Other examples for other approaches are Dingwall (196.., 196..), Hymes (1961, 1963, 1964, 1970a), McDavid (1951a, 1951b), A. Makkai (1972:58–116), Neustupný (197..), Pike (1954–60, reprinted in Pike (1967)) on the general field, and Pike (1966) on tagmemic work. Articles considering a period from a somewhat personal standpoint include Benveniste (1954), Bloomfield (1946b), Cassirer (1945), Hall (1946), Haugen (1951, 1972), Hill (1955), Jakobson (1962, 1971), Joos (1962), Malkiel (1959), and contributions by Bach, Fillmore, Pike, Lamb, and Friedrich to O'Brien (1971).

It would be impossible to inventory even a representative sample of statements that take stock, or define a period, from articles, books, and reviews, but the opening paragraphs of these are a rich source of them. As related examples, let us mention Pike (1947:155), Bloch (1948:4), and Bolinger (1950:117); (cf. also the sketches in Hymes 1971:51–2, 1972:7–8). Reviews especially are a major resource. Let us suggest that reviews by Householder (of which 1951, 1963, 1970 in our references are instances) would in themselves provide a useful chronicle of a generation of linguistics from an independent vantage point.

2.2.7 Lexicons and bibliographies

Lexicons are a symptom of development (though in what particular ways we are not sure). Note Voegelin (1948), concerned with the recent developments in the field as to commonalty and neologism, and Hamp (1957), compiled at the request of an international body to clarify terminology in use in the United States that might offer difficulty elsewhere. See also the informative critique by Joos (1958b), which suggests a terminological criterion for traditions, and finds four in the

United States at the time in question. The two works perhaps reflect a stage at which structural linguistics in the United States was perceived as freshly distinctive, and not yet widely international. A project for a dictionary of linguistic terminology by H. A. Gleason, Jr., is known to us, but its present state is not (cf. Gleason 1951b). Koerner (1971c) is a valuable overview of a twenty-year period.

There are no bibliographies devoted particularly to our subject, but there is one recent bibliography in the history of linguistics with some coverage of it (Salus 1971, reviewed by Koerner 1973d); see ch. XI, "The twentieth century", 42–53. There are of course the *Linguistic Bibliography* (*Bibliographie linguistique*) published since the end of World War II by the Permanent International Committee of Linguists, and the linguistic component of the MLA international bibliography (see Koerner 1971). Special note should be taken of the exemplary bibliographies on histories of linguistics now made available by Koerner (1974). Finally, some bibliographies to source materials contain entries of relevance. The two of which we know are both concerned with the Franz Boas collection and related materials in the Library of the American Philosophical Society (Voegelin and Harris 1945, superseded by Freeman 1966).

2.2.8   *Biographies*

The major genre of biographical writing remains the obituary article. A number of these are noted in connection with individual scholars in (3.2). As mentioned, the one collection for our subject is Sebeok (1966), which includes articles on Boas (Emeneau, Jakobson), Kroeber (Hymes), Sapir (Voegelin), Bloomfield (Bloch, Sturtevant), and Whorf (Carroll). (See reviews by Austerlitz (1972), Hoijer (1968), and Malkiel and Langdon (1969), all interesting assessments.) Mounin (1972) has chapters on Sapir (82–96), Bloomfield (111–25), Harris (170–88), and Chomsky (189–224). Significant personal assessments may of course appear in a variety of forms, the review of selected writings or classic works most notably. Here we mention one example for its thoughtful interpretation of the 'figure in the carpet', the extra-scientific motives, informing the life work of Roman Jakobson (Whitman 1973).

3.   EMERGENCE OF AN ACADEMIC PROFESSION

The historiography of structural linguistics in the United States must be institutional as well as intellectual. In this we perhaps differ from Koerner (1972b:257), who considers the subject to belong to the history of ideas, as perhaps its best exemplar. The subject does belong there, in part, but it is also part of the history and sociology of science, and failure to go beyond ideas is a principal cause of the present weakness of the subject. The intellectual and institutional sides are especially intimate, when as in the United States, the growth of a structural focus in the study of language is inseparable from the growth of an independent profession of linguistics (1.3).

The events and personalities involved in the founding of the Linguistic Society of America, the launching of its journal *Language*, and the provision soon after for summer Linguistic Institutes would be a good starting point for a variety of studies. Who were the early members of the LSA? Did they tend to change their other professional affiliations after the founding of the LSA in 1925? Were they concentrated in certain institutions and departments? Can they be picked out from the ranks of their other groups before 1925, and be seen as potential rebels? By some common pattern of study and publication? Did this pattern change markedly after 1925? Sheer numbers are a consideration important here, and to later evaluation of the intellectual accomplishment of the period. Hockett (1952b:88) notes that Sapir trained no graduate students before 1925, and Bloomfield trained very few himself during his career. From 1910–1930 there were virtually no newcomers to linguistics in America, save for those in historical-comparative linguistics and Boas' graduate students in anthropology.

There are a few published sources for the *LSA* and *Language*: cf. Boomfield 1925a, 1925b, 1946b; Marckwardt 1962; Moulton 1966, and of course the *Bulletins*, *Announcements*, and other documents of both. The significance of the Linguistic Institute is treated in Sturtevant 1940 and Hill 1964, and is evident in the announcements and records of each Institute; still, much of crucial importance, as to what actually was taught and learned, remains undocumented. Sturtevant (1950:304), Voegelin and Voegelin (1963:16) and Joos (1967:9) comment as to the impact of Bloomfield, and Pike (1967:3, 53–54) as to that of Sapir.[9] A history of the LSA

---

[9] The period from the first Institute through the first post-war years is of most concern to us here. It is documented in the *Bulletins* of the LSA as follows:
1928. Kent, Record of the Linguistic Institute ... 1928 (*Bull.* 2);
1928. Sturtevant, Announcement of the LI ... 1929 (*Bull.* 3);
1929. Kent, Record of the LI ... 1929 (*Bull* 4);
1930. Sturtevant, Announcement of the LI ... 1930 (*Bull.* 5);
1930. Kent, Record of the LI ... 1930 (*Bull.* 6);
1931. Sturtevant, Announcement of the LI ... 1931 (*Bull.* 7);
1931. Kent, Record of the LI ... 1931 (*Bull.* 8);
1936. *Bull.* 9, pp. 12-13 (report of the 1936 plans; the announcement is no longer part of the *Bulletin*);
1937. *Bull.* 10, pp. 13–14 (report of the 1936 LI);
1938. *Bull.* 11, pp. 16–17 (report of the 1937 LI);
1939. *Bull.* 12, pp. 18–19 (report of the 1938 LI);
1940. *Bull.* 13, pp. 20–21 (report of the 1939 LI);
1940. *Bull.* 13, pp. 83–101 (Report of the Special Committee on the Linguistic Institute);
1941. *Bull.* 14, pp. 25–27 (report of the 1940 LI);
1942. *Bull.* 15, pp. 18–19 (report of the 1941 LI);
1943. *Bull.* 16, pp. 15–16 (report of the 1942 LI);
1944. *Bull.* 17, pp. 12–14 (report of the 1943 LI);
1945. *Bull.* 18, p. 15 (report of the 1944 LI);
1946. *Bull.* 19, pp. 16–17 (report of the 1945 LI);
1947. *Bull.* 20, pp. 12–13 (report of the 1946 LI);
1948. *Bull.* 21, pp. 14–15 (report of the 1947 LI);

has been announced by its Executive Committee in connection with the Golden Anniversary of the Association in 1974 — perhaps it will be more than a Golden Anniversary document. Interest groups within the LSA deserve special study, e.g., the Group for Phonemics (1937–1949), whose existence is an indication that interest in structural analysis was not general, and the Group for American Indian Linguistics (1937–1942) (cf. Hymes 1971a:237–239). The Committee on Native American Languages sponsored much of the new descriptive research during the period; its activities are reported in *Bulletins* of the American Council of Learned Societies, as is a little as to Sapir's project in the 1930s on English grammar (cf. Kroeber 1939, Hymes 1971a:239, n. 16, and 240, n. 19). The Library of the American Philosophical Society contains important information as to the first: perhaps archives of Yale University and of the ACLS may illuminate the second.

The career of the Linguistic Circle of New York, and its journal *Word*, deserve a case study (cf. Jakobson 1971b: 536–538), as does the shifting pattern of linguistic involvement in already existing journals (notably in Classics and Germanics before World War II), and the formation of many new journals after World War II. There is, for example, a marked shift in the allocation of Bloomfield's journal publications, as before and after the founding of the LSA and the journal *Language* in 1925. In rank order, before 1925, they are: *Journal of English and Germanic Philology* 8, *Modern Philology* 4, *American Journal of Philology* 3, *Transactions of the American Philological Association* 2, *Monatshefte für deutschen Unterricht* 1, various others 6. In rank order, after 1925, the list is: *Language* 27, *Modern Philology* 10, *Journal of English and Germanic Philology* 7, *Maître Phonétique (MP)* 3, *Monatshefte für deutschen Unterricht* 2, *International Journal of American Linguistics* 2, *American Speech* 2, various others 6. Most noticeable is that the *TAPA* and *AJP* disappear and *Language* emerges massively; this change can be explained as a shift in interest away from philology toward descriptive studies (thus also the addition of *MP, IJAL, AS,* as well as some of the papers in *Language*), but Bloomfield did not cut himself off from philology, especially Germanic philology (witness *JEGP*). The more general implication is that the community of traditionally trained, philologically oriented scholars and language teachers would increasingly have to seek the publications of linguists in journals of their own, and that those entering the profession as linguists might less and less find philological journals relevant.

In general, means of expression and means of support for linguistic work need investigation. Obviously the history of our subject has not been simply a formal ballet of theoretical positions; often enough it has been a surge of groups now this way, now that, struggling for, sometimes following, sources of support The *ACLS*

1949. *Bull.* 22, pp. 12–13 (report of the 1948 LI);
1950. *Bull.* 23, pp. 17–18 (report of the 1949 LI);
1951. *Bull.* 24, pp. 12–13 (report of the 1950 LI);
1952. *Bull.* 25, pp. 12–15 (report of the 1951 LI).

has played a central role in all of this from early years, and its institutional files and perceptions would cast an interesting light. The records of sources of support in private and governmental agencies and foundations, together with oral traditions and recollections, need to be gathered and examined. Some sources of support have had long-standing purposes, independent of particular theoretical interests, e.g., the Library of the American Philosophical Society and its Phillips Fund (cf. Harris 1946, 1947, Voegelin 1949c, Voegelin and Harris 1945b, Hymes 1971a: 250–251, and the volumes of the *Yearbook* of the APS generally), and missionary organizations (cf. Wonderly and Nida 1963). In every case one needs to seek the conception held of linguistic research and its relevance to the purposes of the supporting institution; the persons and procedures involved in the giving of support; and the results of it. In many cases the questions, 'What is linguistics' and 'Why support linguistics?' will have had to be answered in terms different from those in use among linguists themselves; but such dialogue with persons outside the profession may have had much to do with institutionalization, maintenance, and change of linguistics in particular places and along particular lines. Again, personalities and social relationships external to the profession itself will have played a part and will need to be known — work will have gotten supported (or not), a certain configuration of colleagues have been made possible (or not), because of such things — an old man too long on the job, or one remembering an early enthusiasm, a young man too new on the job, especially congenial, prickly, inheriting an old antagonism, etc.

University connection with intellectual development is signalled by certain labels — a 'Yale school' (Bloomfieldian), a 'first Yale school' (Sapirian — Hymes 1971a), a 'Harvard school' (Ivić 1967:236–309), 'Mitniks'; but such labels do no more than call attention to a prominent location of an approach. The actual circles require investigation, and propinquity never accurately defines them. Historians should not make the student's mistake of assuming that names in a common catalogue imply conversations.

With regard to university programs and departments, even statistics as to the development would be helpful. (The LSA and Center for Applied Linguistics have compiled some.) Sebeok and Hammer would have been a valuable resource. One wants evidence as to the local 'structures of feeling' and personal relationships. How did programs and departments come to have their initial characteristics, and how have these been changed? Who really read most doctoral dissertations at a given time? Whose courses had to be taken by everyone? Who deferred to whom on certain topics, and why? What sort of performance was expected in examinations? What ingredients entered into the launching of successful careers from the particular place? Much of the history of the general field will have its explanation here. Patterns of stimulation and support, of discouragement and omission, will appear, and roles essential to any discipline—kinds of teaching, management functions, will become visible.

The fact that departments of linguistics are common today should not conceal their recency. The origin and growth of separate programs and departments since World War II is in special need of study. Where linguistics began as a program or committee, linking persons from diverse departments (as at Indiana), it is important to know the disciplines involved, the sources of initiative, the crystallizing factors. Local histories may illuminate the question of the emergence of a separate discipline just as much as the history of the national organization; in certain respects, local histories may be essential to understand important careers and the attitudes of certain scholars. One would like to relate some of Bloomfield's animus toward certain kinds of traditional philology to his academic experience. The discipline as a whole, and individual scholars, have often found recognition more easily at a national level than in a local setting. A leading contributor to the developing discipline might be accepted by colleagues at the LSA (including eminent philologists), yet be opposed at his own institution. (Thus, Zellig Harris could not teach linguistics in his home department of Oriental Languages, at Pennsylvania, and had to do so in Anthropology, under the guise of analysis of unwritten languages.)

The fact that departments of linguistics are common today, and linguistics well established, should not obscure the fact that links among disciplines remain important throughout the history of the subject. The question of the independence, or interdependence, of linguistics and other disciplines does not end with the formal emergence and success of the profession (cf. Jakobson 1971b, part E, "Interdisciplinary outlooks", and, in a similar vein, Hymes 1968b). On the one hand, centripetal and centrifugal attitudes seem to be present throughout. Thus, cf. Sapir (1929) to Bloomfield's remark in his 1932 review of Hermann's *Lautgesetz und Analogie* (Hockett 1970:249, n. 6):

It may not be amiss to state in this connection that Sapir and I are perhaps diametrically opposed as to proximate non-linguistic matters, such as psychology and the synthesis of linguistics with other sciences.

On the other hand, the one or the other attitude may dominate in a certain period. Indeed, one can suggest one developmental pattern, whose closer examination would be worthwhile. There would seem to be an alternating contraction, then expansion, of effective scope. For a case in a personal career (Sapir), cf. Hymes (1970:258–268); with regard to the 'cutting edge' of the profession, one can suggest that (Hymes 1970:268):

An emphasis on the separateness of language and linguistics, a sense of achievement with regard to linguistic form, a beginning to seek out a broader relevance to social life on the basis of that achievement — such can be said to be the course, very roughly, of linguistics, first under Bloomfieldian, then under Chomskyan, auspices.

Interest in 'metalinguistics', paralinguistics, kinesics and communicative behavior generally in the 1950s represent the broadening under Bloomfieldian auspices; Chomsky's attention to language acquisition comes a few years after the launching of his formal approach (though perhaps recent work in psycholinguistics (cf.

Dingwall 1970a, Derwing 1973) and in variation represent the broadening corresponding to the early 1950s). Perhaps such a pattern is inherent in a succession of formal advances, each initially restricting interest, but expansion of relevance coming inevitably.

A sense of the relevance of these matters may help insure a frame of reference for the history of linguistics that is ample enough to include them (as well as motivate collection of data that may later be unobtainable). Such a frame of reference would be that of a general 'field of linguistics', comprising all studies of language that implicate linguistic structure. Within the general field, the actual state, or effective scope, of a department or discipline of linguistics of course varies. The relation between the general field and the discipline, or department, indeed, may be different for different scholars at the same time, and of course changes in the relationship are an important part of the changing profile of linguistics itself over time.

Patterns of employment would be one important line of evidence for the changing history of such links. Hockett has implied a subtler kind of link, that of an implicit division of intellectual labor, such that a historian looking back within a single named discipline might consider absent something actually present under another label (1952b:90):

[American linguistics] has often tended to leave to general anthropology certain problems which, though found in language, are not unique thereto; European linguists have attacked some of these problems on their own. The outstanding example is the *langue* and *parole* problem. . . . The average American linguist is either unimpressed or else actively repelled; but it should not be overlooked that there has been a half-century-long debate in general anthropology in this country on the nature of 'culture' and its relation to 'behavior', which in good measure parallels the European *langue-parole* discussion.

(Hockett cites Kluckhohn and Kelly (1954) as a germinal reference; in the year of his review there appeared a major monograph on the concept of culture, by Kroeber and Kluckhohn, the nature of language having some part.)

Hockett's 1952 interpretation of the American scene underscores the need to study shifts over time in disciplinary linkages. In 1962 the *langue-parole* discussion was activated within linguistics in the United States as 'competence-performance', and by 1972 psychology would be as likely as anthropology to be the setting of general debates implicating language, and known to linguists. Cross-section at ten year intervals might indeed be one way to get at significant shifts.

The first period of emphasis on the separateness of linguistics involves the disciplines already engaged in research on language, notably *philology* generally (and as components, the several *language and literature* professions), *dialectology*, and *ethnology*.

Philology, dialectology, and ethnology, these three, are the fields of most immediate importance, because it is from these three fields that participants in the formation of a separate profession mostly came; with which the new profession would be most in competition, regarding position and preference within academic and other contexts; and which it could expect most to influence. One would expect to find varying ingredients of conversion, competition, and condescension, the choice of 'linguistics' being just that, a choice, not an inevitable or impersonal development. It was a choice, moreover, without institutional support in the form of departments of that name for almost a generation after the founding of the LSA. 'Linguists' would have to retain or seek employment in departments with language names, or in anthropology.

3.1 Philology

Concern to establish the new, descriptive work, as against domination by philology, can be readily documented (e.g., cf. Harris 1940, Lane 1945, Trager 1946, Malkiel 1969:535–536, 549, and Lyons 1970:30, n. 1). Critical response by some philologists to work such as that of Bloomfield can be traced in journals of the period; see, e.g., reviews of his book *Language*. At the same time it is important to note the decisive acceptance of Bloomfield's book by a number of leading philologists (see reviews by Edgerton, Kroesch, Sturtevant, Kent and Bolling in Hockett 1970: 258–278). At Yale in the 1930s Edgerton was a major factor in what Sapir (and after him, Bloomfield) built. In general, major philologists played a vital role in development of the new profession, and of the new approach which became central to it, even when not fully comprehending or welcoming some of its consequences.

Thus, Voegelin reports that

Bolling, the editor of Language, complained that the paper [Swadesh and Voegelin 1939] was not intelligible to him, and that he was publishing it only because he was urged to do so by Bloomfield and Sapir (letter to T. Lightner, October 6, 1970; copy supplied by Voegelin).

There was also something of a generational difference that linked Bloomfield with 'philologists', rather than with the new generation of 'linguists' (despite Bloomfield's animadversions on 'philologists' in certain contexts). Hockett reports that

In general, Bloomfield, Edgerton, and some of the elder statesmen of the Linguistic Society were gently urging Bloch, in the early years of his editorship, to try to cut down on the number of articles on phonemics and to focus more attention on other aspects of language (Hockett 1970:369–370).

Trager (1946:461) commented on Lane (1945) that

It is not, I believe, historically accurate to set up Bloomfield as the one name around whom to center descriptive linguistics as contrasted with the older historical techniques. Bloomfield's contributions to all kinds of linguistics have been so great that all of us linguists are basically Bloomfieldians; but he has always had the deepest interest in historical work . . . he has, it is my impression, rather tended away from precise and explicit formulation and codification of doctrine. . . .

On the other hand, a scholar whose work was entirely devoted to Indo-European studies could write a sketch of the history of linguistics for a philological journal in which he entirely accepted Bloomfield's point of view, that of a gradual liberation from 'the heritage of speculation which burdened descriptive linguistics from its very beginning' (Lane 1945:476) to a purely formal basis of approach to language analysis (p. 480), accepting even Bloomfield's name for the necessary approach, 'mechanistic' (480, 483).

When we have to do with 'mechanistic philologists' and 'philological mechanists', it is clear that no simple picture of a struggle between philology and Bloomfieldian structuralism, even if the picture is sometimes painted by Bloomfield himself, will suffice.

Nevertheless, Koerner (1970a:162–3) begins a study of Bloomfieldian linguistics with the statement that:

American structuralism has had to face two main criticisms by linguists of different backgrounds and various approaches to language. Firstly, it was argued that structuralism excludes the historical aspect of a given language insisting on the 'merely' descriptive synchronic method of linguistic analysis.[1] Its preoccupation with language systems appeared to render the traditional historical approach, which deals with linguistic change of various kinds, rather difficult.

Footnote (1) goes on to say (p. 163):

Since we are not concerned here with the relation of structural linguistics to historical-comparative or 'diachronic' approaches to language description, we may simply refer the reader to the criticisms of T. B. W. Reid (1956 and 1960) and A. Nehring (1962). . . . That these charges cannot be laid against Bloomfield himself can clearly be seen from the fact that he devoted almost half of his main synthesis of the study of language to problems of historical linguistics. . . .

It is indeed true that structural linguistics in the United States has been criticized by practioners of comparative-historical linguistics, or philology, but it is difficult to be sure what Koerner is saying. His exemption of Bloomfield (n. 1), because of attention to historical linguistics, suggests a conflict between historical and structural approaches as such. The following sentence of the main text, however, suggests that what is meant is only that the kind of descriptive method adopted in the United States made historical work difficult, and that what was excluded was not history as such, but historical factors and insight from descriptive grammar. (The first sentence of the footnote also suggests this interpretation, in speaking of 'approaches to language description'.) If so, then the charge can be laid against Bloomfield contrary to Koerner's note, and no amount of pages on historical linguistics in a textbook would excuse him. But the matter is further confused. The English-language criticisms, cited first by Koerner in his note (Reid 1956, 1960), are not only not critical of neglect of history, but also not criticisms of neglect of linguistic change as much. As to the first point, Reid presumably knew that his main target, Hall, practices history as well as description. As to the second, his criticism can be summed up as a charge of unworkable narrowness, particularly in neglect, not of history, but of meaning, and of social complexity and variation. Whatever the confusion in Koerner's brief exposition, it is important to consider the two types of criticism to which he alludes. The descriptive approach that crystallized in the United States was often enough attacked both for what it did not do (history) and for what it did (description of a certain sort). It was attacked from the standpoint of an older tradition, that of comparative-historical work, as a departure from its concerns and its conception of language. But it is essential to locate such criticisms carefully, and to assess them against the record of the actual emergence of descriptive, or structural, linguistics in the United States. To do so will show that the issues can in no way be reduced to a simple conflict between philology and structuralism. Descriptive issues as to the nature of language divided structuralists themselves, and had an admixture of philosophical and cultural position; and the relation of descriptive linguistics to comparative-historical work, and to philology as such, has been very complex. Let us consider first the general relation to philology, and in particular to comparative-historical work.

In Europe, opposition to structuralism, involving restricted numbers of professorial chairs and limited opportunities for academic advancement, as well as other factors (such as Germanic vs. non-Germanic scientific tradition), continued as an issue in various places into the post-war period,[10] despite the opportunity for integration of structural and historical work offered by the perspective of Jakobson and the Prague School (cf. statements from 1919 onward by Jakobson, reprinted in Jakobson 1962:20, 218, 502f., 651). Nevertheless, there was integration of the two kinds of work in some circles in Europe, and from at least 1930 on the issue can be said to have been, not the doing of comparative-historical work, but the kind of comparative-historical work that should be done. Bloomfield's integration of descriptive and comparative work in his book *Language* (1933) shows that such a situation was international. The deeper truth of the situation in the United States, however, is that conflict between the two kinds of work was never as much an issue. Leading structuralists practiced comparative-historical linguistics, 'contrary to a widespread impression' (Hall 1969:198), the leading structuralists being outstanding examples (Bloomfield, Sapir). Such work went on partly within established fields, Bloomfield maintaining his interest in Germanic scholarship (cf. Moulton 1967), and Sapir working afresh on Indo-European and Semitic in the last years of his life. A striking feature of the situation in the United States is that scholars who participated in the founding of structural description participated also in the founding of the comparative-historical linguistics of a great many language families. Comparative philology was effectively introduced to these families by structuralists — Bloomfield in Algonquian, Sapir in Uto-Aztecan, Athapaskan, etc. (cf. Haas 1953b, Hockett 1948, Hymes 1971a:231, 242–252).

The descriptive-structural movement also laid the foundations for the philology

---

[10]   Thus Haugen (1958: 499) notes that J. R. Firth was 'often quite belligerent towards the historical linguists who were dominant when he first wrote'.

of a number of languages in the sense of textual study as well (cf. citations of statements of principle in this regard in Hymes 1959). An anthropological context, and the interest in American Indian languages, defined philology and synchronic analysis as mutually relevant; one required knowledge of structure, of history, and of culturally authentic text, all three, and often required description for the sake of history and texts.

It might be, of course, that structural linguists accepted comparative-historical work, but that scholars trained in comparative philology rejected the new descriptive approach. Such scholars sometimes did reject the new approach, but others did not. Indeed, attitudes that we may today associate with the rise of the new approach in the 1930s are to be found early in the century. Their continuity is one of the most striking and most neglected aspects of the history of modern linguistics. We associate a sense of mission to bring the results of linguistics to public attention, a sense of righteous indignation that linguistics goes unheeded (especially in language teaching) with the Bloomfieldians, but Bloomfield himself expressed such views early in the century, well before he discussed phonemes or behaviorism. Again, the view that linguistics is a science does not arise with structural linguistics, or the behaviorist Bloomfield, but spans the century and is shared by eminent philologists. Note the references to 'linguistic science' and 'scientific study of language' in reviews of Bloomfield's 1914 book (Hockett 1970:50, 51, 54, 55), and the use of 'linguistic science' throughout his publishing and teaching career by Sturtevant (see below on his course, "Introduction to Linguistic Science" at Linguistic Institutes from 1930 on, and his book (1947)), as by the Indo-Europeanist Lane (1945, 1949).

It would seem that structural work *became* the central focus and ideology of an organized profession, and contributed to the development of an organized profession, but was not alone responsible. Far from it. There is a tendency to interpret the years before the Second World War in the light of the situation after it. We notice work of foundational importance as early as the middle twenties (notably Sapir (1925) and Bloomfield (1926)), and are tempted to think that the story of those years is the story of the work of Sapir, Bloomfield, and the students of theirs who became central to field in the 1940s. That is far from the whole story. Much more needs to be known, but it is clear from institutional records and personal recollections that structural linguistics was a subordinate theme in organized linguistics in the 1920s and 1930s. The formation of the Linguistic Society of America, the founding of the journal *Language*, and the initiation of Linguistic Institutes — the three major expressions of professional institutionalization — were not expressions of the rise of structural linguistics, but more, it would seem, an expression of the desire of scholars with primary interest in language itself, conceived as an object of science, for a common forum and home for that interest.[11]

---

[11] See the concise, clear retrospective statement by Sturtevant in his history of the Linguistic Institute (*LSA Bulletin* 13:83–84 (1940)).

Consider the survey of linguistic studies undertaken by Kent and Sturtevant for the new LSA (1926):

The term 'linguistic course' has been taken to mean one that deals with the principles and the history of language in general or of a group of languages or of a specific language; with phonology and morphology, syntax, semantics, phonetics, with general (descriptive) or experimental phonetics, whether or not illustrative of a single language; with the psychology of language.

General linguistics is linked with historical perspective ('the principles and the history of . . .'). The topics that we associate with descriptive or structural linguistics, and consider central to general linguistics today, come second (phonology and morphology, syntax, semantics, . . .), and are linked with the study of particular languages and language families (as the qualification for phonetics 'whether or not illustrative of a single language' suggests). The summary tables of the report show as much. Their headings (pp. 6–7) are as follows:

I.   General Linguistics and miscellaneous Indo-European
II. Greek, Italic, Romanic
III. Germanic
IV. Semitic and Miscellaneous.

In short, from the point of view of a survey of training available in general linguistics in the mid-twenties, conducted on behalf of the professional organization devoted to linguistic science, phonology, morphology, syntax and semantics do not appear as primary headings. They are not general linguistics, and will not be for ten or twenty years.

The same picture appears from the history of the Linguistic Institute in the period. The first Institutes were quite small in attendance (1928–31), those of the resumption in the mid-thirties (1936 onward) notably larger, but throughout the basic course of the Institute was an "Introduction to Linguistic Science". As taught the first two years by Prokosch (a Germanicist much admired by Bloomfield), and subsequently for many years by Sturtevant, its character was that of comparative-historical linguistic science. Here is the description of the course as announced by Sturtevant for 1931 (*LSA Bulletin* 7:8 (1931)):

The origin of the science, and some of its chief results. Phonetic law; its importance and some suggested explanations. Analogy: contamination, analogical creation, analogy in syntax. Other changes of form. Change of vocabulary, including word-formation. Change of meaning. A survey of the known languages.

The other courses of the Institutes in these years are predominantly in Indo-European languages and studies. For the first Institute Pliny Earle Goddard was to have offered "Linguistic Anthropology" and "Methods of Studying Unrecorded Languages", but had to withdraw because of illness (as it proved, fatal). J. Alden Mason took up the second of the courses, having the Polynesian specialist Stimson as his one student. Neither course was offered in subsequent years. As for anthropological and social science approaches, the initial proposer of an institute, R. Saleski, offered "The sociological study of language" in 1929, but no one enrolled (*Bull.* 4 (1929), p. 15); Boas visited to give one lecture, "The relation between grammar and lexicography" on July 10 of the 1930 Institute; but no work in American Indian languages or in descriptive linguistics as such, even field work with unwritten languages, is offered. The sympathy and interest in study of American Indian languages is present in the Society (cf. Kent and Sturtevant 1926: 14, reproaching American universities for the fact that only five offer facilities for training in the study of such languages), and the Institute early on stood sponsor for work on American Indian languages supervised by a committee chaired by Boas (cf. *Bull.* 3 (1929), p. 4).[12] But the main activity directly involving the Institute is sponsorship of the organization and conduct of a *Linguistic Atlas* (cf. *Bulletins* 3 (1929), p. 4; (1931), p. 5; 7 (1933), p. 4; Sturtevant 1940:87–88). It is not until Sapir's course in 1937 that descriptive linguistics (in the context of work with unwritten languages) is offered,[13] and not until the 1939 Institute that emphasis upon descriptive techniques is noteworthy (*LSA Bull.* 13 (1940), p. 20). (We do not presently know the character of the "Introduction to Linguistic Science" as taught in 1937 by Sapir and 1938 by Bloomfield (on the great attention to these courses, see Edgerton (1940 — excerpted in Hockett 1970:530).

This picture is supported by Voegelin's remark that historical linguistics 'enjoyed top-billing' in Linguistic Institutes until World War II (1959:110), though not with the remark that 'the close-knit membership of the LSA . . . could talk about nothing else [save Bloomfield's wholly American, wholly explicit linguistic theory] at the half dozen Linguistic Institutes preceding World War II' (Voegelin and Voegelin 1963:20). For one thing, Bloomfield was not 'present at every one of these LI's *(idem)*; he taught throughout the 1938 Institute, and visited one or two days (weekends) in 1939 and 1940 (Bloch 1949, in Hockett 1970:526, and Hockett 1970:541). Voegelin's 1963 remark no doubt reflects the perspective of the close-knit younger group that was to emerge to prominence, beyond the setting of Linguistic Institutes, in the years after World War II (the context indicates that Voegelin has in mind specifically structural description). This perspective will engage us in discussing Sapir, Bloomfield, and especially Bloomfieldians, in later sections.

Assumption of editorship of the LSA's journal, *Language*, by Bernard Bloch in

---

[12]   The Commitee on Research in American Native Languages was launched with sponsorship of the ACLS in 1927, with funds from the Carnegie Corporation. LSA *Bull.* 3 (1929): 4 reports were accomplished in 1928 and projected for 1929. For further discussion, and sources as to the Committee, including its reports in the *Bulletin of the ACLS* in these years, see Hymes 1971a: 237–239, esp. n. 16.

[13]   The innovation is not noted at the time in the official report (*Bull.* 11 (1938): 16), but its organized successor the next year (urged by Sapir) is noted in terms of cooperative research with Native American Indian informants (Voegelin and Harris with Hidatsa, Bloomfield with Chippewa; see *Bull.* 12 (1939): 19). Sapir's 1937 teaching of Field Methods in Linguistics, and the phonetics of Navaho is later noted by Sturtevant (1940:88), and Hill (1964:4).

1940 may be seen to register a decisive change. With regard to the dominance of philological interests within linguistic science until this time, it is worth noting that in his first report, Bloch commented (*Bulletin* 14 (1941):25):

> It appears that some members of the Society regard LANGUAGE as a journal devoted chiefly to the ancient languages. If the distribution of articles published during the past few years seems to support that view, it is not through any choice of the Committee on Publications, but because the scholars at work in the ancient languages have sent in more material than others. In order that our journal may more fully represent the varied interests of our membership, the Committee would welcome a larger number of contributions in the field of the modern languages, especially English. Any apparent one-sidedness in LANGUAGE can only be corrected with the active cooperation of all our members.

Notice that the discussion is in terms of languages, ancient versus modern, not in terms of perspective or method (historical vs. structural).

A few years later Bloch felt compelled to justify his editorial work against the charge of favoritism to a single field, 'school', or even university (*Bull.* 18 (1945): 14). A year later he reported lack of enough material to make up the next number, and presented statistics as to the distribution of articles in the entire 21 volumes of Language so far published (15 under Bolling, 6 under Bloch). The differences are calculated. As in the comment in Bloch's first report, the tables are organized in terms of language families and groups. The organization may have been disingenuous (in that suspicions and complaints were at least in important part concerned with perspective and method, rather than with language of application), but the organization continues a conception found in the report by Kent and Sturtevant that constituted the first *Bulletin* of the Society (1926, discussed above). Given the terms of organization, the tables show, as Bloch states, no differences in proportion of space per topic that can not be accounted for by number and length of acceptable contributions treating the topic.

Given that *Language* did serve as the place of publication of major articles by the emerging group of structural linguists (Hockett, Harris, Trager, Bloch himself, and others) and that after 1944 the rival journal *Word* was found or felt to be more hospitable to certain topics and kinds of exploration, nevertheless, so far as comparative-historical and Indo-European work is concerned, *Language* continued to publish it, as it does today.[14]

The continuity of comparative-historical work is further indicated in the fact that general books and textbooks in the United States were expected to include it (cf. Sapir 1921, Bloomfield 1933, Gleason 1955, 1961, Hockett 1958) throughout the period in which structural perspective became central. In their descriptive work, indeed, structuralists in the United States were far from denying links with history. Thus, Sapir (1922:95):

---

[14] Note that Andrews and Whatmough (1961) depended almost entirely on a survey of Language 1930-1959' for a rather extensive survey of comparative and historical work, despite . . . decline for the subject (p. 58 and n. 1).

Of this large number of types (of stem-formation in Takelma) about half are of frequent occurrence, while of each of the rest but few examples have been found. . . . It is very probable that some of these are ramifications of others, while some types show more or less petrified suffixes that for some reason or other became specialized in certain tenses. As comparative linguistic material is entirely lacking, however, we can not make a genetic classification of types; a purely descriptive classification must suffice.

Such an approach remained with Sapir, and in a letter to Voegelin (August 17, 1934), giving a detailed commentary on an analysis of Shawnee phonemes, one finds Sapir treating a strict synchronic perspective as something publicly prescribed but privately to be circumvented for the sake of insight:

I should think the comparative evidence might give one a valuable hint. Theoretically, all phonemic matter should be discussed and settled without reference to history; practically, it is sometimes a real help to take a forbidden peep at comparative evidence and then rationalize thus acquired insights as best one can on descriptive grounds.[15]

In his book Sapir (1921:153) had joined descriptive and historical grammars as sources of knowledge of linguistic structure, and turned to historical persistence for evidence of structural depth. Bloomfield's postulates (1926) to include historical linguistics, and his 1933 book is of course a masterful integration of historical linguistics within a structural framework; the major contribution to Algonquian studies published in his lifetime (1946) is in a comparative-historical framework, as is the series of lectures he chose to give to the 1939 Linguistic Institute (on comparative Algonquian).

Certainly there came to be structuralists who did not do comparative-historical, or textual work, and particularly there came to be many who did not continue philology in its Indo-European embodiment. Pride of place did shift. Thus, Trager (1946:462) states, 'all linguistics is descriptive', historical linguistics being considered 'diachronic description of several stages of the same language'. By 1949, looking back on the emergence of descriptive linguistics, Lane (1949:333) could begin a paper with the claim that:

For more than a generation now the bulk of scientific linguistic publication in America has been devoted to descriptive linguistics and the vast majority of the last generation of students of linguistics have devoted themselves largely to that field. The larger measure of scientific advance has accompanied the larger measure of devotion . . . notable exceptions have been due to the continued labors of an older generation of scholars.

---

[15] Thus it is an error to infer (Koerner 1970a:164): 'Since the analysis of these native languages could not be based on any written record, a synchronic descriptive method turned out to be the only adequate procedure for linguistic investigation.' This flat statement overlooks the use of internal evidence for the history of a language – Boas recurrently noted such evidence, Sapir employed it brilliantly and systematically in analysis of Chinookan, and Radin insisted upon it in his grammar of Wappo. Moreover, descriptive analyses themselves provided a written record that could be used for comparative-historical perspective. The exigencies of the data did not determine the theoretical perspective with which the languages were studied. In particular, Boas, rightly singled out by Koerner, brought to the data a fundamental interest in historical process. A strict synchronic compartmentalization came to the fore, as a principle, much later, when much more data to circumvent it was available.

Lane is likely wrong in terms of bulk of publication, concerning the preceding generation (that would imply a period from 1924 or earlier), but the prospective bulk of publication for the next generation (1949–1974) would of course bear him out. What he overstated, but perceived correctly, was the seed which had been growing within the covering for linguistic science provided by philologists within the LSA, Linguistic Institutes, and *Language*. He was right, not as to statistics, but as to center of gravity. Even so, there is a misleading equation between 'the 19th-century brand of linguistic science' and comparative Indo-European grammar (333). Many descriptivists continued that 'brand', as it had developed in the twentieth century, only with regard to languages other than Indo-European.

One must, to be sure, take into account experiences such as that described by Malkiel (1969:536), the experience of a drastic effect of polemic overtones in some of Bloomfield's remarks on the relation between the established philological traditions and the new generation's mode of work. The Bloomfieldians had often a sense of building from scratch, and many things were gaily rejected or abandoned temporarily. With many Bloomfieldians, synchronic, static arrangement and classification of the observed came to be identified with a scientific approach, as against representation and imputation in terms of diachronic or dynamic process. Even so, those most active in fostering this outlook often did historical as well as synchronic work. Indeed, it is only in the concentration on methodological models, from Harris (1951) through Chomsky (1957, 1965), that comparative-historical linguistics is almost lost from sight. Even here one can detect something of a division of labor in the Harris approach (cf. Hoenigswald 1960), and in recent years there has been increasing concern among adherents of Chomsky's approach to deal with historical problems. Close textual analysis, of the sort known to Germanists, anthropologists, and folklorists, does almost disappear for a time, but the applicability of linguistic analysis to literary and other texts is never wholly neglected, and has a certain history throughout the domination of Bloomfieldian and early Chomskyan approaches.

In sum, the rise of descriptive, or structural, linguistics often enough was accompanied by aversion to 'philology', as a label for some practices, attitudes, and styles of work, but there is no simple relation of rejection or supercession. Therein lies one of the major positive features of the rise of structural linguistics in the United States. Leading scholars saw their work, not as the denial of the valid content of philology, but as its extension, indeed universalizing, to peoples and languages without philologies of their own. In this extension there arose, and remain, strains and tensions between established European philologies and the newer ones. Work on the new basis challenged received opinions as to languages and cultures, especially 'primitive' languages and cultures; there were no doubt conflicts of role and personality as well. Nevertheless, structural linguistics in the United States developed on the assumption that it helped to complete the impulse that had created the philogies of classical antiquity and Asia.

Let us deal more specifically with the criticism of the emergent descriptive linguistics with regard to descriptive practice. As with the charge of neglect of history, it is essential to locate the criticisms in terms of source, time, and focus. As has been noted, the criticisms of Reid (cited by Koerner) accuse Bloomfieldian descriptive practice of the 1940s, as exemplified especially by Hall, of an unworkable narrowness. It is important to bear in mind that such criticisms did not have philologists as their only source. Criticism of descriptive practice of Hall's sort for neglect of meaning came from many sources (cf. Gray 1945–9, Pei 1944, Schlauch 1946, 1947, Sperber 1960, Spitzer 1946, Swadesh 1948a, Timpanaro 1970). The bases are in part philological perspective and philosophical idealism, but they include Marxism (Schlauch, Swadesh), from which perspective the Bloomfieldian behaviorism was mechanical materialism, not historical materialism, for which attention to social relationships and meaning was essential. And the critics included early leaders of structural linguistics in the United States (Swadesh, Pike, Nida).

The crucial respect in which structural linguistics in the United States separated itself from the views of some linguists associated with traditional philology (and some linguists associated with structuralism as well) was with regard to what may be called *methodological relativism* (cf. Hymes 1973a:24–25). This perspective owed much to the anthropological tradition in the United States, but one must distinguish between objections to it as a general principle (encompassing its anthropological role), and objections to certain uses of it in linguistic description. The latter objections are concentrated on treatments by Bloomfieldians such as Hall and Trager of languages such as French. Criticism in terms of the general nature of language had even more force, and motivation, it would seem, when the nature of certain languages was in question.

The general anthropological principle has often been taken to have been expressed by Joos (1957:96): 'the American (Boas) tradition that languages could differ from each other without limit and in unpredictable ways.' (It is quoted as 'unpredictably and without limit' in Teeter (1964:8) and Stankiewicz (1966:495, n. 1)). Insofar as the statement is taken to express a radical relativism, it is mistaken, and it is misleading in its failure to show the other side of the coin, namely, that all languages could be regarded as *equal*, both in the eyes of linguistics and of mankind.

Joos presents the statement as contradictory to the universalism of Trubetzkoyan phonology. (It is European ideas, especially those from Prague, Joos says, that were most often called 'structural' by the Bloomfieldians, who favored 'descriptive' in the early 1940s.)[16] There was indeed insistence, warranted by experience, as to the danger of imposing a priori categories on languages. The tension between an inductive and an a·priori emphasis persisted throughout the development of struc-

---

[16] In other words, for participants in the linguistics of the period, 'structural' tended to be associated with general linguistics and universals – just the opposite of the association given to the term and period by many adherents of Chomsky. (Cf. discussion of the term in (1.2).)

turalism, and there was some noticeable difference between dominant American and European outlooks in this regard. But Boas (and Sapir, and Kroeber — see Hymes 1961a:21–2) did not at all consider that languages could differ from each other without limit. They held definite conceptions of properties, and an analytic frame of reference, valid for all languages (cf. Boas 1911, Sapir 1921). Each indeed saw the importance of linguistics as residing partly in the universal properties it warranted (cf. Boas 1908, Sapir 1921). Whorf, the person in their tradition most prominently associated with the idea of radical difference, held that there was an underlying universal realm of form (cf. Hymes 1971a:235–236). There were Boas and Sapir models for description, and a Whorf formulation of a general guide to the plan and arrangement of languages (cf. Hymes 1961c:23–27, 1972b).

A continuity can be traced from Boas to Chomsky in the assumption of a universal analytical method. The notion acquires richness of content through the years, to be sure. In Boas it is comprehensive, but with little detailed content; the emphasis is upon avoiding ethnocentrism in description (of which much was present). In Sapir (1921) the Boasian (and Humboldtian) form of general linguistics, focused on typology, is much enriched, and followed by specific investigations of universal semantic dimensions (i.e., grading, and the ending-point relation). With the Bloomfieldians the attempt to develop strict canons of description amounts to specification of the form of language in some detail, and the mathematical bases of such specification are explored by Harris, Hockett, Greenberg, and others. With Chomsky such specifications take a different and fuller form, but form of possible descriptive statement is similarly restricted.

The earlier structuralist work can be evaluated, and criticized, properly enough, for limited accomplishment with respect to general linguistics and universals, but, as we have seen, the impression that there was no theory in this regard, no attention to general linguistics and universals, is false, both as to the status of general frameworks for analysis of language and as to empirical investigations. The impression is the more misleading, because it was *precisely* the universalism of the approach that offended many critics, some writing from the standpoint of 'traditional grammar'. With description, as with history, the work was seen as extending universal principles of regularity uniformly to all languages. The approach might equally be called 'methodological universalism'. The relativism was heuristic with regard to specific languages, and it was a Boasian, and anthropological, way of making one's scientific work what today would be called 'vulnerable'. The surprises in newly described languages could lead to revision, if necessary, of the appropriate level of the general framework. But the fundamental properties of the framework were not 'up for grabs'. Indeed, it was thought to be the triumph of linguistics that its universal categories were just that, concrete universals, allowing for the specific phonological patterns and entities of individual languages within a framework of principle applying to all (cf. Harris 1951:8, n. 6).

With regard to the heuristic relativism in the methodology, it is striking to find that non-European languages again play the role of making universal frameworks vulnerable. Lightner (1971:574) writes:

People are going out and looking, e.g., at non-Indo-European languages and they're finding a large number of things they didn't expect to find.

In this respect it is worth remarking that Matthews (1972) suggests that the structural integrity of different types of language be taken as a methodological principle (cf. Lyons 1962 on the value of this in phonology). Matthews writes out of concern to do justice to Latin; his suggestion is reminiscent of the Boasian view which often tagged an attack on the 'Latin model' (cf. Bolinger 1968:194, Hymes 1963: 94–5)!

In the light of such statements it would be tempting to sketch a cyclical course for the relation between general frameworks and specific languages; one could see priority to one alternating with priority to the other (e.g., pre-Boasian, then Boasian, then Chomskyan, then post-Chomskyan emphases). Such a sketch may have some justification in so far as dominant public ideologies are concerned. At any time, however, and with regard to any type of general framework, one can distinguish work that is more a priori, and work that is more inductive (cf. Hymes 1963:80). The problem of the relation between imposed framework and exposed language may be the more significant for being unrecognized. (Precisely these points are made by Hockett (1966:70–71) with regard to one tagmemic mode of analysis.) A historical sketch of this dimension of American structuralism, then, will show, not a rising and falling line, but variously located clusters.

With regard to the universalism (egalitarianism) in the methodology, no doubt the climate of opinion after World War I was favorable to the tone taken with regard to it; perhaps something of the social origins of linguists in the United States also played a part. The most militant spokesman for the egalitarian implications of the position has been perhaps Hall. Thus he wrote (1946:33–4) of 'socially biased value judgments which European scholarship has inherited from the aristocratic, theological background of mediaeval and Renaissance intellectualism'. There were indeed real biases with which issue had to be joined, and it is misleading for a scholar (known for egalitarian views in other respects) to write somewhat condescendingly (Bolinger 1968:194): 'The categories of classical grammar were gone — they were good for Latin but not, so it was thought, for Hokan or Chinook.' A diverse language family (Hokan) is unfortunately paired with a language (Chinook), and the genuine problem of universalizing descriptive concepts adequate to American Indian languages is missed; cf. Sapir 1922:52–3:

If we study the manner in which the stem unites in Takelma with derivative and grammatical elements to form the word, and the vocalic and consonantic changes that the stem itself undergoes for grammatical purposes, we shall hardly be able to find a tangible difference in general method, however much the details may vary, between Takelma and the languages that have been dignified by the name 'inflectional'.

Sapir reviews the relation between processes in Latin, Greek, German, and Takelma, in the typological terminology of the day, and concludes (54):

Not that Takelma is in the least thereby relegated to a peculiar or in any way exceptional position. A more objective, unhampered study of the languages spoken in various parts of the world will undoubtedly reveal a far wider prevalence than has been generally admitted of the inflectional type. The error, however, must not be made of taking such comparatively trivial characteristics as sex gender, or the presence of cases, as criteria of inflection. Inflection has reference to method, not to subject-matter.

There were those who seemed quite unconvinced of the desirability of losing the prejudices (embodied sometimes in the use of typological terms such as 'inflection' and 'incorporating') that the Boasian tradition (accepted by Sapir, Kroeber, Bloomfield and others) was designed to eradicate. 'Culture languages' with a written literature continued to be distinguished from other languages, whose speakers, to put it bluntly, were considered uncivilized, in respects that had nothing to do with culture. Culture languages are considered to require special handling to capture their richness; techniques and theories designed for 'unwritten languages' are simply not good enough.

Hence the force in the early period of Sapir's aphorism (1921:234): 'When it comes to linguistic form, Plato walks with the Macedonian swineherd, Confucius with the head-hunting savage of Assam.' And although prejudicial attitudes might be thought to belong only to the earlier period, there are many manifestations of them in the postwar period as well. Thus Pei (1944:170):

. . . is it quite fair to treat a language like French, which is the vehicle of a great culture and civilization, exactly as we treat some little-known tongue of central Africa that has no literary, cultural or esthetic values, or even a written form?

(Cf. Messing 1951, Reid 1956:34, n. 1, and Malmberg 1964:183, with apt rejoinder by Langdon (Malkiel and Langdon 1969:572).) There are theoretical underpinnings for such a viewpoint, but it would be a mistake to miss the role of plain snobbery in it. Echoes of fights against such snobbery were to be reawakened in those raised in early structuralism by the deductive aspect of Chomskyan grammar, its justification of the written form of language, and its downgrading of languages other than the linguist's own. Bloomfieldians had perhaps turned from the 'mentalism' of Boas and Sapir, and some of their interests, but had accepted wholeheartedly, as a common tenet of faith, the themes of equality, diversity, and scientific relevance of all languages. For them, the new approach could not but smack of reaction (cf. Hall 1969:220–223).

The methodological relativism (egalitarianism), while an important part of the *solution* to the problem of creating a general linguistics on a universal basis, appeared as a problem to others, the problem of an approach which might deny their vital interests (and often did). Cases of such response are difficult to assess, however, because the immediate target may be open to criticism for narrowness of data base or method. Criticism on these counts, indeed, could come from other structuralists. Thus Martinet (1949:30–31) does not object to use of the same methods for French as for 'Polynesian and Hottentot' (his examples), but to their procrustean character when applied to French. His evaluation reflects a settled opinion as to how French morphology really works, but the analysis to which he objects, by Hall, really *is* procrustean, in its abundance of zero morphs, stretching French forms to fill the descriptive format. Still Martinet can be read as arguing, not against use of zero forms in general, but against use of them for French; he implies that they may be good enough for the exotic languages he seems to think Hall to be schooled in. In contrast, Bloomfield (1945b:8) was sharply critical of Trager's analysis of French morphology (1944) on the grounds of lack of clarity and of pedagogical value. Bloomfield went so far as to say that 'a less rigorous statement may be more useful even for scientific purpose'. (Cf. Trager's remarks (1955: 511–512) and cf. Hall (1951–52) for a list of other attacks on his analysis of French.)

In sum, we have to distinguish two dimensions of the controversy (a controversy quite important for the image of a distinctively 'American structuralism', perceived in a Bloomfieldian image by both parties, as it bid for attention and acceptance). There was the issue of a uniformitarian approach to description of languages, and there was the issue of the particular methods employed by those American linguists who analyzed languages such as French under the uniformitarian banner. Some critics could distinguish between the two issues. (See the measured evaluation by Malkiel (1962:63–91).) And some American linguists could undercut the uniformitarian approach by accepting the distinction some critics wished to make, and inverting the evaluation. What was disdained by the former in the name of literature and civilization was esteemed by the latter in the name of science. Thus, to the objection that Indian languages were not of interest because they had no 'literature', no Shakespeare, a linguist could reply that that was their advantage. The reply reflected perhaps the attraction to linguistics of students interested in language but not in literature, and no doubt reflected the assumption that unconscious patterns were most regular and readily described (cf. Hymes 1970 on the history of this assumption from Boas through Lévi-Strauss). Again, structuralists working with American Indian languages might assume homogeneity and the representativeness of a single informant, and proclaim it an advantage, as if to prove the case of the philologist who could document easily the heterogeneity of French (cf. Reid 1966).

In this interplay between philological tradition and emergent structural linguistics, then, we have a history more complex than 'good guys' vs. 'bad guys'. The universalistic principle could be implemented by a procrustean methodology, and even compromised by workers in its tradition. Those who criticized the methodology might do so from a parochial base, but might also point to slighted phenomena with which later linguistics would have to deal. So far as we know, however, the critique did not itself rise to a universalistic plane, calling on structuralists to recognize the unsung Miltons and interesting heterogeneity that escaped their net in pools all their own.

The controversy helps to characterize the period of the 1940s and 1950s. In a longer time perspective, the relationship between philological traditions and structural linguistics shows important continuities, as we have seen. The details and dynamics of this, in terms of persons, teachers as well as practioners, and in other respects, deserve thorough study. As time elapses, the perspective in which we perceive the controversial issues will become more complex, for a critique of the limitations of the egalitarian outlook has begun, in the light of a renewed evolutionary perspective (cf. Hymes 1968a, and 1971a:v–x). It will come to seem not merely a recognition of permanent truth, but an interesting question, as to why Bloomfieldians, not themselves engaged in work with American Indian languages, so thoroughly embraced the egalitarian perspective originating in anthropology (cf. Hill 1952, and references in Hymes 1964c, part II, 82–4, esp. Bloch 1956).

Linguists with a philological background were associated with language teaching, of course, and much of the continuity in the relation between philology and structural linguistics, as well as a source of discontinuity, lies in the relation to language teaching of both (cf. Robins 1967:231–232).

3.2   *Language Teaching*

Certain aspects of language teaching were of course of concern to missionary linguists from the outset (cf. the practical implications of the title of Pike 1947). For social reasons, educational practice with regard to language was also of concern to other pioneers of American structuralism, although often outside the college classroom (e.g., Bloomfield's concern with the teaching of reading, and Swadesh's work with literacy (cf. Hymes 1971a:243–4)). Language teaching proper provided an important means of livelihood for many linguists, and, during World War II, was the focus of an identification with the national interest. There resulted a concentration of practical and theoretical activity that was to be crucial for the success of the Bloomfieldian approach that came to be identified with American structuralism (cf. Voegelin and Voegelin 1963:24). Moulton (1961:85) points out that two pioneer introductions to linguistic analysis (Bloomfield 1942 and Bloch and Trager 1942) were prepared initially for use in the Army Specialized Training Program. Joos (1957:108) writes:

It is doubtful whether the matter will ever command enough interest from non-linguists to attract any expert historical research worker; but if it does, there may yet be a fascinating history written on what our linguists did as their peculiar contribution to what was called 'the war effort'. . . . The most visible result is a couple of dozen sets of books, with phonograph records, for learning various languages. First made for the government, these became commercial publications after the war, and their royalties are mostly being used to support linguistics today, for instance by making the publication of the present book possible. A substantial portion of these royalties is currently being used, aside from the main purpose of supporting research, for grants in support of study at the Linguistic Institute of the Linguistic Society each summer. There is a certain justice in this, for it was just such grants, made from foundation funds, which before the war sent many young students to the Institutes and thus substantially helped to build up the number of linguists who could be called on to do that wartime work.

Joos goes on to indicate the ways in which

In the hothouse atmosphere of the wartime work, American linguistic theory was to develop far more swiftly than it had before . . . after the war, fully a quarter of the content of this collection was published in two years . . . .

One can hope that the history suggested by Joos will be written, and the research for it begun while personal knowledge can still be consulted.[17]

The wartime work produced the 'Army method', which in pedagogical contexts became identified with the new linguistics and its anthropological sources (cf. Haas 1953b). The issue of methodological relativism (or equality) was joined on this front, as well as on that of structural grammars, and with perhaps more consequence for the place and support of linguistics as a profession. Certainly the new group of linguists saw their approach as expressing the values of both science and democracy. Indoctrination of beginning linguists in the value of the profession commonly included warnings against biases to be expected from those schooled in traditional grammar (cf. Householder 1969, Bloomfield 1945a:625–626, where the lucid statement of relativism may surprise those who know him second hand as a 'mechanist' who rejected all consideration of meaning, and Nida 1949). This climate of opinion became unfamiliar; as Hodge (1963) points out, most students came to have already learned a relativistic outlook, and to be nearly innocent of traditional grammar. Imaginative recapture of this climate of opinion, with its populist overtones, is essential, however, for the historian who would not be guilty (Chomsky 1966b:3, n. 4) of 'complete lack of comprehension of the goals, concerns, and specific content of the work that he was discussing'.

Miller (1970:xxxvi) considers the experience of language teaching as a factor also in the differentiation of American and European varieties of structuralism:

Unlike many of their later students, the first- and second-generation American descriptivists were familiar with other ways of doing linguistics, and above all, they were well read in the standard corpus of European linguistic literature. . . . Their rejection of other traditions of linguistics was in the main based upon nothing more or less profound than their simple empirical observation that, by and large, the traditions did not work. Historically, this rejection was deeply rooted in the fact that most of the American

---

[17]   Cf. *LSA Bulletin* 17 (1944): 13; 19 (1946): 16; 20 (1947): 13; and 21 (1948): 15, with regard to the link between language teaching and the growth of descriptive linguistics at Linguistic Institutes in these years.

descriptivists (Bloch included) were also involved in language teaching for much or all of their academic careers in a way that their students and the later generations of American linguists have generally not had to be. Europeans know foreign languages; Americans must learn them. . . . What began as simple, practical considerations for overworked language teachers evolved into a new theoretical convention in linguistics. . . .

It appears likely that language teaching was not merely an application of linguistics, and source of employment, but also played a vital part in formation of consciousness of an autonomous linguistics with distinctive outlook. Whether or not the changes were due mainly to discovery that traditional ways simply did not work, Bloomfield, Sapir (to some extent), and their followers should be seen against the background of language study in higher education in their time. There were powerful interest groups among philologists and modern language (i.e., literature) teachers. Both groups were schooled in traditional grammar, and had been exposed to, if not steeped in, an atomistic type of comparative phonology (e.g., prospective Milton scholars being required to take Old English and in it to learn Germanic sound correspondences). These groups, and their professional societies, were often committed to a conservative or puristic attitude toward the cultural values of literary and historical study. Such a background may help explain the attention given by descriptivists to exotic languages and nonstandard dialects: these were varieties of language study not firmly in the control of established groups of scholars (just as phonology was the sector of language structure not so dominated). By moving into these areas, two purposes were served (not necessarily consciously): an entrenched opposition was outflanked, and a favorable position occupied. Study of these forms of language, together with the field work image associated with them, may have helped the new profession challenge claims of established method and traditional values in language teaching with claims of universality and practicality.

Many linguists had a sense of the relevance of their linguistics to language teaching and learning on a comprehensive scale. Besides foreign language instruction, literacy work in other languages was important (cf. Hymes 1971a:243–244 on Swadesh, besides the well-known work of missionary linguists); the teaching of English, both to speakers of other languages, and in courses for native users, became important; so indeed did the teaching of reading itself. On all this Bloomfield had a consistent and thoroughgoing point of view (cf. Hockett 1970:35, 49, 51, 54, 57 384–395, 400–405, 426–438, and references to 1940 and 1961 in the bibliography (pp. xxvii, xxix)). The reported division of labor between Bloomfield and Fries in the early period of American structuralism, and the long conjunction of the Linguistic Institute in Ann Arbor with a major center for the teaching of English, are significant in this regard, as is the later appearance of 'linguistics' based textbooks in schools at all levels. We have a few helpful studies: King and Tondrían (1950), Haas (1953), Fries (1955), Moulton (1961), Hodge (1963), Kelly (1969).

3.3 Dialectology

If the image of 'American structuralism', arising in the post-war period, was largely shaped for philologists of European languages and in Europe by analyses of languages such as French, and methods of teaching them, the image at home in the United States was shaped to a great extent by analysis of English, and the implications of a new basis for domestic instruction in it. Exotic languages and anthropological field work on the one hand, behaviorism and operational methodology on the other, provided motives and idioms in both respects, but dialectology contributed directly to the definition of what a satisfactory analysis of English ought to comprise. For Harris' methodological studies (1951a:9, 13, 199) dialect was extricable, but for Trager and Smith (1951) and others who joined in the discussion of English proper, known variation (in inventory) was something to be accounted for.

Dialect studies, then, can be reckoned as a factor comparable to the study of exotic languages. Both were sponsored by the early Linguistic Institutes, and dialect studies were directly nurtured there (cf. Sturtevant 1940:88, Hill 1964:3, and *Bulletins* of the LSA for those years). Dialect studies have a major but mostly unnoticed importance in the generation following Bloomfield. Bloch and Joos had both been field workers on the *Linguistic Atlas* project directed by Kurath; Bloch continued to use the *Atlas* and its contents to illustrate classroom lectures in the 1960s. Henry Lee Smith, Jr., worked independently for many years on American dialects, and through a popular radio program helped to stamp in the public mind the image of a linguist as someone who could tell people whence they came. Trager and Smith (1951) devoted much attention to details of regional pronunciations as well as to the theoretical question of an overall pattern to accommodate them. It is largely forgotten, in fact, that some of those most prominently associated with the study of exotic languages were also involved with analysis of English in the period before World War II. Sapir had an English grammar project, in which Swadesh and Newman participated; Swadesh was active in the continued debate over the phonemes and particularly the syllabics of English; Whorf developed a model of English phonemic distributions (analogous to recent 'morpheme-structure rules') and described his own dialect of English (cf. Hymes 1971a:233–234; 262, n. 36). One mark and possible cause of the character of the period after World War II is that Sapir's students by and large soon cease to participate as such in the discussion of English. Swadesh published one further article on English phonology, but turned his main attention to carrying out Sapir's legacy with regard to historical relationships among American Indian languages, and was associated with the European-oriented journal *Word*, rather than with *Language*; Newman published one article on English stress in *Word*, but his great demonstration of the mature Sapir model was with Yokuts, and published in an anthropological series (where its unintelligibility to some anthropologists soured the sponsor on linguistics for some years).

It may well be that a distinctive analysis of English is necessary to the success of an approach, or would-be 'paradigm', in linguistics in the United States. In the 1940s and 1950s, it was dialectologists, rather than anthropologists, who pursued this.

A principal source of the influence of dialectology on Bloomfieldians was Bloomfield himself. His effort to integrate dialectology, historical linguistics, and structuralism occupied much space in his *Language* (1933). (If he did not succeed in reconciling change and dialectal diversity with a structural model of description, the same remained true of linguists in general until very recently.) The Voegelins (1963:19) recall that Bloomfield, late in his career, was interested in starting field work on an Ojibwa dialect study which would be phonemic.

There are least three ways in which the influence of dialectology on the course of development has been felt: as an object of interest and specialization for its own sake; as a source of pressure on the development of phonemics, leading to the Trager and Smith 'overall pattern' model, which dominated the early 1950s, and provided a frame of reference and data for methodological discussions (cf. Joos 1967); as a source of a steady flow of anomalous data which called into question the accuracy of standard analyses of American English and the validity of the general approaches behind them. Some dialectologists indeed constituted a kind of loyal opposition to the descriptive structuralists. Kurath (1945) criticized the rejection of meaning, and objected to the solution of American English vowels and the use of zero elements in morphology; he noted contradictory views of meaning on pp. 6 and 53 of the Bloch and Trager *Outline* (1942). McDavid (1955), reviewing Trager and Smith (1951), is respectful but firm, listing five points of disagreement. Four are matters of dialectological accuracy; the fifth goes to the root of the Trager and Smith approach (390):

Probably a linguist should restrict phonemic analysis to one dialect at a time; when he makes an analysis involving more than one dialect, he should label this *diaphonemic* (cf. Harris 1951a:8).

Use of dialectology against the overall pattern model can be seen also in McDavid (1953), Weinreich (1959), and Sledd (1955). (The thinking about language generally of Weinreich, of Einar Haugen, and of William Moulton has been intimately bound up with their training and research in dialectology, on Haugen's development, cf. now Neustupný (1974)). Gleason interpreted such comments (citing McDavid 1958:492–493) as a rejection of phonemics, but they can be so interpreted only if the overall pattern approach is taken as indispensable to phonemics. The point of McDavid (1953) and many others was that the overall pattern approach was a distortion of phonemics.

We have in this controversy a significant instance of the internal diversity of linguistics in the United States in the Bloomfieldian period, a diversity rooted partly in a tradition and data not usually taken into account in later assessments.

For transformational grammarians, and the years dominated by them, the history of interest was the history of methods and theories bearing on formal models abstracted from the diversity of American speech. Transformationalists might be resented by dialectologists, but returned indifference. There was little or no direct contact with the dialectological tradition, and variation in English was commonly held not to be of interest, but to be superficial. Curiously enough, it is with the rise of a new approach to variation, mediated by Weinreich in the case of the work of Labov, that the older dialectology comes to be felt to be a relevant target for rejection (cf. Shuy 1974, Gilbert ms.). We have here an instance, perhaps rare, of what might be called delayed confrontation.

The institutional and personal continuities and discontinuities in attention to dialectal diversity in the United States greatly need study. Social forces outside linguistics, notably the rise of Black militancy, obviously have played a part. The character of the social diversity within the country may be a perennial source of partial distinctiveness for American linguistics. We have badly needed historical treatment of this subject. There is one sketch for the earlier period (Pound 1952), and a book-length general history now by Mundell (1973). Mundell organizes the subject in terms of early work from the eighteenth century until the late nineteenth century; the Dialect Society period (1889-1931); the *Linguistic Atlas* period (1931–1954); and the sociological-theoretical period (1954–). He emphasizes methodology and theory.

3.4   *Anthropology*

At the outset of part (3) we observed that anthropological study of American Indian languages, and behaviorist 'rejection of meaning', are two themes nearly always evoked in tracing the history of linguistics in the United States. Koerner (1970a:165, n. 8) observes:

Many analysts agree that, besides behaviorist psychology of the thirties, the investigation of Amerindian languages has had an essential impact on the development of American structuralism; cf. R. A. Hall (1951:112ff.), H. H. Christmann (1958/59:29), A. Nehring (1962:21), M. Bierwisch (1966:100). (Cf. also Bolinger 1968:191.)

The difficulty is to assess the nature of the impact correctly.

It is curious that scholars who reject a mechanistic approach within linguistics should resort to something of the sort in historical explanations of linguistics. The concentration of earlier American structuralism on phonology is often traced to the situation of field work with an unknown language (e.g., Levin 1965:92). One had to establish a transcription, hence phonology, or so it is reasoned. This explanation ignores two crucial facts. On the one hand, the American anthropological tradition that led into structuralism began with grammar (cf. Voegelin 1952a, Hymes 1970,

Stocking 1974). On the other, phonology, when it came, was not American, but international. Let us take these two facts in turn.

Boas, who largely established the modern pattern of anthropological activity in regard to language, did not concern himself much with sound systems, but rather with grammatical categories and processes (see Boas 1911). Indeed, it was not to be taken for granted that anthropologists would describe American Indian languages intensively at all (or that other linguists would pay attention to them). Boas came upon a scene in which the dominant activity was collection of vocabularies for the purpose of classifying languages. The novelty of his introduction of grammar as a focus, and his 'psychological' interest in it, was remarked upon at the time. Boas' orientation, then, cannot be explained as a mechanical response to an external necessity, but only as a choice. The reasons for the choice have not been closely studied in unpublished materials, but much is already made clear (cf. Stocking 1968a, 1974 especially, and also Hymes 1961c:23–24, 1970:255). Amidst the multiplicity of activities and interests in anthropology, as he pursued it and helped to establish it, Boas gave a great deal of attention to language because he saw in it a key to the general theoretical problem of ethnology, the origin, maintenance, and modification of culturally distinctive categories of thought. Boas employed the Humboldtian term 'inner form' with regard to languages at a crucial point in his major statement of his theoretical approach (1911:81, Hymes 1964c: 123; cf. Chomsky 1966b:2, n. 4). He had met Steinthal, an expositor and developer of von Humboldt's ideas, and once avowed to Lowie that his work was based on Steinthal's principles. He worked, indeed, in a period of international and interdisciplinary interest in 'cognitive psychology', with regard to the bases of 'folk' categories. That climate is apparent in Bloomfield's first general book (1914), in which the route back to W. von Humboldt, as founder of the kind of general linguistics shared by Bloomfield, Boas, Sapir, and others, is explicitly traced and praised (see ch. 10 on the history of linguistics; cf. 1933:18).

As to phonology, the development of the subject in Prague, Copenhagen, and London can hardly be explained as due to work with American Indian languages. Analogous empirical work may be found to have played a part, but clearly phonology has been a stage in the *general* development of modern linguistics, and has to be explained as such. Part of the reason probably is the opportunity afforded by phonology. The study of speech sounds had been largely set apart as phonetics and a natural science. Initially, then, the study of phonology appeared, not as a narrowing of attention, but as an expansion and integration of the scope of linguistics proper (cf. Sapir 1925). Participants in phonology could have the exhilaration of capturing and exploring a sector of speech that had previously seemed to lie outside the human sciences. (The spirit would seem to have been similar to that felt by young linguists a generation or so later in exploring syntax with a new methodological principle.)

In this regard it is important to recall that students of both Sapir and Bloomfield, of both mentalist and behaviorist persuasion, joined in the discussions and contributed to the analyses.

Gleason (1965:44) goes so far as to trace both supposed traits of American structuralism to the influence of anthropology — not only focus on phonology, that is, but also 'rejection of meaning'. Experience of difficulty in translation, and the inadequacy of meaning-based descriptions of parts of speech, are said to have conspired to create a suspicion of meaning. 'The movement of thought among American anthropological linguists was toward total rejection of meaning as a basis for analysis.' Bierwisch (1971:39) also links the two traits to anthropology:

Two main sources have given it (American linguistics) its particular stamp: research on hitherto unexamined North American Indian cultures and languages, and behaviorist psychology. Both influences converged at one point: in the rejection of all speculation, of all mentalistic notions, and of Sprachgefühl as linguistic criteria.

Bierwisch's explanation in succeeding sentences is along the same lines as that of Gleason. Thus, he writes (39):

When the linguist himself does not speak the language under analysis he cannot analyze his own intuitions about it, and he can only rely on properties of the acoustic signal and study their patterns.

The statement assumes that meaning is available only through inspection of one's own intuitions, and, presumably, not available through field work and ethnography.[18] It bespeaks a woeful ignorance of the practice of linguistic and anthropological fieldwork, as exemplified and inculcated by Boas and Sapir. As indicated above, the shapers of anthropological research into American Indian languages were interested precisely in relations of meaning (cf. Kroeber's foreword to Hymes 1964c). Here is Boas on the guiding principle of his grammatical work (1911:81 = Hymes 1964c:123):

. . . the grammar has been treated as though an intelligent Indian was going to develop the forms of his own thoughts by an analysis of his own form of speech.

Throughout his lifetime Boas insisted on grammatical categories as a focus of description, as shown by his chapter on "Language" (1938) and his stimulation of Whorf to write on the universal dimensions of grammatical categories in the same period (the 'Bloomfieldian' thirties). In connection with the design of an international auxiliary language, Sapir undertook studies toward "Foundations of language, logical and psychological, an approach to the international language problem" (cf. Mandelbaum 1949:5). Two of these studies were indeed published with

[18] Cf. Reid (1956:34, n. 1), where a purely observational study of behavior as stimulus and response is granted theoretical possibility, but where it is said that 'This anthropological approach could not be expected to give satisfactory results for a language of civilization such as French'. The equation of behaviorist method = study of little-known languages = anthropological approach is here complete.

the aid of the International Auxiliary Language Association and by the LSA as *Language Monographs* (Sapir 1930, Sapir and Swadesh 1932), the third posthumously (Sapir 1944). Sapir's technique and goal have striking resemblance to current work in case grammar (see, e.g., the investigation of locative relations in Sapir and Swadesh 1932).

Sapir's students gave attention to semantic definition of formal categories, in their published work and in papers at LSA meetings in the 1930s; Whorf's attention to the category of aspect reflects this concerted interest. Thus, Swadesh's dissertation (1933) is subtitled *A semantic study of word structure in a polysynthetic language*, and Whorf defined the essence of linguistics as the quest for underlying meaning (1956 — written ca. 1936; cf. Whorf (1945:1–2 = Carroll 1956: 87–88).

The major demonstration of Sapir's mature methodology in grammar was described in 1944 by Harris as follows (202):

The great attention to meaning evident in Newman's work is not common in modern grammars. In this Newman's work is undoubtedly superior.

It is true that during these years a number of scholars, linked to the anthropological tradition, joined in a growing ambivalence toward, or downright eschewal of meaning as a basis of analysis. In each case, a distinction was made between heuristic use of meaning and principled exclusion of it from the methodological foundations of final statement (cf. Harris 1951b:311, n. 21, 365, n. 6, Trager and Smith 1951:81, Bloch 1948, n. 8); however arrived at, structural relevance had to be justified by formal consequence (see further in (3.3)). But two things must be noticed. *First*, the methodological principle did not exclude meaning as an acceptable object of analysis. Harris' own conception, expressed in his review of Newman, was seen by him as in continuity with that of Sapir, and expressed also in his major treatise of this period (1951b:311, n. 21):

. . . The fact that distributional methods are able to bring out the major grammatical meaning categories is merely an indication that the old results are not lost in the new methods.

(Cf. 347–348, the chapter ending with citation of Lotz on Hungarian with regard to semantic categories of grammar.) In the methodological statement most influential, beside Harris (1951b), Trager and Smith (1951), like Harris, excluded meaning as part of rigorous statement of 'microlinguistic levels', but reserved an important place for it in 'metalinguistics' (82). Indeed, they saw their approach as continuous with that of Sapir's student, Whorf, four of whose articles they republished and rechristened (Whorf 1950) in this connection.

The central position of the period is perhaps best evidenced in Hockett (1948b). Hockett was Bloomfield's student and, indeed, disciple. In reviewing the grammatical sketches in the volume initiated by Sapir, Hockett praises Whorf's contributions, here and elsewhere, because he reminds us that the formal clues of real significance in assaying the structure of a language are often very subtle and must be looked for long and diligently; he underscores the fact that a language DOES have a semantic structure in addition to its formal structure, and that there is an intimate relation between that structure and the other aspects of the culture of the speakers of the language, however difficult it may be to get at such matters (185).

At the same time, Hockett criticizes Whorf because 'It would be pleasant if we could rely on the type of semantic statement that Whorf makes; at present we probably cannot.' His great praise goes to the Eskimo sketch in the volume — 'the finest descriptive analysis in the book, and one of he finest known to me anywhere' (186), in important part because,

The analysis reflected by Swadesh's presentation was clearly based on good objective methodology, using form and distribution, rather than meaning, as the fundamental criterion. But he does not rest content with that; he is not satisfied to give the bare formal structure, like a skeleton, but instead states, at every point, the features of meaning which seem to correlate with morphemes and classes of morphemes; and in some cases, when formal analysis has gone as far as it apparently can, he subdivides a formal category on a purely semantic basis. The use of meaning INSTEAD of form is of course unacceptable; but Swadesh's SUPPLEMENTARY use is highly commendable; it puts flesh on the skeleton, and contributes largely to the high degree of readability of the sketch. By this device he manages to approach Whorf's procedure, so far as it is on relatively sure ground, without leaving formal structure out or unexplained. (187)

Hockett's position, which we judge to be representative, can be said to distinguish between varieties of 'interpretive' and 'generative' (constitutive) semantics, and to insist on the former. In this Hockett is in manifest agreement with Bloomfield's position (cf. Bloomfield 1933), and somewhat in disagreement with the Sapir of the studies of grading, totality and ending point relation.

In short, the issue was not the inclusion, but the place, of semantics.

The second thing to notice is that meaning was consistently important in the line of fieldwork from Boas and Sapir to Newman, Swadesh, and Voegelin, and that the outstanding field workers of the post-war period, Swadesh and Pike, were particularly prominent in opposition to the tendency to neglect meaning. The sketches in Hoijer et al. (1946) were written by field workers and were all based on field work (though not in every case the personal field work of the author), and, as Hockett's review has shown, included significant attention to meaning. Voegelin, who had helped initiate field work courses with actual informants present at the Linguistic Institute in 1938, sometimes sought to extrapolate the trend away from meaning in theoretical essays, but in his own practice in the period pursued another course. The ambivalent observer of trends in climate of opinion in the discipline was in practice the explorer of paradigmatic and lexical organization of semantic features, and of the balance between internal semantic creativity and borrowing (Voegelin 1948b, 1952b, Voegelin and Hymes 1953, Voegelin and Voegelin 1957). He, like others, illustrates the applicability to linguistics of the sociological distinction between public norms and personal behavior. One might think, from public statements, that the linguists of the period had deeply internalized an aversion to meaning, such that it could be overcome only slowly or by cataclysm. Far from it. Many a linguist who observed a public norm of distrust of meaning, for the sake of the regard of his fellows, and perhaps the shocking of others, was quite prepared to change when respectability permitted. (On the 'social identity' approach to the relation between norms and social action, see Cancian 1974.)

In sum, if the so-called 'rejection of meaning' was a consequence of anthropological tradition and field work experience, why is there no sign of it in the founders of both, Boas and Sapir? Why so little sign of it among the men who followed them in tradition and experience? The truth of the matter is that the so-called 'rejection of meaning' was a phenomenon specific to the 1940s, having more to do with conversations in New York City than with experience in the field. There was in linguistics a climate of opinion, rooted in philosophy (behaviorism and operationalism), methodology (the carrying through of formal possibilities), and professional ideology — the mix of these sources varying a good deal from person to person. The central fact is not field work, but the establishment of a formal idiom of a certain sort. The point of transition can almost be dated with Harris' 1944 review of Newman — probably the most important article for understanding this period, since it deals with work and a colleague both of which are admired, rather than with an older generation or foreign school. (The continuity of the position stated there by Harris to Chomsky's syntax and interpretive semantics is clear.)

How then explain the error on the part of some interpreters close to the actual scene? The general problem would appear to be that participants in the development of linguistics in the period habitually justified ideas, judgments, orientations in terms of the requirements of field work. It is not that all of them engaged actively in field work, but that they shared an image of the tasks of linguistics in which the analysis of a little-known language loomed as representative. The description of others' languages, for teaching and for science both, from data freshly obtained, was taken for granted, deeply presupposed.

Interpreters of this work have too often accepted the idiom at face value. Thus it is tempting to explain concern with so-called 'discovery' procedures as a natural development out of the need to discover the structure of little-known languages. Yet the linguist most articulate and influential in defining formal phonological procedures (Bloch) was out of a background in English and English dialectology, and the man most thoroughly committed to exploring and defining operational procedures in grammar (Harris) was connected with the anthropological tradition by fraternity more than by research involvement. The theoretical, not practical, motives of Harris could not be more painfully clear (cf. 1944, 1951a, 1951b). In contrast, as we have seen, the field workers par excellence, Pike and Swadesh, were as critical of a unilinear algorithmic approach to formal foundations of method as they were to eschewal of meaning. The origin of formalized foundations (later miscalled 'discovery' procedures) of the sort developed in the 1940s and 1950s — a generation after the establishment of the field work tradition, and against the objections of preeminent field workers — must be sought in a conception of science.

It is true that an environment of concern with describing little-known languages, as with teaching languages, is conducive to an emphasis on discovery, in the sense of an emphasis on the ways in which one makes inferences as to units and relations from one's data (cf. Robins 1967:231–232). To a great extent, this is what teaching linguistics in the period meant. But what was taught was not algorithms, but principles and heuristics. The principal texts of the period (Pike (1947), Nida (1946, 1949), Gleason (1951, 1965, with workbook)) are evidence enough of this. They accurately reflect the influence that the field work, descriptive context had. One might think that those who wish to characterize the period would go to these works, but they have gone instead to attempts at formal foundations, and filled the gap between these formulations and field work by imagination. (This analysis does not account for Gleason (1965); we are baffled, except to suggest that he imputes to the anthropological tradition as a whole an attitude encountered among a few participants at the time he entered linguistics in the early 1950s; see immediately below.)

We must immediately add that imaginary explanations are not entirely without warrant, if one trusts inheritors of a tradition to be its accurate historians. Some well-known figures came to define 'anthropological linguistics' as merely the study of unknown or little-known languages (Voegelin 1959:122, 1965, and elsewhere), or of the languages of peoples who have no writing (Hoijer 1961:110). Hoijer does go on to give the subject some substance, organizing his essay in terms of a Sapir tradition, responsive to the needs and interests of anthropology, and carried on particularly by work of Swadesh, Greenberg, and Whorf; but the one section (#6, on ethno-linguistics, especially Whorf, 121–123) that directly exemplifies in a distinctive way Sapir's conception of 'linguistics as a social science' (111) also belies the initial definition. Such definitions of the scope of the anthropological tradition — or of the term 'anthropological' — lost from view much of the theoretical motivation of work of Boas and Sapir, and lent themselves to an impression that the entire tradition historically lacked concern for theory. Perhaps it had largely come to that after World War II — Hymes recalls Voegelin in lecture posing the question, why was Boas interested in grammatical categories, and Hoijer concludes a discussion of Greenberg's reconstruction of Sapir's typology as follows (1961: 120–121):

Morphological typology, it should be noted, has interested very few modern American linguists. ... The reason for this may lie, as Kroeber has suggested, in the question 'What do we do with a morphological classification of world languages when we have it?' The question is not easily answered, and the lack of a clear answer unquestionably affects both the interest in, and the nature of, morphological typologies.

Boas and Sapir would have thought there to be obvious import, historical and social psychological, to any adequate typology, though 'adequate' would have meant to them semantic as well as formal content (cf. Hymes 1961c). New techniques of semantic analysis, published in an issue of *Language* dedicated to the anthropologist Kroeber; tools for analysis of social interaction, developed within a tradition derived from Sapir; a methodology for general structural analysis of behavior, inspired by Sapir's example — all were developed in the period preceding the narrow definitions of 'anthropological linguistics' just quoted. Curiously enough, such work finds a place in a survey of general linguistics (Hamp 1961 — see citations to Goodenough, Lounsbury, Trager, and Pike), but not in the same volume's survey of 'anthropological linguistics' and the Sapir tradition (Hoijer 1961).

In sum, an 'anthropological linguistics' in the years after World War II might have been expected to enrich linguistics with anthropology, but the momentum and hopes flowed in the other direction. Leading spokesmen defined the subject in such a way as to impoverish it as if it were no more than an ad hoc division of labor.

A further complication is that prominent Bloomfieldians in the same period claimed the anthropological label, as defining the place of linguistics as a social science. Thus, Hall (1950b:118 (= Hockett 1970:549)):

If a worker in linguistics, even in its more traditional branches (e.g., Romance, Indo-European), is today entitled to view himself as a social scientist, working in a branch of anthropology, and not (in Bloomfield's phrase) as a mere 'crow-baited student of literature', this change in his status is largely due to Bloomfield having placed the entire study of languages on a truly scientific basis.

And Hockett (1952b:90), describing American linguistics as institutionally at least in part a branch of anthropology, goes on to say:

Logically, every bit of linguistic activity, from field-work with an Indian language to the counting of mute e's in Chaucer, is part of cultural anthropology.

Such a conception of the place of linguistics may seem natural enough, but we must be wary. An extreme example of what could happen to linguistic use of an anthropological motif is found in Garvin (1967), where it is claimed that the advantage of the study of American Indian languages is that the linguist can be an observer pure and simple, having no incentive to learn the language, because of the small size and small socio-political significance of the society. But Boas, Sapir, and Bloomfield learned to use languages with which they worked (as indeed did Garvin when he worked on Kutenai), and specially demanded a practical knowledge of language as part of anthropological field work (cf. Voegelin 1959:114 and Teeter's important assessment of Bloomfield's practice, to which he contrasts the Garvin claim (1970a:531, n. 12)). Nor does the claim fit the current practice of field workers (e.g., Hale (1965) and Silverstein), for whom a working knowledge of the language is an intellectual (and moral) obligation. Even when one does not or can not achieve a fluent active command of a language, one uses one's growing understanding of it to guide and inform research. Indeed, much information is simply not available to an 'observer pure and simple', and the adequacy of one's work may be directly proportionate to how much one knows and can share. (These observations are independent of the question of using one's own knowledge of a language as data, but the training of native speakers as linguists, where possible, is obviously desirable (on inadequate training, cf. Trager 1945:86).)

The Garvin claim is a travesty of actual practice, past and present. It is a case of post-hoc adoption of the mantle of the anthropological, American Indian tradition for reasons extraneous to it, and points up how much we need close study of the process by which that tradition was taken up as part of general justification of outlook and approach in linguistics. In each case in which reference is made to the tradition, the context and intent of the writer should be examined with care. The tradition has been invoked with differing purposes, and to differing effect, by participants and observers alike.

It does seem likely that the tradition was adopted by Bloomfieldians, not themselves direct participants in it, or only marginally so, for at least four reasons:

(1) acceptance of the goal of preserving knowledge of languages, as diverse expressions of human experience and creativity;

(2) acceptance of the egalitarian thrust of the methodological outlook, in its relativism and universalism, an outlook which they made their own;

(3) use as an arena of training and experience that could free linguists, especially students, from preconceived biases. Thus Bloomfield (1945a:630) writes:

. . . it was largely through the observation of American Indian tongues that linguistic students learned to describe the structure of languages in realistic and intelligible terms — and not in the traditional pseudo-philosophical jargon of our school grammars.

(4) as a way of defining linguistic study of language as scientific (cf. the quotations from Hall 1950b and Hockett 1952b above).

The last three reasons are closely linked, as the Bloomfield quotation implies; and to it may be compared Sapir 1947, Whorf 1956 (both posthumous), and Hall 1951–52:103), and other writers. But to go from the Bloomfield quotation to identification of the anthropological tradition, as a whole, with the whole of the Bloomfieldian approach would be illegitimate. It was a possible step, but still a step, and one not taken by everyone.[19]

It remains to trace the process of generalization among those who took the step through direct evidence. 'The 'Army method' of teaching languages, mentioned

---

[19] Thus Levin (1965:91), in tracing the 'American preoccupation with speech' to study of native Indian languages, cites supporting statements from Bloomfield and Harris, but gives a contrasting account of Whorf. The latter, and his own preceding contrast between Bloomfield and Sapir (90), should have alerted him to the mistake. And Whorf, Sapir, Swadesh, Newman, Pike, and others patently did not subscribe to use of the informant as a source simply of a corpus, but considered his judgments essential.

above, may have been one important matrix. In any case, part of the generalized image held by other and later scholars is false, if for no other reason than that the Bloomfieldians did not collectively abandon meaning at all (see further below (3.3.)). The anthropological tradition, being common to all sides of the debate about meaning, cannot explain the disagreement. Further, it would seem that eschewal of reliance on meaning, as a goal, appealed most strongly, not to those deepest in the anthropological tradition, but to those who came to it, and to linguistics, out of traditional philological fields. Men such as Bloch, Harris, Joos, Trager, and Twaddell had backgrounds in English, Semitic, Germanic, Romance, Germanic again, with which they partly broke. It would seem that the appeal of various forms of operationalism, positivism, and behaviorism, at least as a style and a public ideology, had a great deal to do with emergence of a new professional identification on the part of young men who might wish to define their difference from traditional fields. Such a motive does not appear to have operated strongly within the anthropological tradition proper. In short, we suggest that a great deal of the flavor of the Bloomfieldian period has to do, *not with the continuity of an anthropological tradition, but with a discontinuity between philological contexts and the new profession of linguistics.* Some anthropological interests in language, indeed, suffered as much as some philological interests in the Bloomfieldian heyday after World War II (cf. Hymes 1961a on Kroeber in this regard, and cf. Malkiel 1959 on a then incipient Sapir renascence; on the complex empirical and ideological relationship between field experience and theory, cf. Hymes (1963:83–85) and Stocking (1968a:133–160)).

A related interpretation of the role of anthropology in the development of American linguistics is in terms of *salvage.* Bolinger (1968:91) writes charitably, but patronizingly:

It is little wonder that linguists in America were so caught up with the urgency of recording and analyzing native American languages that they had little time or patience for anything else.

There is truth to the motive singled out here, a motive repeatedly stressed, and acted upon, by Boas, Bloomfield, and others, but the implication of general lack of anything else is false, as we have already seen. Two further things may be said. In its own time (a time still with us) the salvage effort has been understood as having social as well as scientific importance. It was seen as laying foundations for valid generalization (cf. Boas 1911:v, 82, Whorf 1956), and its significance for general theory was recognized by sociologists, such as Mauss, philosophers, such as Cassirer, and others. It was also understood as part of an orientation of respect for the integrity, value, and right to equality of each language and way of life, in a tradition extending from Herder. The humanistic implications of the earlier salvage work have come to the fore in a concrete way in recent years. For Native Americans today, and those who work with them, the value of what has been preserved, or is being preserved, for maintenance of cultural identity and pride is no small thing. A climate of opinion is conceivable in which linguistic work will be evaluated for its contributions to oppressed peoples as much or more than for its contributions to formal models. Such a climate of opinion would provide an alternative perspective on the historical development of American linguistics. Some linguists working with Native American peoples today experience something of such a climate of opinion.

There is a considerable literature on the anthropological tradition in relation to linguistics. Much of it is concerned with the perennial problem of defining and reconciling the interests of the two general disciplines, and the possibility of a named subdiscipline as mediator. See references in Hymes (1964c:32–33, through about 1962; Hymes (1963, 1964a, 1964b); the discussion initiated by Teeter (1964b), followed by Voegelin (1965) and Hymes (1966b); Hammel (1965); and Friedrich (1971). On the history of the American Indian work, see Landar (1974).

3.5 *Psychology*

In the earlier period the link with psychology was not so much disciplinary as intellectual. Boas, Sapir, and Bloomfield each were familiar with, and influenced by, particular lines of psychological thought: Wundtian (and perhaps Herbartian) in the case of Boas, *Gestalt* in the case of Sapir and Whorf, Wundtian and then behaviorism in the case of Bloomfield (see (3.3)). Disciplinary relations seem to have had to do more with issues of race and intelligence than of analysis of language directly (cf. Stocking 1968a:270–307). In the very recent period the interplay of persons, institutions, journals, etc., is obviously important, but not yet documented or discussed in historical perspective.

3.6 *Phonetics*

The relation of American structuralism to phonetics has been of crucial importance to its development, yet we know of no historical study. Three major foci would be the separation of phonology, as phonemics, from technical phonetics in the 1920s and 1930s; the development of phonetic analysis within the context of structural phonology, by Pike, Bloch and Trager, and others; and the expectations and consequences of acoustic phonetics, and experimental phonetics generally, in the postwar period. There is something of a sequence of condemnation for spurious objectivity that obscures structure (cf. Sapir 1925, the beginning of a sustained attitude); hopes for laboratory objectivity that would resolve structural uncertainties; and a more complex, dialectical relationship, with different degrees of trust and distrust, interest and disinterest, as prevails today. The interrelation between attitudes toward phonetics as a discipline, and toward phonetics as a sector of language, very much needs to be traced as well. If we consider 'sound' and 'meaning' as the two substantive poles between which structure has been thought to mediate, then implicit or explicit designs of language, and analytic practices, have varied just as much in treatment of 'sound' as in treatment of 'meaning'. Sometimes both, sometimes one and not the other, have been excluded from 'language' (as the object of linguistics). It is 'meaning' that has received all the attention, but the history of attitudes toward 'sound' may be equally revealing.

The emergence of a separate discipline, linguistics, ultimately must be studied in terms of the interrelations of three planes of activity. On the public plane, contrast in terms of named disciplines is in question, the leaders of American structuralism can be said to have brought about its autonomy from philology, psychology, phonetics, and from older forms of dialectology as well. A number would have considered linguistics to be in principle a part of anthropology, but not to be dependent on it. On the personal plane, scholars would not escape what Malkiel (1969:548) describes as 'the complications arising from most linguists' split commitments to several disciplines that compete for their time and loyalty'. Individual bibliographies, and teaching schedules, would show as much. On the plane of ideas and practice, any scholar's work would show assumptions and influences, explicit or implicit, with regard to the handling of text materials, the handling of speech sounds, the handling of variation, the nature of meaning, learning, and interaction, and the role of language in social life — in short, would show dimensions of the sort that officially belong to disciplines such as philology, phonetics, dialectology, psychology, and anthropology.

The effective configuration of influences and orientations at all three levels can be best studied perhaps in terms of individual scholars, and their particular networks of intellectual and social relationship. Indeed, the reference group of a scholar will commonly include persons not normally counted in the history of his discipline, but nevertheless significant to his or her own work. The role of admired and privileged friend from another field especially needs to be noticed. Whatever the public place of a discipline or scholar, the configuration of organizations joined, meetings attended, and journals published in, needs to be described. We do not now have much work of this sort, but let us turn to what we do have, in kinds of material, and issues raised, with regard to the principal figures in the history of our subject.

4. PRINCIPAL FIGURES

As is not surprising, there is material focused on individuals for the earlier period more than for the later. Except for Chomsky (cf. Lyons 1970), living figures have not been much subject to biographical sketch or overall assessment in print. (Papers of this sort, from seminars and visits of scholars, do come into existence, and would be worth collecting.)

For the earlier period, the figures of Boas, Sapir, Whorf, and Bloomfield have been the foci of attention. For the more recent period, scholars tend to be treated collectively, as Bloomfieldians, tagmemicists, transformationalists, etc., and the history of particular topics looms larger in what is written. We will follow this roughly chronological order of prominence, taking up interpretations of major issues associated with individuals (e.g., meaning with Bloomfield) then with groups, then topics. We shall want to stress that the chronological order is indeed rough, and can be misleading. There were early groups, not much discussed as such, around Boas and Sapir, and later scholars have individual profiles of importance. The history of repetition and discussion of examples is a rich one, replete with minor modulations and occasional sea-changes, throughout the long history of the study of language.

4.1 *Boas*

The best general study of Boas, relevant to linguistics, is in Stocking (1968a). By and large, biographical sketches of Boas, of which there are many, do not shed much light on his linguistic work. The obituaries and tributes by linguists, however, are of interest (see Bloomfield (1943b), Emeneau (1943), Harrington (1945), Jakobson (1944, 1959)). A good deal of light is shed on Boas' role in the development of both linguistics and anthropology in an important study by Darnell (1969). Something of a later generation's view of Boas' mature linguistic practice can be gained from reviews of the posthumously published Kwakiutl grammar (Swadesh 1948, Newman 1950, Hall 1950a). Explication of the nature of his linguistic approach has been offered by Voegelin (1952a) and Stocking (Stocking 1974a, 1974b); cf. also Hymes (1961b, 1963:79–80). Controversy as to the place of Boas' practice in relation to contemporary theoretical concerns has been raised by Voegelin and Voegelin (1963), and responded to by Postal (1964b); see discussion in (2.2) above. Most writings by American anthropologists and linguists with an historical orientation mention Boas, and may comment significantly. This literature is too great to give here; for references through about 1962, see Hymes (1964c:7–9, 23–25), and cf. Lesser (1968:164–165). For fairly extended discussion in works on the history of linguistics, cf. Ivić (1965:152–153) and Hymes (1970:255–258). There is extensive documentation of Boas' career available to scholars (cf. Voegelin and Harris 1945b, Freeman 1966, Stocking 1968b, 1974b).

Much of the significance of Boas has been discussed in connection with general articles (2.2) and anthropology (in 3.4). We need to consider further the interpretation of Boas offered by Teeter (1964), for it has apparently remained unchallenged with regard to a contention that illuminates the role of textual evidence and the necessity of interpreting terms and notions in context. Teeter gives a short, apt account of Boas' work, except for one, central point. He takes Boas to have held two contradictory views, namely (a) that there are linguistic universals, but (b) that *all* preconceptions about language must be avoided. No direct evidence for the second view is given. Boas certainly warned against the kind of preconception caused by inadequate theory and experience, as Teeter notes (198), but it is nowhere evident that 'he often seems to be advocating a more extreme view' (198), or that 'we find Boas, then expressing incompatible ideas at different times' (199). These statements imply the existence of supporting quotations; we doubt that any can be found. The evidence, so far as we know, is all on one side. Boas was quite aware of the point, noted by Teeter, that conceptual schemes are universal and inevitable; he could be said to have established that point as a central interest of American linguistics and anthropology. (Cf. Stocking 1968:159 on the centrality of an early analysis of perceptual/cognitive error with regard to speech sounds for all of Boas' later work (the analysis, first made in 1889, is utilized again in 1911: 16–18).)

Teeter supports the supposed contradiction in Boas' thought by setting up a contrast between Boas' theory and actual practice. He describes Boas' concern to avoid preconceptions as being restricted to those shown inadequate by experience; notes that Boas frequently wrote of specific universals, though considering (correctly) that too little was known for a comprehensive theory; but all this is assigned to 'Boas' actual practice' and 'work' (198–199). A reader of Boas (1911) will find that these features do not need to be inferred from Boas' practice; they are explicit in his principal statement of his approach. It is hard to know what could count as a theoretical statement on Boas' part, if his statements in the "Introduction" to the *Handbook on American Indian languages* do not (cf. pp. 16, 18, 23, 24, 27, 28, 33, 35, 36, 43, for instances of Boas' concern to establish 'necessary elements of articulate speech' (36)). In general, Boas' 'analytic' approach can not be understood as anything other than the establishment of what appeared an essential, minimal universal framework of formal universals; he stated general characteristics of language and instructed students to describe languages in terms of them.[20]

Teeter proposes that Boas avoided the dilemma of his contradictory views by a compromise, such that linguistic universals are not specifically linguistic, but due to

---

[20]   We see more fully here the falseness of the attribution to Boas of the view that languages could differ from each other without limit and in unpredictable ways (Joos 1957:96), or, as put by Joos in his Preface (1957:v): 'American Linguistics derives, ultimately and also currently, from the brute necessities of stating what has been found in a particular language. It got its decisive direction when it was decided that an indigenous language could be described better *without any preexistent scheme* of what a language must be than with the usual reliance upon Latin as the model. It is usual to name Franz Boas in this connection . . .' Joos' statement of the supposed Boasian position so closely resembles Teeter's account of Boas' supposed second, contradictory view as to seem a likely source.

human psychic makeup. The compromise, like the contradiction, is fictitious. Boas did hold that some attributes of language are evidence of universal properties of the human mind (Boas 1908, for example, and 1911:71). He also held that some attributes of language are found in *all* languages (Teeter cites one such proposition (199, n. 4), and we have indicated a number of them in the paragraph just above).

The inferred reduction of linguistic universals to psychological traits is apparently made plausible by a misreading of Boas' use of the term 'mental life' in a famous statement from the 1911 "Introduction". We have to consider what Boas himself meant in writing of 'mental life', and what, for him, linguistic theory might comprise.

Teeter (1964:199) quotes Boas to the effect that language is 'a manifestation of mental life'. Let us consider the correct, and full, quotation. Boas wrote (1911:63 = Hymes 1964c:17):

If ethnology is understood as the science dealing with the mental phenomena of the life of the peoples of the world, human language, one of the most important manifestations of mental life, would seem to belong naturally to this field.

With the full quotation we can avoid two misinterpretations. First, 'mental' did not mean 'psychological' in the sense of belonging to the domain of the discipline of psychology; Boas was patently discussing the domain of the discipline of ethnology.[21] He was expressing a general conception known in German as that of the *Geisteswissenschaften*, and 'mental' here is an equivalent of *Geist* — in other words, he was defining ethnology as equivalent to the cultural sciences. Psychological, yes, in the sense that all of culture can be taken to have a psychological basis, but ethnological too, with reference to the distinctive mental configurations of particular cultures and languages. The relevant psychology for Boas would have connotations of Wundt's folk psychology (although Boas did not accept Wundt's line between folk and civilized).

Second, as indicated above, 'mental' did not imply purely universal attributes. Boas not only considered that some features are universal to languages, but also that all languages reflect the history and culture, and more particularly, the psychological makeup, of the community of which they have been a part. This universal thesis, with its particularistic implications, was for him a part of linguistic theory, of general linguistics, in the tradition of von Humboldt and Steinthal. We do not see this context of theory for studies of individual languages today — it is a functional, rather than a substantive, universal. So we do not see, looking back, implications of any theory in the work in which such a context was assumed. Yet this context of theoretical significance, associated with language typology, has been continuously recognized from Boas to Harris. Cf. Boas (1911:v):

---

[21] The difference is nicely brought out in a passage from Bloomfield's book of the same period (1914:318): '...perhaps the student of a mental science could an ideally should refrain from any running psychologic interpretation.'

The object of the whole work has been to describe as clearly as possible those psychological principles of each language which may be isolated by an analysis of grammatical forms.

And (1911:82):

It is planned to give a comparative discussion of the languages at the close of these volumes, when reference can be made to the published sketches.

The interest of Sapir (1921) and Whorf (1956) in comparative study of language types is well known. With reference to psychology subordinated, the interest as a justification for analysis remains in Harris (1951b:3):

The greatest use of such explicit structural descriptions will be in the cataloguing of language structures, and in the comparison of structural types.

Stuart (n.d.) has called attention to this context of theory in Boas in an interesting explication. It is essential to bear this context in mind, if the work from Boas onward is to be understood.

Only a full-scale monograph could do justice to Boas' place in the development of American linguistics. The work that has been done, however, allows us to venture a brief summing-up. Institutionally, Boas was a major force in defining, organizing and supporting the work of linguistic description throughout much of the century. Intellectually, an effective, sustained tradition of description of language can be said to begin with him. The tradition was systematic, synchronic, universalistic, but in retrospect it seems a precursor of structuralism proper, not an instance of it, if by 'structuralism' one means an approach that defines the status of elements explicitly and consistently in terms of internal relations. The step from Boas' analytic approach to structural analysis proper can be seen as the step from Boas 'every single language has a definite and limited group of sounds' (1911:16) to Sapir's 'sound patterns' (Sapir 1925); from recognition of 'inorganic sounds' in a mixture of phonetic and phonological representation (Sapir in Boas 1911–1922–1934, Part 1: 674, n. 2, Part 2: 35, 51) to explicit recognition of the principle of functional contrast (cf. Hymes 1961b, Voegelin and Voegelin 1963:16, Hymes 1970:256–258, and discussion of Postal on Boas in (2.2)). The continuity from Boas to Sapir and Bloomfield in outlook is nonetheless great. If Boas and some of his students were skeptical of the 'phoneme', as an abstraction that lost information, phonology can be seen as in keeping with the thrust of Boas' concern for validity of analysis in terms of the relations within a language.

4.2   *Sapir*

Sapir has been the subject of a comprehensive and penetrating study on the occasion of his selected writings (Harris (1951b)). A study of one aspect of his thought is presented in Hymes (1970:258–288); cf. also Guxman (1954 — not seen). There are a number of personal tributes and evaluations, all of some interest: Benedict (1939), Boas (1939), Chao (1968:vi), Edgerton (1939), Haas (1953a), Hall (1969), Hjelsmlev (1939), Hymes (1969b), Mandelbaum (1949:v–xii), Swadesh (1939a), Voegelin (1942, 1957), Woolfson (1970), Mounin (1972:82–96). Sapir figures in Mead (1959), where some of his letters are reproduced, and in another biography of Ruth Benedict by Mead (1974). Lowie prepared a collection of Sapir's letters to him, with an introduction, which, having been declined by the University of California Press, was issued privately by Mrs. Lowie after her husband's death (Lowie 1965). Sapir's practice has attracted renewed interest (e.g. McCawley 1967); the articles by Harris (1944, 1951b) are of special historical importance, not only for what they have to say, but as examples of sympathetic exposition of an approach from which the author himself has chosen to depart (cf. Harris 1951b:301, and 1951a:373).

As with Boas, the literature that contains comment on Sapir is too great to list here; for principal references through 1962, see Hymes (1964c:10, 23–25). Much of the significance of Sapir is discussed in other parts of this essay. Here let us take up three points of special importance to the general historiography of our subject.

(1) Sapir's reputation, as reflected in comments, has been marked by notable discontinuity. On the one hand, there are remarks such as those in Joos (1957:25, 31, 115, and also 96 and 80), reflecting an image of Sapir as intuitive or even mystical, rather than responsible; such comments were current in the late 1940s and early 1950s, although it is important to note that the leader in abstract methodology did not share them. Thus Harris (1944:198) said of Newman's grammar of Yokuts:

This grammar takes on special methodological importance as perhaps the fullest example of Sapir's mature linguistic methods. Sapir had a consistent and very productive way of handling linguistic material.

And (1951b:7, n. 5):

The most explicit statement of the relative and patterned character of the phonologic elements is given by Edward Sapir (citing Sapir 1925).[22]

[22] If documented refutation is needed of remarks such as 'the essential irresponsibility of what has been called Sapir's "method"' (Joos 1957:25), perhaps the following will suffice: 'Sapir ordered me to write it (Swadesh and Voegelin 1939) when I first came to Yale, and assigned Swadesh to me as a tutor since Swadesh knew morphophonemic theory, so far as Sapir had then developed it, while I did not. I put in more time writing it than I had when writing the Tübatulabal grammar. Swadesh put in so much tutorial time that I insisted he be listed as senior author – he was certainly my senior in terms of linguistic knowledge. Sapir told us that he put in much more time than he anticipated; what he did was to find exceptions to what we would today call rules (e.g., his uncanny sense for anticipating what would occur in Tüb. from his knowledge of Southern Paiute on which he was then reading galley proof). Sapir insisted that we reformulate until there were no remaining or apparent exceptions' (Carl F. Voegelin to Theodore M. Lightner, October 6. 1970; carbon sent Hymes by Voegelin). Voegelin and Voegelin (1963:18) note Sapir as a collaborator (the silent partner) in the paper. Notice that the paper was written some years before publication (Harris 1951b:293, n. 10), and given at the 1937 meeting of the LSA in Philadelphia.

On the other hand, there is the emergence of a positive revaluation at the end of the 1950s (some 20 years after Sapir's death); cf. Pike (1967) (first issued in 1954), Malkiel (1959), and the interest shown by transformational generative grammar in Sapir's phonology, including adoption of the term 'sound patterns', and in Sapir's mentalism (cf. Bierwisch 1971:40). Sapir's later writings have been treated as unheralded beginnings of a form of sociolinguistic research (Hymes 1970, 1972b).

The fortunes of the reputation of someone as important and many-sided as Sapir can be taken as something of a projective test for distinguishing subsequent groups and periods.

(2) Some of the recognition accorded Sapir has the effect of implying a periodization of American linguistics, such that Sapir precedes Bloomfield. There is an element of truth in this, one well stated by Robins (1967:209):

Bloomfield's interpretation of linguistics predominated in the attitude and outlook of most American linguists during the thirties and forties. Much of the work done in these years was conceived by the scholars involved in it as the articulation or development of some of the ideas or suggestions expressed by Bloomfield; and the ensuing period has now come to be known as the 'Bloomfieldian era', although it cannot be said that every one of its characteristics can be directly traced back to Bloomfield's teaching.

The catch has to do with 'the thirties', as we shall now see.

Robins goes on to say that in a survey such as his, 'Bloomfieldian linguistics' can reasonably be treated as a unity, and assigns it the period (1933–57). A similar choice is implicit in Waterman (1963:92), Bolinger (1968:193), and V. Makkai (1972). Makkai presents a four-fold grouping of approaches in phonology: I Bloomfieldian phonology, II Prosodic analysis, III Distinctive features and generative phonology, IV The Copenhagen school and stratificational phonology. Particularly relevant here are the subdivisions of Part I: (a) Formation of the phonemic principle; (b) The early Bloomfieldian era; (c) Further development of Bloomfieldian phonology.

The diversity within American structuralism is represented well enough by Makkai to dispose of misconceptions of it as monolithic; this is one of the important services rendered by the book. The order of contents, however, relegates Sapir to the 1920s, as if entirely succeeded in the 1930s by Bloomfield. This is a serious error. It is in fact an important task to investigate the relation between the phonologies developed *within* the 1930s by both men, and to study the relations between these and what followed in the 1940s and 1950s. (Derwing 1973:181 recognizes that the later developments are distinct, but in labelling their period 'the post-Bloomfieldian era' (175) implies that their predecessor was 'Bloomfieldian' alone; cf. the implication of Koerner (1970a:167), 'as Sapir before him', in reference to Bloomfield; the next citation being to Bloomfield (1933)).

American abstract morphophonemics would appear to have its start in the post-doctoral collaboration, about 1933–36, of Newman and Swadesh with Sapir (cf. Hymes 1971a:233, n. 7). Thus it is misleading to place articles by Swadesh under 'Bloomfieldian' heading (indeed, Swadesh's main influence other than Sapir was apparently Trubetzkoy); and it is misleading by omission not to discuss Newman's analysis of Yokuts in this period. (Since restatement of Newman's Yokuts has become a minor linguistic industry, a telling selection might have been garnered from Newman, Harris, Hockett, Kuroda and others (cf. Hockett 1973 and Pullum 1973).)

Not only was Sapir active in the development of phonology in the 1930s; to some he would appear to have been the leader at the time. Thus the Proceedings of the Meeting of 1936 (of the LSA) report:

Professor Edward Sapir spoke also of the proposition to form an American society which should be one of a group of societies loosely affiliated with other national societies, to form the International Association for Phonology (Phonemics). The Executive Committee instructed the Secretary to correspond with Prof. Dr. R. Jakobson, Secretary of the proposed International Association, with regard to arranging a plan of affiliation between members of the Linguistic Society and the International Association for Phonology (Phonemics). (*Bull.* 10 (1937), p. 12)

In reviewing for philologists the progress of linguistics towards an adequate (mechanistic) approach, Lane (1945:482–3) nevertheless, when discussing activity in phonology, did not cite Bloomfield, but wrote rather:

The greatest amount of activity in pursuit of the 'phonemic theory' has perhaps been shown in Europe by the Cercle Linguistique de Prague and in America by Sapir and his students, and, as in the case of all new theories, much unnecessary vehemence has been expended on the pros and cons of this or that particular conception.

In raising a few points of disagreement with Lane, Trager (1946:461–2) went even further:

It is not, I believe, historically accurate to set up Bloomfield as the one name around whom to center descriptive linguistics as contrasted with the older historical techniques. Bloomfield's contributions to all kinds of linguistics have been so great that all of us linguists are basically Bloomfieldians; but he has always had the deepest interest in historical work . . . in his book *Language,* and in his lectures and in conversation with colleagues, he has, it is my impression, rather tended away from precise and explicit formulation of doctrine. The actual codifying and formulation of descriptive theory and techniques have been much more explicitly carried out by other linguists, beginning with Sapir's 'Sound patterns in language' . . . and continuing through to the work of the group among whom Eugene A. Nida and Kenneth L. Pike are the outstanding figures, and in the basic investigations of the linguists who participated in the Army's recent language program.

Sapir also, of course, had the deepest interest in historical work; and it is hard to read Bloomfield's *Language* as not concerned with codifying and formulating descriptive theory and technique. But the striking thing is that Sapir is mentioned in this way at all. To one leader in the development of descriptive linguistics in America (a leader curiously absent from Joos (1957), incidentally), it was reasonable in 1946 to trace the main line of development of codifying and formulating descriptive theory and technique from Sapir, more than from Bloomfield.[23]

Trager's phrase, 'basically Bloomfieldians', of course recognizes the pervasive influence of Bloomfield in the period. The general effect of his remarks is to recognize the joint influence of the two men in the period in question (and of their younger followers). Failure to recognize this joint influence makes the account of the history of phonology in Stark (1972) misleadingly incomplete. Stark contrasts Sapir's conception of sound pattern to Bloomfield's critique of phonetically organized tables of phonemes, and brings out clearly Bloomfield's conception of phonologic structure as concerned with 'the working of the language' in terms of privileges of occurrence. But Stark follows Bloomfield in opposing such a conception of structure (essentially distributional) to a conception in terms of phonetic character. From this one might infer that Bloomfield introduced the distributional approach to phonologic structure, and that Sapir did not employ it. Neither inference would be correct. Sapir's doctoral dissertation, written in the first decade of the century (Sapir 1922), contains a highly detailed analysis of the distributional structure of Takelma sounds. One can point to a tradition from that dissertation, through the work of Sapir's students, and students' students, that employs both the tabular (phonetic) presentation and the distributional analysis. The grammatical sketches in Hoijer et al. (1946) generally show this: Swadesh (Eskimo), Hoijer (Chiricahua Apache), Voegelin (Delaware), Trager (Taos), Newman (Yokuts), Halpern (Yuma), Hoijer (Tonkawa), Haas (Tunica), Li (Chipewyan). (Curiously, only Whorf's Hopi and Milpa Alta Aztec, and Swadesh's Chitimacha, do not clearly show this; and Whorf may have considered distribution sufficiently accounted for in his innovating treatment of allophones as positional variants.) Phonemic articles in *IJAL* after World War II frequently show both presentations (Newman 1947, Garvin 1948, Hoijer and Dozier 1949, Garvin 1950, Wonderly 1951), though not all do (e.g., Wolff 1952).[24] Furthermore, in contrast to the Bloomfieldian theoretical neglect of subphonemic detail, stressed by Stark, descriptions such as these continued to give considerable phonetic detail. Moreover, the presentation of phonetic detail commonly was in terms of the dimensions that underlie phonemic tables. The table itself might be presented in an offhand or perfunctory fashion, but its phonetic dimensions were regularly employed to organize phonetic facts. That such dimensions were found useful, even indispensable, to

---

[23]   Perhaps an echo of Sapir's prominence in the development of phonology lies behind the statement (Koerner 1970a:165): 'Edward Sapir's book *Language* (1921) represents the first general attempt (in America) to investigate languages on the basis of their phonological systems ("patterns") . . . .' In fact, of course, the core of Sapir's book is concerned with grammatical systems, and phonology as such has only a few pages (55-58).

[24]   Garvin 1948 does not give a table, but employs the dimensions of a table to list the phonemes in paragraphs. Wolff's omission of a table may be due to the focus of his paper on historical phonology, or editorial intervention (an initial discussion of style having been truncated (V. Hymes, personal communication)).

coherent presentation of phonetic relationships was indeed an implicit refutation of Bloomfield's position that the dimensions were an ethic imposition (1933: 129–130):

Tables like these, even when they exclude non-distinctive features, are nevertheless irrelevant to the structure of the language, because they group the phonemes according to the linguist's notion of their physiologic character, and not according to the parts which the several phonemes play in the working of the language.[25]

In sum, it is quite misleading to write (Stark 1972:392–393):

That Bloomfield's syntagmatic and formal notion of the phoneme and phonemic structure *replaced* [emphasis added] Sapir's mentalist and paradigmatic conception of 'sound-patterns' is indicated by the virtual absence of phonological paradigms from Bloomfieldian descriptions of particular languages and by the downgrading of phonetic substance to 'pre-linguistic data' or 'phonetic habits'.

Bloomfield's notion replaced Sapir's only in the sense of insisting on exclusive attention to one-half of Sapir's approach, so far as ideas are concerned. So far as linguists are concerned, the phrase 'virtual absence' obscures a considerable amount of work throughout the period. Bloomfield's notion replaced Sapir's notion for *some* linguists, including the most prominent. But even here Harris, who vigorously upheld the Bloomfield view in his analysis of Trubetzkoy (Harris 1940:347–8), echoing Bloomfield's own words as to 'what work each phoneme can do' (348), and completely subordinating phonetic pattern to distributional pattern; and who carried distributional reduction and organization of phonemes to virtually unintelligible (and distorting) extremes (cf. Harris 1945:245b, para 3, Bender and Harris 1946); even Harris assimilated Sapir to the role of predecessor (1968:13):

Sapir was, with Leonard Bloomfield, a founder of formal descriptive linguistics and the distributional method that characterizes it.

In this biographical article Harris is consistent with his methodological treatise written two decades earlier (1951:7):

It is a matter of prime importance that these elements be defined relatively to the other elements and to the interrelations among all of them.[5]

[5] The most explicit statement of the relative and patterned character of the phonologic elements is given by Edward Sapir in Sound Patterns in Language . . .'

And Harris' treatment of process statements of phonology, as exemplified in work of Newman, Hoijer, and others, is always couched in terms of alternative idioms. While Sapir's use of process formulation (Harris 1968:13):

[25] The concern to avoid alien imposition on native structure can lead to ironic paradox. Boas established a tradition of avoiding the European derived alphabetic order in listing lexicons of American Indian languages; the lexicons so organized are very hard to use for American Indians (like the rest of us they rely on alphabetic order for such purposes). Bloomfield, the advocate of speakers' habits and a physicalist creed, sought to supersede traditional phonetics and a traditional mode of presentation, and so deprived of theoretical status a very real part of speakers' habits, leaving to mentalists such as Jakobson and Chomsky the defense of the status of this facet of the physical reality of speech.

reduced the incisiveness and generality of the distributional theory he was developing, it did indicate some of the other systemic factors (factors of equilibrium, of dynamics, etc.) that may be required to understand the sources of aberrant phenomena or of the place these phenomena occupy in the descriptive system. These additional factors may even aid ultimately in understanding the source of the system itself.

Stark recognizes the presence of more than one approach in syntax in the work after Bloomfield (398), but only within the Bloomfieldian heritage. It is necessary to recognize more than one approach in phonology as well as in syntax, and without as well as within a strictly Bloomfieldian heritage. Careful study of practice and of terminology in the literature of the period would demonstrate as much (cf. Joos 1958:281 on terminology as evidence of multiple American traditions). The discussion just given, especially the quotations from Harris, show the underlying presence, continuity, of features of the work of Sapir. To miss these features is to limit one's historiography to aspects of surface structure, so to speak.

The source of the limitation is lack of close study of the primary sources, but this lack has its source in turn in the 'mainstream' model, and the simplistic periodization that results from it. A period, it seems, must have one center, one hero or heroic thrust. So Sapir is put 'before' Bloomfield, and in consequence structuralism in the United States comes to be equated with the Bloomfieldian model. Stark slips into just such an equation. He parallels Makkai in writing (1972:385):

In the United States it is possible to distinguish three theoretical models that have their moments in the scientific study of language. They are the pre-Bloomfieldian models of Franz Boas and Edward Sapir, the model worked out by Leonard Bloomfield and his successors which dominated American linguistic thinking from 1926 to 1957, and the transformational model that surfaced in 1957 . . . .

The models of Boas and of Sapir were of course not identical, so that one has to do with four, not three; but the main point is the neglect of the work of Sapir, Newman, Swadesh, Voegelin, Whorf, and others in the period in question. Having assigned the chronological period to Bloomfield and his successors, Stark comes shortly to write (381) of 'American structuralism' as if it and the Bloomfield model were the same thing.

This mistake leads Stark astray with regard to grammatical analysis as well as with regard to phonology. Thus he puts in quotes the term 'status', as used by Trager and Smith (1951:79), implying that the term is idiosyncratic and unexplained. The term was in fact a technical term within a descriptive system for the analysis of grammatical categories (see Whorf 1938:279 = Carroll 1956:117). The term and system were well known to Trager, who indeed is thanked, together with Swadesh, in Whorf's general article on grammatical categories (written at the request of Boas; see Whorf 1945, n. 1). Trager had previously employed the category of *status* to integrate treatment of several positionally diverse prefixes (factive, negative, narrative, definite, comparative, interrogative) in his contribution to the set of grammatical sketches planned by Sapir (Trager 1946:202). Not knowing this, Stark applies a mistaken connotation of the term 'status', and infers (1972:402):

What this term seems to mean is that the question 'Is he talking' is a completely unique utterance that is not related to 'He is talking'.

This inference does not follow from the Whorf, Trager, or Trager and Smith use. The latter in fact speak of frames (1951:79) in a manner analogous to later work on batteries of syntactic transformations; frames, not unrelated unique utterances, are what their examples (p. 80 of their booklet) illustrate.

Again, Harris' use of form classes and sentence patterns, rather than ICs and constructions, appears to Stark (1972:405) as 'not simply un-Bloomfieldian but . . . in fact anti-Bloomfieldian'. Form classes, however, may not be un-Sapirian. Like others, Stark overlooks two articles (Harris 1944, 1951b) that are essential to interpretation of the development of syntactic analysis in the United States. Harris' treatment of Sapir directly (1951b), and via Newman's Yokuts (1944), is expressly intended to capture (in a metalanguage of elementary unitary operations) the insights and indeed 'productiveness and elegance of Sapir's and Newman's method' (1944:205). Stark expresses curiosity as to Harris' motivation (403). Harris himself states it directly enough (1946:161) — in the first instance, it is a mathematically inspired uniformitarianism, seeking the most general statements by means of the simplest units and (repeatable) operations. In the second instance, an answer would seem to be at hand in Harris' transformation of Sapir's and Newman's method (Harris 1944:198–201, 201–205) from 'essentially aids in the process of research' into a 'description in terms of a catalog of elements and a minimum of most general statements about their occurrence' (205). Harris saw Sapir's (and Bloomfield's) use of process terminology as a stage in the history of science (1951b:291), but also, in Sapir's case, as having the

advantage of opening the way to a more subtle descriptive analysis — something always dear to Sapir's heart — by giving a special secondary status to some parts of the descriptive structure.

Harris added:

There is need for further elaboration of descriptive techniques, in order to make room for such refinements among our direct distributional statements.

In Harris' exposition of his reasons for replacing 'configurational interpretation' with 'structural statement' (1944:201–205), replacing classification and naming (203), and picturing of the particular relation as supporting or controlled by the general relation (204), by simply the most general statements of relations, arrived at by working up — one can see an attitude that would apply to forms of IC analysis as well. Not that Harris ignores IC analysis, but it is treated briefly, as one possible use or outcome of his general method (1951a:278, 363), and later as a complementary but obviously less adequate analysis (1965:365, 366 and n. 8). It does not seem too much to infer that in distributional analysis (as opposed to any primarily classificatory, categorizing approach) Harris found, and sought to develop, both generality, and *flexibility*, the latter being a capacity to respond to descriptive detail in a way akin to Sapir.

This interpretation appears to be supported by Harris' way of contrasting the analytic manners of Bloomfield and Sapir (1965:363):

Traditional grammar established various distinguished segments of sentences which were hierarchically subdivided into smaller segments (in a manner made explicit by Leonard Bloomfield, as the method of immediate constituents), or were altered by a grammatical process (in a manner developed, for example, in the work of Edward Sapir).

In point of fact, it can be argued that IC analysis is neither derived from nor strictly compatible with traditional grammar, and has its origin in Bloomfield's work (from 1914 on) in the work of the psychologist Wundt (Percival ms.). Be that as it may, Harris' comparison of IC analysis vis-à-vis transformational analysis (1965:364–365), his summary of the virtue of the latter:

Transformational analysis is of particular interest, first, because it can be described and investigated with algebraic tools, and second, because it provides exceptionally subtle analyses and distinctions for sentences (365),

and his discussion of acceptability-ordering, sense, and nuance (368–371, and n. 17 on 371) strongly suggest a continuity from grammatical process to grammatical operation. If the desire to design a formal instrument is due to Bloomfield, the instrument seems tuned for transcription of Sapir.[26]

In sum, for a linguist concerned to develop explicit formal method in the 1930s and 1940s, there was saliently Bloomfield's book of 1933 (cf. Harris 1951a:v). Besides Bloomfield's book, there was, for linguists, as source and precedent, as there should be today for historiographers, the contemporary work of Sapir (cf. Fries 1961:198, n. 1).

Neglect or ignorance of the Sapir tradition leads also Bierwisch into error. The salience of Bloomfield's *Language* is perhaps responsible for the mis-statement (1971:39) that 'The theoretical foundations of linguistic research in the United States were formulated in the 1930s.' Sapir (1925) — cf. Harris 1951b:292 — and Bloomfield (1926) are of course earlier, essential foundations. As for the 1930s, Bierwisch joins with those who view theoretical foundations in the United States as having rejected all mentalistic notions. Sapir and his associates in the 1930s of course did not. In assessing the decade one must note explicit statements of mentalistic notions, as in Sapir (1933b) and Whorf (1956 — written about 1936), together with the way in which meaning enters naturally into the grammars written under Sapir in the decade, such as those of Newman (1932b), Swadesh (1933), and Haas (1935). (Note the subtitle of Swadesh's dissertation, "A semantic study . . .", and his M.A. thesis of 1931 on Nootka aspect.) Indeed, not only is the Sapir grammatical model of the 1930s a neglected part of our general topic, but also it has a historical development of its own that should be traced. Newman's first sketch of

---

[26]   Harris (1945) also shows his interest in this period in coming to terms with Sapir's mature work (239): 'Sapir's Navaho analysis was even more interesting in the morphology than in the phonology. It is therefore to be hoped that Hoijer will soon give us a detailed presentation of Navaho morphology as a companion volume to the present excellent publication.'

Yokuts (1932a), for Boas, when first back from the field, is different from his dissertation (1932b), and the dissertation is revised and expanded in the published monograph (1944, completed about 1936). Swadesh's 1933 dissertation was published in revised and reduced form (1939b).[27] Haas' 1935 dissertation was revised and expanded in 1939 for publication (1941). Hoijer recounts (personal communication) that Sapir approved his Chicago dissertation on Tonkawa, while expecting revisions before publication (1933). These grammars, and others influenced by Sapir, are represented also by succinct typological sketches in Hoijer (1946), a volume planned in the 1930s by Sapir.[28] This material, and correspondence (e.g., of Sapir to Newman about his revision of Yokuts for publication), together with interviews, or written recollections, on the part of still living students of Sapir, would make possible an analysis of crucial importance to an adequate understanding of a 'Sapir model' and the actual development of 'American structuralism'.

Teeter (1964) recognizes the mentalistic dimension of Sapir's phonology, but, through neglect or ignorance of the scope of Sapir's linguistics as a whole, takes him to be evidence of the supposed development of a rejection of theory and of universals (see discussion under Boas above). According to Teeter, the dictum of Boas that we must put off a comprehensive theory of linguistic universals hardened to the dogma that there are no linguistic universals — the 'post-Boasian fallacy' (1964:200). This is to ignore Sapir's typology (1921) and universalizing investigations in semantics, and the early revival of a typological interest in general linguistics in the 1950s by Greenberg, Hockett, Voegelin, and others, a revival in a pre-Chomskyan mold with consciousness of Sapir as major precedent. And the error illustrates vividly the need for (Teeter 1966:84) 'a restudy of the sources with special attention to the theoretical concerns of the past'. Teeter writes (1964:200) that 'we find even Sapir calling it an "obsession" to "desire to apply an absolute and universal phonetic system to all languages" ', and later refers to acceptance of the post-Boasion fallacy (1964:202) 'as Sapir implicitly did in his phonemics'. But the quotation (from Sapir 1925 = Mandelbaum 1949:36) is taken out of context and misread in terms of a Chomskyan view of what 'universal phonetic system' should mean. What Sapir calls an obsession is the desire to *mechanically* apply a phonetic system, concerned solely with the physical characteristics of sounds, to

---

[27] Notice that in the publication in 1939 Swadesh describes his analysis as 'of the *semantic* relations of morphemes' (emphasis supplied). Notice also that the analysis is described as a study of 'the general *theory* of Nootka word structure'; reference is made to a working theory already shaped by Sapir, and it is claimed for the theory presented in Swadesh's paper that it is based on a broad sampling of native material (1939b:77) (emphasis on the word 'theory' supplied). Attention to the semantic characteristics of grammatical elements resembles that of Newman with regard to Yokuts; in addition Swadesh establishes a classification of lexemes into seven semantic classes, which have formal concomitants (99).

[28] The planning of the volume began in the period of post-doctoral collaboration between Newman, Swadesh, and Sapir (about 1933-36), as evidenced by this extract from a letter of Sapir to Newman: 'I hope your abbreviated Yokuts grammar comes through. So far I have only Morris' Eskimo in the docket.' (Sapir to Newman, August 12, 1935, from Gilmanton Iron Works, N. H.; courtesy of Newman).

the *exclusion* of functional, i.e., structural relations. What he rejects is not the place of a universal phonetics, but failure to recognize the existence, beyond phonetics, of a level of phonology! The remark occurs in the context of distinguishing a mechanical physical interpretation of relations among sounds from an interpretation in terms of a mentalistic linguistics. The very next sentence (Mandelbaum 1949:37) goes on to say:

for the objective relations between sounds are only a first approximation to the psychological relations which constitute the true phonetic pattern.

Sapir himself sums up his thesis at the end (Mandelbaum 1949:45):

The whole aim and spirit of this paper has been to show that phonetic phenomena are not physical phenomena *per se*, however necessary in the preliminary stages of inductive linguistic research it may be to get at the phonetic facts by way of their physical embodiment. The present discussion is really a special illustration of the necessity of getting behind the sense data of any type of expression in order to grasp the intuitively felt and communicated forms which alone give significance to such expression.

In sum, a paper that is the first published argument for the theoretical existence of phonology (in the United States) is interpreted as a step in the elimination of theory from American linguistics.

Similarly McCawley's claim (1967:110) that Sapir 'rejected' universal phonetics and 'used the terms "universal" and "absolute" as if they were interchangeable' is not borne out by an examination of the passages he cites. Sapir criticized those who 'are obsessed, like so many linguists, by the desire to apply an absolute *and* universal phonetic system to all languages . . .' [emphasis supplied]. Sapir himself is at pains through this entire paper to show the importance of relativistic and distributional classifications of sound units, and to do so in terms which are drawn from the prevailing 'universal' articulatory classification of sounds. At the very least he is entitled to have his choice of conjunction in the quoted passage taken seriously: he said *and*, not *or*, implying that the two traits are distinct rather than interchangeable. Nor is the paper in this section 'guilty of unusual vagueness, inconsistency, and ex post facto rationalization' (McCawley 1967:110) as we read it. Indeed, it seems quite clear.

European linguists and linguists in the Prague tradition have commonly noted the dimensions of Sapir's work neglected or ignored by linguists in the United States. For example, with regard to Teeter's assignment of Sapir to a step in the loss of theory (= universals), Stankiewicz noted at about the same time (1936: 495, n. 1):

The quest for generalization was cogently stated by Sapir: 'It would be easy to relieve ourselves of the burden of constructive thinking and to take the standpoint that each language has its unique history and therefore its unique structure' (1921:200).

It is time for the pervasive, but piecemeal, attention to the work of Sapir and his students today among American linguists, to give rise to a systematic, full-scale study.

(3) The discontinuity in the reputation of Sapir, and the consequent neglect or ignorance of his work and tradition, together frame a major historiographic problem: given a period (the 1930s) in which both Sapir and Bloomfield were active, with students who developed their approaches, why did just one of the two come to dominate the following period (the 1940s and early 1950s)?

Robins (1967:208–209) suggests reasons, contrasting Bloomfield's concentration on methodology and formal analysis to Sapir's wide ranging interests, and noting the status of Bloomfield's *Language* as a student's textbook. There is something to both points, and yet, as we have seen, there is more to the picture than that. Both Bloomfield and Sapir ranged from descriptive methodology in the late 1930s to problems of comparative-historical linguistics, Bloomfield working intensively on comparative Algonquian, and Sapir pursuing problems in Indo-European, Tocharian, and Semitic. And in 1937 Sapir might have seemed as much or more an active leader in the development of the central descriptive concern of the time, phonology. Sapir did give much of his attention to the emerging field of culture and personality, of which he was indeed one of the founders, and his plans for a book in the 1930s were not for a linguistics textbook, but for a text on the psychology of culture.[29] But it would seem that one must point above all to biographical and personal facts in chronological context. Sapir taught once at the Linguistic Institute (1937), where the emerging generation of the new profession was inspired and trained, and with impact (cf. Pike 1957), but his health, although not his ideas, had already begun to fail (Voegelin, personal communication). Bloomfield succeeded him for a full summer (1938) and part times of two more (1939, 1940), and his 1938 introductory course was the first held in the evening, i.e., at a time when other faculty and all students could attend. (The change was prompted apparently by the interest in Sapir's 1937 course.) Bloomfield's years coincided with the introduction of work with informants in cooperative sessions (an innovation proposed the year before by Sapir (Voegelin, personal communication)). And Sapir died in 1939, leaving Bloomfield as the only living 'father figure' for methodologically inclined young linguists, during the concentration of such in the war work in New York City. The locations and interests of younger scholars of course must have been a factor. Bloch became editor of *Language* in 1940, and was shortly at Yale; Whorf died (1941); and of those who had been closest to Sapir, Swadesh was without a teaching position after the war, save one year, while Newman, Hoijer, and Haas were in the west (Albuquerque, Los Angeles, and Berkeley, respectively). Not that these facts should be taken to imply party lines or sharp factionalism among either Sapir and Bloomfield, or their successors. Although Sapir and Bloomfield were not close, not even easily congenial company

[29] One might interpret Sapir's attention to social psychology at this time as a response to the depression and its political climate, but Stanley Newman (personal communication) reports that Sapir's interest was a natural development from work in the 1920s, and Zellig Harris (personal communication) has agreed (1970 conversation, thus revising Harris 1951b:315).

for each other, their relationship was one of mutual respect (cf. Hockett 1970:439, Harris 1973; R. A. Hall, Jr., has testified to this in a personal communication). As to their successors, there were of course differences of affinity, but also many and diverse links of friendship and interest, as acknowledgments and footnotes in these years disclose. To be sure, the relationship between *Language*, after 1940, and the founding of *Word*, in 1944, would repay study. Although in important part a sign of difference between European orientation and the emerging Bloomfieldian orientation, it is also significant for the association with *Word* of Swadesh, and the publication there of papers by Newman and Pike. Still, it is equally significant that the two men whose books of 1951 were salient expressions of the methodological outlook of the post-war years, Harris and Trager (with Smith), both associated their work with the Sapir tradition, including its interest in cultural pattern (Harris 1951b giving it sympathetic expositon, and Trager developing with others a language-centered model of culture (cf. Hymes (ed.) 1964c: 274–280)). There was something in the idiom and set of problems bequeathed by Bloomfield, or taken to be bequeathed by Bloomfield, that served to legitimate and motivate an autonomous linguistics, building knowledge of language afresh, as its adherents thought, as the idiom and problems bequeathed by Sapir did not. Or, though Sapir could be radicalizing and inspiring (witness his impact on Amerindian comparative work, and on study of culture and personality), there was something else more in keeping with the climate of opinion of the new generation.

For it remains that in the 1940s and early 1950s there was a downgrading of Sapir on the part of some who admired Bloomfield, although there was no corresponding downgrading of Bloomfield on the part of linguists who admired Sapir. *This imbalance in reputation partly defines the period, indeed, and points to what needs explanation about it.* The ascendancy of Bloomfield's idiom and ideas, and the consequences for the effective scope of discussion in the mainstream of linguistics in the United States, was not, in 1938, an inevitable or predictable next phase. There was in the work of Sapir and his students the prospect of an idiom and scope that would have considerably resembled the Prague School in outlook and concern. A glimpse of what full scale continuation of the Sapir tradition might have been like can be gained from the contributions to Spier et al. (1941) and Hoijer et al. (1946). Each paper in Spier et al. in one or another way indicated a use of linguistics in cultural analysis (Voegelin, Swadesh, Herzog, Emeneau, Newman, Whorf) and/or an expansion of the scope of linguistics analysis itself (Trager, Newman, Whorf). The grammatical sketches in Hoijer et al. show consistent concern for semantic function and the interdependence of features within a configuration of language as a whole. In sum, there was distinguishable in 1940 a Sapirian strain, whose fortune might have been other than it proved to be.

Hymes (1970a:229–231) has attempted to characterize a Sapirian variant of structuralism as a 'First Yale School' (extending an appellation associated with the Bloomfieldian approach) in terms of five tasks:

(1) to develop the methods of the nascent structural linguistics and to test their application in the analysis of both exotic and well known languages;
(2) to sustain the profession of linguistics, where almost no recognition existed so far as departments, chairs, specific courses, and autonomy of the discipline were concerned;
(3) to continue to rescue disappearing languages;
(4) to pursue proof and establishment of genetic relationships among languages;
(5) to relate the results and methods of linguistic inquiry to other things — to other disciplines in the humanities and social sciences; to particular problems within these disciplines . . .; and to practical affairs, such as education.

The careers and scope of the work of Swadesh and Whorf (cf. Hymes 1970a: 262) can be placed in these terms, and elements of the work of Hockett, Newman, Pike, Trager, and others, not usually discussed in connection with the development of linguistics in the United States, can be seen as response to such a tradition (e.g., Hockett's work on psychiatric interviews, in relation to that of Trager, Smith, McQuown, Hall, Birdwhistell on paralanguage, kinesics and verbal interaction generally, Newman's work in psychology of verbal behavior, the intended scope of Pike 1967, Trager's work with Whorf and Swadesh on Macro-Penutian, and with Whorf on Uto-Azteco-Tanoan, Trager's conception of 'metalinguistics', Whorf's comparative linguistic work and attention to grammatical categories, such as aspect, as well as his concern with the relation of language to culture).

Flatly stated, the set of five tasks does not clearly distinguish the scope of a Sapir tradition within the general tradition of structural linguistics in the United States, except perhaps in the absence of a task of work on the diversity and dialectology of American English. (Even in this regard one must note that Swadesh and Whorf each contributed description of their own dialects.) In thrust and emphasis, however, the context of anthropology made the last three tasks more pressing for students of Sapir than for those who came to Bloomfield from backgrounds in languages, philology, and dialectology. Bloomfield and his immediate followers endorsed these tasks, but for students of Sapir they were responsibilities. Although involved in earlier methodological discussions (cf. Hockett 1942, n. 1), Mary Haas has devoted herself to description of disappearing languages and genetic relationships. Swadesh was deeply involved in methodological developments in the 1930s, but after World War II turned almost exclusively to demonstration and extension of Sapir's insights into remote genetic relationships. Those who took up the general problem of the relation of linguistic method to method in the analysis of culture, and problems of specific methods for paralanguage and kinesics, clearly did so in terms of the heritage of Sapir (cf. Newman 1951:184–186, Hymes 1970a).

Robins' point, then, as to Bloomfield's concentration on methodology and formal analysis, is descriptively apt, as part of the explanation of the character of the 1940s and early 1950s. The point needs to be fleshed out in terms of individual careers and disciplinary context, not only of Sapir and Bloomfield, but also of their followers, as indicated just above.[30] And there remains to be explained the fact that development of descriptive method, in and of itself, would be the primary task, the task among other possibilities, indeed, that amounted to a definition of linguistics proper, or at least of a contribution to the mainstream of linguistics. This is a matter not only of scope (concentration on the first task, development of method), but also of idiom. For some linguists in the period, Sapir became almost unintelligible. For many, Bloomfield represented not only a foundation on which to build, but a criterion of acceptable style, in both linguistic presentation and extralinguistic attitudes. This viewpoint is faithfully expressed in Bloch's obituary (1949—quoted from Hockett 1970:530–531):

There can be no doubt that Bloomfield's greatest contribution to the study of language was to make a science of it. Others before him had worked scientifically in linguistics; but no one had so uncompromisingly rejected all prescientific methods, or had been so consistently careful, in writing about language, to use terms that would imply no tacit reliance on factors beyond the range of observation. To some readers, unaware of the danger that lies in a common-sense view of the world, Bloomfield's avoidance of every-day expressions may have sounded like pedantry, his rigorous definitions like jargon. But to the majority of linguists, the simple clarity of Bloomfield's diction first revealed in full the possibilities of scientific discourse about language. It was Bloomfield who taught us the necessity of speaking about language in the style that every scientist uses when he speaks about the object of his research: impersonally, precisely and in terms that assume no more than actual observation discloses to him.

Bloomfield gave recruits to the aspiring science, not yet anywhere a recognized discipline, an overt criterion of identity, an idiom of boundary maintenance, in a way that Sapir did not. (Harris 1940, 1944, 1945:246 gives a judicious, libertarian account of analytic motives for the idiom, but it became a shibboleth as well.)

Part of the outlook that went with membership in the new discipline, especially attitudes about the equality and relativity of languages, and the value and importance of American Indian studies, did indeed derive from the anthropological tradition (shared in by Bloomfield as well as by Sapir). A part that came to identify those who regarded themselves, and were widely regarded by others, as central to the emerging discipline derived from Bloomfield's attitudes and idiom. (On elements of both kinds as badges of membership in Bloomfieldian linguistics, cf. Householder 1969:886–887.) Various of Bloomfield's specific tenets and proposals might be criticized or rejected by his own followers, and linguists influenced by Sapir might contribute (Lepschy 1970:77–8 (quoted in Dinneen 1971:288)):

in maintaining among American linguists a healthy dissatisfaction with the stifling limitations imposed on research by a mistaken sense of scientific 'responsibility' on the part of some of Bloomfield followers;

[30]   One scholar central to the period has spoken of it almost as if at the end of World War II the task of development of formal method, and the task of development of 'ethnolinguistics' (relations between language and culture), were alternatives on whose profitableness one could bet, the first having won.

but those who accepted the methodological task as primary, and of Bloomfield's idiom as necessary, would define the 1940s and early 1950s as Bloomfieldian in the eyes of admirers and critics alike. Perhaps Ivić (1965:156) offers an apt summary of such a view of the outcome in those years:

The difference in the historic role of these two great Americans lies in the fact that Sapir determined the scope of interest and type of general culture proper to a typically American linguist, while Bloomfield laid the foundations of typically American linguistic method.

An interpretation specific to linguistics in its disciplinary context, and one that seems to us correct, is given by Newman (1951:185).[31] On the one hand, Newman points out, Sapir

. . . was as thoroughly committed as Bloomfield to the view that a valid linguistic science must be a coherent and self-consistent body of concepts. It must not look for extra-linguistic formulations to support or, still worse, to validate its findings.

On the other hand,

At the time that Sapir was seeking to expand the horizons of language study beyond the linguist's traditional universe of discourse, history played a cruel trick on him by directing linguistics into contrary channels. Under the influence of Bloomfield, American linguists in the 1930s turned to an intense cultivation of their own field, sharpening their methodological tools and rigorously defining the proper limits of their science in terms of what Trager has identified as 'microlinguistics'. They became increasingly efficient microlinguists. Certainly no one can deny that this involuntary trend has given linguistics a disciplined clarity and power of analysis that it never had before. But it is equally true that this trend carries with it the seeds of an ever-narrowing parochialism. And it was Sapir's main purpose to make linguistics a more cosmopolitan member of the community of sciences.

4.3 Whorf

The relation of Whorf's work to the Sapir tradition has been indicated in the preceding section. Like Sapir, Whorf has experienced a cycle of interest and neglect, and has suffered even more than Sapir from neglect or ignorance of the true nature of his work.

Some of Whorf's papers remained unpublished at his death in 1941, and his ideas were not much discussed until the end of that decade. This posthumous interest came to a focus with the issuing of four of his papers by Trager (Whorf 1950), and empirical development of one of his leading ideas by Hoijer (1951b), followed by discussion at the major anthropological conference of the era (Hoijer 1953), an important conference of anthropologists and linguists (Lévi-Strauss et al. 1953), and a conference entirely devoted to the 'Sapir-Whorf' hypothesis (Hoijer

---

[31] Except that the fourth sentence quoted reads the 1930s in terms of what had become dominant in the 1940s, and was still so at the time Newman wrote. As the sentence stands, it forgets the range of concerns shown in Spier et al. 1941, including those in psychology of Newman himself.

1954). Whorf's writings had something of an almost revolutionary impact, but for only a few years. The association of his name with the notion of linguistic relativity is remembered, but there has been little work on the subject, or on his own ideas, for a decade or more.

Inaccurate conceptions of the role of Whorf's ideas have been common enough, and continue to recur. A specialist in the history of linguistics has recently written (Koerner 1973c:683):

Basilius 1952 appears to have started the debate among linguistic anthropologists on the 'Whorfian hypothesis', but had no effect on linguistics proper.

In point of fact, the paper by Basilius, whatever its merits, played little or no role in anthropological discussions, which centered among Trager, Hoijer, Kluckhohn, and other former associates of Whorf and students of Sapir. Such an error, by a specialist, shows how much even the rather recent history of structural linguistics in the United States is in need of study. It is ironic that the error comes in a review of a translation of W. von Humboldt's great work on the Kawi-Sprache; gradual recognition of the precedent of von Humboldt was a feature of the posthumous discussion of Whorf's ideas.

Misconceptions with regard to the Humboldtian tradition seem indeed to show something of a pattern in American linguistics, a pattern of recurrent, or successive, amnesia. We have seen earlier (under Anthropology) that Boas was aware of a tradition linking his work to that of Steinthal (and hence W. von Humboldt), and that Bloomfield (1914) recognized von Humboldt as founder of general linguistics; Sapir wrote a Master's thesis on Herder in which his influence on von Humboldt was argued. A generation later, Whorf was aware of the tradition stemming from Boas and Sapir, but not, apparently, of von Humboldt (Whorf 1956). After World War II, indeed, Boas' own motive for attention to grammatical categories came to seem obscure to some linguists, although clearly stated in his well known "Introduction" (1911). More recently, detailed attention to grammatical categories by Boas, Sapir, and Whorf seems to have been forgotten, von Humboldt being installed as a predecessor in general linguistics by a leap across the interval between the present and the early 19th century (Chomsky 1964b).

There are now discussions which document the Humboldtian (and Herderian) sources of the tradition of structural linguistics in the United States, through Steinthal and Brinton (cf. Darnell 1967) to Boas, Sapir, and Bloomfield; cf. Robins 1967:152, Brown 1967, Christmann 1967, Gipper 1972:130ff, and also Cassirer 1945, Hymes 1961c:23–24, 1963:72–73, 1970b). A full-scale study is needed. It would have a great theme, and historical scope; it would deal with a continuous tradition that links European and American linguistics in a fundamental, yet little noticed way. Behind the impact of anthropology on structural linguistics in the United States stands not only work with American Indians, but also German intellectual tradition (cf. Stocking 1968a:133–160).

Neglect of Whorf's historical place is one side of the coin; misconception of his actual views and work is the other. He is famous for an extreme view of linguistic relativity which he did not in fact hold or invent (cf. Hymes 1966c, 1970a:262, Robins 1967:87, 93). The extensive literature on the 'Whorf hypothesis' through 1962 is indicated in Hymes 1964c:149–153; Whorf is also discussed in Dixon 1965:97–101, and extensively in Gipper 1972. The only general introduction to his work and career remains the valuable book edited by Carroll 1956; Part I of Carroll's introduction has been reprinted in Sebeok 1966:563–585, and cf. Trager 1968. There is now a unique unpublished study, considering Whorf from the standpoint of the development of American society and thought, including attitudes toward the relation between science and religion (Rollins 1972). Rollins takes into account a remarkably prophetic unpublished novel by Whorf, and provides a perspective on the significance of the man in his time and place that is lacking for most contributors to our subject.

Perhaps the chief irony of Whorf's reputation is that he became famous for a single portion of his work, through articles not published by himself or addressed to non-technical audiences, and this posthumously, in the very different climate of linguistics after World War II and the immediate post-war years. His interest in direct study of meaning then seemed a polar opposite to the priorities of the dominant tendency in linguistics proper. He became a symbol of the significance of language in culture, helping to legitimate continuing connection of linguistics with cultural anthropology; but all this occurred in a changed disciplinary context. The naturalness of culturally oriented semantic interests in the broad tradition of the 1930s was not apparent to students entering linguistics in the 1950s without benefit of anthropology, and there was not a continuity of semantic inquiry sufficient to bridge the gap between the 'Whorf hypothesis' and the ordinary practice of linguists. His name became at best a symbol of a promissory note (cf. Trager 1968).

In the event the full range of Whorf's work was lost from view, even though available for sampling in Carroll (1956). Whorf was in fact an active contributor to the development of linguistics in terms of all the the tasks that can be identified as salient to the Sapir tradition (Hymes 1971a:262, n. 36; cf. above under Sapir). He helped to develop phonology in both exotic languages and in English; publicized the science of linguistics most effectively — his claims of universal significance are the counterpart and precedent, in a different climate of opinion, to those of Chomsky; he helped formulate Uto-Azteco-Tanoan and 'Macro-Penutian' families of languages; and he sought to integrate linguistic theory with anthropological theory and with practical affairs. Whorf indeed invented 'allophone' as a technical term.[32]

---

[32] See discussion in Joos 1958:285. Makkai 1972:4 notes attribution of the term to Whorf. Trager and Bloch (1941), containing the first use of the term in print, acknowledge unspecified debt to Bloomfield, Hockett, and Whorf (n. 4). Whorf's own use of he term is attested in the posthumously published sketches of Hopi and Aztec (Hoijer et al. 1946:160–161, 371–372).

Most serious for understanding of the actual history of our subject is neglect or ignorance of Whorf's semantic work and views. Within the context of the Sapir tradition, Whorf most consistently and penetratingly developed semantic description. His writings make most explicit in general statement the concern for underlying semantic configuration that Harris, for example, explicates and transforms in his review of Newman's Yokuts (Harris 1951b). Whorf discussed his views with Trager, Swadesh, and others during the 1930s (cf. Whorf 1945, n. 1), and articles published then and after his death make clear his insight; but he is not recognized, as he should be, as a close and true predecessor, not only for a Humboldtian interest in language and social knowledge, but also for a Humboldtian interest in inner, underlying form. Consider these statements (cited from Whorf 1956 — written about 1936):

'any scientific grammar is necessarily a deep analysis into relations'
'A covert linguistic class may not deal with any grand dichotomy of objects, it may have a very subtle meaning, and it may have no overt mark other than certain distinctive "reactances" with certain overtly marked forms'
'Grammatical research up to the present time has been concerned chiefly with study of phenotypes [i.e., overtly morphemically marked categories]. A certain type of grammar proceeds as if linguistic meaning dwelt wholly in them. The anthropologist should not be satisfied with such a grammar . . .'
'linguistics is essentially the quest of MEANING'
'The complex structure of English is largely covert, which makes it all the harder to analyze.'

4.4   *Bloomfield*

A general, book-length study of the life and work of Bloomfield does not exist and is greatly needed. In the interim the anthology edited by Hockett (1970) and the article by Fries (1961) provide a good introduction to the character of his contribution to linguistics.

Bloomfield appears to be unique in the annals of structural linguistics in the United States, in that two appreciations of his contribution appeared during his lifetime, unprompted by any occasion of book review or survey. Both treat his application of comparative-historical linguistics to the Algonquian family of American Indian languages (Sapir 1931, Hockett 1948a). At his death there appeared tributes and evaluations such as Bloch (1949), Hall (1950b), Sturtevant (1950), all of interest and importance. In the *International Journal of American Linguistics* tribute took the form of republication of his 1926 postulates with a headnote by the editor, C. F. Voegelin (*IJAL* 15:195–207 (1949)) — evidence enough of the symbolic significance of both man and article. General discussions of his work and approach began to appear a decade later, occasioned by review of posthumously published work (Voegelin 1959, Malkiel 1962–3, Teeter 1970a, 1970b), associated with continued work with Algonquian materials and evaluation of his own practice (Bever 1963, 1967, as well as Teeter and Voegelin just cited, and Teeter 1969), commissioned (Fries 1961, Hockett 1968c), or necessitated by any review of major predecessors (e.g., Dixon 1965:78–84). Very recently there has come to be assessment of the relationship between Bloomfield's own views and practice, on the one hand, and those developed in his name (cf. Hockett 1968a, 1970:367–376, Huddleston 1972, Stark 1972, Harris 1973, Silverstein ms.). (On Bloomfield, see also Davis (1973, ch. 4) and Mounin (1972:111–125.)

Unpublished correspondence figures in Fries (1961) and Hockett (1970), and Hockett also provides valuable additional personal data (532–544). As with Boas and Sapir, the literature that contains comment on Bloomfield is too great to list; his name enters into any discussion of the development of structural linguistics. Much of his significance has been noticed in preceding parts of this essay. Here we shall take up three aspects of the issue that is most salient in subsequent linguistic discussion: Bloomfield's conception of linguistic science, especially as associated with his views on psychology and meaning. But first let us note a contrast with Sapir. The initial attitude of most linguists today is sympathetic to Sapir's name, and the thrust of a critique of historiography is to show that his role was more comprehensive, in content and time, than often assumed. One must build up knowledge of much that has been forgotten. There is an initial lack of sympathy on the part of many today toward Bloomfield's name, and the thrust of a critique is to show that his role was less encompassing (but in some ways, more complex) than often assumed. One must disentangle Bloomfield from much that has been attributed to him.

In a sense the fundamental problem is the same as it is for any figure: to provide an accurate picture of the scope and content of the work, and of its place in relation to what preceded and followed it. But Bloomfield poses the complication of a scholar who has become a symbol for an entire period, indeed prehistory (the prehistory of Chomskyan transformational grammar). One can find even a historian of linguistics writing (Koerner 1970b:419):

To be sure, European linguistics has never suffered a period similar to that which American linguistic science underwent between 1926 (see Bloomfield's *Postulates*) and the Ninth International Congress of Linguistics held at Cambridge, U.S.A. in 1962, on the occasion of which Chomsky felt obliged to show that transformational theory is 'much closer to traditional grammar' than post-Bloomfieldian structural 'taxonomic' linguistics . . . .

The statement is internally contradictory — post-Bloomfieldian linguistics can hardly have begun with Bloomfield's 1926 *Postulates* — but the image of thirty years or more dominated by one man's views is common enough. If historians can make such statements, it is not surprising that writers of textbooks single out Bloomfield (Grinder and Elgin 1973:30) as 'the man whose philosophy of grammar dominated the field of linguistics in the United States until recently' for the 'arbitrary' beginning of a chapter on "The historical antecedents of transformational (generative) grammar" (ch. 3, 30–44). The initial discussion shows nicely the need to disentangle Bloomfield's relation to work that preceded and followed his own specific contribution. Grinder and Elgin write (31):

If one were asked to choose the most significant and valuable contributions made by Bloomfield, it is probable that the following two would be the ones most frequently selected:

1. The object to be described is not the written language but the spoken one, and the relation of the linguist to the language must be that of a nonmanipulating observer.

2. The set of structures that the linguist discovers in the language he is studying must be characterized in an absolutely explicit manner, without any overt or covert appeal to the general cognitive or linguistic abilities of the individuals using the description.

The first of these ideals is one that Bloomfield himself attributed (correctly) to Boas (cf. Fries 1961:217–219), and was general to the tradition shared by Sapir and others. The second ideal, insofar as it can be approximated in any human inquiry, is most thoroughly developed in work of Harris and Chomsky, and, if Bloomfield gave it impetus, still its roots are to be found in the 'analytic' method of Boas, wherein descriptions are stripped bare of traditional preconception to focus exclusively on what is there in the language. The authors later refer to 'these two clearly formulated, if not original, theses issued by Bloomfield' (34), but they have in fact presented the theses to students as Bloomfield's, for they present them as product of Bloomfield's attempt to work out a philosophy of grammar within the boundaries of behaviorism (which in turn is taken as the reflex in psychology of positivism) (30–31). It is of course impossible to attribute to behaviorism or positivism the adherence of Boas and Sapir to nonmanipulative, explicit analysis of spoken language.

Our central thesis is that Bloomfield's views on behaviorism had perhaps more influence on others than they had on Bloomfield, and that insofar as they were necessary to his linguistic work, the necessity appears to have been personal and social, rather than linguistic. The three aspects under which we will consider this thesis have been noted by others before, but continuing neglect of each indicates the need of reassertion.

(1) Fries (1961:200–2) correctly summarizes the import of Bloomfield's early work:

This emphasis upon the basic scientific importance of the assumption of 'regularity' [in sound change] appears in Bloomfield's earliest linguistic writing and continues to the end. It is the starting point from which all the other emphases upon so-called 'mechanism' arise.

The flavor of Bloomfield's outlook from the start is indicated in the concluding lines of a review of Prokosch (Hockett 1970:33 (originally 1912)):

If we had had such books twenty years ago the *Nation's* and many others' criticism of our modern-language teaching (to wit and namely: that is has been a complete failure) would never have been made. Nor may a modest hope be out of place, as this book has come from the pen of a linguist (or 'philologist'), that the science of language may in time come to hold, in America also, its proper place among the sciences.

Elsewhere in these reprinted pages from the second decade of the century (about two decades before *Language* (1933) and some years before meeting the behaviorist psychologist Weiss) we find

what great harm is done by the barbarous ignorance of our whole school-system about matters of language (35);

we find that the 'mentalist' psychologist Wundt's work is criticized for failing to carry through in language its 'methodic precaution' of 'the exclusion of reflective rationalizing explanations' (39, 41–42); and we find, Wilhelm von Humboldt having been hailed ('this great scholar's intuition' (62)) for recognizing the priority of the sentence to the word, that speakers' division of sentences into words is not reflective, but (64):

it is a matter of implication, and is due to the associational connections of the parts of the sound-sequence which constitutes the sentence . . .

in short, a matter of habits.

In sum, Bloomfield's known career *began* with a commitment to the status of linguistics as a science, and to a rejection of teleological, logical, or other post-hoc or a priori explanations of linguistic facts (cf. his papers on "Sentence and word" (1914) and "Subject and predicate" (1916) in Hockett 1970). Rigor of method as against speculative interpretation; the facts of science as against popular misconception and entrenched intellectual prejudice — these are there at the start. Their origins in Bloomfield's work must be sought earlier and deeper than the psychologies of either Wundt or Weiss. Bloomfield's shift from use of Wundt's social psychology in his first general book (in 1914) to the idiom of the behaviorist psychology of Weiss in his second (1933) is now rather well known. The shift is interesting and it has some causes and consequences of interest; but what we know as the characteristic tenor of Bloomfield's linguistics must be traced to the interaction between his personality and the linguistic science that he embraced as a career.

(2) Bloomfield's conceptions of psychology, then, are secondary to his commitment as a linguist. It is possible to imagine Bloomfield as having developed the substance of his linguistic work without reference to psychological positions of any kind. This is indeed the point at which Bloomfield himself explicitly arrived. Fries (1961: 203–209) discusses "The 'exclusion' of psychology", and notes that Bloomfield's postulates of 1926 begin with reference to psychology only to exclude it (cf. the passages from 1914, 1922, 1924, 1926, 1933, 1939 cited by Fries in this connec-

tion). Bloomfield's position (suggested as early as 1914) was that the autonomy of linguistic science required it to be independent of psychology.

To say this is not to deny a constitutive role to psychological assumption. No theory can avoid psychological premises, whether made explicit or not. Where there is no talk of psychological matters, there still may be some underlying 'representative anecdote' (to use Kenneth Burke's term) of the user and acquirer of language. Such an anecdote (perhaps conceived as an antidote to a preceding dominant approach) will be compatible with work in some directions, rather than in others, allow some possibilities rather than others, indeed, create some problems internal to itself, through the boundaries and terminology it supports. The norms of correctness in terminology adopted by followers of a Bloomfield or a Chomsky are especially influential and revealing. In this respect the Whorf who as a fire insurance inspector noted the consequences of calling a vapor-filled drum 'empty' offered a permanent lesson to linguistics itself (cf. Hockett 1968:97). Terminology, then, and representative anecdote, interact with the goals, practice, and commitment of linguists to shape what is done.

In a later period historians may discover that what was done and what was lastingly accomplished must be distinguished, and may conclude that terminology and anecdote, fused in the idiom or rhetoric of the approach, had more to do with what was done than with what was lastingly accomplished. The temptation is then to dismiss the rhetoric as merely decorative or superficial. And superficial it is, to those who must discard it to find kernels they wish to use.[33] But since no approach appears to succeed without a rhetoric, it would seem that it is not superficial, but a functional prerequisite. Perhaps the particular rhetoric was not indispensable. Perhaps, given other circumstances, one or several other rhetorics might have done as well. The circumstances, however, were not other, but were composed of definite institutional arrangements, personal characters, abilities, climate of intellectual opinion, and inherited knowledge and problems. From the standpoint of any one factor, the others might well have been different, and certain contingencies can be retrospectively brought to light. One hates to write history from the standpoint of the Whigs or victors, but there is the presumption in favor of a successful rhetoric that it spoke to the condition of those who employed it to advance the subject. The scholars on whose intellectual and organizational work we build were not fools.

In our judgment neither Bloomfield's nor Chomsky's rhetoric is adequate to a theory of language conceived as part of a theory of social life; indeed, both cut off

[33]   Harris (1973) takes Bloomfield's distributional linguistics (to which he sees Sapir as also a contributor) as a precondition for the development of formal transformational grammar. According to Voegelin (1974), he also says (untruly) that in effect no one paid any attention to Bloomfield's psychological notions: "Bloomfield's espousal of a particular current school of behaviorist psychology as an interpretation of linguistics was arbitrary and not supportable. This was clear to almost everyone from the start, and neither his students nor his readers took it up" (p. 253).' We think that Voegelin is correct in finding Harris' exposition of linguistic theory 'fair and penetrating', but also correct in countering Harris' dismissal of Bloomfield's psychological rhetoric as having been without effect (cf. Hockett 1968a: 24-25).

successful inquiry into the bases of such a theory. This defect, however, appears from a conception of the goals of study of language that goes beyond the problems which the approaches in question partly found, partly constituted as tractable normal science. In each case, one seems to have assumptions and terminology congenial to the personality and capabilities of an original mind; the state of the discipline is such that personal preferences and needs answer to the situation of a new generation; and the outcome is a 'world-historical figure' (in Hegel's term), a named subject for essays such as this. As with the rhetoric, so with the figure: there is a tendency for the profession to treat the person and the work as a single entity, and for historiography to sever the two, regarding the accomplishments of the work as necessary, but the personal element as accidental. Ultimately historiography must analyze the interaction of accomplishment, person, and rhetoric.

Bloomfield's relation to psychology has been discussed in particular detail by Belyi 1967, Esper 1964, 1968, Fries 1954, 1961, Lepschy 1973, and Olmsted 1970. There is additional analysis of the relation of linguistics to psychological theory, as to its history and implications at the time, in Alkon 1959, Blumenthal 1970, Currie and Currie 1973, Marshall 1970, and Schlauch 1946, 1947. (Voegelin 1974 cites a forthcoming book by Esper (in press) as well, which neither he nor we have seen). In his writings, and in a letter quoted in Hockett (1970:545–6), Esper affirms the debt of Bloomfield's *Language* (1933) to Weiss, a debt which Hockett had personally heard Bloomfield insist upon. Esper affirms this debt in contrast to the view of Fries (1961:204, n. 1) that Bloomfield's very qualified characterization of the relation of the 1933 book to psychological foundations must be read literally. Bloomfield there states that he has tried to avoid any dependence on psychology, and Sturtevant (1950 (in Hockett 1970:545–6)) suggests that in a third edition Bloomfield would have proceeded to declare the dependence of psychology on linguistics. With Bloomfield more than any one it is wise to take what he says literally. In the absence of additional evidence, we have, then, testimony by Bloomfield to a debt, and published statement by Bloomfield that *Language* (1933) is not based on any specific theory of psychology. The resolution would appear to be that Bloomfield got from Weiss, not linguistics, but a conception of science. In using Wundt early in the century he had already been critical of teleological and a prioristic elements. Given the view, shared by many, that psychology was the discipline elementary to a general science of man, it would seem most likely that Weiss showed Bloomfield that there did indeed exist within psychology the kind of scientific outlook Bloomfield wanted. This must have provided both confirmation and motivation. Social personality being what it is, the phenomenon is familiar — the innovator in one field (scientific or humanistic) finding requisite support in another. Linguists today know this phenomenon, often uncomfortably, as other fields borrow tools, ideas, terms, prestige, from them. Our conjecture as to Bloomfield is only that, but it is the hypothesis with which we would approach new evidence.

In this connection it is important to bear in mind that the period in which Bloomfield worked, between the end of the first and second World Wars, was one dominated in much of its intellectual life by a climate of opinion very sympathetic to positivism, behaviorism, and the like. It was a period of loss of faith in the traditional categories and cultural symbols of Western civilization; the evolutionary optimism that had informed liberalism and socialism alike before World War I was shattered. Within this general climate the success of the writing of Gertrude Stein, W. C. Williams, and Ernest Hemingway is related at a distance to the linguistic idiom of Bloomfield and the Bloomfieldians. The widespread distrust of semantic content in language, and the widespread interest in building up knowledge or art from simple, fresh elements, is reflected in the work treated in Black (1949) and Urmson (1956), and in the lifelong opposition of language as symbolic action to conceptions of language as mere motion in the work of Kenneth Burke (cf. Burke 1967). The effect, then, of Bloomfield's stance was not due to Bloomfield alone.

Bloomfield's views on meaning are of course bound up with his views on psychology and the nature of science, and the two topics have together received most of the attention directed to his work. Among younger linguists who do not know his work directly, indeed, Bloomfield is probably best known today for a position he never held at all: the 'rejection of meaning'. It is not usually specified whether Bloomfield is thought to have rejected meaning as a heuristic tool in linguistic analysis, or as an element of definitions and characterizations in linguistic description, or both. In point of fact, Bloomfield favored the use of meaning in both analysis and description, and said so plainly in many publications. In two careful studies Fries (1954, 1961) tried to clear the record, but despite abundant evidence, the 'rejection of meaning' is still routinely charged to Bloomfield and to his followers collectively. Thus, Ivić (1965:159):

Bloomfield's methods were further elaborated by his pupils who kept strictly to his principles; the category of meaning had to be excluded from analysis; the criteria used had to be rigorously objective and mechanical.

Bloomfield's pupils were clearer on the point. Bloch (1948:6) wrote:

Since our approach differs in some respects from Bloomfield's — chiefly in that Bloomfield invokes meaning as a fundamental criterion and . . .

This paper in phonology was expressly considered as an attempt to formulate a new start, a stock-taking, in the spirit of Bloomfield's work but in response to new developments. In the first years after the war Bloch had relied on Bloomfield's definition of the morpheme, a definition which entailed meaning (cf. his 1946 "Studies in colloquial Japanese II: Syntax" and 1947 "English verb inflection", pp. 155, n. 4 and 243, n. 4 in Joos 1957). But shortly 'meaning' would be displaced here as well. Here is Trager, reconsidering his opinion of Nida's textbook presentation of morphology on the appearance of the second edition (1951:127):

As for morphemes themselves, let us leave meaning out of the discussion. Morphemes are recurring partials of structure, identifiable by distribution and correlation in patterned arrangements. It will be time enough to worry about meaning when we have worked out all our morphemic (morphological and syntactic) analyses.

The joint view that meaning is not necessary to the task at hand, and is to be considered later, is the same as that of Harris, who takes note of semantic, stylistic, and cultural studies, but as separate, later activities (see discussions indexed to 'meaning' in his 1951 book).

Bloomfield himself could not have been more explicit than he was in a letter to Fries (Fries 1961:215; also cited by Akhmanova and Mikael'an 1969:9):

It has become painfully common to say that I or rather, a whole group of language students of whom I am one, pay no attention to meaning or neglect it, or even that we undertake to study language without meaning, simply as meaningless sound. . . . It is not just a personal affair that is involved in the statements to which I have referred, but something which, if allowed to develop, will injure the progress of our science by setting up a fictitious contrast between students who consider meaning and students who neglect or ignore it. The latter class, so far as I know, does not exist. (Letter of January 29, 1945).

The issue, for Bloomfield, was not between presence and absence of meaning, but between its proper and improper use.

Hockett has been consistently clear as to the fact that form-meaning covariation was essential to Bloomfield's linguistics. Thus (Hockett 1952a:117):

Bloomfield's system recognized two initial criteria for the analysis of a language: sameness or difference as to *sound,* and sameness or difference as to *meaning,* of utterances and parts of utterances.

He correctly locates the departure from this view in *some* of Bloomfield's followers and in a period of about ten years, the 1940s (Hockett 1968a:24–5).

Bloomfield's own views can be consulted pointedly and at length in two of his last publications (1944b, 1943:102). What he rejected was not meaning, but what he called 'mentalism', meaning thereby the imputation of a causative role to unobservable factors. This position is further to be distinguished from Bloomfield's physicalism, i.e., the belief that physical causes can be imputed to all effects (observed and unobserved). Bloomfield was both an insister on observables and a physicalist, but the two positions can be held independently of each other. As to his conception of the place of semantic analysis within grammar, Bloomfield's position, as outlined in chapters 9 (Meaning) and 10 (Grammatical Forms) of his book (1933), would seem to be equivalent to what is now called 'interpretive semantics'. Each unit of lexical and grammatical form is matched with a unit of meaning, and the meaning of each form is taken to be constant and definite (morphemes are matched with sememes and tagmemes are matched with episememes). There would seem to be a continuity of outlook from Bloomfield through Harris to Chomsky in the postponement and parallelism of semantic analysis.

An adequate understanding of Bloomfield's views appears to be gaining ground. Chomsky early on (1957:235, n. 2) rebuked Hockett for his phrasing of Bloomfield's view:

Incidentally, the implication (p. 12) that Bloomfield held any such oversimplified view of meaning as this is surely unfair. In fact, Bloomfield quite explicitly rejects this view and discusses the remoteness of the connection between stimulation and linguistic response. Cf. L. Bloomfield, Language (New York, 1933), pp. 23, 141.

To which compare Hockett (1968a:22), where the interpretation of Bloomfield as identifying meaning with stimulus — response, or behavioral antecedents and consequences (an interpretation of meaning pervasive in Harris 1951) is rejected. Hockett says that Bloomfield's terse definition may give such an impression, but he is quite certain that that was not his view.

Stark (1972:412) concludes:

although meaning was not part of Bloomfield's conception of language structure, it was part of his linguistic theory so that it was included in all his theoretical discussions.

It is difficult to see how a theory that postulated a strict parallelism between units of form and units of meaning, such that (Stark 1972:411):

for Bloomfield a *linguistic form,* whether a morpheme or a tagmeme, is not a meaningless shape, as we now take it to be, but a correlation of units of form with units of meaning

can be said to exclude meaning from the structure of language. It would be closer to the mark to reverse the statement, and to say that Bloomfield included meaning in his conception of language structure, but not in his short-term linguistic theory. But it is surely wrong to oppose 'linguistic theory' to 'conception of language structure'. Stark brings out Bloomfield's views quite clearly, and shows that skepticism as to the practical possibility of incorporating meaning explicitly in linguistic analysis led to shifts (among some) to reliance on distributional patterning (meaning in the generic sense being assumed), among the Bloomfieldians.

The term 'theory' is troublesome in another account of Bloomfield that is nevertheless insightful. Teeter (1970:530) writes:

The Menomini language shows clearly that, while Bloomfield indeed lacked an explicit theory of language, neither discovery procedures nor limitations to immediate observables (another favorite modern charge) played any important part in his linguistic practice.

The work discussed by Stark, and which exercised so decisive an influence on the course of linguistics, was an explicit SOMETHING of language. 'Model', perhaps, but then so is transformational generative grammar, as a theory, a model. Such a use as this of the term 'theory' implies that current linguistics has provided something that was missing, whereas the polemics and controversies associated with the rise of Chomsky's views make clear that the issue was the *replacement* of something that was there, a theory of the nature, and study, of language.

Teeter's account is nevertheless invaluable for its attention to Bloomfield's actual procedures in the analysis of a language. Teeter does seem to misread what Bloomfield meant by saying 'No preconceptions' (1972:530–1). Bloomfield did not mean 'no theory', 'no conception of the nature of language', 'no model of language structure'. The rest of the quoted sentence makes clear what he meant; it reads:

find out which sound variations are distinctive (as to meaning) and then analyze morphology and syntax by putting together everything that is alike.

(The letter is Smithsonian Institution Office of Anthropology document 4365–a, dated December 23, 1919, and was called to attention by Michael Silverstein.) Teeter comments that the saving grace of the remarks is that Bloomfield (unlike post-Bloomfieldians) did begin with preconceptions; but of course what Bloomfield meant was that he did not begin with preconceptions as to which sound variations would be distinctive as to meaning. Surely Teeter is not recommending that we abandon the principle of contrast and repetition in phonology! But the preconceptions to which Teeter calls attention are equally important, namely that for Bloomfield,

Linguistic analysis begins with the productive control of a language and its social manifestations, and this is why a grammar not only describes a system but considers its use. . . . It is not too much to say that this theory involves no less than the ethnography of speaking. . . . If we can distinguish a speaker's KNOWLEDGE of a language from his COMMAND of it, Bloomfield begins with command.

(3) Teeter observes that it was only with his study of the Menomini grammar that he became fully aware of the extent and sharpness of the differentiation to be made between Bloomfield and the Bloomfieldians. Bloomfield's attitude toward actual descriptive work, and his practice of it, are indeed crucial considerations. They have been too far submerged beneath discussion of his views on psychology and meaning. As we have seen, it has become almost a tradition to pay more attention to these aspects of Bloomfield than to any other facet of his work. (Thus Ivić (1965:156–8) devotes about half her discussion of Bloomfield to his behaviorism, and relegates his life-work in comparative Algonquian to a footnote (156, n. 38).) Yet Bloomfield showed himself far more concerned with description and comparison of languages than with model-building. Hockett (1970:369) reports of his correspondence with Bloomfield at the time of his development of a system of descriptive phonology:

My concern with Ojibwa was more as materials for theoretical discussion than as data. Bloomfield was primarily concerned with accurate reporting of facts. As a result, much of the latter part of this correspondence was at cross-purposes.

The letters support Teeter's interpretation of Bloomfield's practice (e.g., 'Living with Fox-speaking family should be very good' (370)). And Bloomfield's attitude on the relation between models and the structure of a language shines forth clearly (370–1):

Not 'rules-of-thumb,' for what is here involved is not merely our convenience, but the speakers' habit of correlating morphologic complexes. To be sure, we take the liberty of inventing a basic (morphophonemic) formula and then telling how it is to be modified to produce the actual (phonemic) utterance, but this is merely a descriptive device: the actual forms do stand in the correlations which we describe.

(The parenthetic terms appear to have been supplied by Hockett.)

The last quotation brings out a point now widely recognized. As formulated by Huddleston (1972:338): 'Bloomfield's treatment of morphological alternation is quite clearly dynamic.' In a painstaking study of the historical development of Bloomfield's treatment of phonology and morphological alternation, Silverstein (ms.) concludes:

... it is clear that by the time of *Language* Leonard Bloomfield's phonology was essentially the same as that of Edward Sapir at this time period.

(Silverstein, like Hockett, stresses the need to read Bloomfield literally and carefully in context, and observes that his terseness could mislead.)

This recognition of the respects in which the work of Bloomfield and Sapir are alike has gained ground in recent years. Hockett himself observes (1968a:34):

But we must remember that transformations are largely a corrective to certain temporary extremisms of the 1940's, a reintroduction, with improvements and under a new name, of certain useful features of the Bloomfieldian and Sapirian view of language, that we had set aside.[34]

This shift is of the greatest importance to an accurate historical picture. Bloomfield, of course, retains his similarity (continuity) with the Bloomfieldians; but it

---

[34] Whereas in a volume published in 1961 the Sapirian tradition could be treated as comprising only interests specially anthropological, set apart from descriptive theory and method. Hamp introduces the article on general linguistics in the United States in the 1950s with the remarks: 'Since other contributors to this volume have assumed the task of treating the Sapir and Bloomfield traditions, the mainstream of distinctive American activity in general linguistics during the thirties and forties of this century will have been covered by implication in those contributions.' (165). There is indeed a contribution on the Bloomfield 'school' (Fries 1961), but the article representing Sapir is on 'anthropological linguistics' (Hoijer 1961). The article focuses on the continuation of the Boas tradition by Sapir, treating descriptive work in American Indian languages, historical and comparative work in American Indian languages, glottochronology and lexicostatistics, linguistic typology, and 'ethnolinguistics' in the sense of 'linguistic relativity' – in short, distinctive contributions of Swadesh, Greenberg, and Whorf along lines opened up by Sapir – but there is nothing on method or theory of description. Perhaps the responsibility lies with Hoijer, not the planners of the volume, for Hamp speaks of the most original aspect of the activity involving the Sapir and Bloomfield traditions as being in the fields of descriptive phonology and morphology, and himself stresses the differences in work stemming from the two traditions (165), so as to counter any impression of a monolithic school in the United States (165–166).

is of the utmost importance to complete the picture by bringing out his dissimilarity (discontinuity) with them, and his similarity with Sapir.

If Sapir and Bloomfield shared essential characteristics, then clearly 'mentalism' vs. 'behaviorism' cannot be the all-encompassing causal factor that it has sometimes been taken to be. It has of course always been ironic that the work of the 'mentalists', Boas and Sapir, should be explained away primarily in terms of practice, and the work of the 'behaviorist', Bloomfield, in terms of a ruling idea. But it remains to account for the common element. Bloomfield himself provided one lead. He said of Boas (1943:198):

> Perhaps his greatest contribution to science, and, at any rate, the one we can best appreciate, was the development of descriptive language study. The native languages of our country had been studied by some very gifted men, but none had succeeded in putting this study upon a scientific basis. . . . The progress which has since been made in the recording and description of human speech has merely grown forth from the roots, stem, and mighty branches of Boas' life work.

Fries (1961:218) quotes this passage, and notes that Bloomfield seriously engaged in first-hand descriptive field work with Menomini in 1920–1921, and later with Cree and Ojibwa, 'stimulated especially by Boas and in some respects by Sapir' (219). Bloomfield had already worked with Malayo-Polynesian languages and published in 1917 *Tagalog texts with grammatical analysis*. It is not known what led him, as a brilliant but orthodox Germanist, to concentrate his research efforts, first on these languages, and then, throughout the rest of his life, on Algonquian. It was not inevitable, and it may have a great deal to do with his development of a descriptive theory.

The published observations on the relations of Bloomfield to Boas and Sapir, as possible sources of this development, are sparse. The Voegelins (1963:36) note that he travelled to Europe more than once in the company of Boas. As of 1921 he was hardly known to Sapir, who wrote to Lowie (Nov. 18, 1921), regarding a possible replacement for himself at Ottawa (Lowie 1965:50–1):

> I have also written to inquire about L. Bloomfield, who has done work on Tagalog. Full-fledged philologists sometimes turn out disappointingly in the field . . . .

As students at Barnard, and of anthropology in a class of Boas, with Ruth Benedict as assistant, Margaret Mead and Bloomfield's younger sister were intimates (Mead 1959:4), this in 1922. But in February of the next year (1923), Marie Bloomfield had committed suicide. That any effective anthropological impetus was transmitted through the relationship thus seems unlikely.

One can agree with Lepschy (1973:127) that Bloomfield's 'thought is more complex, at times more torturous and contradictory, and certainly more interesting than it is made out to be'. We would suggest that a crucial factor in understanding the complexity, its sources and its development, lies in replacing the two-dimension picture of Bloomfield as behaviorist and theorist with a three-dimensional picture that includes Bloomfield the Americanist.

Let us consider the roots of Bloomfield's descriptive work more closely. It would seem to have begun with an American Indian language, Fox, which he mentions in two publications of 1914 (cf. Hockett 1970:94, headnote). At the present time we do not know when he began to work with Fox data, but do know that he began philologically, excerpting materials from publications by Jones and Michelson. Hockett infers that his first extensive descriptive work was with Tagalog; certainly it was his first descriptive work based on his own recording from a speaker of a language, and the first substantial descriptive work published.

Work on Tagalog was possible due to the presence at Ohio State of a fine speaker of the language, Alfredo Santiago, in 1914–1917. Hockett places Bloomfield's work in the years 1915–1916. As to reasons for the work, Bloomfield himself speaks of discovery of hitherto unnoticed or inadequately treated features of phonology as a result of taking phonetic notes (Preface to *Tagalog Texts*, in Hockett 1970:79). He does not say why he took phonetic notes — why Tagalog? A factor of national (governmental) interest in the Philippines may have been involved (as it was in an ethnological study of Philippine culture by Kroeber in the same period), but this is not known. Certainly a sense of scientific mission was involved, once the work had begun. Bloomfield explains that his initial work had two obvious limitations: the data were translations or isolated sentences, and the relation of Mr. Santiago's speech to Tagalog generally was unknown. The first limitation was overcome by texts, narrated with (Hockett 1970:79):

that vivacity of intellect and freedom from irrelevant prepossessions which we seek and so rarely find in people whose language we try to study.

Bloomfield adds that the quality may be due in part to education in Spanish and English, so that

his speech-feeling for his mother-tongue has not been deflected by the linguistic, or rather pseudo-linguistic training of the schools, so familiar to us.

(Notice use of the notion of *Sprachgefühl*, to be exorcised by the Bloomfieldians a quarter-century later.)

The second limitation could not be overcome, in the absence of adequate description of dialectal differentiation, indeed (and here we come to the main point) of any form of the language at all. Some data might have been collected from a different region, and from printed Tagalog books, but a single clearly defined set of data is preferable (Bloomfield writes) to a necessarily incomplete attempt to describe the whole language in its local and literary variations. (Note that description of the language as a variegated whole is set aside for practical reasons, not in principle.) Moreover, Bloomfield goes on to say (Hockett 1970:80–81):

In most cases where my results deviate from the statements of the Spanish grammars, the evidence of printed books (and not infrequently the internal evidence of the grammars themselves) shows that the divergence is due not to dialectal differences but to the fact that the grammars are the product of linguistically untrained observers, who heard in terms of Spanish articulations and classified in those of Latin grammar.

One can see in the first defect a factor in the emergence of structural linguistics internationally in conjunction with intensive study of phonology: there was a great gap that was empirically, as well as theoretically, patent. Bloomfield himself goes on to stress this point:

This study presents, then, the first Tagalog texts in phonetic transcription and the first scientific analysis of the structure of the language. . . . No experience could show more clearly than the reading of these books (all the accessible treatises on Tagalog) the necessity of linguistic and especially phonetic training for anyone who wishes to describe a language. Not one of the works in the following list [34 titles] contains an intelligible description of the pronunciation of Tagalog.

Phonological description was needed for Philippine as well as American Indian languages, needed for flourishing languages (such as Tagalog) as well as for languages about to die; it was, in short, a need of universal scope in the slow growth of empirical adequacy in linguistic science.

One should not miss as well the import of 'Latin grammar' and 'first scientific analysis of the structure of the language'. Their import for the Tagalog description is brought out in the criticism of a reviewer, Frank Blake (probably the leading American specialist in Philippine languages at the time — cited from Hockett 1970:88):

In a grammatical work like the one under discussion, in which the author follows an entirely new plan of arrangement, some attempt, at least, should be made to show where the new arrangement and the older and more familiar forms touch. The fact that practically no concessions to this natural demand are made by the author is responsible for much of the obscurity that mars his work. The least that could have been asked for in such a book would be a brief index of the familiar grammatical categories with references to the places in the grammar where they are treated, but not even this is furnished. Any grammarian is, of course, thoroly [sic] in sympathy with the invention of new terms and the setting up of new categories in the study of a new and peculiar form of speech, but familiar terms and categories should not be thrown overboard, as they are here, without good and sufficient reason, especially when the new terms and categories offer no special advantage over the old, or are in many cases decidedly inferior to them.

In short, distrust of traditional grammatical categories, and of meaning-based description, is present in Bloomfield's first descriptive work. (Cf. Hockett 1970:88, n. 1: 'The Tagalog Grammatical Analysis demonstrates in detail his policy of working from form to meaning . . .'.) Bloomfield associates his descriptive approach with need for accuracy and the overcoming of ethnocentrism (recall 'Spanish articulations . . . Latin grammar'). This suggests Boas, but not any structural or psychological doctrine. Indeed, the Tagalog work was done before Bloomfield could have read de Saussure's 1916 Cours (whose 1922 edition he was to review); about a decade before the term 'phoneme' began its career of centrality to structural linguistics; some years before he met the behaviorist Weiss; a decade before the first of the writings (Bloomfield 1926) which directly shaped the next generation of academic linguists. All this reinforces the view that Bloomfield's outlook had a fundamental continuity throughout his career, and can best be explained by an early interaction between his personality and 'neo-grammarian' attitude, on the one hand, and obvious scientific needs, on the other. If there is a further early influence, in the form of an intellectual context, then it is the anthropological tradition, as defined by Boas in the *Handbook of American Indian languages* in 1911 (work cited by Bloomfield in his own 1914 book).

As for the choice of Algonquian as a family in which to specialize, the fact that another trained philologist, Michelson, had provided data may have been a factor; but it is important to notice that the aboriginal languages of the regions of Bloomfield's birth, childhood, and education were Algonquian. As for the choice of Menomini as language with which to begin field work, the absence of any adequate account of the language (confirmed by Michelson in correspondence to Bloomfield (M. Silverstein, p.c.)) was a factor, but the same was true of other Algonquian languages. The spirit in which the fieldwork was conducted (cf. letter to Mr. Carl Haessler in Hockett 1970:[90], and the end of "Literate and illiterate speech" (in Hockett 1970:155–156)) suggests a personal reason. The Menomini had lived aboriginally in northeastern Wisconsin, and a number of them were settled near Green Bay, Wisconsin, some 50 miles or so north of Elkhart Lake, the village in which Bloomfield's family had lived from the time he was nine (not a great deal farther north, indeed, from Chicago, where he had been born, attended high school, and received his doctorate). Bloomfield was not himself steadily at Elkhart Lake for more than a few years, and it is not known to us whether or not he had contact with Indians as a child and youth; but it seems likely that the choice of Menomini (and Ojibwa, also spoken in northern Wisconsin) had more than scientific significance. His praise of the work and character of Boas in later years may owe something to his own sensitivity to juxtapositions of Indian and non-Indian in the state from which he came.

In sum, fascination with the sources of Bloomfield's psychological assumptions and idioms must give way to analysis of the deeper structure of his purposes and commitments. Insofar as the style is the man, the style included a rejection of teleological explanation, and ethnocentric categories, together with a commitment to empirical validation, from the earliest work; and it included patient hours of handling data unstudied by more than two or three others; frank admiration and respect for the qualities of members of minority cultures, including linguistic and narrative skills invisible to others in the communities from which he came; patient learning from old people whom most of his neighbors would deem needing to be taught. Attention to the mature written style alone can be healthy for understanding of the development of our subject; even today Bloomfield's writing has power to charm and change readers who approach it with preconceptions of a narrow-minded mechanist (this has been the experience of several of our students). But further information on the formative years of his life and career, if it can be obtained, is greatly to be desired.

Let us return briefly to a comparison of Bloomfield and Sapir, in terms of their similarities, as against their successors. These two great figures, presiding over the development of structural linguistics in the United States, shared two things which, while not themselves features of linguistic theory, may have been integral to their role. As we have noted, an autonomous society, journal, and teaching forum for linguistic science came into being in the United States in association with the academic dominance of Indo-European philology and comparative-historical research. Both Bloomfield and Sapir were respected scholars, indeed leaders, in this regard[35] (as, one should recall, had been de Saussure in Europe). The major indigenous tradition of linguistic research was that of anthropological philology; description of American Indian languages was conceived as an obligation, as against widespread neglect and misappraisal of their scientific and their human value. Bloomfield's Algonquian work identified him with this tradition.

The two men thus were at the center of the convergence of two streams essential to the shaping of the institution of linguistics in the United States. The Indo-Europeanists (Bolling, Edgerton, Kent, Sturtevant, et al.) could appreciate the Americanist purpose;[36] perhaps Boas and the bulk of his students could appreciate Indo-European work (it would be helpful to have documentation of their attitudes). Bloomfield and Sapir were native to both, as their students, by and large, were not to be.

One can suggest, then, that Bloomfield and Sapir were uniquely in a position to legitimate the emerging structural approach. This would apply both to descriptive work and to a descriptive (structural) perspective on comparative-historical studies. Men without Indo-European, and comparative-historical, qualifications perhaps would not have been called to Yale, or have been able to participate effectively in support of a new generation whose interests were predominantly descriptive. Yet

---

[35] An interesting case in point (Hahn 1952, quoted from Sebeok (1966 (2):380)): 'Interest in laryngeals began again in that very year, 1927, with the work of Kuryłowicz, who later came to Yale to study with Sturtevant, but above all it was his colleague Sapir who kindled Sturtevant's ardent zeal for the subject. It must have been during the thirties, probably in the first part of the decade, that he wrote me in great excitement of a meeting of the Yale Linguistic Club when Sapir presented his views on laryngeals, and showed how they cleared up a number of cruces – twenty-six of them, I think – in Indo-European comparative grammar. Sturtevant went on where these men began . . . .'

[36] Cf. Kent and Sturtevant (1926:14): 'In spirit of the peculiar duties and advantages which our country has for the study of the American Indian languages, only five of our universities offer facilities for training in them. It is perhaps natural that museums and other non-teaching institutions should take the lead in gathering and interpreting the records of these rapidly disappearing idioms; but the American universities must train scholars to perform the task.'

by the same token, neither Bloomfield nor Sapir can have seen descriptive linguistic theory as the (or at least, his) only goal in the progress of linguistic science. We may read them that way today, but to do so is to forget the Bloomfield who chose to lecture on comparative Algonquian to the Linguistic Institute of 1939, and the Sapir who explored Tocharian and Semitic in the same years. It is the emergence of descriptive linguistic theory as *the* goal of linguistics that more than anything gives a distinctive stamp to the 1940s and the Bloomfieldians.

5. SUCCESSIVE APPROACHES

We enter here upon years in which no single figure dominates. None looms as large (at least to present eyes) as Boas, Bloomfield, and Sapir, or stands out as distinctively as does Whorf (Harris may prove the exception). One has to do with a group, perceived by itself and by others as cooperating in a common task. It is conscious of itself as distinctive in relation to predecessors, to contemporaries in other traditions and countries, and, in the event, to successors. One has to do, in short, with the 'Bloomfieldian' years.

Much that pertains to these years has been discussed in connection with the roles of philology (3.1) and anthropology (3.4), and the influence of Sapir and Bloomfield (4.2 and 4.4). In this section we shall focus first upon what we take to be the fundamental historical problem, namely the existence and success of such a group. The problem has two salient aspects: delimitation, and characterization, of the crucial period. In attempting to deal with either aspect we find ourselves necessarily considering the other, and both are treated together in (5.1). Characterization there has to do with the historical role of the group as a whole: we indicate ways in which the period appears to represent a qualitative change, suggest the dimensions of the change (partly by considering previous groups which might have had such a role), and define what we take the historical role to be. The substantive traits of the work are considered in a second section (5.2) in terms of diversity among participants and over time. This leads to consideration of attempts to characterize, and to explain, the period, by historically minded and other recent writers. Assessment of these attempts brings us full circle to a second characterization of the period.

5.1   *The Bloomfieldian Period*

There is general recognition of a specific, dominant trend in the work of the period, under various names ('post-Bloomfieldian', 'neo-Bloomfieldian', 'Bloomfieldian'), and there is growing recognition that the period of time to which these terms chiefly apply is quite limited. Chomskyan criticism of 'structural linguistics' tended to cast a shadow over all preceding work in the century. Nevertheless, appreciation of the thrust of Sapir's work, signalled by adoption of terms associated with him, such as 'sound pattern', and structural restatement (*à la* Harris) of analyses done or influenced by him (Southern Paiute, Tübatulabal, Yokuts) lightened that shadow; and there has been an increasing reassessment of Bloomfield himself (notably his analysis of Menomini morphophonemics). Students of the development of linguistics in the United States are increasingly willing to distinguish Sapir and Bloomfield from their successors.

The retrospective remarks of Joos (1957:108) and the Voegelins (1963:20, 24) on crystallization of an 'American' approach in the late 1930s and early 1940s have been discussed, as has Hockett's remark that in the late 1930s he and Bloomfield were writing past each other with regard to Hockett's Potawatomi work, Bloomfield being concerned with the facts of the language, Hockett with the use of the facts for theory. Other testimony to the distinction between Bloomfield and the Bloomfieldians has been cited in connection with both Sapir and Bloomfield; let us mention here Trager (1946), Teeter (1970a), Huddleston (1972), Stark (1972), and Silverstein (ms.).

5.1.1 *The rise of descriptive linguistics*
'Bloomfieldian' linguistics is usually discussed in terms of ideas. That is, the ideas held by linguists of the period are assessed, and perhaps explained, while the existence of a field of descriptive linguistics, in which models of language structure are argued, is taken for granted. We should like to suggest that *the key to Bloomfieldian linguistics is precisely that it could not take either of these things for granted*. The significance of the Bloomfieldian generation is that it is the first to be employed (or seek employment as *linguists*; that is, to claim a place in academic life in virtue, not of knowledge of a language or language family, but of knowledge of a methodology for the study of any language, of language in general. The content of Bloomfieldian ideas may be seen as less significant. In part those ideas were shaped by a general stage in the development of structural linguistics, the stage of transition from revolutionary breakthrough in the traditionally weakest sector, phonology, to consolidation in terms of the central sector, syntax-semantics. In another respect, the cast given methodological ideas in the United States was probably due to their institutional value, combined with the common tendency of a younger generation to delight in shocking an established order. Extreme differentiation of 'scientific linguistics' from 'philology' probably had adaptive value in efforts to secure a novel place in the academic sun. This essential *social* role of the Bloomfieldian idiom goes far to explain its general acceptance as central reference point, even by linguists whose own work continued or developed ideas in conflict with it.

The records of the Linguistic Society themselves provide interesting evidence of the emergence of descriptive linguistics to prominence. They indicate an interaction between scientific and national problems. Let us cite some of this evidence, before considering further the significance of the Bloomfieldian group.

Recall that 1937 was the year of formation within the LSA of the Group for Phonemics, and also the year in which Sapir taught at the Linguistic Institute. He initiated plans for descriptive work with informants, realized the next year with Bloomfield, Voegelin, and Harris; and the success of his introductory course led to its being scheduled the next year in the evening, so all could attend, when Bloomfield taught it. 1938 was also the year in which the LSA began to hold a summer meeting in conjunction with the Institute (cf. *Bull.* 12 (1939):18–19). In 1939 a study of the future of the Institute was voted, and a questionnaire sent to all who had ever attended it. The report of responses (following upon Sturtevant 1940), notes that 'There is demand for work in phonemics' (*Bull.* 13 (1940):98), and concludes with a Postscript from the head of the Department of Phonetics of the 'Summer Institute of Linguistics' at Siloam Springs, Arkansas (the anonymous author obviously was Kenneth Pike). The Postscript, the only response to be printed in full in the *Bulletin*, stresses the enormous practical and scientific value of the Institute's training for the contribution of missionaries to both description of languages and world literacy (*Bull.* 13 (1940):101):

The success of this movement depends to a considerable extent upon the continued training of the Linguistic Institute which you represent. Already through its phonemic instruction seen in the courses given on descriptive linguistics, it has had a large part.

The letter also states (101): 'We hope that the courses on descriptive linguistics will not be curtailed.' The hope suggests that there may have been uncertainty. In the event such courses took the center of the stage. The report of the 1939 Institute is interesting in this regard. Despite a sharp reduction in resources available for the session, the same number of courses was offered as in 1938, and in addition 'Dr. Trager generously gave a course in Phonetics and Phonemics for an eager group of 8 students.' The report goes on to single out two aspects of the session as especially noteworthy: the first attempt to present systematically the changes in the Egyptian language throughout its recorded history, and (*Bull.* 13 (1940):20):

the emphasis upon descriptive techniques which characterized much of the work. Dr. Voegelin worked with a Delaware Indian; Dr. Emeneau with a native speaker of Tamil; and Dr. Trager with a Lithuanian informant.

Furthermore (20):

Apart from the research work carried on with these informants the demonstrations of principles and technique by Dr. Emeneau and Dr. Voegelin proved the most valuable part of the evening course in the Introduction to the Scientific Study in Language. And Dr. Trager's course in Church Slavonic was also new in the thorough use that he made of the more modern methods of descriptive technique.

The point, of course, is that these things were newsworthy in 1939, as such things were again the following year (*Bull.* 14 (1941):26):

Three aspects of the work of the 1940 session deserve brief comment:
(a) The work with actual informants (a Chippewa and a Cherokee) proved valuable not only for the particular courses in which they were used but also for the effect which the presence of such work, by giving emphasis to descriptive techniques, had upon the Institute as a whole.

Significant as well is that the precedent of collective attendance at the 'introductory' course, begun with Bloomfield in 1938, is noted again for 1941 (*Bull.* 15 (1942):18), when taught by Sturtevant, assisted by Trager (for descriptive linguistics?), and for 1942 (*Bull.* 16 (1943):16), when taught by Kurath. Introduction and frontier of interest coincide.

Connection with World War II appears first in the report of the 1943 Institute under Haugen at Wisconsin (*Bull.* 17 (1944):13):

Some students came primarily for the purpose of learning particular languages so that they might be able to use them as teachers or otherwise. . . . Among those whose interest in language had an immediate objective were those who expect to make a direct contribution to the war effort and reconstruction.

The paragraph continues with several specific examples. The report of the 1945 session brings practical purposes very much to the fore (*Bull.* 19 (1946):16):

. . . the largest single group consisted of teachers of foreign languages attracted by the emphasis upon the discussion . . . of the contribution which linguistic science can make to a successful dealing with the practical problems of learning and teaching language. . . . That these teachers were also attracted by the courses and lectures in linguistics is evidenced by the large registration in such courses as 'Phonetics and Phonemics' (23 registrations) and the consistently satisfactory attendance upon the lectures of the 'Introduction to Linguistic Science' (average attendance 37) . . .
Although the chief emphasis of the 1945 session of the Linguistic Institute was put upon the practical matters of sound descriptive analysis as underlying satisfactory teaching materials and the implications of linguistics for teaching procedures, other aspects of linguistic science were not neglected. Professor Voegelin dealt with the descriptive approach to American Indian languages and an analysis of their structural types. All the work with actual informants was the center of much interest and Dr. Kenneth Pike's lecture demonstration using a speaker of Ibo as an informant attracted an audience of 285.

The report for the 1946 Institute continues the story (*Bull.* 20 (1947):13):

As in 1945 considerable interest centered in the classes and discussions devoted to a consideration of the contributions which linguistic science can make to a successful dealing with the practical problems of learning and teaching a foreign language. The supporting courses for this practical work (Phonetics and Phonemics, for example) had large registrations.

Notice the term 'supporting'; it suggests that 'American structuralism' was shaped in the post-war period by field work experience directed, not toward anthropology, but toward the international involvements of the United States. The work in the Army Language Program of course suggests it also.

The 1946 report continues to find descriptive work newsworthy (13):

The special interest in descriptive structural linguistics showed itself not only in the registrations for the courses regularly announced (Linguistic Field Methods and Structural Types of American Indian Languages) but also in the requests for special work which was organized in an additional course carried by Professor Voegelin.

The 1947 report (*Bull.* 21 (1948):15) notes redressing of a balance that had been upset by the prominence of descriptive work:

Descriptive linguistics, linguistic geography, and new methods of language teaching were well represented in the program; historical and comparative linguistics, which had been slighted during the War years, were again given more adequate attention.

A year later neither descriptive nor historical linguistics is news as such. Sturtevant is first Collitz Professor, J. R. Firth is first foreign staff member since the beginning of the war, but in each case it is the persons who are of note (*Bull.* 22 (1949):12–13), not the fields they practice (historical, descriptive, respectively). The relation between the two fields does appear once more, again in a spirit of balance. Kurath reports of the 1949 Institute (*Bull.* 23 (1950):17):

One had the feeling that the structuralists and the historical linguists are getting to understand each other better.

We can assume that by this time the centrality of descriptive linguistics had been established, and that the equation between introductory course and Indo-European, prevailing before World War II, had been replaced by the equation between introductory course and structural analysis. The Kurath report suggests that 'historical linguists' indeed is becoming temporarily a marked term. There are structuralists who do history (cf. items 7, 8, 15, 28, 29, 30, 31, 37 in Joos (1957), nearly one-fifth of the total); those who do not do history structurally are 'historical linguists'.

Much more needs to be known about this process; many more lines of evidence need to be pursued. Even with what is known, however, one can sense that these years are a watershed. The intellectual change combines with institutional change in such a way as to redefine the context in which intellectual change will henceforth occur. This change is a *displacement* (of comparative-historical by descriptive work); the next change will be a *replacement* (of one conception of descriptive work by another). Before this change, so far as conceptions of linguistic structure are concerned, there were *circles*; now there is a *center*.

5.1.2 Predecessors

Let us try to suggest the characteristics of the difference, and some of its causes, beginning, as one must, with Boas. Linguistic work under Boas can be seen as having a distinctive character, relative to what had preceded it. Adopting Prague School notions for definition of a standard language, we can say that there were attitudes of loyalty, pride, and awareness of a norm; the loyalty was associated with features that had both separatist and unifying functions, the pride with sources of prestige, and the awareness of a norm with a frame of reference. The *Handbook of American Indian languages*, and the analytic method embodied in it, provided a salient frame of reference. There was pride in providing analyses that answered to both scientific and humanistic needs. The Boasian work could be distinguished from preceding Americanist work by its concern with grammar, by its mode of statement, and indeed by its orthographic practice (especially after agreement upon an Americanist orthography (Boas et al. 1916)). But by and large, the loyalty, pride, and sense of norm were not specific to linguistic work. All of Boasian anthropology, not just its linguistics, set itself apart from the evolutionary and ethnocentric pre-conceptions of predecessors and less scientific contemporaries; it held out the goal of analysis of all of a culture in terms of its own patterns; and linguistic work itself was seen as a contribution to the general field.

The Boasion circle continued both as part of the new LSA and alongside it. Boas' journal, *IJAL*, continued, as did his monograph series (and Bloomfield published in both); the field work sponsored by Boas' committee was a major source of support in the late twenties and early thirties. All this was one facet of the emergence of an autonomous society, journal, and teaching activity for scientific linguistics. So far as comparative-historical work, particularly Indo-European, is concerned, there is no indication of crises or issues of a 'paradigmatic' nature. The dominance of Indo-European scholarship would seem to have been inherited, not brought about at the time. Structuralist restatement of historical linguistics in the 1930s, by Bloomfield in this country, and by the Prague School in Europe, does not seem to have provoked conflict at the time. The leading comparative-historical scholars would seem to have formed a circle with common interests, a circle over-lapping perhaps with the new focus of attention they helped create in the 1930s, dialectology. So far as attitudes and functions are concerned, the dominant focus is apparently the existence of an autonomous linguistic science, rather than any one approach within it.

In the 1930s one can find some evidence of separatism from preceding anthro-pological tradition in the circle around Sapir, manifested in the adoption of new orthographic symbols (e.g., *š* for Boasian *c* — see Herzog et al. 1934). The adop-tion of the notion of 'phoneme' causes some separateness on a larger scale from older Boasians who do not accept it (Boas, Radin). Some younger linguists are close to Sapir, as indicated, some closer to Bloomfield, but there is overlap and interaction. Comparative-historical work retains its central place, and is shared in by Bloomfield and Sapir themselves. There is no indication, so far as Bloomfield and Sapir are concerned, either of attempt to replace comparative-historical work by a new 'paradigm', or to outstrip one another in a race to become a paradigm's progenitor (cf. Harris 1973 on the attitudes of Bloomfield and Sapir in this regard). So far as one can tell, the common concern is with the general growth of linguistics, although with different emphases in each case.

As we have seen, with the late 1930s and the 1940s, a new conception of the essence of 'linguistic science' comes to the fore; what is taught at Linguistic Institutes, what counts as the core of an introductory course, changes. Descriptive, or structural, linguistics emerges as a frame of reference for a generation; supported by Bloomfield (1933), Bloch and Trager (1942), various articles, and an idiomatic norm. Separatist and internally unifying effects appear, and a new source of prestige. The impetus of descriptive linguistics indeed gives rise in the post-war period to separate programs, and departments, of linguistics. Competence can now be defined, to some degree at least, independently of departments of anthropology and of particular languages. There will in fact be much continuity in both regards. What seems most distinctive and important is the emergence, or legitimation as central, of a concern with methodology itself. Many linguists will continue to know anthropology and various languages, and contribute research in these; but it is now possible to imagine a career based upon contributions to, and teaching of, phonology and morphology (and syntax) as such.

5.1.3 Intellectual core and representative genres

The program of distributional analysis, of rejection or suspension of meaning, and of item and arrangement formulation — three traits associated with the Bloomfieldian advance — all this seems to us of secondary importance. The active contributors to linguistics in the period were themselves far from agreement on these points, and there is some reason to think that the program was being superseded, or at least significantly extended, by the beginning of the 1950s (see discussion in next section). The dynamic of the program was essentially within the 1940s, and the dynamic was there, we suggest, because the particular traits were believed to embody something essential and general — namely, *the establishment of a formal, fully explicit theory of linguistic structure.*

From this point onward, none of the many involvements of language in other kinds of problem — historical, cultural, social — could claim the center of attention within linguistics itself, until (and if) the possibilities for development of a formal, fully explicit theory of linguistic structure had been exhausted (or found exhausting).[37] Chomsky's significance, in these terms, is to have shown a new

---

[37] This is not to say that leaders of the Bloomfieldian effort meant that linguists should think of their role as that of pure theorist, or, so to speak, theorist-at-large. Method and theory of synchronic analysis defined the center, not the boundary, of 'what linguists do'. From student days at Wisconsin and Yale (1957–1965), Fought remembers hearing the view that older linguists had of the field, viz., that linguists described languages; that their primary focus was, or should be, mastery of the details of a language or group of languages; and that linguistic theory should not become the subject matter of linguistics. (At Yale this view was attributed (very plausibly) to Bloch in the context of the appointment of Lamb. Each member of the Yale department had been primarily a language specialist, including Bloch himself (Modern English, Japanese)). One can see that the inductive style of Bloomfieldian theoretical discussion was not due to a positivist outlook alone. The style also owed something to loyalty to a very traditional (almost philological) conception of one's professional role.

possibility of exfoliation of such theory, just when leaders of the preceding theoretical development had come to take an interest in extending the scope of their work into the study of texts, personality, cultural patterning, psychiatry, and communication. Whereas these leaders implicitly assumed that a desire for greater human relevance was to be satisfied by broadening the scope of one's work beyond linguistics proper, Chomsky proposed that such relevance could be gained by further inquiry within linguistics. In doing so, he did not bring a concern for theory to a field in which it had been lacking, as some have mistakenly argued (see further (5.3) below), but replaced one conception of the constraints and direction of theory with another. He did not convince linguists for the first time of the need for formal, explicit theory (as has sometimes been suggested). Rather, he convinced a vanguard, and through them a majority, of the superiority of a particular formalization of theory. Chomsky's success was possible because linguistics had been prepared, not for his particular mathematical logic and philosophy of science, of course, but for claims based on such formal argument.[38] The new claims dealt more adequately with a level of analysis which the long progress from conquest of phonology had reached, but not satisfactorily handled, namely, syntax, and turned syntax into a vantage point from which to recast familiar territory. All this was accomplished in terms of three genres which had been established as central to linguistics by the Bloomfieldians.

The underlying continuity from the Bloomfieldian generation onward can be seen in terms of these genres. The first is the wholly theoretical article. Bloch (1948) is of special importance, as a sign that Bloomfieldians consciously formulated general theory and were conscious of difference from Bloomfield himself. Bloch remarks on the need for reconsideration of fundamentals, Bloomfield (1926) having remained the only formulation of some basic assumptions for more than twenty years. Bloch's statement is true with regard to the most elementary, general notions, but otherwise can be misleading; other articles do not reach to assumptions about 'speech community' and the like, but they do formulate analysis of entire sectors of language in general terms.

The second genre is that of presentation of theoretical points in connection with analysis of data from a specific language. Joos (1957:vii) describes the genre in these words:

---

[38] Bloomfield most of all had made mathematics and philosophy of science sources of legitimation in linguistics in the United States. Bloomfieldian theory, particularly the reliance on distributional criteria, was widely and correctly seen as an effort to mathematicize linguistics. In this regard it is useful to note the response of a distinguished participant in the development of American linguistics. Haugen (1951:222 (= Joos 1957:363)) speaks of the theorists as quite distinct from ordinary linguists: 'There is a growing cleavage between the mathematical linguists, or metalinguists, and the physical linguists, whom I should call just plain linguists.' (Physical linguists admit phonetics and semantics, as well as the formal relationships between.) And fifteen years later Haugen (1971 – presented in 1966) sees transformational grammar as successor to the efforts of both Harris and Hjelmslev towards formalization, and possibly the common metalanguage, or algebra, whose need he had urged in 1951 (53-55).

When a contribution to theory is advanced, the steps are apt to be more or less these: (1) a warning is given what the theoretical points will be; this step is facultative. (2) a collection of data from a single language is presented. (3) a way of 'handling' the data is proposed, which means a way of 'stating' them in my terminology above, with consideration of as many alternative ways as may be known to the writer or occur to him at the moment; the treatment of alternatives constitutes due warning that this is a theoretical paper (in case step 1 was omitted), whereas it is almost de rigueur to avoid mention of alternatives in describing a single language. . . . (4) the theoretical implications of the chosen descriptions are stated. (5) [this step may be placed before the fourth mentioned] other languages are drawn upon for data lying around loose or not well covered by current practice; thus Bloomfield's remark 'we are obliged to predict' (1926; in Joos 1957:26) which he used to characterize linguistics as a science, is now used to classify general theory as a science also — this gives the theoretical paper, American style, a familiar air to the American reader accustomed to reading descriptions of particular languages, wherefore both kinds of paper are read with a similarity of appreciation which, for all I know, may be unique as well as characteristic of the American scene. (6) the aforesaid theoretical implications get their formal statement as a contribution to theory; this last step, like the first, is facultative.

The third genre is that of 'structural restatement', launched by Harris with his review of Newman's Yokuts (1944; cf. Harris 1947a, 1947b), although Swadesh and Voegelin (1939) is a partial precedent. Harris' series shows pure concern with mode of analytic statement; and at the time it was regarded by some as not quite respectable. The data, after all, had not been gotten by Harris. Such an attitude, of course, reflected a world common to anthropology and philology, a world in which, for many languages, provision of accurate new data, through field work, editing or searching of archives, could be a primary contribution and a source of solution to problems. It was a world in which abstract methodological proposals were rare, and mastery of preceding scholarship, and of all the data available to use for a given problem, bases for respect and advance of knowledge. It was a world that the genre of structural restatement, reinforced by mathematical bases, and exalted as a quest for universal human nature, was to quite displace.

The overall development of these three genres appears to be as follows. There is precedent for each in the 1930s, in connection with phonology, on the part of students or followers of Sapir and Bloomfield. Swadesh (1934), and the pertinent chapters of Bloomfield (1933), launch discussion of phonology as such, and there are theoretically relevant treatments of particular data, e.g., Chicago English (cf. V. Makkai 1972 on these matters). Newman's final statement of Yokuts and the Swadesh-Voegelin reanalysis of Tübatulabal (1939) might be considered structural restatements, but in each case the restatement involves the collector of the original data and the guidance of an academic mentor. The 1940s bring several changes. Morphology becomes the subject of a series of articles purely theoretical (notably Harris 1942, 1946, Wells 1947b, Hockett 1947, and Nida 1948) — this is the respect in which the period is a transition, substantively, between the phonological focus of early structuralism and the syntactic focus of structuralism under Chomsky.

Discussion of phonology intensifies, in terms of the new Bloomfieldian idiom, and reactions to it (see again V. Makkai 1972). The systematizing concern extends beyond articles to pamphlets and books, intended both to teach and to codify (Bloomfield 1942, Bloch and Trager (with participation of Bloomfield) 1942, Nida 1944ff., Pike 1947, and Harris 1951 (completed by 1946)).

All three genres are of course familiar to us from the 1950s onward. The substantive content of course extends to syntax, and more recently, semantics. With regard to structural restatement, there is an interesting continuity of attention to American Indian grammars and analyses, but with regard to theoretical articles based on a particular language, there is a difference. Recall Joos' characterization of 'the specifically American habit . . . of using the inductive tone of voice in arguing pure theory . . .' (quoted above). Joos goes on to indicate that his characterization is an ideal reconstruction; not only are the patently theoretical steps facultative, but (1957:vii):

Omission of the first step [see quotation above] is preferred: readers might, if any theoretical point is stated before its data, feel that the case has been prejudiced. And the last is very likely to be omitted, for a similarly very American set of reasons: the formal statement is felt to assign to theory an emphasis that properly belongs to facts and the stating thereof, or is felt to encroach on the reader's right of opinion. . . . The second step is mandatory. . . . It must not be mixed with the fifth. . . . The third step is not just mandatory; it is essential: otherwise the paper is not Descriptive. The fourth step is apt to be veiled, or fragmented and dispersed throughout the paper; my readers may test their comprehension of the American style by formulating a suitable reason or two. Altogether, then, there is ample reason why both Americans and (for example) Europeans are likely on each side to consider the other side both irresponsible and arrogant.

Joos perhaps overstates the 'ideal type' American contribution to theory, in the interests of the contrast to a 'European' style, although he is profoundly right about the 'inductive tone of voice'. Certainly many of the papers in his collection are quite explicit that they are dealing with theory (cf. Swadesh and Voegelin 1939 (p. 92 in Joos 1957), Hockett 1942, n. 1, Wells 1947, first paragraph, Hockett 1947, first paragraph — both Wells and Hockett speaking of theory in connection with matters that Harris (1942, 1946) chose to write of as 'technique' and 'procedure') (cf. also Bloch 1948:58.5 (end), 59.1, and 1953:44). And Joos perhaps implies that the leaders of structuralism in the United States did not need to advertise the theoretical implications of their work, since the work would be read by an in-group familiar with the style and alert to the implications (1957:vii):

We may request the Europeans to try to regard the American style as a tradition comme une autre; but the Americans can't be expected to reciprocate: they are having too much fun to be bothered, and few of them are aware that either side has a tradition.

The remark itself is anachronistic, given the active revaluation of European work already undertaken by 1957 (see 5.2. below 'Second phases'). In any case, the successors to the legitimacy of theoretical activity would not treat it with diffidence.

The spirit of the second genre — a contribution to theory entailed by a contribution to analysis of a language or sector of a language — would continue, but with the former commonly the justification for the latter, not the reverse.

5.1.4 Growth and pace

The Bloomfieldian years mark a decisive change, not only in the legitimation of abstract theory and its associated genres (Haugen's 'courants . . . vers une linguistique algébrique' (1972:53)), but also in number of participants in the development of theory, and its pace. All these things likely are interdependent; moreover, to assess the growth in linguistics, we would need to know something about other scholarly fields in the same period. To some extent the situation of the forties was one of new opportunities for scholars already committed to the field; but there was also a growth of audience and of sense of significance. These last may be due to the accomplishments, and attractiveness, of linguistics, as well as to external, or general, social trends. In any case, concentration of linguists together at Linguistic Institutes and in work for the government increased interaction, so that the pace of working through an idea, and the life of a term, would seem to have greatly shortened. Proliferation of terminology would itself seem to be one major sign of the new situation. Haugen (1951:211 (= Joos 1957:357)) comments on 'the rapid growth of a new linguistic terminology' in apparent reference to the past decade. (Note also Joos' comments in his review of Hamp's glossary (Joos 1958b), and the dated entries in the "Comments on certain technical terms" in Joos 1957:419–421.) The first 'working paper' publication appears in 1942, *Studies in Linguistics*, edited by Trager (cf. Joos 1957:vii). One could say that by 1945 the profile of publication outlets was such as to link structural linguistics in the United States with each of its major contributory traditions — *Language* with Indo-European and comparative-historical philology, *IJAL* with Americanist and anthropological work, *Word* with European and Sapir orientations insofar as marginal to the perceived dominant trend. Work that the Bloomfieldian circle considered central to theoretical advance was framed by presentation in *Language*; internal discussion found expression also in reviews in *Language*, in *IJAL*, and in contributions to *SIL*.

The range and pace of work constitutes a qualitative change. This change is not only a sign of the onset of the Bloomfieldian period, but also an expression of its nature. One must take the change into account in assessing the outcome of the period. It would be quite mistaken to regard the period as a fortress of fixed opinions. Minds changed within the group, partly in response to criticism from without but also partly through the working out of the implications of ideas themselves. In this respect the work was always work in progress. What would have been insisted upon was the necessity of the *kind* of work — development of explicit, abstract, wholly general models of the nature of linguistic structure. With regard to the particular formulations which dominated attention during the 1940s, Hockett writes (1968a:29):

Slowly and painfully, largely under the leadership of Harris, we constructed a view of the design of grammar based on our view of the design of a phonological system, freeing our procedures and terminology of any vestiges of the 'grammatical process' (or 'taxeme') kind of thinking, until we had achieved what we seemed to have been seeking: a pure *item-and-arrangement* model of grammar.

This particular term, true enough, appeared in print only in 1954; but the article I published in that year had been written four years earlier. It is interesting to note that we no sooner achieved a pure item-and-arrangement model (not yet called that) than we began to wonder whether it was really what we wanted.

Hockett's comment points up the fact that Bloomfieldian work must be understood with reference to its development over time. The temporal development provides a framework, indeed, within which to consider the diversity of Bloomfieldian work generally.

5.2 Diversity and Development of Bloomfieldian Work

Most discussion of Bloomfieldian work concentrates on its approach to linguistic structure, and does so in terms of its contrast with the Chomskyan approach. Such a focus gives a unity to the work, and agrees with the common opinion of the profession (to judge from remarks and presuppositions in papers, proposals, and conversations) as to what is significant. Sometimes such comment suggests that the recent history of the field can be described by comparing a known Chomsky with the inferred content of a Tomb of the Unknown Bloomfieldian. Historiography is primarily concerned with an ideal Bloomfieldian, in a completely homogeneous scientific community, who embodies its implicit model perfectly, unaffected by such irrelevant conditions as historical limitations, shifts of attention and interest, and personality (random or characteristic), in applying his knowledge of the model in actual practice. Or so it sometimes seems.

The popularity of Kuhn's notion of revolutionary paradigm may play a part (a distorting part) here. Ideological forces, reinforced by ignorance, are no doubt at work (and it is noteworthy that Chomsky's own citations of immediate precedent, and generosity to critics, appear to attenuate as between 1955 and 1962 or so). No doubt there is a purely poetic motive as well: polarized conflict, focused on a single issue, enhances any narrative (cf. Burke 1968:380–409).[39]

---

[39] Insofar as the appeal of a profession, and of an approach within a profession, has always an element of persuasion and identification, hence of rhetoric, one would want to analyze the differential success of Bloomfieldian and Chomskyan styles of appeal. One would want to consider the relation between the attitudes of prospective linguists, the general climate of opinion, and the typical styles of work, and attitudes toward work, held forth by each (these would be relations between acts, scenes, and agents, in Burkean terms). Both share an appeal to participation in a further sphere, that of scientific advance in general, even though the conceptions of science are different; both perhaps share an appeal to participation in a further sphere of human welfare as well, the one through relevance to practical affairs, the other through relevance to knowledge of human nature. But the Bloomfieldian approach has an appeal in terms of 'sacrifice' (the self-denial of its conception of methodological rigor and substantive

The Bloomfieldian work has had neither precisely the degree, nor kind, of unity often accorded it with regard to analysis of linguistic structure. We shall consider the mapping of its degree of diversity in 'positional', 'interactional', and 'developmental' terms, and then take up the nature of its unity in contrast, and continuity, with Chomskyan conceptions.

5.2.1   Mapping the diversity

The roster of Bloomfieldians is generally well known. Lists differ in extent, but certain names recur in all. Haugen (1951) mentions Bloch, Harris, Pike, Nida, Wells, Voegelin, Chao, Hockett, Joos, Trager, and Pittman (n. 4 = Joos 1957:353, n. 4). Bar-Hillel (1954:231) names Bloch, Harris, Hockett, Smith, and Trager as 'representative'. Lounsbury (1962) cites Bloch, Harris, Hill, Hockett, Trager, Smith, and Joos. Ivić (1965:163) refers to Harris (1951), Bloch and Trager (1942), Trager and Smith (1951), and Harris (1954) as elaborations of the 'distributionalistic method'. Robins (1967:210ff.) discusses prominently Harris (1951) — 'the development of certain aspects of Bloomfieldianism to their extremes', and Trager — 'the "separation of levels", though not found as such in Bloomfield, was pressed by some linguists, G. L. Trager, for example, to such lengths that . . .'; and finds 'Bloomfieldian' linguistics as it ultimately developed to be presented in Hockett (1958), Gleason (1955), Hill (1958); he also notes Joos (1957). Pike's work receives separate discussion as a 'somewhat divergent development of Bloomfieldian immediate constituent analysis in grammar' (212). Finally, Hockett (1968a:17) lists in alphabetical order 'the names of some of these post-Bloomfieldian descriptivists: Bloch, Haas, Harris, Hockett, McQuown, Nida, Pike, Swadesh, Trager, Voegelin, Wells'. The difference between this list from recollection, and that of Haugen (1951), is largely due to the fact that Haugen was citing pertinent publications during the decade of the forties — thus, perhaps, no Haas, McQuown, Swadesh (although phonological analysis by Swadesh might have been noted); that Hockett omits Joos may be explained by the fact that he has just discussed Joos (1957). (On this group, see also Davis (1973, ch. 5), Posner (1970:509–519), and the surveys by Apresjan (1966), Arutjunova et al. (1964), Fries (1963), and Guxman (1964).)

The main lines of distinction within the Bloomfieldians are clear enough to knowledgeable participants. With somewhat broader scope and unfortunate cuteness, Joos (1958b:281) writes that inspection of Hamp (1957):

reveals three or more American traditions; merely to clarify this statement and without invidious intent, one name may be given for each: Hockett, Pike, Jakobson, X.

Hockett (1968a:26, 32ff.) sharply distinguishes 'Trager, Bloch and I' vis-à-vis Pike. Hall (1969) initially distinguishes Bloch, Trager, Smith, 'and (in the 1940s and early 1950s) Hockett and Harris' (193), from Pike and Fries (196–197); he later

---

scope) that is not so readily apparent in the Chomskyan period. (On these two fundamental types of appeal, and transformation, see Burke 1968:189–192, 200.)

summarizes the two groups with the name-sets 'Bloch-Trager-Smith' and 'Fries-Pike' (198), in relation to a number of other scholars belonging to no sharply identified 'school' at all.

A somewhat different perception of groupings is found in Akhmanova and Mikael'an (1969:13–23), where Bloomfield and Fries are discussed, and then Wells, Pike, and Harris; with regard to the Bloomfieldians, they sum up (22):

In contrast with Pike, Wells may then be said to belong to the 'left' wing of the Trend, which is most brilliantly represented by Z. S. Harris.

Koerner (1970a) distinguishes two groups, one of which he terms 'moderate Bloomfieldians', and in which he includes Gleason, Hall, Hill, Hockett, and Nida, on the ground that they (168):

tend to employ the concept of meaning either in their definitions of linguistic items or analytical procedures, whereas others tend to admit only its heuristic use or even to deny its use at all.

In contrast (172):

One group of pupils seems to have misinterpreted their master's failure to offer a definite method of handling 'meaning' in language description, and attempted an almost entire deletion of the semantic aspect(s) of language. Besides C. C. Fries the most eminent scholars who may be said to belong to this group are . . . Trager, . . . Bloch, . . . Smith, and . . . Harris.

(We omit Koerner's citation of full first and middle names, and dates.)

We will consider the adequacy of the general picture of the period projected by Koerner a little later. Here let us note the strangeness of opposing Fries and Nida, the two scholars who most 'shamelessly' used meaning directly throughout the period in question. Koerner seems to have misconstrued certain isolated quotations. Fries rejects reliance on meaning, when the issue is understood as reliance on meaning *rather* than on form, and especially when reliance on meaning is understood, as in much traditional grammar, as reliance on *a priori* labels. The quotations from Fries given by Koerner amount to the claim that a language has an explicit structure, and that it is the business of analysis to disclose it. As the evidence that Fries approached the viewpoint of tending to exclude meaning almost completely from procedures of linguistic analysis the following Fries statement is quoted (on p. 172):

I should like to insist that as a general principle any use of meaning is unscientific whenever the fact of our knowing the meaning leads us to stop short of finding the precise formal signals that operate to convey that meaning . . . .

In the context of the time, and perhaps in the context of any time, the statement is simply a justification of formal analysis. It is hard to imagine grounds on which any linguist interested in meaning could in fact object to it. For the converse is this: any use of meaning is scientific so long as the fact of our knowing the meaning does not lead us to stop short of finding the precise formal signals that operate to convey that meaning (cf. discussion of 'mentalism' in (5.3)).

Stark (1972) states well the relation between individual positions, their ongoing development, and an underlying unity. Finding Hockett, Bloch, and Harris most important for his study, he adds (387):

My term 'Bloomfieldians' should not imply that these men are mindless carriers of an inflexible dogma. Quite the contrary. Hockett is as much an innovator as a codifier; Harris is known for a 'hocus-pocus' bent that is distinctly non-Bloomfieldian; and Bernard Bloch, probably the truest Bloomfieldian of them all, reshaped Bloomfield's doctrine in many fundamental ways.

We shall want to consider the role of 'truest Bloomfieldian', in the sense of answering to a later period's stereotype, a little later. Here let us note that Stark treats Bloomfieldian morphemics as uniform (393–397), in contrast to syntax (389):

no single approach to syntax ever dominated Bloomfieldian linguistics in the same way that IA dominated morphemics and the building-block phoneme dominated phonemics.

In syntax he considers Bloomfield's 'taxeme/tagmeme' model, Hockett's constructional grammar, and Harris' morpheme to utterance model (cf. discussion earlier in regard to Sapir's influence). This restriction slights an axis of contrast the Bloomfieldians themselves found important (and that has continued to be important), namely, the place of syntax. Joos (1957:153) observes that Harris completes his picture of English without intonations, in spite of recognizing them as meaningful and in construction with the rest of sentences. Joos proposes that one should experiment with the converse, starting from intonation (and juncture and stress), to build up a syntax as far as possible, bringing in Harris' morpheme substitution classes only insofar as needed to complete the system without redundancy. Joos adds (153):

just such an anti-Harris procedure ('anti' here is logical not polemic) is to be found in the Smith and Trager syntax work (very little published as yet: early hints in their Outline [1951]).

Trager-Smith phonological syntax was indeed a major development within the period, not least because it was the target, in syntax, of Chomsky's first attacks on the dominant approach. But Trager and Smith are discussed only briefly by Stark within the context of Hockett's IC approach (402), and of general comments on Trager and Smith, as the fullest flowering of the Bloomfieldian approach (414ff.).

Stark is right as to the unity to be found in Bloomfieldian morphology — a central, distinctive focus of the period — but a closer reading is possible and instructive. In this respect we are fortunate to have Matthews (1972, Part II). His account of the item and arrangement model of the Bloomfieldians is attentive to points which differentiate Bloomfieldian work from predecessors, including Bloomfield himself (e.g., on the definition of 'morpheme' (41, n. 6; cf. 57, n. 2), and from contemporary and later critics (see also his discussion of criteria for evaluation of morphological theories (ch. 3), and of the scope of a linguistic theory (ch. 2)). Matthews acknowledges a persuasive force for 'item and arrangement' morphology, in terms which confirm, and in many ways complement, Stark's observations on the general model. He brings discussion of Bloomfieldian work to the level at which one can perceive developing and cross-cutting differences of position.

Each participant in the work did indeed have an individual constellation of views and interests, developing over time, and it will prove necessary to study these, in the light of materials beyond the published books and journals, as well as through close reading of what is already available. Here we can serve historiography by indicating ways in which the diversity of the period in actual content belies stereotypes based on a dominant idiom and first-order approximations. Let us first point to evidence of links and debts that cut across salient positional alignments, and then consider evidence of the development of Bloomfieldian work over time. This will involve particular attention to Trager and to Harris, as sources of the standard conception of Bloomfieldian work, and will entail as well attention to evidence of ways in which the period was not in fact typically 'Bloomfieldian'. These matters will bring us full circle to an assessment again of the role of Bloomfieldian work.

5.2.2 *Networks of interaction*

The assessments of diversity among the Bloomfieldians so far given may be called 'positional', in that they are based on assessing the position of scholars on one or more issues deemed criterial. To some extent, the assessments implicitly reflect a knowledge that may be called 'interactional', having to do with networks of interaction, cooperation and influence. No careful study of these networks has been made. There is a tendency to link Fries and Pike, perhaps, because of a common interest in practical work, and location at Michigan, as well as certain kinds of continuity from Bloomfield; and a tendency to link Pike and Nida because of a common interest in practical work in the context of missionary activity, as well as a common distance of sorts from what Akhmanova and Mikael'an call the 'left wing' of Bloomfieldians. Such groupings may overlook the ways in which scholars at the same institution may be differentiated in their work by that very fact (occupying complementary niches), and so have a different range or emphasis than would have been the case in a different immediate set of colleagues. Such groupings may also overlook significant differences in network that exist alongside similarities; the American Bible Society (in which Nida works) is not the same as the Wycliffe Bible Translators (with which Pike is associated).

Acknowledgements in books and articles give us some clues to networks that cut across apparent divisions. Consider the following brief selection:

We are indebted also to several of our colleagues, especially Prof. Leonard Bloomfield, Dr. Charles F. Hockett, and the late Benjamin Whorf, for criticism and for many valuable suggestions on English phonemics. (Trager and Bloch 1941, n. 4)

The present paper derives from the phonemic systems of Bloomfield, Sapir, Trubetzkoy, and their followers. It owes most to Bloomfield, though rather to the methodological rigor of his work than to his phonemic theories. Apart from published material, the writer's chief stimulus has been his correspondence and discussion with George L. Trager and Bernard Bloch. He owes thanks also to Morris Swadesh for many suggestions in the past, to Mary R. Haas for specific criticism of the present paper; and above all to Bloch for advice and active assistance in giving the paper its final shape. (Hockett 1942, n. 1)

I wish to acknowledge my great indebtedness to the outstanding recent contributions of such structuralists as Bernard Bloch, Charles F. Hockett, Zellig S. Harris, C. F. Voegelin, and Rulon S. Wells. (Nida 1949:vi)

The procedures of analysis discussed here are the product and outgrowth of the work of linguists throughout the world, to whose investigations the meagre references cited here are an inadequate guide. This book owes most, however, to the work and friendship of Edward Sapir and of Leonard Bloomfield, and particularly to the latter's book Language.

In preparing this book for publication, I had the benefit of many discussions with C. F. Voegelin and Rulon S. Wells III, and of important criticisms from Roman Jakobson, W. D. Preston, and Fred Lukoff. N. Chomsky has given much-needed assistance with the manuscript. (Harris 1951:v (dated January 1947))

Harris' bibliographic notes are indeed catholic with regard to diverse approaches.

These samples show perhaps unexpected crossings of 'Sapir', 'Bloomfield', and even 'Prague School' boundaries, and they indicate the importance of influences not represented in discrete books or papers. The name of Rulon Wells, for example, recurs significantly, not only in acknowledgements from Nida and Harris, but also, in his major general paper, from Bloch (1948, n. 7):

In arriving at the present formulation of these postulates, I have profited immeasurably from the criticisms and suggestions of many colleagues. I am especially indebted to Yuen Ren Chao, Charles F. Hockett, Henry M. Hoenigswald, Martin Joos, W. Freeman Twaddell, and — above all — Rulon S. Wells.

Correspondence and personal recollections can make possible an accurate reconstruction of these networks and their roles.

Some light is shed on these matters by obituary and other articles on participants now dead; see, with regard to Bloch, Hill (1967), Joos (1967), and Miller (1970); on Fries, Marckwardt (1968); on Swadesh, Newman (1967), McQuown (1968), and Hymes (1971a); on Weinreich, Malkiel (1967). More can be said about individual positions, differences, and relations on the basis of the mutual criticism of participants in the period, but that can best be done in relation to the 'developmental' diversity.

We have said that the work of the period was work in progress, such that a fixed image of it would be inadequate. The true nature of the unity to be found in the period can be brought out by considering diversity of viewpoint in relation to time. The scope of work to be considered is itself defined by unity with regard to the task of establishing descriptive linguistics, notably phonology, and increasingly morphology and syntax, in terms of explicit analyses with explicit justifications. Throughout the period there would be controversy as to the proper starting point of explicit analysis, the steps by which properly to proceed, and the point, perhaps, at which it was necessary to stop. There would be disagreement as well as to the proper relation between analyses and justifications. But throughout the period a characteristic idiom, and definition of the center of the situation, gained dominance. Successive clusters of reviews document this process, and provide material essential to its study.

5.2.3   Development in time

The first group of reviews serve to define the direction of the emerging group as against the views of others in the United States and abroad. It is impossible to overemphasize the importance of two reviews by Harris in this regard, one of a general book by the Indo-Europeanist Gray (Harris 1940), the other of Trubetzkoy's major phonological treatise (Harris 1941). Harris' change from the world of Semitic philology, in which he had begun, to the world of the Bloomfieldian idiom, comes forth full-blown in the first of these, and is developed in the second. (One might compare Bloomfield's mildly stated opposition to Gray's 'psychologism' in his own review, reprinted in Hockett 1970:365–366.) The review of Gray appears in the first issue of *Language* edited by Bloch. In the review Harris has little to say about the comparative-historical content of the book (so much is this the case that a supplemental review, dealing more with these things, by D. Swanson, is appended (231–235)). Harris' theme is stated in his first paragraph (216):

... the value of the book is vitiated, especially for the layman, by a major shortcoming. This is the neglect of the method of structural analysis, i.e., of organized synchronic description. ... It is the chief purpose of this review to show that an appreciation of linguistic structure is necessary for any interpretation of linguistics, and that its neglect leads to undesirable results in practice.

It is significant that such a theme had to be argued in a lead review in the journal of the LSA in 1940. It is equally significant for the course of linguistics in the United States that the claims of structural method (Harris consistently uses the term 'structural') are identified with theses as to 'the irrelevance of semantic classification' (224), and of 'the logical analysis of ideas, which is used by several European linguists today' (224), as well as that 'psychological explanations' are 'particularly undesirable' — 'They add nothing ... and are often circular' (225), leading to the conclusion that mentalistic statements are not only necessarily circular, 'since our only evidence for thought is language', but also that association of different languages with different psychologies 'has dangerous social implications' (226–227). Almost every paragraph of the long review has a forceful topic sentence, but the heart of the emerging view of linguistics — the view which cuts off analysis of structure from analysis of functions — comes in one paragraph worth quoting largely in full (228):

With an apparatus of linguistic definitions, the work of linguistics is reducible, in the last analysis, to establishing correlations. Correlations between the occurrence of linguistic forms and the occurrence of situations (features of situations) suffice to identify meanings; the term 'to signify' can be defined as the name of this relation. There is therefore no need to regard 'sign' or 'symbol' as primitive terms of linguistics. To say that linguistics is a 'science sémiologique' is to push its foundations back to a 'science' which cannot be studied objectively, to a relation of 'signifying' . . . which requires something like teleology for its understanding. And correlations between the occurrence of one form and that of other forms yield the whole of linguistic structure. The fact that these correlations may be grouped into certain patterned regularities is of great interest for psychology; but to the pattern itself need not be attributed a metaphysical reality in linguistics. Gray speaks of three aspects of language, . . . basing himself on the langue-parole dichotomy of de Saussure and many Continental linguists. This division, however, is misleading, in setting up two parallel levels of linguistics. 'Parole' is merely the physical events which we count as language, while 'language' is the scientist's analysis and arrangements of them. The relation between the two is the same as between the world of physical events and the science of physics. The danger of using such undefined and intuitive criteria as pattern, symbol, and logical a priori, is that linguistics is precisely the one empirical field which may enable us to derive definitions of these intuitive fundamental relationships out of correlations of observable phenomena.

Here is the goal, the general significance of linguistics, held out in the concluding sentence of Sapir's "Sound patterns in language" (1925), but taken to require renunciation by the scientist to reach it.[40] One must not speak of these 'intuitive fundamental relationships' until the rigors of the quest have been completed. The danger, of course, is that those who began with a personal experience of what the promised goal might be like (say, from contact with Sapir) might retain a sense of it, but their students, and readers, lacking the initial experience, would come to lack a sense of the goal as well.

Harris' review of the work of the major European colleague, Trubetzkoy (cited in the 1930s and early 1940s by most Bloomfieldians in their systematic work), brings the position to bear at a second crucial point. The argument for structural linguistics, as against its neglect in a general book, might have been made in quite other terms by Swadesh or Newman or Whorf. The argument against Trubetzkoy is for an essentially positivist conception of scientific practice within the sphere of structural linguistics. Thus, Harris writes (1941:345):

[40] Sapir's sentence is: 'The present discussion is really a special illustration of the necessity of getting behind the sense data of any type of expression in order to grasp the intuitively felt and communicated forms which alone give significance to such expression.' (Mandelbaum 1949:45). The recurrence of 'intuitive' in Harris' statement is perhaps significant. Sapir's examples imply a general canon of not restricting attention to observable form at any level of analysis. One example (from Nootka) involves stylistic values and genres (songs, chants, ordinary speech), i.e., ethnographic knowledge. If one replaces 'teleology' in the passage from Harris by 'ethnography', one sees how drastic the position is, and one sees also an equivalence with Chomsky. Harris rejects, as 'teleology', unwanted metaphysics (philosophical or perhaps religious); Chomsky rejects, as 'behaviorism', unwanted social science. Both bracket, and postpone for a later day, whatever might show linguistic analysis to depend on foundations in analysis of another kind. The effect is to exclude from linguistics whatever makes of sentences social actions.

The point at issue is the Prague Circle's occasionally mystical use of philosophical terms. . . . Such talk may be considered a matter of taste. It makes no difference what picture each linguistic worker has of a phoneme, so long as each performs the same operations upon it.

The Prague Circle terminology, however, has two dangers: first, it gives the impression that there are two objects of possible investigation, the Sprechakt (speech) and the Sprachgebilde (language structure), whereas the latter is merely the scientific arrangement of the former. Second, talking about function, system, and the like without defining them in terms of operations and relations, fools even the linguistic worker. For by satisfying him with undefined psychological terms it prevents him from continuing his analysis.

Rigor of duty is the quest.

Other reviews of European, particularly Prague School, work occur in the same issue of *Language* as Harris' review of Gray. Trager (1940) sympathetically expounds the character of Van Wijk's book as a useful companion to Trubetzkoy's *Grundzüge*, bringing together the views of all his school and making it possible to trace their development; but the general criticism must be made that the book suffers from a mentalistic attitude (248):

This may all be so [that la langue is the psychic equivalent of la parole], but as linguists we can describe only linguistic facts, objectively recorded and analyzed, and have no means of knowing anything about 'psychic' values.

The specific Bloomfieldian point, that true phonemic relationships, and tables, must be based on function and structure, not on type of sound, is also made (250; cf. Harris 1941:347–348), following Bloomfield himself. The search for linguistic form, the drive to establish linguistic form as central object of study, is being institutionalized as requiring, like Hjelmslev, the casting out of 'content' (or 'substance') on either side of the nexus between sound and meaning. Voegelin (1940) expounds some of the contents of a diverse phonological volume, ending with an extended discussion of Bloomfield's *Menomini morphophonemics*, and emphasizing the way by which Bloomfield avoids elaborateness (257):

Bloomfield's Menomini may be distinguished from the Nootka, Tübatulabal, and Potawatomi studies in that it alone is good to the reader: it gives him few theoretical forms and only simple rules to remember.

See also Trager (1941) on Hjelmslev's work on case, and Hockett (1942, section 7.2., n. 14), whose citation of Trubetzkoy is appended to this terse dismissal (Joos 1957:101):

The simple statement of distribution made above gives the facts without any complications; any talk of neutralization or cancellation or archiphonemes (n. 14) confuses the facts without adding anything.

It is this paper of which Joos says that 'the task of codification was taken on by — indeed, in a way it was assigned too — the youngest of the persons spoken of, Bloomfield's disciple C. F. Hockett' (1957:96) (Note that Joos is speaking of codification of phonology, as developed by Bloch and other Bloomfieldians, not, as Stark (1972:398) has it, of 'Bloomfield's ideas'; in other words, not of ideas as to the whole of structure, nor of ideas specifically those of Bloomfield). Joos (1957: 108) speaks of the paper as a stock-taking report that shows where phonological thought stood at the time, and, with all allowance for Hockett's personal originality and skill, what Bloomfieldian phonemics was pretty sure to develop into through those years of 'war effort' discussion: 'Very little of that discussion had so far been reflected in print, which accounts for the shock effect of this publication.' Note as well Hockett's report (1970:369) that Bloomfield himself 'did not like my 1942 paper, though he took pains not to let me know this (I learned of it indirectly)'. With this systematic exposition of phonology, and an exposition of a purely formal method to determining the minimal units of grammar proper in the same year in the central journal (Harris 1942), the distinctive Bloomfieldian thrust was well under way in public view.

By 1946 a full-scale treatment of language structure as a whole in such terms existed in the form of the manuscript of Harris' *Methods in descriptive* (later: *structural*) *linguistics*, recommended for publication by the LSA's committee on such matters, but languishing for lack of funds. There are of course Bloomfield's book, and the two pamphlets, issued through the LSA, Bloomfield (1942), and Bloch and Trager (1942) (participated in by Bloomfield with regard to syntax). In the 1940s there appear the first of what was to come to be regarded as a textbook style peculiarly American, both in Bloomfieldian and in Chomskyan versions, namely, the exposition of principles together with practical lessons. Pike (1947) was the first in phonology. Reviews of the book illustrate the range of opinions as to the new American approach. The book was praised for its usefulness by some European and United States scholars (e.g., Martinet (*Word* 5:282–286 (1949)), and Voegelin (*IJAL* 15:75–85 (1949)), and condemned for methodological inadequacy from opposing sides cf. Trager (*Lg* 26:152–158 (1950)) and Hockett (*SIL* 7:29–51 (1949) = V. Makkai (1972:200–210)), as against Evans (*BSOAS* 13:531–534 1950)). See also reviews by Thomas (*QJS* 34:384 (1948)), Echols (*JEGP* 48:377–379 (1949)), Haugen (*AmSp* 24:54–57 (1949)), Fischer-Jørgensen (*Acta Linguistica* 5:104–109 (1949)), and O'Connor (*Maître Phonétique* 3(28): 34–36 (1950)).

The successive editions of Nida's work on morphology, and the reactions to them, are especially interesting. The first edition of the morphology, and also of the dialogues to introduce linguistic topics (*Linguistic interludes* (Glendale, Calif: SIL, 1944)) are given a joint lead review in an issue of *Language* by Hockett (1944:252):

Our science has been sadly in need of the two types of material which Nida herewith gives us: interesting presentation of the fundamentals of linguistics for the layman, and good teaching material for the most elementary phases of analysis.

There is no comment on Nida's use of processual terminology; Hockett states

(253): 'Nida wisely sticks close to what we know, avoiding areas which are still in dispute.' Nor does Harris' student, and advocate of rigor, Preston (1948) comment on the processual approach, except perhaps by implication in observing (56):

Nida's book is eclectic in that it presents terminology, procedure, and theory as derived mainly from Bloomfield and Sapir.

A very few years later, however, Hockett finds himself concerned to review the reissuing of the first edition, with some revisions (Nida 1946), not because of the revisions, but because it seems to him that his statement (quoted above) is no longer true (1947:243):

perhaps, however, it is the word 'wisely', rather than the phrase 'what we know', on which I want to recant.

In this regard, Hockett adds a footnote (2) to say that the point of view he develops owes a great deal to Harris, particularly to his "Morpheme alternants in linguistic analysis" (*Lg* 18:169–180 (1942)). The concern to avoid circularity, and reliance on native speaker reaction, in favor of an explicit, unidirectional procedure, is evident (279):

If words have been determined without resort to immediate constituents, one can perform the operation of analysis into immediate constituents on words. Bloomfield is not very helpful (Language 161: 'Any English-speaking person who concerns himself with this matter is sure to tell us that . . .'); Nida also asserts that immediate constituents exist, but does not tell us very clearly how to go about discovering them.

Concern to do without 'process' is even more evident, on grounds of redundancy, and implications of hierarchy (282, 283):

. . . in Nida's presentation 'morphological process' is just as fundamental as 'morpheme'. We don't need both. . . . Despite the general applicability of the test [devised by Hockett], therefore, it might be better to refrain all together from using terminology that suggests priority of one constituent over another.

Nida's contribution is nevertheless still valued, and the hope expressed that he will find the criticisms useful in a further revision.

Nida's second edition (1949) is indeed a revision, not only in the replacement of fictitious data by sample data from actual languages, but also in that (v):

. . . instead of setting up morphological and phonological processes as basic to the descriptive methodology, it treats the morpheme together with its allomorphs as the fundamental feature.

The context of the changes, and the value of the book, are both recognized by Martinet in his review in *Word* (1950:84):

In a way, Nida's second edition of his morphology, which we may prefer to consider as a completely new book, is the outcome of theoretical discussions that we find mirrored in a number of papers, mostly published in Language, by scholars like Hockett, Harris, Bloch, and Nida himself. Nida's standpoint has thus been made clear in advance.

In comparison with that of his opponents, it was frequently characterized by a superior concern with facts. . . . The book itself shows most clearly that Nida is not ready to let theoretical bias distort facts out of recognition.

Despite the morpheme-alternant basis, Nida does allow description of types of phonological environment in terms of processes, such as assimilation, dissimilation, and palatalization (21ff.); but Sapir's Southern Paiute, though its principal divisions into grammatical processes and word classes are 'much more valid than they appear', has the difficulty that 'it requires a double listing. The same morphemes must be treated under processes and also under the word class' (233; recall Hockett's criticism above).

Elimination of 'process' idiom was not enough for Trager, however, who concluded (1951:131):

In a way, this book marks a terminus ad quem: linguistics based on meaning has done all it can, and here is an example of what it can do. We must now go on, for progress is an imperative in our culture, and science is part of our cultural activity.

The year of Trager's review can be considered the high-water mark of the initial Bloomfieldian wave. It was the year of publication of two books that were widely regarded as major public expression of the new linguistics, Trager and Smith (1951) and Harris (1951a).[41] We need to consider their status as representatives of Bloomfieldian work, their relation to each other, and their impact, both in the short and long run. The next two parts are devoted to this.

5.2.4   *Trager and Smith*

Because of its focus on English, and its use in circles concerned with English in practical ways, Trager and Smith's small book had great impact. It influenced subsequent work on English by leading linguists (Fries, Hill, Gleason, and others), and shaped the 'linguistic approach' to composition, reading, and the like, for a decade. Attention in the book to American dialectology played a part, of course, as did the linking of the analysis of language to analysis of other communicative codes (paralinguistics, kinesics) and to the communicative consequences of language itself ('metalinguistics', under the aegis partly of Whorf). Educators, diplomats, anthropologists, and others were presented with a promise of a linguistics that was rigorous, central, expanding, and useful.

Stark describes the book as a (1972:414): 'codification of Bloomfieldian theory

---

[41]   Thus, Matthews recurrently links the two. Of the Bloomfieldian conception of morphology (central to the thrust of the 1940s), he observes (1972:113, n. 1): 'The extreme position, as Bierwisch points out in his useful survey of definitions of the morph, is most consistently taken by Harris (1951a, 1954; but see also Trager and Smith 1951, particularly 53f., 58).' Elsewhere (42, n. 3): '. . . The ultimate, post-Bloomfieldian, generalization of the morpheme is reached with the incorporation of 'suprasegmental morphemes' of pitch, etc.; cf. Trager and Smith 1951: 55ff.; . . . also, e.g., Harris 1951a:281–283'. And on extreme inductivism, he cites Harris, and also Trager and Smith (112, n. 1).

and practice that became the structuralist paradigm of rigorous linguistic description'. He considers it the fullest flowering of the extension of distributional assumptions to all of language, and the place in which the shift from Bloomfield's form-meaning correlation (as basis of linguistic analysis) to the Bloomfieldians' slant is completely realized (414, 415). By 'Bloomfieldian slant' (a term adopted from Hockett (Stark 1972:410)), Stark means a step taken along the following lines. Bloomfield in effect conveyed a picture of the relation between linguistic form and meaning, such that meaning is not in the form, but in the world around it (or, in stable associations between the form and features of the world around it (cf. Hockett 1968a:22)). Bloomfield retained both forms and meanings in his conception of language, while insisting on starting analysis with forms. At the same time he stressed the great difficulty of studying meanings. The Bloomfieldians, understandably enough, not only started with forms, but stopped with them, so far as grammar proper was concerned. The use of meaning to get analysis of grammar (and phonology) started was one thing; the study of meaning, semantics, was another, beyond grammar itself. Hence, for example, the Trager and Smith notion of 'metalinguistics', beyond phonology and syntax, as a sphere completing the field of linguistics, and embracing the study of meaning as part of the study of culture (1951, Part III).

Two points require clarification: what was meant by exclusion of meaning, and what was put in its place.

Trager used 'meaning' commonly in the sense of translations, or any other informal mode of knowledge of the content of meaning. Sometimes he put this use in quotes (Trager and Smith 68), as if to suggest that once linguistics itself got to 'meaning', it would be something else, semantics (or metalinguistics). More than any one else in the period, perhaps, he maintained that exclusion of meaning from linguistic analysis was not merely an ideal, or an alternative, but a necessity. Introducing a renewed series of studies of the Taos language of New Mexico, he stated (1948:156):

And I obtained the necessary phonological basis on which to try to construct an objective syntax not founded on translation meaning.

And he maintained his view of the exclusion of meaning from such levels long past the decade of insurgent Bloomfieldianism. A decade later he criticized Hockett's 1958 text (1959:79):

A morphemics based on meaning cannot be successful in fully analyzing a language. It is not meaning but distribution and arrangement of recurrent partials that is the basis of morphemes, as well as for any other level of grammatical analysis.

Hockett's definition of morphemes as the 'smallest individually meaningful elements in the utterances of a language' (1958:123) was judged to be 'meaningless as well as unfortunately misleading' (cf. discussion in Koȩrner 1970a:168).

Trager did admit use of meaning in the sense of difference, as in his review of Lounsbury's Oneida monograph (1953):

The reviewer contends that microlinguistic analysis works with *difference of meaning* only: it asks, 'Are these two items the same or different?' It is not until one gets to metalinguistic analysis that one begins to use *referential meaning*, or meaning in the more or less ordinary sense.

Difference of meaning, like the result of the pair test proposed by Harris for differentiation of forms, is required as an initial observation (or assumption, with testing of the correctness of the assumption being resorted to in difficult cases). Such differentiation answers to the fundamental assumption stated by Bloomfield, that in a speech community some utterances are the same. Put otherwise, the criterion is a way of meeting the requirement of recognizing repetition and contrast. The use of the criterion in no way implies prior analysis of meaning on the part of the linguist, or prior ethnography, at least in principle (cf. Trager and Smith 1951:83). Trager (1955:511–512) is full and explicit:

I hold that a morphemic analysis can be accurate and satisfactory only in direct proportion to the accuracy of the phonemic analysis in which the morphemes are expressed. It must be performed without the use of referential meaning, except that DIFFERENCES of meaning may be used as a guide [not foundation] to structure. It is a statement or construct by the linguistic analyst, and must be arrived at wholly from the corpus of material available and in terms of the methods explicitly followed. It must be internally consistent and systematic, and it must be as rigorous in these respects as possible. Any departures from rigorousness in the direction of pedagogical 'easiness' or the like should be made by starting from the full analysis and with explicit description of what is done and why.

(The last sentence is in response to criticism of an earlier Trager analysis of French, by Bloomfield himself (1945b:8): 'A less rigorous statement may be more useful even for scientific purposes.') Much later, Trager (1968:82) 'endorsed' two of three recantations specified by Hockett as part of a reevaluation of Bloomfieldian linguistics, as to the rigid separation of synchrony from diachrony, and item-and-arrangement style of description: Trager denies that he ever accepted either during the fifties. Hockett's third item is separation of semantics from grammar-and-lexicon; this position Trager remains unwilling to give up. The essentials of his position are preserved in his latest book (1970).

Trager's views on meaning, however, hardly differentiate him from Harris, as a representative of Bloomfieldian work. If anything, Trager is less extreme. He provides a specific place for semantics ('metalinguistics') and talks about reaching it. While maintaining a rigid purity in phonology, morphemics, and syntax, he sees to the republication of papers of Whorf, formulates paralinguistics, conceives a general scheme for the analysis of culture, and so forth. While Harris does not exclude such activities, he does not much provide for them. He goes further than Trager in excluding meaning, inasmuch as he proposes that systematic experimentation with doubtful pairs of forms, randomly presented to obtain judgments as to shape, would suffice. In other words, one would not need even so much of meaning as judgments of sameness or difference; one need only ask for judgments of sameness or difference as to shape (that is, ask an informant to identify each of series of presented forms as A or B).

Stark concludes that Trager and Smith are the fullest realization of the Bloomfieldian slant, because they base linguistic analysis on phonology. For Trager and Smith, 'objective syntax' (1951:68) means 'phonologically based syntax'. We have to disagree with Stark's analysis. Harris breaks with Bloomfield's form-meaning correlation just as do Trager and Smith. And Harris finds a point d'appui in phonological shapes, one even more 'meaningless' than that found by Trager and Smith. Nor is it correct to trace the path toward the full realization of the Bloomfieldian slant crucially through Bloch's phonological postulates (1948). Insofar as Bloch eliminated meaning by means of a highly formalized analysis of sound features and their distribution, his approach was in keeping with that of Harris, not of Trager and Smith. Trager and Smith, as we have seen, retained differential meaning in phonology (Hymes recalls Smith insisting on this at the Linguistic Institute in 1952). Harris had very early proposed that phonological units could be established on the basis of distribution, rather than on the basis of phonetic differences (and, a fortiori, semantic differences) (cf. quotations from reviews of Trubetzkoy (1941) above, Bender and Harris 1946:21; and Harris 1941b, 1942, 1945). Bloch does share with Trager and Smith a concern for phonological bases of syntactic analysis, and such bases are the Bloomfieldian approach par excellence — but only if our criterion is that of maximum difference from the dominant succeeding approach.

The difference between Trager and Smith, on the one hand, and Harris, on the other, does lie in 'phonological syntax' (recall citation above of Joos 1957:153 on an 'anti-Harris procedure, and note as well that Chomsky's first assault on Bloomfieldian positions was on phonological syntax). The reason for the difference would seem to lie in a factor not taken into account in Stark's (or so far as we know, anyone's) analysis. Harris, as well as Trager and Smith, Bloch, and others, shares in the 'fundamental assumption that underlies all the other notions of the Bloomfieldian model', namely, no 'tacit reliance on factors beyond the range of observation' (Stark 1972:388, and 387 (quoting Bloch 1949:92)). All share the expanded picture with which Stark concludes his analysis (418):

The Bloomfieldian search for an operationally defined and homogeneous theory was balanced by the requirement that the description rely on factors within the range of observation; taken together these two requirements characterize the foundations of the Bloomfieldian model and the particular representation of sounds, words, sentences, and meanings that it presents to us.

Trager and Smith, indeed, share with Harris the statement that the analysis is the linguist's construct, though they may think the analysis also real, because of its grounding and procedures. But though Harris is more than anyone instrumental in establishing the idiom of behavior, induction, and arrangement in the period, his relation to it differs from that of most.

5.2.5 *Harris*

Harris' 1951 book had great intellectual impact, as an epitome of the new discipline in purest form — abstract, mathematical, hard to understand, with palpable facts of language (of which Trager and Smith offered a fair number) replaced by symbols and manipulations. Looking back, we can see that it represented the line of work that would be most productive, both immediately in terms of work in syntax, and ultimately, in terms of the next major change in the discipline (cf. Stark 1972:403–404). Nor is this retrospective view in conflict with opinion at the time. The book was hailed as a milestone when it appeared (cf. discussion of reviews below). Yet there are ironies, if not seeming contradictions, in this significance and acclaim. Whereas Trager and Smith were explicit as to a single schedule of procedures, and their book was considered for a time a 'bible' in some circles, Harris was officially entirely diffident about the specifics of his proposals, and those who accepted his book as a major event were highly critical of it. In the ironies, there are clues to the character and diversity of the period. Let us consider them in turn. (On Harris, see now also Mounin (1972:170–188).)

Harris expressly denied unique virtue for what he presented (1951:6):

> The only preliminary step that is essential to this science is the restriction to distribution as determining the relevance of inquiry. The particular methods described in this book are not essential. They are offered as general procedures of distributional analysis applicable to linguistic material . . . the whole framework of basic procedures presented below could be supplanted by some other schedule of operations without loss of descriptive linguistic relevance. This would be true as long as the new operations dealt essentially with the distribution of features of speech relatively to the other features within the utterance, and as long as they did so explicitly and rigorously. Any such alternative operations could always be compared with the procedures presented here, and the results of one could always be put into correspondence with the results of the other.

Indeed, Harris' thesis that 'the logic of distributional relations . . . constitutes the basic method of structural linguistics' (v) is open to a range of interpretations. One could accept 'the principle . . . of relative distribution, the method . . . of controlled substitution' (McQuown 1951), and the statement quoted above, on an interpretation that allowed for appeal to native speakers' judgments, beyond observable parts of utterances; for use of meaning; for investigation of meaning; for statement of relations in terms of processes; for base forms in morphology and in phonology; for absence of bi-uniqueness in morphophonemics; for going beyond linearity in phonology to analysis into features; for analysis of morphological elements in terms of features; for analysis of morphology independently of phonology, or of phonology in terms of morphology; for prediction of sentences not in one's corpus; for formulation of a grammar as a deductive system; for investigation of styles in context. Harris himself allows for all these things.

These supporting statements are from Harris (1951a), with one exception (from Harris 1951b).

Native speaker's knowledge:

273, n. 27: 'Objection might be made at this point that the potentialities of substitution cannot be used to distinguish portions of speech; for these should be distinguished by their internal structure, independently of what substitutions occur in partially different utterances. However, experimental work in the psychology of perception, especially that due to Gestalt psychologists, leaves little doubt that an utterance is perceived not as an independent structure but in its relation to other utterances. Therefore any differences in substitution potential which can be recognized from the structure of an utterance are relevant even to that utterance alone (and are certainly relevant to the whole language).'

Use of meaning:

365, n. 6: 'In determining the morphemes of a particular language, linguists use, in addition to distributional criteria, also (in varying degrees) criteria of meaning difference. In exact descriptive linguistic work, however, such considerations of meaning can only be used heuristically, as a source of hints, and the determining criteria will always have to be stated in distributional terms (Appendix to 12.41) [cf. esp. p. 189]. The methods presented in the preceding chapters offer distributional investigations as alternatives to meaning considerations.'

311, n. 21: 'As in the case of many of the procedures discussed previously, the method of this chapter enables us to state on distributional bases results, such as paradigms, which are often (and much more easily) obtained by considerations of meaning. However, again as in the case of the other procedures, the method enables us to check the distributional relevance of the meaning differentia, and enables us to find patternings over and beyond those whole meanings we consider 'grammatical'. The fact that distributional methods are able to bring out the major grammatical meaning categories is merely an indication that the old results are not lost in the new methods.'

Investigation of meaning:

(1951b: 301): 'The formal analysis of language is an empirical discovery of the same kinds of relations and combinations which are devised in logic and mathematics; and their empirical discovery in language is of value because languages contain (or suggest) more complicated types of combination that people have invented for logic. In much the same way, we have here [in Sapir's semantic papers] an empirical discovery of elements of meaning in natural languages, instead of the seemingly hopeless task of inventing basic elements of meaning in speculative abstract semantics. ... Such isolating of 'elements of meaning' is not subject to the usual criticisms directed against semantic work, because it is an empirical linguistic investigation. It does not derive elements of meaning from some deductive system of presumed basic meanings, but discovers what elements can be separated out from the total meaning of each word; and it discovers this by comparing the various words of a semantic set, by seeing the linguistic environment in which these occur, and the social situation or meaning of each use. All these investigations involving meaning, when carried out with the kind of approach that Sapir used, have validity and utility.'

Process statements:

373: 'In using such models, the linguist would speak, for example, of base forms . . ., of derived forms, . . . or processes which yield one form out of another. In all these types of presentation, the elements are seen as having histories, so that the relation of an element to sequences which contain it becomes the history of the element as it is subjected to various processes and extensions.'

[While it is clear from the context, and the whole book, that Harris does not himself wish to use process statements, his discussion of them is straightforward (It begins, 'Other types of presentation which have frequently been used . . .'), as are his comments in his review of Newman (1944) and other remarks relating to use of process and configuration by Sapir and his students (see discussion earlier under Sapir). Footnote 18 on this page gives process statement an algebraic formulation, followed by a suggestion that the two modes of presentation are complementary, the one [process] studying variation of morphemes (one at a time) in respect to the utterance, the other studying the variation of utterances (or environments) in respect to a morpheme contained in them.]

Base forms:

226, n. 18: 'The new one-spelling morphophonemic writing of the previously plurimembered unit is sometimes called the base form or theoretical form, from which the phonemically written members are derived.' (cf. 235, n. 38).

307, n. 14: '. . . However, in selecting a member of the . . . class . . ., we cannot avoid deciding for one member as against the others. . . . The criteria for selecting a basic alternant are not meaning or tradition, but descriptive order, i.e. resultant simplicity of description in deriving the other forms from the base.' (cf. 367, m. 9, and Harris 1944:245).

Non bi-uniqueness in morphophonemics:

362–363: '. . . the distinctions between sounds are in general only in one-many correspondence with the distinctions between morphophonemes: two distinct morphophonemic sequences may represent identical segment (or phoneme) sequences; such different morphophonemic sequences are phonemically equivalent. (cf. Harris 1944, n. 23).

(In the 1944 note, Harris expressly permits partial overlapping among phonological components — the same sound feature may be represented in different environments by different components — and states that it is no bar to phonemic writing.)

Beyond linearity:

144: 'Another consideration is the availability of simultaneity, in addition to successivity, as a relation among linguistic elements [citing Saussure and followers, in n. 41 — cf. Harris 1944, especially the last sentence (Joos 1957:138)]. The possibility of having elements occur with each other is left open by the previous procedures (except in chapters 6, 10 [which do use components, of more than unit length]), where the operations involve only the relation of segments being next to each other . . . The consideration of elements among which there obtains the relation of simultaneity involves removing the limitation to one dimension from linguistic analysis. Removal of this limitaton is all the easier in view of the ease of arranging letters on paper two-dimensionally, and of the ready availability of mathematical terminology for two-dimensional relations.' [There follows an exposition, clear, concise, Harrisian in logic, of distinctive feature analysis as a technique of linguistics, including reference to a phonological problem in Danish, accompanied by the footnote (52, p. 148): 'The example and the final solution were given by Roman Jakobson in a lecture at the University of Chicago in 1945'.]

299: 'This section considers the relations of selection (government, etc.) among morpheme classes. It leads to the recognition of paradigmatic patterns, and of components which express the distributional relations among morphemes.'

No unique order or dependence of levels:

23: 'If, disregarding phonology, we have first determined the morphemes of a language, we can proceed, if we wish, to break these morphemes down into phonemes.'

195: 'Morphological elements are independent. It is also possible to determine the morphological elements of a language without relation to the phonemic contrasts and with no prior knowledge of them.' [The procedures for doing this, and for going from morphological to phonological elements, are then indicated.]

299, n. 1: 'Whereas chapter 16 covered primarily what is called syntax, chapters 17 and 18 parallel most of what is usually considered morphology proper. This order of treatment was most convenient for the methods developed here. It is also possible, however, to treat the morphemic relations within whole-utterance environment (syntax) after the relations within smaller domains (morphology proper).'

Prediction beyond corpus:

280: 'From the statements of chapter 16 alone we shall be able to learn what sequences of morphemes, and what utterances, do and do not occur in the language.'

Grammar as deductive:

372–373: 'The work of analysis leads right up to the statements which enable anyone to synthesize or predict utterances in the language. These statements form a deductive system with axiomatically defined initial elements and with theorems concerning the relations among them. The final theorems would indicate the structure of the utterances of the language in terms of the preceding parts of the system.'

[This statement is in section 20.3, 'Description of the Language Structure', and is followed shortly by the statement on process presentation quoted above.]

Stylistic and other investigations:

364: 'It may be noted that there are not just two descriptive systems—phonology and morphology—but rather an indefinite number, some of these being phonologic and some morphologic. It is thus possible to extend the descriptive methods for the creation of additional systems having other terms of reference. For example, investigations in stylistics and in culture-language correlations may be carried out by setting up systems parallel to the morphologic ones but based on the distribution of elements (morpheme classes, sentence types, etc.) over stretches longer than one utterance.'

And finally, with regard to rigidity (as distinct from rigor), and algorithmic constraints, Harris begins his survey of the operations presented in the book (365):

'As was seen in 2.1, the only over-all consideration which determines the relevance of an operation is that it deal with the occurrence of parts of the flow of speech relative to each other. Beyond that, there is freedom in the choice of operations.'

Munz, a close student of Harris, has traced the development of his theoretical views from the 1940s, and concludes that the importance of the distributionalist program (and program is all that it was for Harris) steadily declined through the period, references to it becoming increasingly perfunctory. In place of it there is a growing concern with semantics in grammar, but this concern is more or less concealed by the continued use of distributionalist terminology (see Munz, forthcoming). Such an interpretation fits with the nonsectarian tone of the 1951 book, and the inclusion, and translation into the book's idiom, of unit distinctive features and process relations. Clearly, however, the book put forward as an ideal the independence of formal analysis in terms of distributional relations, and the very catholicity of scope in the book had the effect of proposing its idiom as a lingua franca for linguistics as a whole. And the book was reviewed in terms of the ideal, and idiom. Given their power and scope, relative to other work known at the time, it is not surprising that the program was reviewed as a package. The demonstration of the possibility of such procedures, the specific procedures proposed, and the attitudes associated with both, especially as they appeared to separate formal analysis from wider grounding and interests, *were pretty much universally criticized*.

The book was greatly stimulating, widely influential, highly respected — but not accepted. It was too abstract and catholic to be a successful text (though it was tried as one); it departed too much from practical work and nonformal assumptions and concerns to be adopted. Cf. the reviews by Fowler (1952), Hockett (1952a), Householder (1952), Mead (1952), McQuown (1952), Newman (1952), Togeby (1953), Voegelin (1952).

The double reviews in *Language* (McQuown, Fowler) and in *IJAL* (Voegelin, Mead) indicate that the book was regarded as an event of the first magnitude. For anthropologists, Newman (1952:404) stated:

This book is the most important contribution since the publication of Bloomfield's *Language* in 1933. It makes explicit the direction in which linguistics has been moving.

But Newman also points out that Harris accepts practical use of meaning. In *Language* Fowler attacks the theoretical premise of doing without meaning, and declares the entire enterprise untenable. McQuown begins by calling the book epoch-making, and concludes (504): 'Harris has provided us with the tool. It is our task to use it.' He says that if he has any criticism, it is not of the purpose of the book or of the methods by which it hopes to achieve that purpose, but rather of certain aspects which ultimately will interfere with its success and with the applicability of its results. Within this frame of praise and admiration, McQuown reviews points which others often made reasons for castigation and rejection. Is linguistic analysis a game? McQuown insists on considering 'psychological (i.e., cultural) reality', the way the data structure for the bearer of the culture (cf. Hockett 1952b:98, Householder 1952:261). Which analysis one chooses does matter, and economy and exactness should not be fetish-like criteria in themselves: 'The protest here is against an attitude, not against a necessary result of the procedures recommended in this book' (497). Again, why tie our hands by limiting ourselves to data of a particular type, articulatory or acoustic, or extra-linguistic, such as accompanying actions, and what is in the brains of the participants in speech? Is not something to be gained by choice of a scheme of 'natural' segmentation of the phonetic continuum, such as Pike's? Why are we not told something about the art of eliciting useful responses? 'Every informant is a walking-talking complete corpus' (500). [Clearly no one misconstrued Harris's book to provide discovery procedures, either in the sense of unique algorithms, with which to discover structure from data, or in the sense of ways in which to discover the data on which valid structure depends; it was understood as a handbook, not a protocol.] The 'stress upon distribution rather than meaning' (Harris 1951a:3) leads to tortured solutions and in the event our choices of solutions and of questions depend upon knowledge and hunches about MEANING (McQuown's caps). There is very little discussion of the basic identification of primary elements; little specification of procedure for getting at crucial distributional facts (McQuown considers that 'It is surely no accident that Harris' most successful examples are from English and Modern Hebrew. Crucial environments present themselves.' (503, n. 9)); little comment on interpreting the informant's reaction.

These points constitute the bulk of a *laudatory* review in the leading linguistic journal in the country! There is perhaps no better illustration of the climate of opinion in which most Bloomfieldians subscribed to the ideal of a rigorous mathematical foundation, while holding a lively sense of the incompleteness of any purely abstract analysis of language, cut off from meaning and native-speaker knowledge. (Hymes recalls Voegelin saying at the time, 'some call meaning a shortcut, but since everyone uses it, it looks more like the royal road'.)

Insofar as Harris held up to the period a mirror of the perfection of one of its tendencies, or aspirations, then, the image was no sooner seen than questioned, and by some, rejected (cf. Stark 1972:418).[42] Insofar as the Chomskyan image, or our own image, of the Bloomfieldian period depends upon Harris' work in those years, it must be complemented and qualified by understanding of what other Bloomfieldians themselves thought of it.

The chief source of an image of Bloomfieldian work, apart from Harris, is in the work of Trager and Smith, as we have noted. The contributions of Bloch, Hockett, Wells, and others were important and influential, but neither developed in book form, as physical candidates for representative of the whole, nor presented as the work of a school considering itself a vanguard (cf. Stark 1972:415, n. 12). It is worthwhile to attempt to delineate the contrast between Harris and Trager more carefully.

One salient difference is in the relation of the two to the revived interest in a linguistic approach to problems of cultural scope in the 1950s (discussed further below). Harris interested himself in these possibilities, but continued to concentrate on method proper to linguistics itself, whereas Trager took an active part in developing a scheme of the larger field, and in working out certain parts of it (cf. Hymes 1970a:287–289). Both entertained the prospect of a general methodology, extendible beyond linguistics (a prospect emphasized by McQuown in his review of Harris), and both placed linguistics at the center of the vast territory of culture; but whereas Harris could be said to have proposed a vehicle with which to explore, Trager and Smith seemed to know in advance just how the territory was allotted and posted, and just what route one had to take. One might say that for Harris, his formal procedures were an experiment he hoped would succeed, and was sure would clarify; for Trager and Smith, their procedures (in microlinguistics) were a necessary foundation for the analysis of communication and culture as a whole. This difference may go together with the Tragerian insistence that microlinguistics itself be done just so.

Within linguistics proper Harris gave the Bloomfieldian idiom (which he had done so much to establish) a content quite different from that given it by Trager, Smith, and many others, a content, indeed, different from what on its face the idiom would seem to have. The difference would seem to come down to a difference, not in general positions, but in motivational core, and it shows in their attitude toward observable data as a starting point of analysis. For Trager, the inductive idiom expresses a conception of linguistics as an essentially *empirical* science in a sense that implies that, given adequate data, there will be one analysis that is *right*. For Harris, the idiom expresses a conception of linguistics as an essentially *mathematical* science in a sense that implies that, given adequate data, there will

---

[42] Stark quotes Bloch, who, two years after the appearance of Harris' book (which he would have known in manuscript for some years before), views as still an open question the possibility of achieving the goal he and Harris shared (Bloch 1953b: . . .): 'My theory of a unified approach to linguistic structure and linguistic analysis, based on a consistent set of assumptions, exploiting a reasonably uniform set of techniques, and provided with a consistent technical terminology, is here only adumbrated. It remains for all of us – for you no less than me – to see whether it can be given substance.'

be a set of adequate analyses that are *convertible*. For Trager, given phonological data as starting point, justification of analysis must show how one could proceed step by discrete step; no circularity, no mixing of levels (to cite two slogans of the period). For Harris, one needs an operational foothold in a corpus of data, but given that foothold, one can take imaginative, inventive leaps. (One can indeed first consider the data from the standpoint of morphological elements and relations, rather than phonological ones; the difference is a matter of convenience, not principle.) One can come at the data from more than one vantage point, then, and can consider alternative formulations, depending on one's purpose (1951:9, and n. 8). Trager, in contrast, held strongly to the position that there was one correct, *linguistic* analysis, from which departures, for whatever reason, were not to be taken lightly, and only with painstaking explicitness as to the nature of the departure (Trager 195:511–512; cf. Hodge 1963:52).

The Trager logic strikes one as not only rigorous, but also rigid, even mechanical (and the confidence of arriving at a right analysis from the data depends on unquestioning acceptance of a format that others may find arbitrary). The Harris logic strikes one as rigorous, but also flexible. Personality differences no doubt play a part, but there appear to be differences in historical role as well. For Trager, validity depended on keeping strict faith with phonological data as starting point, and on doing so by singleness of procedure. Within the singleness of procedure, strict separation of levels was considered essential (cf. Trager and Smith 1951:54, 81, 86, 87). These characteristics reflect the experience of linguistic structuralism in defining an object of its own and in making it the fulcrum of disciplinary success. *More than anyone else in the United States, Trager converted the lessons of this experience into a general system and definition of the field.* Future conquests would be won in the same way as the war of the past (and to some extent, present). What was possible depended on how far one could push and deploy that starting point and procedure (phonology = objectivity (Trager and Smith 1951a:77), scientific = separation of levels).

For Harris, validity depended on keeping strict faith with one's algebra. To be sure, Trager and Smith spoke of the essence of linguistics in terms of distributions, terms that are quite Harrisian (191a:54); and Harris' starting point was in observable, phonologically describable, data. But for Harris what was possible depended on how far one could push a generalized starting point and procedure that was far less dependent on inherited formulations and the specific experience of the emerging discipline, far more capable, because of an abstract, algebraic core, of adaptation. In the event, the procedure was to prove adaptable to a conception of starting point, and purpose, almost antithetical to what leaders of the discipline took its experience to be.

There would seem to be two sources for this character of Harris' work. We have discussed the implications of the fact that Harris considers his work continuous with that of Sapir. Admiration and respect for the work of Sapir may have been a factor in his predominantly 'live and let live' tone, such that he would refer to different 'manners of speaking', rather than to 'scientific' vs. 'unscientific', or 'right' vs. 'wrong' analytic styles. Certainly it is because of the flexibility of procedure in his approach that Harris could be Bloomfieldian in idiom and in drive toward formalization, yet seek to emulate Sapir, Newman, and others as to scope and delicacy of analysis. Behind the approach, however, there is also an extra-linguistic factor, a specific conception of the role of formal investigation in science. It is known that Harris has had great respect for the logician Carl Hempel, and for the work in the traditional reconstruction of concepts for scientific use associated with Hempel. (Hymes recalls a conversation in Bloomington in 1953 or 1954 in which Harris recommended Hempel (1952) strongly to him.) It is plausible to interpret Harris' view of the relation between distributional, item-and-arrangement analysis, and the Sapir-Newman 'configurational' approach (which he also considers distributional (Harris 1968)), as analogous to the relation between a common sense concept and its logical explication. The relation is not one of contradiction, or complete replacement, but one of restatement and incorporation. The test of a formal analysis is in part substantive: does it preserve the valid content of the informal notion to which it gives explicit foundation?

Confluence of regard for Sapirian work, on the one hand, and a conception of the role of formal analysis like that of Hempel, on the other, would seem to explain much of the special character of Harris' work.

Harris in effect took the purposefulness of speakers for granted, and drew attention to the purposefulness of linguists. There being more than one admissible analysis of a given language, the linguist was responsible for the analysis chosen, in terms of some purpose of his own. Such a view is very much in keeping with current reflections on the reflexivity of scientific inquiry (cf. Scholte 1973), although omitting the intentionality of speakers would not be. In any case, such a view was not in keeping with the quest for certainty of many in the emerging profession. Neither the subjectivity of the speaker, nor of the linguist, was wanted (cf. Nida 1949:1–2), and Householder noted with some amusement how many linguists, confronted with the freedom rampant in Harris' pages, declared themselves for 'God's truth' as against 'hocus pocus'. Householder' dichotomy oversimplifies, however; it is clear that Harris has considered some things to be true of language, not others, and that he has specifically held that procedures such as those proposed in his first book would be a way of ensuring general linguistics that differences in descriptions were not due to differences in linguists' methods, but due to the languages themselves (1951a:3). Such an attitude is not fairly described as 'hocus pocus', as game-playing (a worry mentioned by McQuown in his review), or as 'theoretical nihilism' (Hockett 1968a:35). That the attitude was perceived in those terms may have been due to a level of focus, and to a difference in the conception of science from which one drew extra-linguistic confidence.

Work focused on particular languages perhaps favored a desire for certainty in the particular case, whereas work focused on formalization perhaps could be treated like experiment in an established science, where truth did not usually depend on a single analysis, and where a variety of experiments, employing different tests, procedures, and angles of approach, might be wanted. In such a context validity could be seen as a long-run matter, growing out of the convergence of many specific results on the part of a number of investigators over time. Insofar as such a perspective accepted a certain degree of indeterminacy in analyses, it had precedent in linguistics in the United States in Chao (1934) and Twaddell (1935), but this precedent was honored more often in the breach than in the observance (Householder 1971:195), whether from practical necessity or theoretical conviction.[43] Most Bloomfieldians at the time conceived of validity, of being right, as something that should be proximately attainable and assertible.[44]

5.2.6 Second phase

The critical reviews of Harris (1951a) must be seen against the background of change in the Bloomfieldian climate of opinion. Hockett (1968a) stresses the half-century mark [1950] as a demarcation (cf. Ivić 1965:159, 161), and there is considerable evidence for this. The decade of the 1950s saw a notable expansion of effective scope, as to intellectual sympathy, content, and diversity of approach.[45]

Haugen (1951) is styled an observer's summing up of a decade; its call for unification of American and European approaches (focused on a comparison of Harris and Hjelmslev) signals what appears to become a conscious effort to come to terms with European work. Haugen's LSA presidential address is followed by the presence of Hjelmslev himself at the 1952 Linguistic Institute, and of his co-worker, Hans Uldall, at the Institute of 1953. The Copenhagen publication, *Recherches*

[43] There was also close precedent in the attitude expressed in Bloomfield's letters to Hockett (Hockett 1970:370–371, 374, 375, 376), but we do not know what influence Bloomfield's attitude had at the time. It does seem to be reflected in Hockett's later distinction between 'gathering' and 'collation' (1955:143ff.), as part of a discussion which has many points of agreement with Harris (cf. especially pp. 176-180 on abstract mathematical systems and convertibility of equivalent analyses — cf. also Hockett 1949, n. 6). See below on the second phase of the Bloomfieldian period.
[44] Chomsky (1957a) catches this note in work of the time, but overgeneralizes it as search for 'discovery procedures' (see discussion of this below). Curiously enough, Chomsky (1957b) criticizes the sensitive and sensible account of the relation between practice and theory in Hockett (1955:143–180) for insufficient objectivity and rigor.
[45] It is to this *second* phase that the frequently used term, 'post-Bloomfieldian', might properly and usefully be applied. The first surge of a distinctive, self-conscious, narrowly focused movement, invoking the name of Bloomfield (cf. Bloch 1949:92 (Hockett 1970:529)), is over and a climate of greater diversity and scope develops. In particular, the relevance of Sapir and Whorf, and their interests, is newly felt, together with an increasing prominence of Jakobson. Cf. Mohrmann et al. (1961), in which the Bloomfield and Sapir traditions are treated in parallel fashion (Fries 1961, Hoijer 1961) and separately from general linguistics (Hamp 1961, in which see especially pp. 165–166). (Cf. also Voegelin 1958b, which begins with a flat statement of the 'general dissatisfaction' expressed over the selections in Joos (1957), and reports alternative titles circulating in the field: 'Blue Book of Linguistic Etiquette', 'Neo-Bloomfieldian Linguistics', 'The Development of Restatement Linguistics in America Since 1925'.)

structurales, was specially noted in *Language* (26(3):443 (1950)), with quotation of part of a letter from Eli Fischer-Jørgensen, and then given a major review by a major link in the development of Bloomfieldian work, Rulon Wells (1951). A review by Hockett (1952b) was perhaps even more an intercontinental stock-taking. Hockett sketches the origins and development of separate traditions in Europe and the United States, summarizes differences, and calls for overcoming the differences (91). By implication, he dissociates himself from a series of unsympathetic reviews of outstanding European works (Harris 1941, Trager 1941); his (Hockett's) own 'completely snide aside' in his 1942 paper (p. 10); a succinct statement of ultra-Bloomfieldian dogma found in a review of works by Hall on the part of W. B. S. Smith (*SIL* 8:5–11 (1950)), presumably expressing views shared by the editor of *SIL*, Trager:

> Again and again it must be reiterated that only a solid sequence of data reliably collected in a fixed way and analyzed according to announced methods based on agreed axioms, step by step, can properly be called scientific;

and what Hockett (89) describes as:

> the last cry from utter despair with our 'benighted' European contemporaries, Trager's one-paragraph review of the volume here under discussion (SIL 8:99 (1950)).

(The last two items in Hockett's catalogue underscore Trager's claim to the role of persistent 'true' Bloomfieldian.)

The significance of Hockett's review is highlighted by the fact that it was the second review of the book to appear in the journal (cf. Garvin 1951). Presumably Hockett submitted it for the purpose of making a personal statement, and the editor printed it as such. As to Hjelmslev particularly, Garvin's lead review in *Language* of an English translation of his major theoretical work is also significant (Garvin 1954).

The views of the Prague School, as represented by Roman Jakobson, become increasingly prominent on the American scene in these years. An important factor is Jakobson's association with anthropology, from his residence with Boas, and association with Lévi-Strauss during the war years in New York, to his participation in anthropological conferences. His contributions to the Anthropology Today conference are found in the volume of discussion (Tax et al. 1953), but European perspectives are prominent in the volume of solicited review papers (Martinet 1953). At a second conference in the same year (1952) Jakobson provides a masterful summation (Jakobson 1953).

Some of the assimilation of European approaches is noted by Weinreich (1959: 323, n. 4) in his review of Hockett's 1958 text, although substantive points noted have earlier dates. (Acceptance of a distinction between 'language' and 'speaking', as equivalent to Saussure's *la langue : la parole* dates from Hockett's review just cited (1952b), and componential features in phonology date from work in the 1940s (Harris 1944, Hockett 1947b).) Not that all European approaches are assimilated at this time; Pandit (1970) rightly complains of neglect of Firth. It is not enough, however, to put the neglect of Firth down to American dogmatism, as Pandit does. In the light of the renewed interest in traditions of Saussurean derivation (Hjelmslev, Prague), some selective factor must have been at work. Since Firth's views must have been at least partly known, through his presence at the 1949 Linguistic Institute, and since anthropologists, so hospitable to Jakobson, were aware of Firth as well (at least in connection with Malinowski), there is a problem here worth investigation (cf. Henson 1974 on the parallel problem in England).

Concurrently with the expansion of intellectual interest geographically, as it were, there is an expansion in substantive, disciplinary scope. Psycholinguistics is christened and launched in summer conferences in 1951 and 1952, and linguistic activity broadens to something like the scope of its inherited anthropological tradition as well, after a few years of published unease (cf. Hymes 1970a:270ff.). Harris had already turned his attention to discourse analysis, introducing it as relevant to the study of culture and personality in a way that descriptive linguistics had not been (Harris 1952a, 1952c; the first paper was given at an anthropological congress held in 1949). Trager, while remaining rigid within descriptive linguistics, promotes the broad ideas of Whorf, and joins with Smith, Birdwhistell, Hall, Hockett, and McQuown in launching study of paralinguistics, kinesics, and communicative behavior generally, along lines broached by Sapir. Both Whorf (alternatively, the 'Sapir-Whorf' hypothesis, or the 'Whorf-Lee' hypothesis), and the psychiatric import of paralinguistics, come to the center of attention; both represent a concern to link the methodological results of linguistics with the general study of man and with human problems. The principal new general approach to linguistic structure, Pike's tagmemics (1954), is expressly linked in its motivation to analysis of cultural behavior as a whole, and linguistics-based approaches to cultural analysis become a staple (cf. Hymes 1970a:277ff.). Ethnographic analysis of semantics, especially of kinship, receives a boost with the launching of 'componential analysis' (in the semantic sense), through papers by Lounsbury and Goodenough in a 1956 issue of *Language* dedicated to Kroeber. General linguistics is pursued in the form of typology, universals, and near-universals, by Hockett, Greenberg, Voegelin, and others, as by Jakobson before them, especially with reference to phonology.[46] The emphasis here, and in psycholinguistics, on universal parameters is in keeping with the general shift of concern to universals in the late 1940s and early 1950s in anthropology. The appeal of linguistics methodologically to anthropology is in part because of its achievement of units at once concrete and universal. Aspects of literature come gradually to attention in discussion of such notions as 'casual

[46] General linguistic questions also arise in connection with the intensified anthropological interest in the evolutionary origins of man and culture (including language) during the 1950s; cf. Voegelin 1951 and Hockett 1959.

speech' (Voegelin), and increasing awareness of structural analysis in folklore, and of work on metrics and style. The historical aspect of the Americanist tradition is given new life in a crucial setting, Berkeley, by Emeneau and Haas, and linked to a highly controversial claim as to method and universality through the work of Swadesh, who turns his attention almost entirely from structure to prehistory. Work of Haugen and Weinreich, with roots in European dialectology and sociology of language, begins to bring questions of diversity of speech community to attention.

The 1950s thus present a picture of many diverse lines of activity, some prominently associated with particular persons, others associated with intersecting circles of friends and colleagues. Debate with regard to models of phonology, morphology, and syntax continue, notions such as juncture come to the fore, new general models are proposed and old ones reconsidered (tagmemics, item and process), but formal models internal to grammar do not appear as an exclusive concern. Indeed, such models do not appear to have quite the same absorbing centrality as before. It is a centrifugal decade.

A student entering linguistics in the United States in the decade would find questions of structural method basic, but not all encompassing. His sense of the field, in terms of mature scholars and role-models, would locate certain linguists as primarily concerned with methodology, with theory in the sense of properties of grammar; but such concern, though commanding attention, would appear as one choice of interest among others. One would expect to have opinions on such matters, and even to contribute something to their discussion; but talent and interest might commit one to the study of any one of a number of aspects of language. There would be no sense of intrinsically secondary, let alone marginal, status in such a commitment. The leading methodological theorists themselves showed varying degrees of interest in such a range of questions.

This climate of opinion did not change with the publication of *Syntactic structures* in 1957. For a few years, Chomsky's views on methodology and structure were regarded as a new position within that sphere, but not as changing, or challenging, the scope of the field as a whole (cf. Hamp 1961:172, and Joos 1961:17, 19, in the context of the whole in each case). Constriction was to come later. At a Linguistic Institute in 1959, a well-known scholar could confidently offer the judgment that Chomsky had some good ideas, but a great deal to learn. The effort of Chomsky and others to redefine the admissible scope and content of linguistic analysis and theory took some years to crest. A reasonable demarcation might be the year of the Ninth International Congress of Linguists, held in Cambridge in 1962, when Chomsky gave the plenary address on linguistic structure, Harris having declined. Even then, Postal (1964:115, n. 149) was to remark a bit later:

I cannot imagine what gives Halliday the severely incorrect idea that a general abandonment of pre-transformational ideas in favor of the approach suggested by Chomsky is taking place in the United States. Neither the journals nor public meetings give this impression to me.

It is important to notice that Chomsky's views were far from full-fledged in 1957. They had not acquired the distinctive phonology, or interest in universals, mediated by Halle out of Jakobson, nor had the methodological position been elaborated into a rejection of the content of social reality and the methods of social science. In 1957 Chomsky's work might appear to be to a great extent a victory for one Bloomfieldian approach to syntax (that of Harris) as against another (that of Trager, Smith, et al.) (cf. Chomsky 1964c, reprinted from the Texas Conference published in 1958). Certainly no departure from official Bloomfieldian canons of objectivity and observables appears in this 1957 chastisement of a backslider (Chomsky 1957b:233, n. 14):

> We touch here on fundamental questions, which have never been adequately treated, and which are related to what Hockett calls 'the fundamental assumption in phonology', namely, that 'the speakers of a language themselves hear some speech-events as the same, some as different', regardless of articulatory variation (p. 144). Put this way, the assumption says very little. We might replace it by a definition of the 'ultimate phonological constituents' for a given language as the phonetic features that distinguish utterance tokens not connected by matching chains, i.e., those that characterize the sets of tokens formed by collapsing these chains. It should then be possible to set up empirical tests to determine whether voicing, but not rate of speed, would qualify as a phonological feature for English. For a very penetrating study of the background and methods for investigations of this sort, see N. Goodman, The Structure of Appearance (Cambridge, 1951), especially Part III).

And again (233, section 10):

> I can see no justification for the position that objectivity in linguistics is in principle something different from objectivity in physical science (p. 211), and that the basic methods in linguistics are empathy and intuition. In linguistics, as in every sufficiently complicated science, the process of discovery, of gaining familiarity with the data, of forming hypotheses, and so forth is very difficult to describe; we can do little more than say that it may involve a large measure of intuition. There must, however, be objective criteria for the validation and justification of grammars, if linguistics is to be a serious science. This can only mean that linguistic theory must be constructed with *explicit and precise definitions and operational tests* [emphasis supplied]. The construction of such a theory should be the major goal of methodological work. It may be that grammatical research can best be described as the attempt to reconstruct precisely and explicitly the 'linguistic intuition' of the native speaker. But it does not follow from this that grammatical theory itself must be based on intuition. In fact only a *completely objective* theory in which empathy, prejudices, unanalyzed notions of 'phonetic realism', and so on, play no part will have any real value as an explanation of 'linguistic intuition'.

The hand perhaps begins to emerge as the hand of the mature Chomsky, but the voice — the use of 'operational tests' and 'completely objective', the placing of 'linguistic intuition' in quotes, the disdain for subjective factors on the part of the analyst — the voice is Bloomfieldian. Here is the passage by Hockett objected to in the second quotation (Hockett 1955:211):

> For a linguist (or a student of any other phase of culture) to be 'objective' means something rather different than for a physical scientist to be 'objective'. A linguist does not

attain usable 'objectivity', in analyzing a given language, merely by abandoning his own personal prejudices: in addition, he must acquire those of the native speaker of the language.

Chomsky seems also to have reference to a passage on p. 147:

> ... the analyst must *empathize,* must to some extent learn the language with which he is working. We know of no set of procedures by which a Martian, or a machine, could analyze a phonologic system — an entity, that is, to which even the basic biologic and cultural common denominator of humanness would be alien and would require specification. The only procedures which can be described are rules for a human investigator, and depend essentially on his ability to empathize. To refuse to do this, to insist on avoiding it as much as possible in the name of a spurious 'objectivity' — as, for example, Franz Boas did — is to place oneself much in the same position as that of a bacteriologist who would refuse to stain his slides.

If students today were asked to match these passages from the book and the review with their authors, Chomsky or Hockett, one wonders how often they would succeed.[47]

In sum, the Bloomfieldian period extends perhaps two decades, from about 1940 until sometime early in the 1960s. One can imagine a curve, or 'life-cycle', from a first distinctive thrust, through a time of centrality, to a time of replacement. Such a curve of course overlaps the curve one might trace for the Chomskyan approach. Its beginning would be about 1957, through a time of centrality beginning in the early 1960s, to uncertain signs of replacement on the present horizon. The curves are alike in that the time of centrality of each has two phases. There is a first phase, intensive forward thrust: the 1940s for the Bloomfieldian model, and roughly the 1960s for the Chomskyan model (really perhaps about 1957–1968). There is the second phase, in which original momentum wanes; a variety of alternative conceptions, and individual directions of interest, come to the fore, although the initial phase continues to define common terms of reference. In the first phase there is, so to speak, a single frontier, and in the second phase, a common base of operations.

In both cases the first phase, although unified in terms of a central direction, shows some internal diversity of conception on close examination. The second

---

[47] Hockett's views in the 1955 monograph are consistent with those of Hockett (1949). Cf. the following passage (quoted from V. Makkai 1972:208): 'Regardless of how much rationalization of analytical procedures we may indulge in, there is an irreducible minimum of *language-learning* involved in any linguistic field project. An entity cannot function as a linguistic field worker and analyst unless it is endowed with the language-learning apparatus and ability that human beings have, which implies, of course, that for the present only human beings can be trained as linguists – we cannot yet construct a machine to analyze languages on the basis of the really raw data which comes from the lips of speakers.' In the 1955 monograph Hockett concluded that work with sound spectrographs demonstrated that such a machine (and hence any literally algorithmic discovery procedure) was impossible. As the beginning of the passage quoted above makes clear, he at no time thought that linguistic theory provided, or could provide, such a procedure for use in field work.

phase shows increasing diversity of direction and scope.

Polarized conceptions of either Bloomfieldian or Chomskyan work are thus inadequate. They get both continuities and contrasts wrong, and assume a non-existent consistent unity. The fault appears most notably in discussions of Bloomfieldian work. As we have seen, it had not one, but two, unifying goals: (1) to establish formal, explicit analysis of linguistic structure, and (2) to relate analysis of linguistic structure to analysis of the rest of social life. These goals came successively to the fore (the second goal, rooted in the anthropological tradition and Sapirian heritage, may be said to have been latent during the 1940s). Historiographic writing, and disciplinary opinion, concentrate attention on work concerned with the first goal. The second goal has been noticed in the context of the history of anthropology (cf. Hymes 1970a) and of sociolinguistics (cf. Neustupný 1974), but generally has been missed.

The diversity and development over time of Bloomfieldian work are important to attempts to explain it in the light of subsequent orientations. We now turn to some additional aspects of Bloomfieldian work in the context of attempts to explain it.

5.3   Explanations of Bloomfieldian Work

5.3.1   Introduction

We come to a point at which it is clear that explanation of Bloomfieldian work must come to terms with personal histories and personal styles, and with the dynamics of their interaction. The work was not static, but was developing into something other than its initial, 'classic', form of the 1940s. In particular, it was becoming transformational in method in one major line of work, and enriched in content and relevance in several. Had Harris' most original student remained of the opinions expressed in his first book (1957a), and in reviews of that year (1957b, 1957c), one would have had a new phase of formal linguistics, but not, we judge, a 'revolution' in linguistics as a whole. The personal history which led to Chomsky's acceptance of a rationalist intuitive epistemology, and of Prague phonology, in addition to Harrisian formalization; and the personal style which led to amalgamation of these in the service of an 'eclipsing stance' that out-Tragered Trager, and captured a generation; these facts of history and style might have been different. The growth in scope of linguistics which we associate with the 1960s, in the sense of investigation of syntax, and then semantics, may be considered to have been more or less inevitable, but not the form in which growth came.

The dependence of the form of the change on personal factors does not detract from Chomsky's importance. Quite the contrary: to stress that the outcome was not inevitable is to stress how important the central actor was. To be sure, to recognize the importance of a historical figure, whose actions have been of great consequence, is not the same thing as to assess those consequences, and to discriminate between ultimate benefits and costs. Suffice it to say here that we find costs, as well as benefits, in the major changes of the 1960s, just as we find benefits, as well as costs, in the major changes of the Bloomfieldian years. What we want to insist upon is that the change from years one speaks of as 'Bloomfieldian' to years which one speaks of as 'Chomskyan' was a specific historical process, or series of events, contingent upon factors of persons, institutions, opportunities, cultural trends, and the like, as are all historical changes.

We insist upon this obvious point because the principal tendency in historiographic writing and comment among linguists has been to describe the change as the replacement of one set of ideas by another (which of course occurred), in such a way as to make the one period seem all of one stripe, the other of another (recall n. 34), and the change itself to depend entirely upon the presence in the one of ideas absent in the other. And this will not do. To a very great extent, ideas associated with the Chomskyan movement are present in the Bloomfieldian period, and not only present, but advocated strongly against some of the period's more salient views. Insofar as Chomsky's success consists of the introduction of ideas, that success must be analyzed into two components: those ideas which were introduced to the center of attention from the periphery, as against those ideas which had not been specifically present at all. And cross-cutting this distinction is another, between those ideas whose role proves to have been essentially ideological and sociological (specific to the success of the movement), and those ideas whose role proves to have been permanently cumulative. A characterization of ideas in the Chomskyan period would be completed by drawing a large circle around the box just described — the circle would contain the many ideas and interests peripheral during the period of Chomskyan dominance.

This heuristic model applies to any period, of course, and applies to the Bloomfieldian period. As instances of the contents of the four inner categories, one can mention immediate constituent (IC) analysis (something specific brought to the center of attention in the period); phonological syntax (something specific and new in the period); structural analysis of units and components of units (something permanent brought to the center of attention in the period); formal, explicit models of linguistic structure (something permanent and new in the period).

Our purpose in this section is to consider more closely the contents of the circle of ideas present in the Bloomfieldian period, as against widespread tendencies in the explanation of the period. Having considered these ideas, we can delimit the range of possible explanations, and indeed suggest factors fundamental to any explanation.

Sufficient studies of individual scholars and topics are lacking, but we can indicate the presence of strong criticism of salient 'Bloomfieldian' ideas within the period, and then show the presence of a number of ideas and interests continuous with salient 'Chomskyan' views.

The philosophical aspect of a religious or political conviction, and loyalty to practical experience, could sustain independence from a dominant trend in the Bloomfieldian as in other periods. The themes of the trenchant critique of anti-mentalism by Swadesh (1948a) are worth pondering. Swadesh analyzed inconsistencies of Bloomfield, and Bloch and Trager, in attempting to avoid use of meaning as evidence of a struggle 'between the fact that meaning is an inseparable aspect of language and the fetish that anything related to the mind must be ruled out of science'. Against the dictum that meaning must wait for analysis until definable in scientific, referential detail, Swadesh pointed out (as did Haugen and Weinreich later) that 'languages are spoken by people who have no such minute and verified knowledge of the whole universe'. As to reliance on observation, rather than the tacit knowledge of native speakers, he states:

It is characteristic of the linguistic mechanists that they have great confidence in the scientist and none in the native speakers of the language, [but] the judgement of the speaker proves to be valuable to the scientist even in the case of subtler problems.

The charge of vicious circularity was a shibboleth in Bloomfieldian argument (comparable to the role of the charge of 'discovery procedure' among Chomskyans). Swadesh maintained that, first, inferences from observable behavior to unobservable 'mind' are like inferences from known to reconstructed languages made by Bloomfieldians themselves (Spitzer had urged the same argument); and, second, such a philosophy of science is inadequate in terms of the very natural sciences it seeks to emulate. It is not considered objectionably 'mentalistic' to speak of atoms and alpha particles, even though they are known mainly by their effects.

This Sapirian critique in a Marxist journal had little effect, and its existence has been generally overlooked. The running challenge to dominant notions provided by Pike has been generally recognized, but not seen as a challenge to historiography. Perhaps one generation of Whig-minded interpreters of history accepts the judgment of another in this regard. Pike is conspicuously absent from rather catholic bibliographic footnotes in Harris (1951a) (thus in n. 1 on p. 59, the citation of literature stops with an article by Swadesh in *Language* (1947) on the analysis of English syllabics, failing to mention an article by Pike, on the same subject, on immediately following pages (cf. V. Makkai 1972:145 for the Pike article)). Hockett (1949) first makes a bow to the practical purposes for which Pike works, and the exigencies they represent, then blasts the theoretical implications of his approach. Joos (1957) includes nothing by Pike. Pike's articles critical of salient Bloomfieldian tenets (particularly on 'grammatical prerequisites') appeared in *Word*, a journal with a strong European and Sapirian orientation (Martinet, Swadesh, and then Greenberg, being principal editors in the 1940s). The fact that Pike, like Nida, *had* to be concerned with analytical procedures as practical devices, and that both were missionaries, worked to deprive their ideas of official acceptance, although together they shaped a very great part of what linguists in the United States actually learned of practical work. (Hymes recalls a lecture at the Linguistic Institute of 1959, at which Pike asked the speaker, Bloch, how his formal principles could work without taking into account meaning; Bloch turned his back and did not answer; on the other hand, Bloch abandoned use of zero-morphemes in English inflection as a consequence of criticism of them by Nida (1948).)

The criticisms advanced by Swadesh and Pike show such ideas were not absent among Bloomfieldians, and that the presence of such ideas was not in itself sufficient. These ideas were not truths such that to know them was to be forced to accept them. Timing, relative to the immediate dynamic of felt progress, and auspices, relative to accepted scientific ideology and occupation, were crucial. (It may be that the productive ideas of a given period are *always* present peripherally in the period that precedes.) An explanation of the continued marginality of Pike's ideas, offered by Hymes (1964d:46, n. 7) has been endorsed by Hall (1969:224, n. 4):

The complex of reasons for the impact of Chomsky in 1957, as against the lack of impact of Pike in 1947–54, may have to do with the span of time needed for 'pattern exhaustion' and Young Turk restlessness to set in; the dramatic superiority of sharp rejection to revisionism; the superiority in prestige and rhetorical effect of criticism couched in mathematics to criticism appealing to facts of experience; the marginal position in intellectual politics of a scholar associated notably both with missionary work and practical skills; and facets of personality (one colleague observed, 'You can't fight arrogance with humility').

Most accounts of the Bloomfieldian work treat its most salient, novel thrust, of course, not its contemporary critics (in the 1940s) or its self-criticism and evolution (in the 1950s). Some accounts are quite specifically, and properly, directed to technical comparison of analyses and the assumptions on which they rest (though such accounts face historiographic problems that will be taken up in the next chapter). Some accounts reflect what we believe to be a widespread impression, namely, that Bloomfieldian work was in some serious sense essentially lacking in theory — lacking in the right kind of theory, certainly, and, one often finds stated or assumed, any real theory at all. (We have noted Teeter (1964) in this regard; Teeter still holds that the period lacked theory (correspondence to Fought).)

A number of themes enter into this characterization of Bloomfieldian work. Most of them are summarized in a fairly representative way in the abstract to Koerner (1970a). In one sense Koerner grants theory to the Bloomfieldians, for he speaks of (162) 'the theoretical bias so characteristic of many eminent linguists of the post-Bloomfieldian era'. The statement suggests that he distinguishes theory in the sense of general philosophy of science from theory that is specifically linguistic. But theory in this sense is almost the same as no theory, so far as the Bloomfieldians are concerned, for he goes on to contrast 'their general data-orientation' to the Chomskyan 'general theory orientation':

Their general data-orientation with a strong emphasis on speech in conjunction with a rejection of any 'mentalistic' speculation about semantic implications, which could not readily be expressed in formalized linguistic terms, fostered an almost complete disregard for linguistic theorizing and led many of them to the 'post-Bloomfieldian fallacy' (Teeter) of taking rigorous data-manipulation for theory. The Chomskyan emphasis on syntax as against the levels of morphology and phonology as well as its general theory orientation has in fact widened the scope of the discussion of linguistic issues by including logic, psychology, mathematics and other fields of epistemological relevance for the explanation of language problems.

The term 'data-orientation' might better be put as *inductive* orientation — a general inductive idiom, and widespread inductive attitude —; and the point as to levels of structure emphasized might better be put as levels of structure reached; but together these two traits, an inductive orientation focused on phonology and morphology, go far to characterizing, and explaining, what was distinctive in the main thrust of Bloomfieldian work, and go together. (Thus, when Matthews (1972: 112) contrasts evaluation in terms of 'the way we arrived at an analysis' (his quotes) to the Chomskyan evaluation within the total context of description, he is of course correct, but evaluation within total context is interdependent with having arrived at a stage at which total description can be reasonably assessed, and no stage before a syntax containing transformational relationships could be such.)

The other traits noted by Koerner do not go together in the way they are often taken to apply to Bloomfieldian work, and, by implication, to explain it. (To characterize Bloomfieldian work in a way that makes it the apparent opposite of Chomskyan work often seems to imply an explanation of why it was succeeded by Chomskyan work, as if good ideas necessarily drive out bad.) Specifically, rejection of mentalism; disregard for linguistic theorizing; exclusion of logic, mathematics, and psychology from relevance to linguistic models or orientation; exclusion of fields relevant to explanation; mistaking data-manipulation for theory — these ingredients of an image of Bloomfieldian work do not explain it, for they do not consistently characterize it nor consistently distinguish it from its successor at the center of the stage.

5.3.2   *Rejection of 'mentalism'*

We have seen already that a number of prominent linguists in the period by no means rejected a concept of 'mind' (Swadesh, Pike, Nida, and others). The significance that 'mentalism' had for those leaders of Bloomfieldian work who eschewed it is clearly stated by Bloch (1949 [in Hockett 1970:531]):

In his long campaign to make a science of linguistics, the chief enemy that Bloomfield met was that habit of thought which is called mentalism: the habit of appealing to mind and will as ready-made explanations of all possible problems. Most men regard this habit as obvious common sense; but in Bloomfield's view, as in that of other scientists, it is mere superstition, unfruitful as best and deadly when carried over into scientific research.

What was at stake, in short, was the possibility of a science at all: the possibility of taking as problematic, exploring, and proving linguistic phenomena, rather than having inquiry cut off by conventional habits of explanation. We may agree that many babies were thrown out with this particular bath water; during the 1940s, the penchant to avoid such 'mentalism', by restricting attention to factors within the range of observation, reached puristic heights far in excess of anything advocated or practiced by Bloomfield himself. The positive implementation on the part of some became extreme, but the negative function, that of separating linguistic science from linguistic misconceptions, and justifying scientific inquiry into language, was shared by linguists of quite different persuasions on the subject of 'mind' itself. Nida (1949) is an excellent illustration of this (cf. also his book, *Linguistic interludes*, as reviewed by Hockett (1944)). An essential part of Nida's textbook is to teach students to make statements about linguistic matters without introduction of non-linguistic material. This is the practical, permanent core of the lesson which Bloch ascribed to Bloomfield (1949 [in Hockett 1970:530–531] see above at end of 4.4). Many members of the present generation, inhabiting a profession already twice established, feel free to link technical argument with considerable playfulness and self-expression, but it is not surprising that a generation still working to establish a profession's claim to a place in the academic sun should regard chasteness of style and thought as an essential virtue. It was so regarded for its own sake, by scholars of diverse views on specific metascientific issues, and it served as a device of boundary maintenance for the movement of which all were a part. Insofar as rejection of 'mentalism' had a common denominator in the period, it was in terms of such an idiom.

We should perhaps repeat, and so insist on, this point. For some, eschewal of 'mind' was not only verbal, but also ontological, or at least epistemological, from the standpoint of some form of empiricist perspective. Some linguists, that is, answered to the sweeping generalization (Teeter 1964:201) that the thrust of the period was to 'drop the assumption of mind, or at the least to reduce it, to the sum total of human input-output correlations'; or, as put by Katz (1964:128), 'taxonomic linguists have denied that theoretical concepts in a linguistic theory can have psychological reality'. But there were many who made no such denial, and many who might have said simply that theoretical concepts *need* not have psychological reality. Katz's and Teeter's generalizations on this point can most charitably be described as ignorant.

For some scholars, eschewal of 'mind' went together with a conventionalist, or neopositivist, view of the status of linguistic analyses. Bierwisch (1971:43–44) notes this position, and finds its alternative equally untenable because of rejection of mentalist notions. Here is how he puts the matter:

Some have held the view that the structures found are merely a useful convention for concisely summarizing the data but do not describe any objective facts. This view corresponds exactly to the neopositivist theory of science, and echoes the views of the neogrammarians, but on a structuralist basis. Others have taken a more 'realistic' view and have regarded the grammar resulting from analysis as a reflection of objective properties of the language analyzed. This led to a new dilemma: how could their findings be objective, when, according to their own objections against mentalistic notions, the only rational explanation, *viz*.: that grammar is the description of the linguistic competence of the speaker, is excluded?

Let us leave aside here the methodological issues involved in attaining objectivity in linguistic analysis — issues far from resolved today (cf. Labov 1970, Derwing 1973) — and note only that insofar as objectivity requires the assumption that analysis answers to an internal ability of speakers, many Bloomfieldians met the requirement. The discussion of productivity a little later in this part provides evidence of this within the heart of the Bloomfieldian camp. To be sure, the Bloomfieldians do not speak of 'competence', but of such things as 'underlying habits' (Hockett 1952b:98); but the point at issue is not the specific psychological interpretation of speakers' abilities, but the factor location inside speakers of a test of validity. For a particular model of a speaker's abilities, one could entertain a variety of hypotheses as to its relation to acquisition, consciousness, and other aspects of psychological theory.

It is not 'mentalism', then, that makes the difference to linguistic theory, but the model of internal ability. Chomsky himself first stressed this technical point against all structuralist comers, mentalist and non-mentalist alike. Only later was the point as to adequacy of model identified with broad psychological and philosophical dispositions (see discussion of *process* below). Bierwisch comes to this point at the end of his discussion (1971:44); it is the one valid part of the discussion.

For some, rejection of 'mentalism' might imply rejection of the intuitions of a native speaker, but it is clear that many linguists in the period strongly opposed such an implication. Pike's insistence on native speaker reaction is well known (1947a, 1947b, 1952, 1954); Hoijer (1958) brings together a number of observations and references. The insistence on the difference between theory and practice in Hockett (1949), Bloch (1948), Harris (1951a), and others allowed for considerable unofficial recourse to native speaker judgment, and meaning, and Hockett consistently regarded analysis to entail becoming something of a native speaker through language-learning (cf. n. 41).

For some, rejection of 'mentalism' might imply rejection of the use or study of meaning, but this view was never general, as we have seen, and it became increasingly unimportant, after the initial flare-up around the turn of the mid-century.[48]

---

[48]   Here is Hockett on the fatal defect of a purely distributionalist program (i.e., one that makes no appeal to meaning, but considers only forms) (1950): '. . . if no additional criteria [other than those used in phonological analysis] are involved, one does not get on to anything that can properly be called "morphology" or "grammar" at all, but simply continues to discuss phenomena or large size-levels on the phonological basis'. In a review of Harris' book, Hockett (1952a) was open-minded but with a choice of words implying considerable skepticism: Harris takes two essential steps beyond Bloomfield's system; only time can tell whether they are steps forward or into some *cul-de-sac*. The first of these is that we are quite explicitly told how to determine

Indeed, Bloomfieldian linguistics in its second phase participates in the general revival of cognitive interests in the 1950s, a revival that occurred *before*, and to a great extent, independently of Chomsky, or in ways contrary to his views. Psycholinguistics develops in this period through the work of Osgood, Bruner, Brown, Carroll, Lenneberg, and others (Brown (1958) is an excellent presentation of a cognitive psychology informed by linguistics and ethnography before Chomsky's advent). Interrelated work in linguistics and ethnography (often called 'ethnolinguistic' in the period) is represented by discussion of Whorf early in the 1950s, and by work in semantic description such as that of Fries (1954), Garvin (1958), Goodenough (1956), Hockett (1948b), Hoijer (1951b), Lounsbury (1956), Newman (1954), Nida (1949, ch. 6; 1958), Pike (1967 = 1954), Voegelin (1948b, 1952d, 1958a), Wells (1954, 1958), and Wonderly (1957).

Finally, it is not clear that attitudes toward meaning were of any consequence, so far as the contrast between Bloomfieldian work and Chomskyan work is concerned. Those structuralists of the time who *did* accept mind, meaning, and semantic inquiry did not develop models with the features considered essential to that developed by Chomsky; yet such structuralists were perhaps a majority, even a large majority, in the world at the time.[49] Chomsky, on the other hand, did not himself deal initially with meaning, or semantics. He continued the Harrisian separation of syntax from semantics, and the common Bloomfieldian postponement of semantics to a later level and stage of investigation (cf. Chomsky 1955, 1957a, ch. 9).

Attitudes toward meaning did eventually change, and in the long run the result is an important difference from earlier work; but it is hard to see that such attitudes played a significant role in the change from Bloomfieldian to Chomskyan dominance.

The story of the term 'mentalism' thus has considerable irony. Often invoked as the key term in explanation of the history of modern linguistics in the United States, it would seem to explain more the color than the content of the subject. (Of course it does not at all explain the relation between Chomskyan linguistics, on the one hand, and the linguistics of Geneva, Prague, Copenhagen, London, Moscow, on the other.) The term was used negatively to avoid an approach and idiom that would short-circuit inquiry into linguistic facts (as indicated in the quotation from Bloch's obituary of Bloomfield). Later such usage would seem to some (Teeter 1964:201) 'an epithet whose use has since helped to short-circuit innumerable attempts at getting behind linguistic facts'. It would seem, however, that the purpose for which Bloomfield and others adopted the term was achieved

---

sameness or difference in sound; the second is that Bloomfield's other fundamental element – meaning – is eliminated entirely.'

[49]   Cf. Swadesh (1948:259): 'It would be interesting to have some concrete measure of the extent to which mechanical materialism pervades American linguistics today. I believe the mechanists tend to be credited with being much more numerous and representative than they actually are.'

by 'mentalists' and 'anti-mentalists' alike in the Bloomfieldian period, and continued in the Chomskyan period. Chomskyan work does not seek what Bloch opposed, ready-made explanations of linguistic facts in terms of 'mind' (cf. Katz 1964:125, on 'theologized mentalism'). Some Chomskyan are tempted into this practice, but the course of research remains essentially one of appeal to linguistic facts and relationships, i.e., to grammar. Indeed, if one replaced 'range of observation' in Bloch's statement by 'range of access' (thus encompassing access to intuitions), Bloch's statement is not far from adequate to current goals of inquiry. The commitment to linguistics as an empirical science is shared. And inferences from linguistic evidence to mental states on entities remains a problem for the Chomskyan point of view.

There are changes in attitude toward 'mentalism', of course, that are associated with decisive change in practice. These changes have to do with the nature and role of mentally available data, and with conceptions of the power of mind (or, internal ability). As a starting point for formal analysis and theory, observational data, commonly equated with phonological data, was replaced by intuitive data, commonly equated with syntactic relationships. Existing models of linguistic structure and internal ability were found inadequate. To assess these changes, we need first to consider the frequently repeated themes of an absence of theory in Bloomfieldian linguistics, and of an absence of the kind of theory associated with logic and mathematics. We can consider these themes together in terms of senses, or connotations, of the term 'generative'.

5.3.3 *Absence of 'theory': 'Generative aspects'*

The statement 'almost complete disregard for linguistic theorizing' (Koerner 1970a:162) describes a widespread impression. The first thing to say is that the Bloomfieldian linguists thought they were concerned with linguistic theory, and in his initial critique of their work, so did Chomsky. A major early paper (1958) begins:

The approach to syntax that I want to discuss here developed directly out of the attempts of Z. S. Harris to extend methods of linguistic analysis to the analysis of the structure of discourse. This research brought to light a serious inadequacy of MODERN LINGUISTIC THEORY, namely, its inability to account for such systematic relations between sentences as the active-passive relation. (Emphasis supplied)

To be sure, the word 'theory' is far less common in work of the period (recall discussion of genres in (5.1)), but it did occur (some references to its use are given in (5.1)). And one must note that other words with the same import were in use, notably 'system' (Hockett 1942, Wells 1947), 'postulates' (Bloch 1948), and 'model' (Hockett 1954, Harris 1959). It is perhaps a reflection of lexical change in the profession that Harris speaks of 'grammar' and 'structure', then 'model' of structure, then 'theory' in successive titles (1954a, 1954b, 1959, 1965), although the essential substantive concerns remain much the same. (We do not know in detail the terminological history of the period, and it is something that would repay study.)

The first requirement, the presupposition, of theory in the modern sense would presumably be taken to be an explicit, formal model of language structure. Most linguists today would speak of such a model as being in some sense *'generative'*. Matthews (1972:8ff.) distinguishes two senses of the term. The wider sense is described in this way:

... the modern concept of generative grammar is the continued search for mathematically precise and exhaustive presentation. ...

The narrow sense refers to:

... any set of rules — or formalized statements about a language — which may be interpreted as defining, specifying or 'generating' some particular set of formal objects.

Matthews identifies the concept 'generative' with Chomsky and his followers, saying (8, n. 5) that brief suggestions may be traced back at least to Harris (1951a: 372–373). The Harris pages do contain a statement of grammar as a formal object that read remarkably like statements associated with Chomsky's work (we have quoted the statement in discussing Harris); but does one need close verbal parallelism to see that the entire book answers to both the wider (common) and narrower senses of 'generative'? What else can *Methods in structural linguistics* as a whole be said to be concerned with, if not with formalized statements interpretible as defining a set of formal objects, as the grammar of a language, and (in the wider sense), continued search for mathematically precise and exhaustive presentation? (Where indeed does one suppose Chomsky received stimulation to work toward such goals?)

Other work toward explicit models of linguistic structure and linguistic analysis in the Bloomfieldian period falls within the scope of the proffered definitions of 'generative'. It is difficult to miss the thrust of the concluding statement of Bloch (1948):

Whoever prefers a different transcription (not merely one resulting from a different set of conventions) must show either that our analysis violates one or more of the postulates that we have stated, or else that these postulates are untenable. If he takes the latter position, we may reasonably ask him to state his own assumptions in equal detail, and put off all argument until he has done so.

The tone is much the same as that of transformational grammarians a decade or so later, setting 'notational variants' aside as not the issue, and challenging critics to show that models of their own will account for the data in question with equal explicitness, or hold their peace. The tone presupposes that explicit theory is prerequisite to debate as to validity.

Again, Hockett (1954) elaborates 'metacriteria' needed for the evaluation of models underlying grammatical descriptions. He states five criteria:

(1) A model must be *general*: it must be applicable to any language, not just to languages of certain types.

(2) A model must be *specific*: when applied to a given language, the results must be determined wholly by the nature of the model and the nature of the language, not at all by the whim of the analyst. . . .

(3) A model must be *inclusive*: when applied to a given language, the results must cover all the observed data, and, by implication, at least a very high percentage of all the not-yet-observed data. . . .

(4) A model must be *productive*: when applied to a given language, the results must make possible the creation of an indefinite number of valid new utterances. This is the analog of the 'prescriptive' criterion for descriptions.

(5) A model must be *efficient*: its application to any given language should achieve the necessary results with a minimum of machinery.

Hockett concludes that neither of the two main types of model available at the time (item and arrangement, item and process) is completely satisfactory, and that there must be more experimentation with each (and devising of further models as well), looking towards an eventual reintegration into a single more nearly satisfactory model, but not forcing that reintegration until ready for it.

This conception of criteria for evaluation of competing models, in terms both of specific grammars and of general types of grammar, was widely read and discussed, and of course preceded published work on the subject by Chomsky. In fact, Chomsky cited the precedent (1962, n. 27 (from a 1958 conference)), and also spoke sympathetically at about the same time of the efforts toward the goal of explicit formalization by Greenberg (Chomsky 1959). If by generative theory, then, one means explicit, formal theory, it is a whopping error to identify the concept with Chomsky and his followers. The term, yes, but the substance, no. This error appears to be widespread in linguistic opinion today; it is one of the rare flaws in Matthews' excellent book.

The character, and failing, of the Bloomfieldian period has been explained by some noted linguists in terms of another idea sometimes associated with 'generative'. Bloomfieldian linguistics might have worked at explicit, formal models, but, according to this view, it did not take into account an essential property of language, its *productivity*. (This aspect of explanation is of course part of the general contrast drawn between 'behaviorist' and 'mentalist' approaches.) Bierwisch (1971: 45) makes this point central to the change from 'American linguistics' (ch. 6) to 'Generative grammar' (ch. 7). Bierwisch writes:

The theory centres on the following simple but essential observation. Whoever speaks a natural language does not simply carry around in his head a long list of words or sentences which he has stored, but is able to form new sentences and to understand utterances he has never heard before. The command of language is thus a productive capacity, not merely the knowledge of an extensive nomenclature. . . . The central question with which linguistic theory is concerned must in view of this productivity be: what is the basis of the ability to form and understand sentences?

There is no doubt that Chomsky made this notion central to the orientation of many linguists. Two implications of Bierwisch's account, however, are false. Chomsky's approach may have come to center on the notion, but it did not begin with it. His initial case to the linguistic public is argued in terms of the adequacy, or inadequacy, of competing formal notions of the concept of grammar. Here is what Chomsky had to say about theory in one of his early, major publications (from a conference in Texas among competing approaches to syntax) (1962, section X):

. . . The central notion to be defined in linguistic theory is, I believe, the notion *grammar of L* for an arbitrary natural language *L*. A grammar of *L* is a device which enumerates the sentences of *L* in such a way that a structural description can be mechanically derived for each enumerated sentence.

And:

The formal definition of *grammar* in general linguistic theory, that is, the careful specification of the form of grammars and the descriptive devices available for grammars . . .;

further,

I have suggested that it can be profitable to conceive of a grammar of L as a theory of the sentences of L and to consider the methodological problem of linguistics to be the construction of a general theory of linguistic structure in which the properties of grammars, and of the structural descriptions and linguistic levels derived from them, are studied in an abstract way.

(Quoted from section X, as reprinted in Katz and Fodor 1964:240, 241, 245.)

Secondly, this simple but essential observation was present through the whole of the development of modern linguistics in the United States, from Bloomfield through the Bloomfieldians, and when it seemed to be lost from view, or denied, was explicitly reasserted (by Hockett and Bloch among others). The reference point is Bloomfield (1926), where the fourth definition reads:

The totality of utterances that can be made in a speech-community is the *language* of that speech community.

We are obliged to predict; hence the words 'can be made'. We say that under certain stimuli a Frenchman (or Zulu, etc.) will say so-and-so and other Frenchmen (or Zulus, etc.) will react appropriately to his speech. Where good informants are available, or for the investigator's own language, the prediction is easy; elsewhere it constitutes the greatest difficulty of descriptive linguistics.

Apart from the term 'stimuli' (which could be reinterpreted to go beyond 'external stimuli', as has been done by some psychologists), it is difficult to see that Bloomfield's fourth definition differs essentially from the point at which Chomsky was to arrive four decades later (Chomsky 1966). Bloomfield's statement might even be taken to go beyond Chomsky, since it considers not only prediction of possible appropriate utterances, but also the features of situations which enter into judgment of appropriateness (cf. Hymes 1971b).

Subsequent linguists called attention to this property of language, commonly under the heading employed by Bierwisch, 'productivity', although Wells (1949) christened it "the Principle of Derivative Meaning' (discussed in Hymes 1964d), in relation to more specific accounts of it by Bertrand Russell and others. To be sure, there was neglect of the implications of the property sometimes, a fact reflected in Nida (1948 (Joos 1957:264)):

As descriptive linguists we are sometimes inclined to overlook such a dynamic aspect of the language [as the productiveness or non-productiveness of a formation]. We tend to imply that productiveness is only a diachronic fact, but it may be a synchronic reality as well.([32]) In syntax it is essential to recognize that the limits of the distribution of many constructions cannot be fixed, as far as the possible collocations of morphemes are concerned; for otherwise a speaker would only be able to repeat verbatim the phrases which he had previously heard.

Nida's note (32) goes on to say:

Any body of material sufficiently extensive to serve adequately as a basis for descriptive analysis must include fluctuations of forms, which are symptomatic of different degrees of acceptability. Synchronic contrasts of this kind are closely allied to contrasts of productivity vs. non-productivity.

In his note (1) Hockett adds a statement parallel to the Chomskian analysis of the factor in language.

Suggestions that the task of the linguist was limited to a corpus were publicly rejected by leading Bloomfieldians. Hockett jumped on a short review by a student associated with Harris to write, in part (1948:269 (Joos 1957:279)):

The task of the structural linguist, as a scientist, is, as Preston implies, essentially one of classification. The purpose, however, is not simply to account for all the utterances which comprise his corpus at a given time; a simple alphabetical list would do that. Rather, the analysis of the linguistic *scientist* is to be of such a nature that the linguist can account also for utterances which are *not* in his corpus at a given time. That is, as a result of his examination he must be able to predict what *other* utterances the speakers of the language might produce, and, ideally, the circumstances under which those other utterances might be produced.([1])

In his note (1) Hockett adds a statement parallel to the Chomskian analysis of the structure underlying novel utterances without investigation of the features that govern appropriateness:

Attempts to include prediction of the circumstances (except in terms of preceding utterances) constitute semantic analysis. Structural analysis can be scientific without being semantic.

Hockett's rejection of any implication that linguistics is a corpus-confined game is warmly endorsed by Bloch (1950:87, n. 6), who refers to 'the admirable statement by . . . Hockett'. Bloch himself, in the context of a discussion of phonology, writes:

. . . the analyst's task is to describe the system in a coherent set of general statements which will enable him to predict the phonetic shape of utterances that have not yet occurred.

The thrust of Harris' major book (1951a:10, 12, 252, 253ff, 374) is to avoid the complications caused by differential productivity of elements, by placing the subject outside descriptive linguistics (374). Hockett writes against this view (1952b: 98–99):

> We require him [the linguist] to produce systematization which in an operational sense matches the habits which we ascribe to the speaker: just as the speaker can produce any number of new utterances from essentially the same set of underlying habits, so the analyst's description must be capable of producing any number of new utterances, each capable of passing the test of casual acceptance by a native speaker. Just as the speaker can understand an utterance he has never heard before providing it conforms to his own speech-habits (that is, is in his language), so the analyst's description must be capable of subsuming, IN ADVANCE, a reasonable proportion of utterances which had not been observed when the analysis was made.

In sum, then, the difference between the Bloomfieldian period and that which followed is not to be found in the absence, vs. the later presence, of the idea of 'creativity' or 'productivity' as an aspect of a 'generative' (explicit) analysis or model. As we have said, the difference is not in idea, but in scope of application (and in the means making extended scope possible). In effect, if a complete grammar is to be thought of as generating all and only the sentences of a language, then the initial structuralist goal was to generate all and only the phonological elements, and sequences, of a language — to generate utterances phonologically. A criterion of 'decidability' (as between what was within and what was not within the language) was established. It is perhaps the clearest way to state the difference between the Boasian conception of each language as having a 'definite system of sounds' and the kind of work that grows from Sapir (1925) and Bloomfield (1926). In the Boasian work there is no explicit set of criteria as to what can count as being a member of a language's 'definite system of sounds'; in the subsequent work, there is (cf. Hymes 1972a:420). The subsequent history of structural analysis is in one respect a history of the successive, successful extension of the principle of decidability.

Perhaps the attitude of Harris (noted above) was taken by Chomsky to be representative or was simply the only attitude with which he was acquainted. In the event, his insistence on the goal, eventually rechristened 'creative' aspect of language use (Chomsky 1966) came to be taken as equivalent to non-existence of the goal before him.

The term 'generative' has often the sense of a model that is 'dynamic', at least in the sense of employing *processes* (cf. Matthews 1972:60), and sometimes in the sense of modelling the actual processes of language-users. Thus, in Katz' argument for the superiority of a 'mentalist' to a 'taxonomic' model, he stated (1964:135):

> As described above, the mentalist explains the facts about a speaker's and hearer's linguistic performance in terms of a model that reconstructs the process by which a message is transmitted from the speaker to the hearer through the speakers encoding the

message in the form of an utterance and the hearer's decoding that utterance back to the speaker's original message. Such a model explains why an utterance has a certain linguistic property, and what function that property has in the process of communication, by locating the property in the causal chain which links the utterance on one side to the neurophysiological mechanisms that perform the encoding and articulation, on the other side to those that accomplish the perception and decoding. But if, with the taxonomic viewpoint, we interpret any of the elements of the mentalist's description of the process of communication as merely fictions, rather than as references to neurophysiological links in such a causal chain, the whole explanation collapses.

Teeter writes at about the same time in the same vein (1964:202):

> Notice also a remark in practically the only post-Bloomfieldian paper which still worries about problems of general linguistic theory: [Hockett 1954] "If it be said that the English past-tense form *baked* is 'formed' from *bake* by a 'process' of 'suffixation', then no matter what disclaimer of historicity is made, it is impossible not to conclude that some kind of priority is being assigned to *bake*, as against either *baked* or the suffix. And if this priority is not historical, what is it?" One might wish to assert the priority mentioned, and to claim that it is psychological, and this proposition is testable either by controlled observation of and hypothesis concerning the behavior of native speakers of English, that is by experiment, or by examination of the possibilities for a theory of English, two perfectly respectable scientific techniques. But even the possibility of such an assertion is not entertained in the passage quoted. The post-Bloomfieldian fallacy has become so ingrained that it does not need explicit statement.

The revival of a process idiom, and the goal of modelling the processes of language-users, certainly had become major forces in linguistics in the United States at the time that Katz and Teeter wrote. The broad strokes in which they draw the issue, however, need considerable historical qualification. Their articles suggest a cluster of processual formulation, mentalism, and adequate theory, as opposed to a cluster of rejection of process formulation, rejection of mentalism (psychological reality), and of course, inadequate theory. The implicit equations do not stand up, either as necessary or as historically clear-cut.

To begin with, a rejection of process formulation appears to be intrinsically attractive to linguists concerned to establish a synchronic, structural linguistics, as against diachronic, non-structural linguistics. Stankiewicz (1966:500) points out:

> the questions of a basic form and of morphonemic 'change' or transformations were seriously considered in the writings of Baudouin de Courtenay and of de Saussure; but they were discarded on the grounds that any reference to 'processes' or 'transformations' evoked for these founders of structuralism the diachronic spirit which they tried to exorcise from synchrony.

Baudouin and de Saussure were of course not rejectors of mentalism.

In the years preceding Chomsky's work, the second phase of Bloomfieldian work, there was by no means a general rejection of process formulations. There had not been even in the 1940s. While the effort then to develop an item-and-arrangement model had been the main thrust, processes, base-forms, derivations, and such were not completely eliminated even from the work of the leading symbol of the thrust, Harris (1951a; see quotations earlier from this book). The thrust began to lose momentum at mid-century — it is of interest to note that Hockett's theoretical discussion of process models was written largely in 1949–1951. We should point out here that Hockett has been unfortunate in his readers. Not only is his 1954 paper far from the only post-Bloomfieldian paper which 'still worries' about general theory (as Teeter puts it), but the passage quoted by Teeter is simply an exposition of the standard objections to process formulations (objections of the sort made by de Saussure as well). Hockett himself reports (1968a:29):

> My 1954 paper has on several occasions been misinterpreted as a defense of item-and-arrangement and an attack on item-and-process.([18]) The paper must have been badly written, since my actual intention at the time was nothing of the kind. I wanted to examine the then prevalent way of thinking and to suggest that the item-and-process model, and perhaps even other models, also deserved serious consideration.

In his note (18), Hockett discusses particular interpretations of the paper as an attack:

> Once by Halle (1962, fn. 9), once by Teeter (1964, p. 203 [read 202]). Their misinterpretation is not entirely their fault; several of my students have said that, until I told them otherwise, they thought the 1954 paper was intended as a defense of item-and-arrangement. Late in 1964 I explained orally to Teeter what had been my actual intention in the 1954 paper and in the particular clause he had quoted from it. He insisted that his interpretation was right anyway.

We have carefully read Hockett's 1954 paper. He says precisely what (in 1968) he said he had said, and indeed provides a formalization of IP (including the *baked* example) to demonstrate its feasibility as an alternative to IA (he had proposed doing just this, as one among other models needing formalized investigation in 1952c:38). That his own students could mistake his words is testimony to the grip of preconceptions in a climate of opinion.

Finally, note that schools which accepted process formulations did not develop the particular model valued by Teeter and Katz, and that the formal starting point of the model, the transformational relation, was introduced into linguistics by Harris. In a longer perspective, it seems clear that process terminology and relationships can have a entirely satisfactory, non-temporal interpretation (Huddleston 1972:336), so that 'the choice between process and non-process terms is simply a matter of style and presentation' (*ibid.*, 382).[50]

---

[50]   Huddleston's long study is an interesting and valuable examination of work of Bloomfield, Bloch, Harris, Hockett, and Lamb. He addresses what linguists certainly took to be the problem, namely, to provide a non-temporal interpretation of descriptive terminology; recognizes the two approaches taken – to devise a metalanguage using only static terms, or to find a non-temporal interpretation of process terms; and concludes that transformational generative grammar (most clearly in work of Lakoff) provides satisfactorily such an interpretation. Our one difficulty with the study is that Huddleston appears to consider the problem as one of substance, only recently resolved (e.g., by Lakoff), whereas the problem appears to us to be one of attitude. Harris, Hockett, and even Bloomfield appear to have resolved it in essentially the same way as Lakoff, namely, by saying how terms (or statements) are to be read. Thus, it is not clear why Huddleston

Teeter and Katz wrote at a time of early confidence in a very close relation between processes in the Chomskyan linguistic model and the processes in language-users. Initial psycholinguistic work by Miller and others in terms of the Chomskyan model seemed to support this confidence, but later work did not. By the end of the 1960s it was generally conceded that the relation between the linguistic model and psycholinguistic reality was quite abstract (i.e., distant and difficult to establish), and some psychologists (Fodor, Bever, Steinberg) began to question the reality (or at least the necessity) of the linguistic model itself. Thus, whereas the ethnolinguistic atmosphere of the early 1950s had stimulated work to find in the products of linguistic analysis a model of parameters of world view, or at least cognitive orientation, the psycholinguistic atmosphere of the early 1960s stimulated work to find the products of linguistic analysis a model of linguistic processing itself. In both cases the initial hopes were severely qualified, both by empirical findings and by theoretical discussion. In both cases the possibility of an alternative mode of organization of linguistc means, congruent with the original goal, was suggested (on the ethnolinguistic side, cf. Hymes 1966c), but not taken up within linguistics itself.

In any case, Bloomfieldian linguists also were often enough prepared to consider models of grammar to be models of psychological processes, whether in Whorfian, information-processing, or other terms. Chomsky indeed severely attacked a particular model of grammar in this regard put forward by Hockett (Chomsky 1957b).

In sum, Bloomfieldian work must be characterized in terms of a central thrust away from process formulation during the first phase, and one can well criticize the outcome (or the possibilities of the general model — cf. Matthews 1972 for a thoughtful mingling of historical and analytical comment); but one cannot explain

---

considers Harris' earlier non-temporal formulation unsatisfactory (336), and he appears to have missed the formulation (Harris 1951a: 373) quoted earlier in this chapter. Harris does speak of elements as having a 'history' in process formulations, but this is the principle of recovery of derivations found in Chomsky's work, which Chomsky has been at pains to dissociate from temporality. (The passage is quoted as epigraph to Part III, "Toward a generative formulation", in Matthews (1972:157).) Like Teeter, Huddleston quotes the passage in Hockett (1954, 1.4) that provides a standard objection against IP, but ignores that Hockett's formalization of an IP model expressly treats the same example (*baked*), and discusses priority within an IP model as a strictly methodological (not epistemological) problem (7.3). He also misses the import of Hockett's comparison of an IP passage by M. Haas to an IA restatement by himself; the comparison leaves IP with distinctive merits of its own (1.6). And directly following the initial presentation of the standard objection (if the priority in IP is not historical what is it?), Hockett expressly rejects criticism of IP statements for having teleological implications: 'This objection is pointless unless it can be shown that such a way of speaking leads its users into errors of fact.' The stated attitude would appear to govern the rest of Hockett's formalization and comparison of the two models. Finally, it is not clear that Lakoff's (or Chomsky's) static interpretation of relations between levels of representation is distinct from Bloomfield's express reference (noted by Huddleston) to descriptive order among processes as a fiction (i.e., as non-temporal).

In sum, the underlying problem appears to have been, not in the properties of models, but in the sensibilities of linguists. Over a period of twenty-five years or so, eminent linguists have solved the problem in essentially the same way, that is, by saying 'Do not read these terms (statements) temporally'. The difficulty has been in getting linguists to accept or be comfortable with the instruction.

the thrust in terms of rejection of theory or of rejection of psychological reality for linguistic analyses. Nor can one explain the success of the Chomskyan approach in these terms. One could have had process formulation, and psychological reality, from other strands of the pre-Chomskyan scene.

It is of course true that Chomsky's specific program of process formulation and promise of psychological reality had decisive appeal. Problem-solving in terms of the new processual mechanism and model was associated with, first, a new sense of the mathematical bases of grammar, and a new sense of the accessibility of theoretical results. The theoretical results first emphasized by Chomsky (and still, it would seem, of most interest to him) were formal. It was a few years before theoretical results in the sense of proposals as to substantive universals of language came to the fore.

In speaking of 'results' we do not imply any evaluation of validity; but it is clear that excitement at the prospect of results within the new model, an excitement not found within the Bloomfieldian approach, gave rise to the sense that the Bloomfieldian approach could be described, and explained away, as 'without theory' (or, without anything worthy of the name 'theory'). There is an important grain of truth here, but, as before, one needs to sort out the historiographic chaff that has surrounded it.

5.3.4   *Absence of theory: Universals and explanations*

The sense of 'theory' implicit in many discussions goes beyond questions of the analysis of grammar (such as we have focused upon in the preceding part) to questions of the 'nature of language'. Two types of question can be distinguished:

(a) generalizations as to the nature of language(s), and

(b) explanations of the nature of language(s).

As with so many other traits, the difference between Bloomfieldian and Chomskyan work cannot be reduced to a matter of absence vs. presence.

Generalizations as to the nature of language(s) stood as a goal of modern linguistics throughout its development. Pike (1947:174) encouraged field practitioners to make their findings available, not only to others who would wish to learn the language, but also to students of linguistics in general, who need precise, accurate, and detailed descriptions of the sound systems of all languages:

They wish to make general studies of the types of structural relationships which are found around the world, in the hope of discovering various language characteristics of a universal nature which will increase their understanding of basic language types. For this purpose they need statements about the large number of languages of which there are as yet no technical materials available.

We have noted that work in typology and universals came increasingly to the fore in the second phase of Bloomfieldian work, the 1950s, before Chomsky's advent and impact (Voegelin, Hockett, Greenberg, Jakobson).

It should be mentioned that in the stage of the emergence of linguistics as a distinct discipline, it was thought of the greatest importance to argue and show that linguistic structure itself existed. As opposed to other approaches, and conceptions, regarding the nature of language, it was considered a decisive accomplishment to show the existence of qualitative structure in a sphere of human life (cf. Whorf 1941). The basic units of phonology and morphology were salient exhibits in this cause. Linguistics was a demonstration of the possibility of rigorous formal analysis of a sort not requiring sampling, statistics, or other techniques derivative of a natural science orientation, and of such a nature as not to permit reduction to such approaches. Phonology in particular was held to teach this lesson (and did so to Lévi-Strauss). It was not for nothing that Jakobson spoke of the international development of phonology in these terms (1953:21):

For years and decades we have fought for the annexation of speech-sounds to linguistics, and thereby established phonemics.

In respect to this point, linguists of all persuasions (mentalist, behaviorist, whatever) were defenders of the distinctive nature of language.

Explanation of the nature of language has been thought to have been taboo in the Bloomfieldian period. A remark by Joos has been widely taken to stand for everyone. Having criticized Trubetzkoy phonology for 'offering too much of a phonological *explanation* where a sober *taxonomy* would serve as well', Joos went on to say (1957:96):

Children want explanations, and there is a child in each of us; descriptivism makes a virtue of not pampering that child.

The element of truth in Joos' comment is that during the initial thrust of the dominant approach there was, as we have noted, concern not to short-cut inquiry by resort to ad hoc explanations. There was in addition a strong sense among leading Bloomfieldians that 'teleological' (functional) statements were out of place (recall Harris on Trubetzkoy).

The limitations of the truth in Joos' comment are three-fold: not everyone agreed; as the second phase of Bloomfieldian ('post-Bloomfieldian') work unfolded, fewer and fewer people agreed; Bloomfieldians in both phases retained a sense of sociocultural context in which some explanations would be found, and some entertained a hope of an eventual unity of science in which underlying explanations might be provided.

It is always dangerous to take one figure's comment as representative of a group, and the history of the use of this remark by Joos is an outstanding example in linguistics in the United States. It is particularly important to recognize that at the time the remark was published, a new, more open current was already well under way, and that if asked to name the most important linguist in the United States, a fair number in that pre-Chomskyan day would have said, 'Roman Jakobson'. The 'means-ends' model of interwar continental linguistics, as represented by Jakobson, won increasing prominence and attention in the United States in the 1950s. With regard to 'explanatory adequacy' (to use Chomsky's term), it is particularly important to recognize that the basic principle involved was already familiar to many linguists in the United States through Jakobson's work. That is, if we take 'explanatory adequacy' to involve what Chomsky (1965) has called a 'systematic ambiguity', such that general linguistic theory, and the principles of acquisition of language, are interdependent, then precisely this thesis was advanced by Jakobson in 1942 (republished in 1962 in his generally available *Selected Writings* I). The claim was noted with great interest in connection with the onset of linguistically informed studies of language acquisition in the 1950s, and in connection with the renewed interest in typology (on which cf. also Jakobson 1958).

5.3.5   *Absence of theory: Discovery procedures*

It remains that there was less interest in generalization and explanation in the Bloomfieldian period, and very little in its first phase. That fact can be accounted for in part by the situation of the group; it was newly self-conscious of its existence and goals, and working to establish a consistent model of language structure in terms of which something meaningful about properties of language might be said in the midst of building a discipline and earning a livelihood. And there were few participants in the work (far fewer than the numbers that entered linguistics in the 1960s). It remains that the initial orientation of the dominant Bloomfieldian group did play an important part. To assess the role of that orientation, however, we must first disabuse ourselves of the widespread impression that an absorption with 'discovery procedures' led many to confuse theory with rigorous data-manipulation.

The term 'discovery procedure' was introduced by Chomsky (1957a:51; cf. Matthews 1972:111, n. 2), and it sometimes comes as a surprise to linguists to encounter mathematicians or philosophers of science who are not familiar with it. It has, unfortunately, a pejorative connotation. The work to which the term properly applies is concerned with 'evaluation procedures' (as Matthews' discussion (1972:14ff, 111–112, 395, and elsewhere), constantly implies without seeming to admit). The 'discovery procedure' models were constantly employed to evaluate descriptions, and the great dissatisfaction with Harris as 'hocus-pocus' or 'game-playing' was because, granted distributional analysis itself, he showed no interest in evaluating one formulation as better than another.

Matthews (1972:111, n. 3) does recognize correctly that 'discovery procedures' were concerned with linguistic theory, and not with practical heuristics; not, that is, with 'discovering' a grammar, but with justifying one. Chomsky himself (1958 (Fodor and Katz 1964:212)) seems in part to recognize this, referring to his presentation as

questioning the adequacy of a certain view of the nature of linguistic theory that has dominated much recent work,

and going on to say:

almost every approach to linguistic theory has attempted to formulate these definitions in such a way as to provide an essentially mechanical method that an investigator might use, in principle, to isolate the phonemes, morphemes and constituents in the analysis of a particular language. This interest in a discovery procedure for linguistic elements has motivated . . . .

The expression 'in principle' suggests a theoretical, not practical, concern, but in a footnote (212, n. 6), Chomsky takes the intent as directly practical. Although some widely held doctrines are not necessary within such a theory, he remarks, they are nevertheless natural requirements 'for a linguistic theory whose immediate aim is to provide a discovery procedure for grammars'.

In Chomsky's most widely read book (1957a), his well known discussion of the goals of linguistic theory distinguishes three types of procedure, and, in coining the name 'discovery procedure', does equate it with practicality (50–51):

The strongest requirement that could be placed on the relation between a theory of linguistic structure and particular grammars is that the theory must provide a practical and mechanical method for actually constructing the grammar, given a corpus of utterances. Let us say that such a theory provides us with a *discovery* procedure for grammars.

To be sure, the subsequent discussion begins with inclusion of a qualification ('if he had the time') that is comparable to 'in principle' in the passage quoted just above (1957a:52):

The point of view adopted here is that it is unreasonable to demand of linguistic theory that it provide anything more than a practical evaluation procedure for grammars. That is, we adopt the weakest of the three positions described above. As I interpret most of the more careful proposals for the development of linguistic theory,([3]) they attempt to meet the strongest of these three requirements. That is, they attempt to state methods of analysis that an investigator might actually use, if he had the time, to construct a grammar of a language directly from the raw data.

(We will take up Chomsky's footnote (3) directly below.) Chomsky goes on to say (52–53):

I think that it is very questionable that this goal is attainable in any interesting way, and I suspect that any attempt to meet it will lead into a maze of more and more elaborate and complex analytic procedures that will fail to provide answers for many important questions about the nature of linguistic structure. I believe that by lowering our sights to the more modest goal of developing an evaluation procedure for grammars we can focus attention more clearly on really crucial problems of linguistic structure and we can arrive at more satisfying answers to them.

In these sentences the heart of Chomsky's true argument is expressed: attempts to formalize linguistic theory in terms of induction are found wanting because of undue complexity, and because of inadequate scope. The central truth of the argument has to do with complexity; Chomsky proceeds directly to discuss simplicity (53ff.) as the notion to use in choosing among grammars (54). All the other objections, and contrasts, turn out on examination to be secondary, and either remediable or not contrasts at all.

Notice first that the contrast at this time is not between observables and intuitions. Chomsky states three main tasks in the 'program for linguistic theory that we have suggested' (53), and the first of the three is this:

it is necessary to state precisely (if possible, with *operational, behavioral tests*) the external criteria of adequacy for grammars (emphasis supplied).

Second, inadequacy of scope is not at issue in principle. Formalization in the inductive mode could be extended to include the properties of syntax of concern to Chomsky — indeed, *this had already been done* in the work on discourse analysis and transformations of Zellig Harris (whose work on this score is *not* cited in the list of works in n. 3 on p. 52, where the only item from Harris is his peripheral exploration of the possibility of finding morpheme boundaries distributionally on the basis of phonological properties). Hockett (1952c) explored this possibility before Harris; neither claimed to have succeeded, and in Harris' system a successful result would have remained a *relation* between phonology and morphology, since, as will be recalled, he maintained that one could analyze *either* morphemes or phonemes first. Third, the 'more modest goal' of an evaluation procedure is misleadingly described. On the one hand, the 'more modest goal' did not prevent transformational generative grammarians in the Chomsky school from seeking, and claiming, 'correct' solutions — in speaking, in other words, just as much as Bloomfieldians in terms of the only right way, and often enough, the only right answer (Voegelin (1958c) early caught this implicit message).

On the other hand, the procedures christened 'discovery' by Chomsky were evaluation procedures too.

Chomsky himself recognizes this fact at one point. In footnote (3) (p. 52) he follows a list of articles with the following discussion:

Although discovery procedures are the explicit goal of these works, we often find on careful examination that the theory that has actually been constructed furnishes no more than an evaluation procedure for grammars. For example, Hockett states his aim in 'A formal statement of morphemic analysis' [1952c] as the development of 'formal procedures by which one can work from scratch to a complete description of the pattern of a language' (p. 27); but what he actually does is describe some of the formal properties of a morphological analysis and then propose a 'criterion whereby the relative efficiency of two possible morphic solutions can be determined; with that, we can choose the maximally efficient possibility, or, arbitrarily, any one of those which are equally efficient but more efficient than all others' (p. 29).

The phrases 'explicit goal' vs. 'find on careful examination', and 'states his aim' vs. 'what he actually does', seem unequivocally to contrast conscious intention ('discovery procedure' in Chomsky's sense) to unconscious effect. This contrast is false, as we shall see in the documentation to follow. It is hard to understand how Chomsky could not have known it to be false on the evidence of the Hockett article itself.

Here is the first sentence of Hockett's article (1952c:27):

In his book *Methods in structural linguistics* Zellig S. Harris attempts to set up formal procedures by which one can work from scratch to a complete description of the pattern of a language.

Presumably Chomsky, who is thanked by Harris for reading the manuscript of his book, knew that Harris presented his formal procedures as a *frame of reference* (recall quotations from Harris earlier and see discussion of his work above), by which one could assess a grammar, and explicitly not a description of how one would in the first instance provide a grammar. It might be, of course, that Hockett misinterpreted Harris, so that the description of Harris applies to the describer, Hockett. This would be in conflict with Hockett's position everywhere else (before and after the 1952 paper), and it is in contrast to what Hockett says in this paper too. His point is that Harris contrasts formal procedures to the many shortcuts of practice, but implies the attitude that the formal procedures (non-semantic procedures) would in principle be possible. He addresses himself in the paper to two questions: Does Harris succeed in displaying a logically coherent non-semantic procedure? If not, can one be formulated? It is clear from the additional two questions that he mentions that his concern is entirely with what is 'theoretically possible' and inherently capable, or incapable, of formalization. In the conclusion, Hockett expresses his belief that outstanding problems of formalization can be solved (he considers his paper only to display 'the beginnings of a complete formalization' (28)). His remarks are worth quoting (38–9):

The general approach involved in the formalization of the present paper is not, of course, the only possible or actual approach in linguistic analysis; there is also the challenge of a clearly worked-out procedure that makes systematic and defensible use of semantic criteria; there is also the challenge of a clearly worked-out 'item and process' model instead of the 'item and arrangement' model implied here and by Harris, either non-semantic or semantic. But to think that any of these alternatives has, as yet, made any *further* [emphasis in original] advance away from rules-of-thumb and toward logical rigor than has the non-semantic item-and-arrangement model would be absurd.[6] Unless we are simply to revert to a medievally obscurantist concentration on *ad hoc* solutions of individual languages or parts of languages, we face and must meet a challenge of clarification greater than any that has yet been confronted in the scientific study of language.

In his note (6), Hockett's purpose is further made manifest (39):

This sentence involves a conscious passing of judgment: the differentiation of kinds of meaning involved in Praguian phonology is not successful; Hjelmslev's procedures in the analysis of 'context' are suggestive but as yet involve some serious methodological contradictions and limitations; Nida's recent direct attack on meaning (A system for the description of semantic elements, *Word* 7.1–14, 1951), is most highly to be commended, and ought to be studied, yet FALLS FAR SHORT OF A REAL FORMALIZATION. (Emphasis supplied)

There seems no escaping the conclusion that Hockett's concern in the article was with explicit *formalization,* as a basis for assessing the adequacy of linguistic descriptions, as a goal and necessity of linguistic theory as a scientific activity. That he was not concerned with 'work from scratch' is obvious from the fact that his starting-place is the normalized result of a prior phonological analysis (28: Hockett notes that 'not all phonemes are linear', but proposes obtaining linearity by various conventions, as a basis for the formalization of the morphological analysis).

Hockett's article is representative of the work of the Bloomfieldians. Theory was understood to require explicit formalization, and explicit formalization was understood to require an inductive model. Chomsky's true argument with the Bloomfieldians was with regard to the *kind* of evaluation procedure, the kind of formal justification of a linguistic analysis, or linguistic theory, that should be followed. To the criterion of theoretically possible induction, he opposed the criterion of theoretically definable simplicity (generality). One may believe that he was right, and yet regret that the issue was not met directly. The effect of the discussion in *Syntactic structures* was to confuse an argument about types of evaluation procedure with an argument as to the presence of an evaluation procedure vs. the absence of any at all. Insofar as presence of evaluation procedures comes to be equated with presence of theory it is not surprising that the charge of absence of theory, or equation of theory with discovery, has come to be so commonly accepted.

In the subsequent discussion in *Syntactic structures* (following n. 3), Chomsky treats 'practical' as a crucial qualification for all procedures associated with the conceptions of linguistic theory and its goals that he discusses, and thenceforward speaks of 'discovery procedures' as 'practical' (as in their introduction (50)). Perhaps there lies behind this usage the thought that a discovery procedure that is not practical would not be useful, and that therefore 'most of the more careful proposals' must have really intended their theoretical statements in the inductive mode to be practically used; they could not have intended, or should not have intended, to propose procedures usable only 'in principle'. The apparent contradiction or inadequacy of course disappears if one recognizes that the procedures 'in principle' were intended for the justification, the evaluation, of description arrived at in other ways. In any case, Chomsky goes on to reiterate a contrast between 'discovery procedures' understood as tools of actual analysis and an evaluation procedure in terms of simplicity. Thus, he writes (56):

It is no doubt possible to give an organized account of many useful procedures of analysis, but it is questionable whether these can be formulated rigorously, exhaustively and simply enough to qualify as a practical and mechanical discovery procedure. At any rate, this problem is not within the scope of our investigations here. Our ultimate aim is to provide an objective, non-intuitive way to evaluate a grammar once presented, and to compare it with other proposed grammars. We are thus interested in describing the form of grammars (equivalently, the nature of linguistic structure) and investigating the empirical consequences of adopting a certain model for linguistic structure, rather than in showing how, in principle, one might have arrived at the grammar of a language.

The confusion is here complete. The statement of goals by Chomsky would equally well apply to the goals subscribed to by Hockett: to investigate the empirical consequences of adopting a certain model for linguistic structure, to which the prerequisite would be to describe the form of grammars (by logical, consistent clarification of their implicit properties). The conflict is not in goals, but in means: 'to show how, in principle, one might have arrived at the grammar of a language' is, as we have said, the mode of evaluation procedure pursued by Bloomfieldians, a mode that they did not confuse with actual processes of discovery.

Chomsky's objection might be taken to be that the procedures sought by Bloomfieldians were in principle not susceptible of becoming practical — but this is an argument between one kind of *evaluation* procedure and another, not an argument between an evaluation procedure and something that is not one.

In any case, Chomsky proceeds in terms of the conflated contrast (56, beginning of 6.2): 'Once we have disclaimed any intention of finding a practical discovery procedure for grammars . . .'; and (59) 'hope of finding a practical discovery procedure . . .' or (59):

. . . the attempt to develop a discovery procedure for grammars. If we renounce this goal and if we distinguish clearly between a manual of suggestive and helpful procedures and a theory of linguistic structure. . . .

This final contrast makes inescapable the reading that 'discovery procedures' are opposed to a 'theory of linguistic structure' and a conscious concern with procedures of evaluation. Given this opposition in this book, it is not surprising that the term Chomsky introduced, 'discovery procedures', has been widely taken up in a literal sense. A few years later, for example, one finds Teeter (1964:203) writing:

It came about, then, that linguistic theory was simply equated with the set of techniques used by the field linguist to arrive at a description of a language. Gradually, since criteria of rightness or wrongness of a given analysis could not appeal to psychology or to a general theory, yet everyone had known that some analyses are more nearly correct than others, justification of a given analysis meant the specifying of the procedures used to arrive at the given result from the data. This became, as it were by mutual agreement, the accepted manner of justification, and a necessary part of all analysis.[15]

In his note (15), Teeter adds: 'This may be clearly traced in the papers reprinted in *RIL* [Joos 1957]. This equation of Bloomfieldian theory with the techniques of the field linguist, and of Bloomfieldian presentation with the showing of how a given analysis was reached, expresses what appears to have become a widely accepted notion. It is worthwhile, therefore, to document that it is false. We can begin with an early contribution, reprinted in *RIL* [Joos 1957].

The conclusion of the first theoretical statement of a Bloomfieldian theory, Hockett's 1942 system of descriptive phonology, establishes a contrast which holds true throughout the period (1942:21 (Joos 1957:107)):

10.3 Analytical procedure is a trial-and-error process, in which the analyst makes successive approximations. He gathers phonological and grammatical material at the same time, though he may emphasize now one, now the other. He makes errors of omission and commission, and later corrects them. At certain stages he may work by 'feelings', but later he substitutes rigorous criteria. Finally the correct statement of the material emerges. In this, the organization depends on what is most efficient for the particular language concerned; if the source material is a body of written records, the very defects of the record may condition the order of presentation.

Thus neither the process of analysis, nor the presentation of the results of analysis, need resemble the general picture of phonology given in this paper. The system given here is a *frame of reference*. If the analyst operates constantly in terms of such a frame, being careful not to confuse the distinctions made in it, and using terms in logically valid ways, the resulting description is the clear-cut, efficient statement of facts which a classificatory science requires.

The only general manual for techniques in reaching phonemic analysis, that by Pike (1947), distinguished clearly between 'analytical procedures' (sections 5–13) and 'descriptive procedures' (sections 15–15). At the beginning of section 5, Pike (67) states: 'we now present a methodology for the analysis or discovery of the phonemic units'. It is clear that Pike based methodology on such understanding of general theory as was available (he specifically noted lack of agreement in the field (64)); in sharp contrast to the implication that has been drawn from Joos' remark about languages differing without limit, the scholar more concerned with field work discovery than almost any other linguist wrote (57):

Such a methodology is valid only if one assumes that all language structures of the world are sufficiently uniform to warrant the application to an unknown language of those procedures which have given adequate results in application to known languages. *Phonemic procedures, then, must be founded upon premises concerning the underlying universal characteristics of languages of the world, lest the orthographical conclusions arrived at by the procedures prove to be both technically and practically inadequate.* (Emphasis in original)

Pike postulated that just one accurate phonemic analysis existed for a given set of data (61), a view interdependent with the goal which he put as follows (64):

The premises for this volume are chosen from existing theory, or postulated for the first time, so as *to lead the student to arrive at an analysis which parallels the vague or explicit observable reactions of speakers to their own sounds.* (Emphasis in original)

Nevertheless it is clear from this book, and from his other writings (especially the end of 1947b), that no algorithm to be mechanically applied was intended in the presentation of analytical procedures, and that no single idealized form of theoretical presentation was in view in the presentation of descriptive procedures. The general strategy of discovery is one of convergence, using all relevant kinds of data, and working back and forth between them (this extends to grammatical data, which Pike accepted as often convenient as matrix for statement of phonological facts (e.g., 146)). The general strategy of presentation (description) is one of adaptation to purpose and audience. Analysis itself might be affected by the latter (cf. discussion of simplicity on p. 149).

It is clear from Hockett's review comments (Hockett 1949) that he considered Pike's presentation of procedures entirely practical in conception, not a statement of theory. Indeed, Hockett ascribes to practical exigencies some features of Pike's theoretical outlook that he opposes. He appeals to the example of the mathematician, who when working out a proof of a theorem, goes where the wind blows him, follows his 'intuition', analogizes on the basis of previous experience, but who has not *established* (Hockett's emphasis) the proof and the theorem until it comes out as a series of statements of a specified logical shape. States Hockett (210):

It is important to keep clearly in mind the distinction between *theoretical frame of reference* and *actual sequence of operations in the field.* (Emphasis in original)

He goes on to say that he does not object to any specific criterion or procedure that Pike proposes as of importance in the total task of achieving a practical orthography (210):

The objections which have been raised here concern the *sequence* in which the various criteria are applied, the various procedures undertaken. And here I mean sequence in the theoretical frame of reference (in the shape of the mathematician's final proof) rather than in actual field work (the mathematician's search for the proof).

The two objections as to *theoretical* sequence concern use of grammatical criteria in phonology, and use of meaning (perhaps substantive meaning) to compare recurrent *parts* of utterances (rather than only whole utterances) at the phonological level (pp. 202–203, 208 in V. Makkai 1972, from which we are quoting). Hockett's view of actual field procedure is clear from another passage (206), which refers to a 'recurrent cycle of prediction, checking, gathering of new data, modification of predictions, and rechecking'.

The standpoint could hardly be clearer. Procedures of discovery in the field are one thing (and a complex, partly intuitive thing). Such things are distinct from theory. Theory is concerned with an ideal frame of reference which justifies analyses, however arrived at.

This standpoint informs the other major theoretical statements of the period, and its other major manual. The latter, Nida (1949), follows a division among procedures similar to that in Pike. Nida's introduction is interesting in this regard. Explaining the arrangement of chapters, he notes that 2 and 3 deal with identification of morphemes and their types, and that (5):

together they constitute the presentation of analytical theory. Chapter 4 introduces the synthetic part of the structural procedures by discussing the distribution of morphemes. . . . Theoretically, Chapter 9, on the organization of the descriptive statement of the morphology, should follow Chapter 6, *but the actual procedures of analysis of a language are quite different from the schematic approach suggested* by Chapters 2–6. Accordingly, it was necessary to introduce first a chapter on *field procedures* and one on *analytical procedures.* (Emphasis supplied)

Like Pike, Nida (2, 192) considered all parts of a language mutually relevant to each other in analysis, and held forth no algorithm of discovery nor single idealized descriptive presentation. Both Pike and Nida, indeed, offer samples of different descriptive presentations.

There were differences in the period in flexibility as to presentation, Trager being less ready to make concessions, for example, in pedagogical presentations. In general, 'description' carried a connotation of 'theoretically proper' (rigorous). There were differences, too, as to where to draw the line between procedures which were part of theoretical justification and those which were practical ('analytic' in Pike (1947) and Nida (1949) — the term recalls Boas' conception of his own approach as 'analytic'). Bloch (1948:5 (V. Makkai 1972:169)) stated:

> The basic assumptions that underlie phonemics, we believe, can be stated without any mention of mind and meaning; but meaning, at least, is so obviously useful as a shortcut in the investigation of phonemic structure — one might almost say, so inescapable — that any linguist who refused to employ it would be very largely wasting his time.

Hockett, like Pike, did not agree with the belief (1949, n. 9):

> Meaning, so defined and focused [i.e., differential meaning] is it seems to me not avoided in Bloch's postulates.

But it is clear that 'assumptions that underlie' are not procedures that discover. Bloch EMPHASIZED that they were not (1948:5):

> Our postulates are intended to state either empirical facts or what are assumed to be facts. They are *not* [Bloch's emphasis] intended to delineate procedures, or to constitute a list of practical rules to be followed step by step in one's work with an informant. On the other hand, the methods of analysis by which linguists usually proceed in arriving at the phonemic system of a dialect are implied in these postulates and can be justified by them.

(As to the role of meaning in phonological analysis, it is of course true that Chomsky sided with Bloch and Harris in denying it a role in determining the basic facts of phonology — see 1957a:94–100).

As we have seen, Harris (1951a) presented distributional procedures as rigorous alternatives to meaning considerations (8, n. 7; 38; 365, n. 6). Meaning was recognized only as a shortcut (7, n. 4; 189; 365, n. 6), or source of hints. Nevertheless, he recognized the use of such shortcuts and hints (1), indeed listing stress upon distribution rather than meaning in setting up of morphemes as an example of cumbersome but explicit procedures offered in place of simpler intuitive practice (3). The cumbersome approach was offered in order to be consistent in the reduction of linguistic methods to procedures. No single schedule of operation was prescribed (1, 6, 365, 371) or any single form of presentation (365, 373). Harris' salient use of the term 'procedures' may likely be the source of Chomsky's sense of its appropriateness in his notion of 'discovery procedures', and often enough Harris sounds like the presenter of an algorithm, when he presents a particular procedure. But, as has been noted, he presents alternative procedures, and he himself makes clear, first, that the procedures are not a plan for obtaining data or for field work (1), but merely ways of arranging the original data (3), and, second, that the use of the procedures is merely to make explicit what choices each linguist makes (2). He states (1):

In practice, linguists take unnumbered short cuts and intuitive or heuristic guesses, and keep many problems about a particular language before them at the same time: they may have figured out the positioned variants of several phonemes before they decide how to cut up into segments certain utterances which presumably contain a phonetically unusual phoneme; and they will usually know exactly where the boundaries of many morphemes are before they finally determine the phonemes. The chief usefulness of the procedures listed below is therefore as a reminder in the course of the original research, and as a form for checking or presenting the results, where it may be desirable to make sure that all the information called for in these procedures has been validly obtained.

Finally, Trager and Smith (1951:54) remark:

This is not to say that in the actual procedure of analyzing a language there is not a constant going back and forth between phonology and morphemics, with refinement and corrections being made in either direction. But the analyst must at all times be aware of the level-differences, and the systematic presentation must always be made in terms of the logical sequence, in one linear order, with the levels carefully distinguished.

One further kind of documentary evidence should be noted. Besides the explicit statements of formulators of theoretical 'discovery procedures', prominently represented in *RIL*; the reaction of one such (Hockett) to a practitioner not there represented (Pike); there is also the reaction of another practitioner not there represented to RIL itself and to the line of work that can be clearly traced there. Voegelin (1958b) writes:

It would be possible to list an impressively high number of interests in linguistics which lie outside of the selection range of the *Readings*. (Some interests seem to be avoided as un-American). The selection of the majority of papers, as already indicated, seems confined to exemplars of the aim *toward a final linguistic analysis* (b), without ever bothering about (a), *techniques for a preliminary analysis,* despite the fact that (a) is prerequisite to (b). However, since every (b) is preceded by an application of (a), it might be argued that every (b) is a restatement of results obtained from (a). The minimum of descriptive linguistics is surely a consideration of both (a) and (b). (The neglect of (a) in favor of an exclusive concern with (b) seems to reflect an unacknowledged stimulus diffusion from European scholarship.) [!] (Emphasis in original, except [!])

The following year Voegelin speaks to the same issue, with 'structural first statements' and 'structural restatements' equivalent to 'preliminary' and 'final' analysis in his review of Joos. Again, he specifically *objects* to *neglect* of the former in favor of the latter (1959:209):

If description can ever be validated as unique in linguistics, it would be efficient to reach this objective in a first statement in field work. Such efficiency would, in one sense, make structural restatement linguistics superogatory (but see 2, in part II of this paper). As matters stand, what precedes in field work appears to many linguists to be a historical prior activity for accumulating archival-like corpora of combinable materials — on the dubious principle that discovery precedes formulation. If the two (discovery and formulation) are interlocking, as is reported by everyone who has worked in anthropological linguistics, then the kind of questions which are asked in making structural restatements have to be asked in constructing the first structural statement — including the relevance of meaning, and the basis of decision when facing alternative analysis.

Here is a call for the kind of unity of theory and practice assumed by those who speak of the period as equating theory with data-handling in the sense of discovery —a call predicated on the *neglect* of such concern on the part of the theorists of the period. This sense of strain between the two activities is further evidence for the difference between the theoretical idiom and the practical inquiry of the period.[51]

In short, Bloomfieldian theorists did not hold that a theory (Chomsky 1957a:50) 'must provide a practical and mechanical method for actually constructing the grammar, given a corpus of utterances'. They did (Chomsky 1957a:59) 'distinguish clearly between a manual of suggestive and helpful procedures and a theory of linguistic structure'. Insofar as they maintained hope of finding grammars that were valid, and argued as to which analyses were more valid, and by what criteria, than others, their work of course is continuous with that today. Even the Bloomfieldian conception of constraint on the form of grammars, so as to permit validation, has a certain continuity with subsequent models. But let us consider that point within a general summing up.

5.3.6 *On explaining Bloomfieldian theory*

We have seen that the most noted Bloomfieldian theorists repeatedly maintained that they were not explicating actual practice, actual discovery of linguistic structure. Several of them disdained to take seriously as theory the views of Pike, who argued for a unity of theory and practice. Indeed, the leading field-linguists of the period (Pike, Swadesh, Voegelin) were outside the circle whose work has been generally taken to represent formulation of discovery procedures, and criticized the direction taken by such theory for its neglect of practical work. Why, then, the idiom, or convention, of presenting theoretical requirements in the guise of an ideally possible analytical procedure?

The essential factors in the development of Bloomfieldian theory, in its first, most distinctive phase, were (1) the creation of abstract, formal theory in the first place, as a systematic and central professional activity; (2) the association of theoretical work with the emergence of a novel discipline within the academic universe; (3) the doing of this at a time when the general existence of structural linguistics (internationally) was based on the conquest of phonology; (4) at a time when a war (a) interrupted communication with international scholarship, (b) concentrated young scholars together under the leadership of the one surviving father-

---

[51] Cf. also Voegelin and Voegelin 1963:28. Voegelin 1959b:207 seems to suggest that it is Chomsky's evaluation procedures that stimulated development of rigorous evaluation procedures for methods of initial (field) description – for the first time! On the whole subject see Miller 1973,

figure among domestic structuralists (c) in the service of a patriotic and humanitarian cause.

These factors contributed to making of the work, not simply a development of linguistics, but a *movement* within linguistics. The movement integrated much that was valued in the tradition on which it drew (anthropology, comparative philology), but much of its direction must be attributed to a sense of being new, and of a need to be new — not merely novelty for its own sake, but a new *autonomy*. Autonomy was grounded in the claim to be a science, or scientific activity, in the description of languages, to be, indeed to be a general science in that sphere for the first time. To be scientific entailed three things: differentiation from established, 'prescientific' work; inductivism (on the presumed model of established empirical sciences); abstract formalism (on the model of mathematics as the language of science).

Models might be built up on the basis of known facts and practices, in the light of general principles, by striving to be as explicit, comprehensive, consistent, as possible; but the tenor of models, like the practice of the field, would take for granted that new facts, substantive generalizations, and revised models would come, case by case, from studies in which the investigator was responsible to data external to him (or her) self. Given the anthropological heritage, both in practice and in critical analysis of inadequate traditional notions; given the pedagogic situation of the war and post-war period; given the small number of linguists and the thousands of languages in the world — all this made perfect sense. For some, positivistic conceptions of objectivity played a part (a part which linguistics is having to reconsider again today), but Pike, who was no positivist, also thought in terms of the accumulation of well described cases as the basis of advance in knowledge of general linguistics. Indeed, the more one insisted, as did Pike, that native speaker reactions, judgments, were essential tests of validity, the more one would want theory to be consistent with practice (as did Pike). Those whose theory-building might put simplicity and other formal constraints ahead of consistency with practice still honored practice, by requiring that (Joos 1961:18) 'the sequence of statements in a description must also be a possible discovery-sequence, whether it is a practicable discovery-sequence or not'. What 'discovery-sequence', as separation of levels, starting with phonology, came to was a way of being responsible to the data with which one was presumed to start. It was the Bloomfieldian way, in Firth's terms, of ensuring renewal of connection with reality, with context. It was part of the morality of commitment to science, but it was also a quite understandable form of bookkeeping.

If one considers the requirement in Chomskyan grammar of the time that the steps of a derivation be recoverable, one can see a clear parallel. The starting points differ: phonic data in the one case, syntactic data in the other; observables in the one case, intuited or inferred underlying structures in the other. But the requirement of being able to trace one's steps, of being able to recover a starting point to which one was responsible, is parallel. Chomskyan 'recovery procedures' answer to

Bloomfieldian 'discovery procedures' (Chomsky himself sometimes speaks of a 'mechanical' procedure (1962, section X, quoted earlier)).[52]

Both approaches, then, Bloomfieldian and Chomskyan, shared ideal ordering requirements, as part of a commitment to accountability. Both might be called 'recovery procedures' with regard to particular grammars. Both participate in 'evaluation procedures', inasmuch as their respective types of model are developed, debated, and revised with the hope of providing criteria for the selection of particular grammars. Some such constraint may perhaps be indispensable to any model or theory with such a goal.

In any case, the particular requirement was indispensable only to some, not all, of these who created the Bloomfieldian period, and it did not remain indispensable, nor did its consequences. Independently, before Chomsky's work, and subsequently in interaction with it, a great deal of descriptive work and descriptive theory developed which differed from Chomskyan work primarily in other respects. One such respect would be simply that of being outside the hegemony of the subsequent movement. Acceptance of transformational relations would not be the difficulty; there would be controversy over specific formalizations, to be sure, and even as to general models. But the main obstacle would be in attitude toward data, in the broad sense in which we have spoken of an inductive orientation, in contrast to a deductive orientation (cf. Matthews 1972:112, who places the change as a switch from extreme to extreme that has been specifically American). The time has not yet arrived (though it is approaching) when one can assess both extremes dispassionately, but let us try to portray sympathetically now the spirit of the earlier, more distant movement (a movement which aggravated considerably the senior author in his student years).

One must refer to the inheritance of the previous world war. The traumatic effect of World War I on established, historically oriented optimism is well known. In many fields there emerged a spirit of having to start from scratch, to build new forms without taking anything traditional for granted. Most immediately relevant

---

[52]   This point was first noted in the literature, so far as we know, by Oller and Sales (1969:213). They state (n. 5): 'The call for a model of language acquisition, or a grammar discovery procedure, appears to be a clear-cut contradiction of Chomsky (1957) where it is argued that a discovery procedure for grammars is too strong a requirement for linguistic theory.' Oller and Sales do not think the requirement in fact too strong in principle.

Derwing (1973:58–60) arrives at the same point. On analysis, he finds Chomsky's use of 'theory' in argument about 'discovery procedures' obscure, as between a theory of a grammar and a general, meta-theory. In any case, Derwing concludes, Chomsky's model for language acquisition, and conception of explanatory adequacy, 'constitutes as much an attempt to provide a 'discovery procedure for grammars' as did any of the earlier more 'mechanical' procedures . . .'. The procedure is displaced in effect from linguist to child. If we distinguish a procedure in principle from an actual process, the point holds all the better, since Chomsky idealizes the moment of acquisition, just as Bloomfieldians idealized descriptive justification – idealized acquisition taking no time, justified description being without limit of time.

Note here also Householder (1971, chs. 11, 12) on "Discovery and testing". The historiography is off the cuff, but the serious attention to heuristics may be a hopeful sign.

is the attractiveness of atomistic philosophy and logical positivism, the 'verification' principle and the like, in the interwar period; there was a desire not to be fooled, not taken in, by traditional authority (associated with the mess in which the world found itself), and in some quarters there was an optimism towards science. Such an atmosphere caught fire, as it were, among young linguists in the United States, who were themselves moving away from traditional humanistic disciplines in which they had first been trained (Bloch, Harris, Joos, Trager), or joining the newly emerging discipline (Hockett). Given commitment to the new discipline, its frame of reference would function as an ideology (in the neutral, necessary sense in which any social group must have an ideology), and be extended beyond the scope of actual work. Given such a commitment, the work itself would have an inner dynamic. There would be an inner logic to work out, to see how far one could carry the perspective and principles that had been accepted, to see how much of language could be dealt with afresh. The momentum of the movement would give a premium in recognition and acceptance to work, statements, notions, which carried further in the chosen direction (even though extremes would be sometimes chastened). To carry matters further along the line of the inner dynamic would be seen, not as folly, but as discovery; criticism from the standpoint of things discarded, or overlooked as alternatives, would be more readily seen as resistance than as wisdom. A 'paradigm', as Kuhn has described it, creates a world in which there is almost daily news. Perhaps such a world is irresistible; certainly it is attractive, not only to contemporaries, but to casual historians, who may lament its tunnel-vision, yet write about it at the expense of close-grained study of actual history.

Kuhn has argued that a paradigmatic community works through to confrontation of its own inevitable anomalies, and such was the case with the Bloomfieldian community. Harris developed transformational relations to go beyond descriptive linguistics, Hockett formalized a process model and entertained prospect of others, a range of interests began to flourish. When forced to choose between their conception of what inductivism required, and what formal abstract analysis disclosed, some Bloomfieldians, indeed, cheerfully enough chose the latter. That is what Joos (1961) did, in welcoming graciously the findings of Chomskyan grammar with regard to a level of deep structure. Though the findings forced abandonment of the hitherto unstated principle that 'text signals its own structure', in favor of a mythical history (Joos specified that 'mythical' had a general, neutral application), the principle of simplicity in formal analysis required acceptance.

The comments of Joos to the contents of his book of readings have been often taken to mirror the true nature of Bloomfieldian work, often misleadingly. This later comment, though seldom cited, deserves to be taken quite seriously, quite representatively. Inductivism and abstract modelling were interwoven in the inital Bloomfieldian phase, but if the historian has to weigh one against the other, then, like the participant Joos, his choice must go to abstract modelling of structure.

Inductivism was the deeply imbedded idiom, but abstract, explicit structure was the work.

Later critics have perhaps taken model-directed theory for granted; Bloomfieldians could not. In their time and place, they might indeed have been different in detail or in degree — processual statement might have been more widely retained, levels less rigidly separated. But one cannot readily imagine discovery of transformational relations, even though Whorf's notion of cryptotypes might have been developed, until phonology and morphology had been worked through. That was the history of the field throughout the world. One can perhaps imagine a development of phonological and morphological analysis without a movement as its center. But without a movement a disciplinary base might not have been created, or created readily. (From a longer or broader perspective, one might question the desirability of an autonomous discipline of linguistics itself.) In any case, the major steps in explicit, vulnerable theory of linguistic structure in the United States have been associated with movements, Bloomfieldian and Chomskyan, that initially sought autonomy for linguistic work.[53] It seems unlikely that a different idiom for abstract theory could have succeeded in the 1940s in the United States; none did, and none was even attempted, so far as we know.

With an inductive idiom, then, the Bloomfieldians created a disciplinary commitment to explicit theory of linguistic structure. Harris more and more revealed a mathematical, inventive kernel within an inductivist skin, leading, in the event, to an invention that would restore much of traditional grammar through formal explication, and find rationalization in an anti-inductive philosophical tradition.

The success of the Chomskyan approach in developing a general, novel frame of reference has had the effect postulated by Kuhn (as noted early by Thorne (1965)), namely, anachronistic misreading of preceding work. In this section we have reviewed characterizations and explanations of the general nature of the Bloomfieldian period. Much of the image of the period has depended upon treatments of specific analytical issues and tenets as well, and in the next section we consider some of these.

6. HISTORY OF PROBLEMS

In examining the history of descriptive phonology as written from the transformationalist point of view, we will look here into only a few facets of the subject, in

---

[53]   Voegelin and Voegelin (1963:28) comment colorfully on the sequence of events: 'When her box was closed, here was such beautiful freedom in structuralizing, amounting almost to anarchy. Now that Pandora's box is opened, anarchy in structuralizing will be eliminated, since structuralizing is model-directed. It can be swash-buckling, as Sapir preferred it to be, only if models are inexplicit. Once a model is explicit, structuralizing has to be restricted, as Bloomfield preferred it to be. If Bloomfield appears to have been sitting on Pandora's box [an image suggested by Chafe], it was in order to slip a key into the lock unobstrusively.'

hopes of showing its depth and complexity. In a sense, however, what this historiographical tradition omits is as significant as what it includes, and we can only allude to some of these areas, suggesting what seems to us to be their purport.

It is difficult at best to reconstruct accurately the arguments of a number of contending parties over a period of years. We have preferred to quote at length in the interests of precision, even at the expense of space and the reader's time, partly because we feel an obligation to let the reader judge matters where we are interested parties, and partly because it seems to us that careful study of sources and thorough exposition have too often been skimped in the works we reviewed in preparing this section. Indeed, we believe that critical and historical writings on phonology, both descriptivist and transformationalist, afford an all-too-perfect illustration of the dangers of the sectarian spirit in scholarship.

On three major issues, criticism of 'taxonomic' phonology and syntax by the Chomsky group has run in parallel. Both are said to slight distributional regularities —to pay insufficient attention to co-occurrence restrictions; both are said to ignore the problem of creativity as manifested by the acceptability of some but not all novel sequences — /blik/ but not /bnik/, *colorless green ideas sleep furiously* but not *furiously sleep ideas green colorless*; and both are said to be unable to account 'correctly' for relations among forms — *opaque* and *opacity*, active and passive sentence forms, and so on.

As for the first of the issues mentioned above, it was an important objective of Harris' 1944 paper on 'simultaneous components in phonology' to illustrate some ways of reducing or eliminating redundancy in phonological co-occurrence patterns through the use of phonological features ('simultaneous components') whose phonetic properties were specified and manipulated by rules referring to their componential environment.

Harris had thus proposed and illustrated in detail what amounts to the use of classificatory phonological features and redundancy rules in 1944. In some respects, notably in its use of long components, and its consequent freedom from the shortcomings of the segment as the domain of phonological specifications, Harris' pioneering work is still superior in flexibility and power to subsequent efforts within the orthodox Chomskyan framework.

The issue of novel but acceptable sequences and their treatment in the two schools of phonology has been discussed in Fought 1973 (see also Kučera 1967 on /blik/ and related matters).

Issues surrounding the treatment of relations among phonological forms will be discussed below, in connection with biuniqueness. Here we will examine one strategem: the reduction of the diversified and lengthy development of some area of linguistics to a few principles said to represent the characteristic or essential traits of the whole tradition. Once the principles are stated, examples or problems of description are then adduced to show that some linguist's practice did not conform to them, or that an analysis which did conform to them failed for that reason to reach the 'correct' solution, that is, one presented as intuitively satisfying, uncontroversial and, of course, in agreement with one's own doctrines.

There have been two main series of such attempts to reduce the practices of descriptive phonology to a few principles, and to summarize 'a body of doctrine . . . to all or part of which a great many linguists would subscribe', while admittedly 'abstracting away from much variation' (Chomsky 1964a:951). The earlier is primarily Chomsky's, appearing first in his review of Jakobson and Halle's *Fundamentals of language* (Chomsky 1957c), and developing in a series of publications up to the mid-sixties, some written jointly with Morris Halle. There has obviously been a reciprocal flow of ideas between Chomsky and Halle on this subject, but Halle's own contributions to the discussion focus in particular on the notion of simplicity in relation to rule ordering and the use of a binary feature system (Halle 1957, 1958, 1959, 1962). The later series, by Paul Postal (1964, 1966, 1968), draws upon the earlier one, but concentrates on certain morphophonemic problems. Other transformationalist writers have frequently cited, paraphrased, summarized, or just alluded to one or both traditions of criticism, giving the appearance of a firm consensus on the inadequacy of descriptive phonology.

In Chomsky's review (1957c) of Jakobson and Halle (1956), he distinguished from their position another 'widely held' view of the phoneme as meeting the following three conditions (1957c:237):

Two phones belong to (are allophones of) the same phoneme only if they are in free variation or complementary distribution. Allophones of the same phoneme are phonetically similar. The set of phonemes must meet certain requirements of 'pattern congruity' and 'distributional similarity'.

In a footnote to this passage, Chomsky mentioned Bloch 1948, 1950, and 1953, and Harris 1951 as 'the clearest formulations of such principles of phonemic analysis' he knew of. This point is of some importance; he refers to Bloch in similar terms again and again (cf. Chomsky 1964b: 83n, 91n, and, indirectly, Chomsky and Halle 1965:128).

The characterization is a fair summary of the definitions of the phoneme found in a number of early papers (e.g. Chao 1934, Swadesh 1934). Something like it might still be given as a brief definition of the phoneme as the term is used by some linguists. Nevertheless, two significant points are omitted in Chomsky's discussion: a phonemic solution was tested by the simultaneous application of these three principles, so that both phonetic similarity and noncontrastive distribution were to be taken into account in examining each putative phoneme's membership; and finally, there were reasons widely accepted for imposing such conditions, and these are quite prominent in early discussion of the phonemic principle.

Each of these three conditions has clear consequences for the design and use of orthographies. Adhering to them results in a writing system whose symbols have consistent sound values, within the limits presumably set by the awareness of the speakers of the language. This was held to make such systems easier to teach, learn, and use than systems whose symbols have more complex relationships to sound. Complementary distribution and free variation, either separately or both together, amount to noncontrastive distribution. With the kind of pattern congruity then sought, this produced further practical advantages, in the view of many of these early writers. Orthographies so constructed employed the minimum number of symbols needed to distinguish the contrasting forms of the language, and arranged them in subsets whose members shared certain phonetic, distributional, and often graphic properties.

Bloomfield, like Chao and a great many of their contemporaries, was concerned with the adequacy of writing systems for the languages he studied and described (including English) (1933:85f., 500f.). Indeed, in the first explicit treatment of the principle which was later to be called biuniqueness, Chao (in Joos 1957:49–50) discussed 'symbolic reversibility' in terms of the 'aspect of reading' and the 'aspect of writing'; the third and last major section of his paper is a still-rewarding discussion of considerations in the design of practical orthographies around the phonemic principle. For obvious reasons, missionary linguists have also been concerned with orthographies from the beginning of their application of descriptive linguistics to Bible translation (witness the subtitle of Pike's *Phonemics*: "A technique for reducing languages to writing" (1947)). It has also been fairly common for field linguists of other persuasions to devise orthographies and teach their use to at least a few informants, and to use them to record collections of texts. There has been a notable lack of comment on the significance of these motives and activities in shaping the development of descriptive phonology, apart from assertions that the study of American Indian languages limited or distorted the methods of descriptivists.

Recent discussions of the biuniqueness relation leave out not only these motivations for accepting it, but also the early, clear expositions of its relationship to morphophonemics, such as those of Harris (1944a, 1944b, 1951). The term itself is first used, to our knowledge, by Harris (1944a:187, also in Joos 1957:128) in a passage explaining that simultaneous components, like phonemes, may be represented by alternating or partly overlapping phonetic values without necessarily losing the biuniqueness of the relationship between sound and symbol.

Chomsky's discussions of the principle deal almost exclusively with phonemic overlapping, as desirable but excluded by biuniqueness, and with the principle of complementary distribution, which he sees as 'biuniqueness converted into a procedure' (1964c:102). His attack on complementary distribution suffers, as we have already noted, from his failure to appreciate that both the phonetic similarity and the noncontrastive distribution criteria had to be satisfied simultaneously in evaluating a tentative phonemic solution. His discussion of phonemic overlapping, as we will have occasion to point out again, involves consideration of morphophonemic alternations, and a tacit assumption that morphemes (underlying representations composed of systematic phonemes) have a single, invariant representation which is acted upon by phonological rules. This tacit assumption, which Hockett (1961) called a principle of *constancy*, is required if sense is to be made of the Chomskyan critique of taxonomic phonology. But it is morphophonemic notations which allow constant representations, and not phonemic ones, as structuralists well understood.

Throughout the duration of the critique, the impression is somehow created, and allowed to persist, that the implications of biuniqueness for phonemic overlapping and for morphophonemic representations were understood only dimly if at all by the structuralists, who went on trying to describe languages according to their arbitrary, unmotivated, and contradictory principles. In fact, there is abundant and clear discussion of the differences between biunique, phonemic notations and non-biunique, morphophonemic notations, including discussion of the implications of the latter for the establishment of base forms, the statement of phonotactic patterns, and the descriptive ordering of phonological rules. An outstanding example of such discussion is Chapter 14 of Harris 1951 (whose preface acknowledges Chomsky's help with the manuscript), which illustrates the morphophonemic treatment of such alternations as *sane, sanity, opaque, opacity,* and other forms which have since become familiar through their repeated appearance in the work of transformationalist phonologists. Harris credits the solution he illustrates to the work of Stanley Newman, whose work on English phonology was undertaken as a part of Edward Sapir's English project about (1935–36, and was published in the Bloomfieldian years (1947).

Criticism of phonemic notations for not having the properties found in the morphophonemic notations of the same linguists seems quite beside the point. It has its most disastrous consequences in the work of Paul Postal, as we will show below; it could just as easily be illustrated in the work of Chomsky and Halle as historians of structural linguistics.

Something of his first characterization of the phoneme remains in Chomsky's later and fuller discussions (1964b:102–3, 1964c:91–5), but it is very much in the background, reduced to a discussion of complementary distribution, with an aside about phonetic similarity.

In the foreground, Chomsky has placed his discussion of 'taxonomic phonemics' in terms of four principles: linearity, invariance, biuniqueness, and local determinacy. Two other background conditions, contrast and phonetic specifiability, are rightly regarded as fundamental both to his and to other approaches to phonology. Although the two are relatively clear, nevertheless important historical questions arise from their treatment in transformationalist writings; they will accordingly be discussed before the other four conditions.

Chomsky and Halle accept the same notion of contrast which underlies other approaches to linguistics, as they point out. Moreover, they present a principle which accurately reflects one consequence of the notion of contrast for descriptivist phonology (Chomsky and Halle 1965:128):

We assume the notion 'contrast' defined on utterances (i.e., *pin* contrasts with *bin, lighthouse keeper* with *light housekeeper,* etc.). All approaches to phonology with which we are familiar require of a phonemic notation that it meet condition (10):
(10) if X contrasts with Y, then the phonemic representation of X differs from the phonemic representation of Y,
where X and Y are utterances (let us assume, phonetically transcribed). Taxonomic linguistics adds various other conditions (e.g., the converse of (10)), but this does not concern us here . . . .

The converse of principle (10) reads as follows:
(10') if the phonemic representation of X differs from the phonemic representation of Y, then X contrasts with Y, when X and Y are utterances.
It is a serious error to attribute this principle to 'taxonomic' linguistics, as we will show later, in connection with Paul Postal's elaboration of this position. Apart from this point, however, there is nothing in Chomsky and Halle's exposition of the notion of contrast which requires comment here.

Phonetic specifiability is the 'requirement that a general linguistic theory must incorporate a universal phonetic theory, with a fixed alphabet' (Chomsky 1964a: 945) in terms of which the pronunciation of linguistic forms generated by the grammar is ultimately specified. It is the imposition of a fixed alphabet as part of this condition which requires comment. The specification of phonetic properties of phonological elements is not otherwise controversial within American structuralism.

Chomsky apparently believes that any discussion at all of phonetic qualities must presuppose a universal system as a frame of reference (1964b:77):

Analysis of actual practice [of modern taxonomic phonemics] shows no exceptions to the reliance on phonetic universals. No procedure has been offered to show why, for example, initial [pʰ] should be identified with final [p] rather than final [t], in English, that does not rely essentially on the assumption that the familiar phonetic properties (Stop, Labial, etc.) are the 'natural' ones.

It is worth noting that the 'familiar phonetic properties (Stop, Labial, etc.)' which Chomsky invoked are not those of Jakobson and Halle (1956) nor those of Chomsky and Halle (1968), although they can of course be brought into some correspondence with those other systems. One is not really faced with the Manichaean choice Chomsky has so characteristically offered. The issue is not whether to use one universally accepted system of phonetic categories all the time or to employ arbitrary or even perverse, *ad hoc* 'features'; instead one must consider a particular scheme of phonetic categories from among the systems in current use to see if it is adequate for the purpose at hand, and if not, how it can be improved.

Knowledge of the details of the production and perception of speech can be and is conceptualized in a number of ways; moreover, some of them, whether physiological or acoustic in content, differ from the others in matters of substance as well as form. A survey of current research in phonetics and phonology would hardly support the contention that one system now in existence is superior to all others for every linguistic application, or even that such a system is a widely accepted objective of research.

Yet, Chomsky seems so convinced of the equivalence of the requirements of a universal or general phonetics and of a fixed phonetic alphabet that he misunderstands the discussions of the role of phonetics in phonology conducted by the descriptivists (Chomsky 1964a:952):

> Bloomfield's apparant rejection of the level of structural phonetics reappears in an extreme form of Joos' (1957) summary of what he takes to be the characteristic view of American linguistics, namely that 'languages could differ from each other without limit and in unpredictable ways' (96), that 'distinctive features are established ad hoc for each language or even dialect', and that 'no universal theory of segments can be called upon to settle the moot points' (228).

This issue has not been very clearly joined, it seems. Joos attributed the 'differ without limit' maxim to Boas (1911), who in fact demonstrated that received theories could not accomodate certain facts of American Indian languages, with phonological, grammatical, and semantic examples showing different 'emic' structures corresponding to roughly the same 'etic' substance.[54] But it is inaccurate to suggest that Boas (or Joos) held the view that each language is totally different from all others, just as it is also inaccurate to say that Chomsky and Halle hold the view that they are all exactly alike. Moreover, since 1957, when Chomsky's review found the Jakobson-Halle universal feature system 'conceptually sound, in its essentials' (1957c:241), it has undergone enough changes, some minor and some cataclysmic, to raise serious doubts about its present, to say nothing of its future (cf. Fought 1973). A great many of these changes have been introduced, or at least proposed, as a consequence of difficulties encountered in describing (or explaining) the phonology of this or that language, in much the same way that structuralists modified whatever phonetic transcription system they had learned in order to suit the needs of the moment. In the one case, however, transformationalists find it possible to sustain their conviction that the system, through all its changes, remains not only universal, but in some sense the same; in the other case they see *ad hoc* floundering.

Finally, it is difficult to read into Bloomfield's chapters on the phoneme (1933: 74–138) anything like a rejection of 'structural phonetics'. It is essential to remember that Bloomfield's remarks about 'acoustics', setting it apart from phonology, are to be taken in terms of the practical and laboratory phonetics of the time he wrote (cf. 1933:84–5, 128). Bloomfield did not reject the acoustic character of distinctive features (indeed, he was to suggest that invariant acoustic characteristics might be discovered and so resolve controversies as to phonemic

---

[54]   Boas (and his students) asserted the existence of linguistic universals, but found that Indian languages differed in their specific organization, such that an a priori framework of parts of speech and categories could not be imposed. At the same time Boas and others sought to universalize *descriptive* concepts (see above 3.2).

analysis). He rejected the possibility of establishing distinctive features and phonological structure on purely acoustic and a priori grounds. Features were established through contrast (presupposing knowledge of meanings), structure through study of relations internal to a language. Perhaps Chomsky has in mind (though he does not cite it) Bloomfield's rejection of phonetic tables as a presentation of phonological structure (1933:129; cf. 4.2 above and n. 25). The issue here is strategy of analysis, and the role of presumed universals in specific analyses (see preceding discussion of a universal alphabet). When Bloomfield is rejecting 'acoustic' features, phonetics, and the like, it is in the context of rejecting that which is non-distinctive in favor of the phonemic principle. And although Bloomfield objected to inconsistencies and accidental omission of features in 'narrow' transcription, he characterized his phonemes as 'lumps or bundles' of distinctive features (1933:79). The difference between Bloomfield's conception of phonetic structure and Chomsky's is not as great as might appear.[55]

This is borne out by Silverstein's searching analysis of Bloomfield's notion of 'distinctive features', which concludes that from the time of his Tagalog work (1917) through 1933, it stood for something very close to 'segmental phonemes' in the work of later structuralists, and that Bloomfield's phoneme was very nearly equivalent to later 'morphophoneme' (defined by reference to automatic and some regular alternations). Silverstein further suggests, without carrying his detailed study of the history of Bloomfield's thought into this period, that it was in reaction to the misreading of his own and the very similar approach of Sapir to phonology that Bloomfield later adopted a three-level model instead of continuing to use his two-level model of phonological description. Silverstein thus suggests that Bloomfield's view of phonology remained virtually unchanging from 1917 or so until at least 1933, but that by 1939 a major restructuring had taken place. He carefully examines the examples in the 1933 chapter, and finds them equivocal on the crucial point of the relationship between distinctive features and the phoneme.

It is possible that Silverstein's explication of Bloomfield is so thorough that more consistency has been imparted to the works from this fifteen-year period than their author would have found in them. Silverstein's readings depend at some points on extremely delicate interpretations of terms used over a long period. But it would be presumptuous to challenge his interpretation, based as it is on an admirably thorough study of the source materials, including Bloomfield's correspondence with Michelson.

[55] Chomsky (1964a:952) quotes Bloomfield (1933:137) as saying that in phonology 'we pay no heed to the acoustic nature of phonemes, but merely accept them as distinct units and study their distribution'. The exact words, in a larger context, are as follows: 'The term phonology is sometimes placed in contrast with the two forms of phonetics [laboratory, practical]: phonology pays no heed to the acoustic nature of the phonemes, but merely accepts them as distinct units. It defines each phoneme by its role in the structure of speech-forms. It is important to remember that practical phonetics and phonology presuppose a knowledge of meanings: without this knowledge we could not ascertain the phonemic features.'

Nevertheless, there are some aspects of the problem, in particular, the crucial period between 1933 and 1939, which still require study before the questions can be answered definitively. It is worth noting in the meantime that, if Silverstein's interpretation of Bloomfield is correct, the resemblances between Chomsky's and Bloomfield's views of phonological units are even more striking, the only major difference being over the question of the indivisibility of segments.

In discussing Chomsky's principles of linearity, invariance, biuniqueness, and local determinacy as a reconstruction of descriptivist phonology, it will be helpful to refer to one or more of the other principles in the discussion of each. They are therefore briefly defined here.

LINEARITY   Each occurrence of a phoneme is associated with one or more successive phones as its manifestation; if a phoneme P precedes (is to the left of) phoneme Q in a representation, then the phone sequence associated with P precedes (is to the left of) the phone sequence associated with Q in the phonetic representation.

INVARIANCE   Each phoneme P is associated with a set of defining features Φ so that whenever P occurs in a phonemic representation there is an associated occurrence of Φ in the phonetic representation.

BIUNIQUENESS   Each sequence of phonemes is represented by a unique sequence of phones and each sequence of phones represents a unique sequence of phonemes.

LOCAL DETERMINACY   The phonemic representation corresponding to a given phonetic representation is determined by strictly phonetic considerations (i.e. is derivable by rules whose input is strictly phonetic).

The relation between this and the earlier set of principles is interesting. The earlier one, which Chomsky condensed from descriptivist writings, has to do with conditions two or more *phones* must satisfy in order to be grouped into a single phoneme (except for some aspects of the pattern congruity condition). The later set has to do with the properties of *symbols* in the phonemic representation as they relate to phonetic values. The earlier, then, deals with what Chao (1934) called the aspect of writing, and the later with the aspect of reading (cf. Joos 1957:49). The orientation of the first is methodological, and of the second, interpretive.

Chomsky defined his invariance condition as follows (1964b:94):

The invariance condition [. . .] asserts that each phoneme P has associated with it a certain set $\Phi(P)$ of *defining features* (that is, P = Q if and only if $\Phi(P) = \Phi(Q)$) and that wherever P occurs in a phonemic representation, there is an associated occurrence of $\Phi(P)$ in the corresponding phonetic representation. The invariance condition has no clear meaning unless the linearity condition is also met; I will assume, then, that it is inapplicable when linearity is violated.

The last sentence quoted is a serious error; we will return to it in the discussion of the linearity principle.

Chomsky then went on to distinguish two varieties of invariance: absolute, required by Bloch, and relative, allowed by Jakobson. The difference has to do with definitions of phonetic features in either absolute or relative terms. We will here be concerned only with the absolute invariance condition and the relation it establishes between phonemes and feature bundles. Hutchinson 1972 contains a thorough discussion of both varieties and their consequences.

Chomsky observed (*loc. cit.*) that partial overlapping, the assignment of a given phone to different phonemes in different environments, is impossible under the absolute invariance condition. An abstract example he gave (1957c:237) will show this more clearly than a discussion. 'There are many circumstances', he wrote, 'under which any phonemicist would choose to assign X in the contexts A and Y in the contexts B to one phoneme, while assigning Y in the contexts A and Z in the contexts B to a second phoneme'. Such circumstances always involve a desire to level out high-frequency morphophonemic alternations by contriving a notation whose interpretation rules allow an unvarying representation to stand for alternating phonemic values in different environments. Here, in any case, is the situation Chomsky described, with the phonetic features added: A and B in this example are environments; X, Y, and Z are segments with (distinctive) phonetic feature-bundles c, d, and e respectively.

$$/ X / = [X] = [c] \text{ in environment A}$$
$$= [Y] = [d] \text{ in environment B}$$
$$/ Z / = [Y] = [d] \text{ in environment A}$$
$$= [Z] = [e] \text{ in environment B}$$

In Bloch's system of phonological description, such a solution would indeed be unacceptable. The following definition of phonetic similarity is basic to his system (Bloch 1950:89, in Joos 1957:330):

Two or more phones are phonetically similar if they contain a quality or a combination of qualities that is absent from all other phones in the utterances of the same dialect. (It follows that if two or more phones are the same they must be phonetically similar, but not conversely.) Under this definition, phonetic similarity has an absolute, not a relative meaning.

The last sentence quoted emphasizes that all and only the phones sharing a particular quality or combination fit his definition of phonetic similarity. Thus, in English, all and only the voiceless labial stops are phonetically similar by virtue of sharing that combination of qualities; likewise, all and only the voiceless stops are phonetically similar by virtue of sharing that more inclusive combination of qualities; the stops form another class of phonetically similar phones, and so on. In later years, Bloch came to call this very special relation *isomerism*, to distinguish it from the everyday sense of similarity.

Having so defined phonetic similarity, he was able to give this concise and careful definition of the phoneme (Bloch 1950:90, in Joos 1957:331):

A phoneme is a class of non-contrastive and phonetically similar phones. [. . .] Each phoneme is defined by the quality or combination of qualities present in all its members and absent from all other phones of the dialect; and every phone that contains such a quality or combination belongs to the phoneme which is defined by it. A phone that contains two or more such qualities or combinations accordingly belongs to two or more phonemes at once.

Compare this statement of the invariance condition in Chomsky and Miller (1963: 311):

The *invariance condition* requires that to each phoneme A there be associated a certain defining set Σ(A) of physical phonetic features, such that each variant (allophone) of A has all the features of Σ(A) and no phonetic segment which is not a variant of A has all of the features of Σ(A).

To return to the example, segments [X] and [Z] are in noncontrastive distribution, and therefore would be assigned to the same phoneme in a Bloch-type solution if they are phonetically similar in the operative sense. This matter can not be decided in the abstract, however. From the context of the example, it seems clear that the three segments [X], [Y], and [Z], are meant to be phonetically different. If this is the case, they would be assigned to three different phonemes in a Bloch solution, as shown below in solution A. If qualities [c] and [e] in the example can be said to be varieties of some more general quality [f], as apical and laminal articulation can for example be said to be varieties of frontal articulation, and if [X] and [Z] are the only segments in the system having this feature [f], then [X] and [Z] would be both nonconstrastive and phonetically similar, and so, would be assigned to the same phoneme, say, / X /, as shown below in solution B.

Phonetic and Distributional Data	Solution A	Solution B
[X] = [c] in environment A	/ X /	/ X /
[Y] = [d] in environments A, B	/ Y /	/ Y /
[Z] = [e] in environment B	/ Z /	/ X /

In this system of phonological description, then, the phoneme and its defining feature-bundle are *equivalent*. An occurrence of one *is* an occurrence of the other. The presence of more than one feature-bundle in some temporal relation, successively *or* simultaneously, implies the presence of the corresponding phonemes in the corresponding arrangement, and vice versa. There is also an important and often overlooked distinction to be made between the phoneme and the written symbol or symbols used to represent it on paper. The symbols in the notation are placed in correspondence with the phonemes by conventions which are usually quite simple and result in one-to-one correspondences, but which sometimes specify the interpretation of some successive combinations of symbols as simultaneous or overlapping arrangements of phonemes, and occasionally specify the interpretation of a combination of symbols as representing a single phoneme.

Now consider representations of forms constructed according to these standards. The rules for interpreting the notation as an arrangement of phonemes and these phonemes as a corresponding arrangement of feature-bundles, make it possible for the user to derive from a given arrangement of symbols the corresponding arrangement of phonemes and of feature-bundles, or alternatively, from a given arrangement of features, to determine the corresponding arrangement of phonemes and the symbols which represent them.

The notation and the phonetic representation are therefore biunique. Since the conversion in either direction makes use only of phonological features, it also has the property of local determinacy as Hutchinson (1972) reconstructs it from Chomsky's statements. Nondistinctive or redundant features are specified in relation to the distinctive features making up the defining bundles of the phonemes, in the familiar way, allowing for phonetic specification to any desired and warranted degree of precision.

Bloch's definition of the phoneme as a class of noncontrastive and phonetically similar (isomeric) phones, quoted above, corresponds very closely to Chomsky's formulation of the absolute invariance condition. With the acceptance of the background notions of phonetic specifiability and contrast, as already discussed, the properties of local determinacy, biuniqueness, and the valid portion of the linearity condition all follow from the invariance relation alone. Representations meeting this condition have a feature-bundle embedded in one or more successive phones as the manifestation of each phoneme; the arrangement of defining feature-bundles conforms to the arrangement of phonemes, and vice versa, but this arrangement is not always one of succession, as Bloch made clear. Nor is the relation between phoneme symbols and feature-bundles necessarily 'linear', but except for this, the arrangement of the one type of element corresponds to that of the other in a particular representation, satisfying as much of the linearity condition as can be salvaged.

In this connection, an unfortunate misunderstanding in Hutchinson's excellent paper should be cleared up. He discusses the effects of the invariance relation between phonemes and feature-bundles upon *overlapping*, which he misconstrues as overlapping in *time* rather than overlapping in *membership* between phonemes. His discussion (1972:17) involves an example of two phonemes, /X/ and /Y/, as shown below; although it does indeed look like overlapping, the key to the example is in the feature-bundles involved, if we take for granted as he does a Bloch-type definition of invariance and of the phoneme.

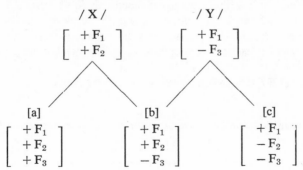

Segment [b] therefore has features belonging to /X/, namely [+ F_1, + F_2], and features belonging to /Y/, namely [+ F_1, − F_3]; it therefore manifests both phonemes at once, but it is the feature bundles which properly speaking *belong* to the phonemes. The two phonemes *overlap in time*, then, in the sense that a single token of the phone [b] manifests both at once; there is however no *phonemic overlapping*, in the sense that two different tokens of the same phone are never assigned to two different phonemes.

The analysis of 'American *r*', [γ], as /ər/ is a case in point. The phone [γ] was analyzed, rightly or wrongly, as composed of the distinctive qualities of /ə/, namely mid-central unrounded vocoid articulation, and of /r/, rather loosely called 'R color', and defined by reference to certain acoustic effects produced by any of several combinations of articulatory means, usually including labialization, retroflexion, velarization, and perhaps others.

It is unfortunate that the term *overlapping* was used for both types of relationship between phonemes.

Even though it is logically dependent upon the invariance condition and, as we will show, largely irrelevant historically, it is the linearity condition to which Chomsky has returned again and again in criticizing 'taxonomic' phonology. His notion is that the linearity condition requires that the phone sequences associated with the elements of a phonemic representation must occur in the same order as those elements (1964b:78, 93, cited in Postal 1968:54–5):

> The linearity condition (32i) requires that each occurrence of a phoneme in the phonemic representation of an utterance be associated with a particular succession of (one or more) consecutive phones in its representing matrix as its 'member' or 'realization'; and furthermore, that if A precedes B in the phonemic representation, then the phone sequence associated with A precedes (is to the left of) that associated with B in the phonetic matrix. This condition follows from definitions of the phoneme as a class of phone sequences (as in post-Bloomfieldian American linguistics, typically) or as a bundle of distinctive features (Bloomfield, Jakobson) or a minimal term in a phonological opposition (Prague circle).

Lamb (1966:540–1) argued that what he called C-phonemics did not impose a linearity condition, and that this condition is found only in Chomsky's T-phonemics, 'a system apparently created by him to serve as the helpless victim of a dramatic onslaught' (loc. cit.). Lamb's discussion of the differences between C-phonemics and T-phonemics is generally clear and useful, raising many of the points repeated here.

McCawley (1967:106–7n5), commenting on Lamb's remarks on linearity, agrees only that

> The 'neo-Bloomfieldian' linguist typically separated segmental phenomena from one or more types of suprasegmental phenomena (stress, pitch) and required his phonemicization of each of these classes of phenomena to meet some criterion of linearity, albeit often one much weaker than that which Chomsky ([1946b]) attributes to them. Deviations from

strict linearity within segmental phenomena were countenanced only to the extent of allowing a single phonetic segment to be phonemicized as a sequence of phonemes which occur elsewhere in the language (e.g. by representing a phonetic nasal flap as /nd/; cf., the passage by Bloch cited in Lamb's fn. 21).

This passage so amplifies the importance Lamb assigned to such cases as to distort and even reverse the point Lamb made very clear in his discussion. In doing so McCawley has not only ignored what Lamb wrote, but also the sources he cited (1966:539–40n12–17) to the effect that apart from Bloomfield and Whorf, there were many (Bloch, Harris, and Hockett) who explicitly rejected linearity as a condition or criterion.

In the same note, McCawley described Lamb's proposed representation of English [p] as /hb/ as 'totally foreign to the notion of "phoneme" in the authors such as Bloch whom he [Lamb] cites . . .', although it is in many ways strictly parallel to the extraction of a 'phoneme of length' from a homogeneous vowel segment, and the representation of the single segment as a digraph, say /a:/, as if it were composed of two segments. Another case is that of English [ɣ], represented by Bloch and by Trager and Smith as /ər/. In the second of these, though not in the first, the constituents of the dyadic representation occur elsewhere, 'alone'; the 'length phoneme' occurs of course only as a feature of some vowel. The steps allowing such an element are set forth in Bloch's postulates (1948, section VI, Duration). He later abandoned this type of solution for nearly all systems with a length distinction in favor of a geminate solution, for reasons of consistency.

The earliest formulation of the linearity principle is Hockett's (1947a; in Joos 1957:218), where it is limited to notations, and *explicitly rejected* from phonology itself:

In the examination of the raw data, we avoid the (usually unstated) linearity-assumption to which our tradition of linear orthography renders us susceptible. Two features, that is, may occur successively (dental closure and labial closure in *hatpin*), or simultaneously (labial and velar closure in some African languages), or in various overlapping sequences. Bundles of simultaneous or immediately adjacent features are given no priority, save precisely for the purpose of deriving an essentially linear notation; this purpose is phonologically irrelevant, though such a notation is useful, if not unavoidable, in making phonological statements.

Practically the same statement, referring to the simultaneous, overlapping, or successive occurrrence of features, appears in Bloch (1948:39); in Bloch 1950:92, the following expression of the priority of features over segments is found (cf. Bloch 1948, part III):

What we hear in listening to the utterances of a speaker is a flow of interwoven, continually changing qualities. These qualities are the irreducible atoms from which all higher units in a phonemic description of the speaker's dialect must be formed. Whether the analyst prefers a description in terms of components or one in terms of phonemes, his data consist ultimately of the qualities that he has heard in the stream of speech, and of nothing else.

The last phrase should be understood in the context of Bloch's continuing effort to provide a strictly distributionalist statement of the otherwise semantically based notion of contrast. A footnote to this passage lists examples of the componential type of description, to which one could add Martin 1951 and a methodological paper by Hockett (1942):

For a theoretical discussion see Zellig S. Harris, Simultaneous components in phonology, *Lg.* 20.181–205 (1944b). For one type of application see Charles F. Hockett, Componential analysis of Sierra Popoluca, IJAL 13.259–67 (1947b), and Peiping phonology, JAOS 67.253–67 (1947).

In the work of those descriptivists — Bloch, Harris, and Hockett — which Chomsky accepts as exemplary, then, *the principle of linearity was no more than a guideline for the design of notations.* It was rejected as a consideration in the analysis of phonological systems proper by Bloch and Hockett; Harris, like the other two, published an influential paper illustrating a componential approach to phonology rather than a segmental one. Thus, although it might be argued that the tagmemic approach to phonology, like that of Daniel Jones, is based on the segment as an ultimate constituent, and that the Prague School and the Indiana group are not fully explicit on this point, there is simply no question as to the priority of components or features over segments within the work of the linguists Chomsky refers to most frequently in his critiques.

With this in mind, it is indeed difficult to understand why Chomsky, Halle, and Postal attach so much importance to the principle of linearity, or what possible evidential value the alleged violations of it could have.

In an effort to shed some light on these questions, we will review the history of the *writer/rider* case, one of the more familiar illustrations of the shortcomings of descriptive or 'taxonomic' phonology.

The class of forms in North American English represented by *writer* and *rider* has been frequently cited by both sides of the dispute between descriptivist and transformationalist phonology. The nuclei of the heavy-stressed syllables and the apicoalveolar flaps which follow both enter into the problem posed by this pair of forms and others like it.

The considerable literature on the status and phonetics of the flaps in American English is usefully surveyed in Malécot and Lloyd (1968), who also report on a perceptual experiment. It is usual in this literature on the flaps to assume that in forms conventionally spelled with a medial *t*, the corresponding flap is a variety of *t*, or in other words, an allophone of /t/ (cf. Haugen 1938, Trager 1942), a question-begging assumption.

The first paper to consider the nuclei together with the flaps as aspects of a descriptive problem is Joos (1942). This admirable note deals with Canadian English dialects where diphthongs composed of low or lower-mid central vowels followed by either [y] or [w] offglides behave in parallel fashion. Below the border zone,

American dialects are comparable in the conditioning of diphthongs with [y] off-glides; the [w] diphthongs often show little or no such variation.

Joos was interested in the patterning of conditioned phonetic variation before voiceless and voiced consonants. While most syllabics are longer before voiced consonants than before voiceless ones, he noted that the diphthongs just mentioned are different in quality. He presented this as a raising before voiceless consonants (fortis, in his paper).

He then observed that the speech of most Canadians shows a merger of the two formerly distinct stops of *writer and rider* as a lenis flap, which he assigned to /d/ in both forms.

He noted that Canadians could be divided into two groups according to the order in which these two changes had taken place. In group A, the raising of the central vowels in diphthongs before fortis consonants preceded the lenition of inter-vocalic fortis apicals; in group B the same changes occurred in the opposite order. Here are the changes for each group, with the characteristic pronunciations of *typewriter* to be expected from each:

Group A	Group B
[a] → [ɐ] / __VK	[t] → [d] / V__V
[t] → [d] / V__V	[a] → [ɐ] / __VK
[tɐɪprɐɪdɚ]	[tɐɪpraɪdɚ]

Joos made it clear that a phonemic split had been produced by the raising of diphthongs followed by the merger of stops as in group A. And he unequivocally assigned the flaps to /d/.

The case next appears in Harris (1951:70), where the flaps are transcribed [r']:

Thus in some dialects the alveolar flap consonant of *writer* is identical with that of *rider*. The preceding vowel qualities, however, differ, so that we have, in terms of segments, [ræyr'ɣ] and [rayr'ɣ]. Before all segments other than [r'] the [æy] and [ay] are complementary: [æy] before voiceless consonants, [ay] before voiced segments, as in [fæyt] *fight*, [pæynt] *pint*, [maynd] *mind*. [. . .] *Nowhere* else in English do we have phonemes with just such a distribution, nor is it elegant to have two phonemes which are complementary through so much of their distribution.

The symbol [æ] designates a lower-mid central unrounded vowel, intermediate between [ə] and [a]; for Harris, the vowel contrast involves tongue-height.

Harris offered three solutions to the problem. The first assigned the *sequence* of segments [æyr'] to the *sequence* of phonemes /ayt/ and the sequence [ayr'] to the sequence /ayd/. The second assigned to /æy/ only those occurrences of [æy[which contrast with [ay] = /ay/; all other occurrences of both [æy] and [ay], where there is no contrast, are assigned to /ay/. Both these solutions involve partial over-lapping or intersection, since the first assigns the flap to different phonemes in different environments, and the second assigns [æ] to different phonemes in different environments. The third solution assigns the different diphthongs to different phonemes in all occurrences, and establishes a separate flap phoneme too, avoiding overlapping, but flying in the face of what seem to be powerful preconceptions about the 'intuitively correct' representations of these forms — a distinction which just happens to agree with the traditional spellings.

Other solutions are not only possible but reasonable. We will outline some of the choices here, to give an idea of the range of possibilities usually skipped over in the literature.

There is first the question of the phonetic facts. It matters whether the nuclei of *writer* and *rider* differ distinctively in length or in height. The two cases would be solved differently in any system of descriptive phonology. If the difference is length, then either a length phoneme or gemination of the first element of the long nuclei would be called for. If the two sets of forms differ in height, one could assign all of the allophones of the higher vowels (as in *writer*) to /ə/; or all to /a/, together with the allophones of the lower nuclei, provided that the contrasts between forms were otherwise represented; or one could assign to /ə/ only those instances of higher vowels where there was another, contrasting form with a lower nucleus. If one establishes a third vowel phoneme, like Harris' /æ/, intermediate between /ə/ and /a/, one can assign all or only the 'contrastive' higher allophones to it, and the other nuclei can be assigned to /a/.

Possible treatments of the flaps are exactly parallel: one can assign all of them to /t/, or all to /d/, or some to /t/ and the rest to /d/, or one can establish a distinct flap phoneme, /D/, and assign all or some of the flap allophones to it.

Not all of these choices are equally attractive, to be sure, and some of them are interdependent. A number have been proposed over the years, however, or are implied by the transcriptions found in the literature. Again, a careful consideration of the possibilities is missing from the transformationalist literature.

It is instructive to follow the presentation of the *writer/rider* example in the works of Chomsky and Halle over the years, and to see the changes of tone and the various uses to which it has been put.

It was first used by Chomsky in an argument against certain views of Jakobson and Halle in his review of their *Fundamentals of language* (1956). He credited the example to Harris (Chomsky 1957c:238), but presented it as a contrast of vowel *length* rather than of height:

. . . an English dialect where medial post-stress /t/ and /d/ merge in a tongue flap [D] and where only the normally redundant feature of vowel length distinguishes *writer* (phonetically, [rayDɨr]) from *rider* (phonetically, [ra·yDɨr]). Jakobson-Halle would be forced to consider length to be a distinctive feature for vowels in such a variety of English, though its appearance, as distinctive, would be limited to this position and to the phonemic opposition /a/ – /a·/.

Chomsky went on to present what amounts to Harris' first solution, accomplishing the allophonic conversion by two ordered rules, and noting that this solution violates an implicit principle he was later to call linearity.

The implications of the shift from a contrast of height to one of length are important; they will be taken up in the next section.

The example appeared next in Chomsky's contribution to the 1958 Texas conference. His solution (or Harris') is offered as an argument against the strong version of biuniqueness (1964b:244):

Consider, for example, the strong ('once a phoneme, always a phoneme') form of the biuniqueness principle, mentioned above. A particular consequence of this principle is that no exceptions can be tolerated on the phonemic level. I have found several speakers for whom there is apparently only one case of an intervocalic, pre-stress, post-weak stress alveolar flap [D], namely in *today*, where it contrasts with the /d/ of *to Denver, adept, to-do (a great to-do)*, . . . and the /t/ of *attack, detest*, . . . If we accept the principle in question, we will have to mark the predictable post-stress [D] in *writer* ([rayDɨr]), *rider* ([ray:Dɨr]) as a phoneme /D/, with consequent complication of tl morphophonemics. But now the two words *writer, rider* differ phonemically only in vowel length, which must consequently be considered phonemic, so that the phonemic transcriptions are /rayDɨr/, /ray:Dɨr/.

This time there is no reference to Harris.

Where formerly it was the alleged length contrast of *writer* and *rider* which was limited in distribution, against the background of the syllabic system of English, here it is the contrastive flap of *today* which is limited and exceptional; *writer* and *rider* have become part of the background. The solution given is taken for granted; the point to be made is about simplicity and the treatment of exceptions (1964: 244–5):

If, alternatively, our goal is, as described above, to construct the simplest grammar of the language, we can merely state this fact about *today* as a peculiar and unique phenomenon, leaving the rest of the phonemic description unaltered, with the transcriptions /raytɨr/, /raydɨr/, /rayt/, /rayd/, /pat/, /pad/, where the phonetic form is predictable by very general and familiar phonetic rules of English, now supplemented by a low-level rule about *today*.

The example appears again in Chomsky's contribution to the Ninth International Congress of Linguists, held in 1962, and in the publications derived from that paper, this time in connection with the four principles he formulated to characterize the taxonomic approach. After presenting the same example, with two ordered rules to produce the same phonetic representations, Chomsky wrote that (1964a:956; 1964b:96)

if phonemic representation is to play any significant role in linguistic description (if it is to be part of a grammar that achieves descriptive adequacy), the linearity condition must be rather grossly violated.

This was the reason he gave (*loc. cit.*):

. . . here words which differ phonemically only in their fourth segments differ phonetically only in their second segments.

However, as soon as we examine the phonemic and phonetic representations of the two forms, aligning the symbols as Hutchinson did (1972:7), it is clear that there is no violation of linearity at all:

$$
\begin{array}{ccccc}
/r/_1 & /a/_2 & /y/_3 & /t/_4 & /r/_5 \\
| & | & | & | & | \\
[r]_1 & [a]_2 & [y]_3 & [D]_4 & [r]_5 \\
/r/_1 & /a/_2 & /y/_3 & /d/_4 & /r/_5 \\
| & | & | & | & | \\
[r]_1 & [a\cdot]_2 & [y]_3 & [D]_4 & [r]_5
\end{array}
$$

Each phoneme has an overt manifestation and the manifestations come in precisely the same linear order as the manifested phonemes. One can only conclude, since Chomsky is so adamant that this constitutes a violation of linearity, that his explicit definition of the linearity constraint is incomplete.

In an effort to reconcile Chomsky's use of the principle with his statement of it, Hutchinson proposes to add the following clause to the linearity constraint (*loc. cit.*):

. . . two phonemic representations differ in their *i-th* segments if and only if their corresponding phonetic representations differ in their *i-th* segments, where *i* is a positive integer.

Such an addition is indeed in agreement with the treatment of the *writer/rider* case in Chomsky and Miller (1963:311–13), where it is offered as an argument against linearity and invariance, again in connection with the first of the Harris solutions. Their statement of linearity and invariance there (1963:313) does not clearly separate the two constraints, but it does lend support to Hutchinson's emendation:

Note, however, that the phonemic representations of these words differ only in the *fourth* segment (voiced consonant versus unvoiced consonant), whereas the phonetic representations differ only in the *second* segment (longer vowel versus shorter vowel). Consequently it seems impossible to maintain that a sequence of phonemes $A_1 \ldots A_m$ is associated with the sequence of phonetic segments $a_1 \ldots a_m$, where a_i contains the set of features that uniquely identify A_i in addition to certain redundant features. This is a typical example that shows the untenability of the linearity and invariance conditions for phonemic representation. It follows that phonemes cannot be derived from phonetic representations by simple procedures of segmentation and classification by criterial attributes, at least as these are ordinarily construed.

However, it is *invariance*, not linearity, which the standard representation violates, because of the phonemic overlapping it produces.

It is perhaps unnecessary to draw further attention to the failure of Chomsky and Halle to sustain either of the key points in their argument, namely, that linearity was regarded by 'taxonomic' phonologists as an essential characteristic of their solutions, and that the *writer/rider* case, whose representation allegedly violates the linearity constraint, thereby demonstrates the futility of the taxonomic approach.

Instead, let us turn briefly to the status of the example as representative of American English pronunciation.

Although Joos and Harris wrote of a contrast of *height* between the first syllabics of *writer* and *rider*, Chomsky presented the case as a contrast of *length*. Householder (1965:29n14) objected to the length contrast in Chomsky's treatments, claiming that a height contrast would be more realistic for American English. In reply, Chomsky and Halle (1965:32–3n27) falsely attributed the length contrast to Harris, and went on to heap scorn on Householder:

The very same argument could have been given for the dialect in which the distinction is one of quality rather than length (i.e., with *writer* = [rʌyDr] = /raytr/ and *rider* = [rayDr] = /raydr/).
Householder comments (fn. 14) that "Halle uses a similar example in which the difference is qualitative (1962:63) [a] vs [ə]. This is more realistic". But this is surely a slip of the pen, for we do not doubt that he is familiar with the fact that in certain dialects of English the difference between the two variants of the diphthongs is one of length (/a:/ vs /a/) whereas in others it is one of tenseness (/a/ vs /ə/) (cf. Kurath and McDavid, 1961: maps 26–27). If indeed Householder means what he seems to be saying and regards the latter dialects as more realistic than the former, then he must also regard German as more realistic than English or Latvian as more realistic than Igbo, a conclusion that seems to us as unbelievable as it is unavoidable.

The tone of this passage seems all the more unacceptable when it is realized that the facts are by no means as evident as they suppose. The two maps in Kurath and McDavid 1961 show the nuclei of *nine* (map 26) and *twice* (map 27); not only do they not show the nuclei in the same type of environment as *writer* and *rider*, but even more interestingly, they do not show a *contrast* of length at all.

There is no area on the maps where the two nuclei differ by length alone. In southern West Virginia and western North and South Carolina, both *twice* and *nine* have low, long, centering diphthongs, [aːə] or [ɑːə]. The rest of the area has a mid or lower-mid rising diphthong [ɐɪ] or [əɪ] or [ʌɪ] in *twice*, and either the same nucleus in *nine*, as in Pennsylvania, New York, and westward, or a low rising diphthong, whether short or long, in New England [aɪ], [ɑɪ], [aːɪ], or [ɑɪ], or a long, low diphthong rising only to mid height, [aːɛ] or [ɑːɛ] , through the South except in coastal South Carolina, which agrees with New York in this particular. In some parts of the area covered by the maps, the two nuclei are transcribed as the same, in others there is a difference of tongue height alone, in still others the difference of height is matched by one of length, the lower vowel being the longer, and in others the height difference is matched by a difference of advancement, the lower vowel being the more retracted. Some New England dialects apparently have all three features, the two nuclei differing in height, length, and advancement.

In short, these maps do not warrant any conclusions at all about the pronunciation of *writer* and *rider* in the territory they cover; moreover, they suggest, if they do not prove, that where there is a difference between the nuclei of *twice* and *nine*, it is height and not length that is distinctive. Elsewhere in Kurath and McDavid 1961 there are hints that there may be a length contrast in some parts of New England, as Bernard Bloch maintained, but the evidence is scanty and not where Chomsky and Halle sent their readers to look for it.

Although the evidence available is inconclusive, and our survey of it is not exhaustive, it does seem reasonable to ask where in North America one can find the dialects whose speakers distinguish *writer* from *rider* by vowel length alone. To Chomsky and Halle they are 'familiar'; like Householder, we do not know where to find them.

For American English in general, in any event, it does indeed seem to be more 'realistic' to speak of a distinction of height rather than of length in such pairs, in the natural sense that the statement is true of many more speakers. Thus, even if it were true, as it is not, that substituting a contrast of vowel length for a contrast of vowel height leaves the logical character of the example unchanged, it does profoundly alter its significance as an example of English, since the data are now different from the usual pattern, the height contrast, shared by most or all speakers, including Chomsky himself by his own admission (1964b:244n32), and the solution must therefore seem that much less appealing on 'intuitive' grounds as a description of English.

This substantive issue is not made any clearer by the ever-widening circle of confusion about the phonetic values of the forms within the literature. Consider the following, for example, as a background for the claims and counterclaims of Householder, Chomsky, and Halle. Although it was Chomsky, not Harris, who introduced the length contrast, Chomsky (1957c:238) attributed it to Harris, a custom followed in many other publications since then, including Chomsky and Halle (1965:132n27) and Postal (1968:24–5); all of them *refer* to the Harris presentation, and at least as late as Chomsky and Halle 1965:133 they still say that a tongue-height contrast is equivalent and could just as well have been used. They go on to misquote Householder, supplying '[a] vs [ə]' for his '[a] vs [ɑ]' (Householder 1965:28n14), which is itself a mistake, since the passage Householder referred to in Halle (1962:63) is really a quotation from Joos (1942:141–4), and he used a tongue height distinction, between [a] and lower-mid [ɐ], the same distinction that Harris used, with [æ] as equivalent to Joos' symbol [ɐ].

In his contribution to the discussion of the *writer/rider* case, David Johns (1969, reprinted in Makkai 1972) notes that vocalic length is associated with voicing of a following consonant (he says the features are in complementary distribution rather than in [nearly] constant association) (1972:550):

. . . what we have is two features which seem to act as a unit and never occur independently together. Yet there are cases where one of the features is not present and the other carries the entire load alone.

This leads him to propose combining the two segmental features, length and voicing, into a 'superfeature':

The superfeature of voicing and preceding length would simply manifest itself as both wherever possible; where the consonant is initial only voicing would be present, and where a neutralization rule applies, as in *writer/rider,* only length would remain. In a word such as *ride,* there would be no need to decide whether length or voicing is distinctive, since they cannot exist independently.

Although the title of Johns' paper is "Phonemics and generative grammar", there are no signs of first-hand knowledge of the literature of phonemics, despite his seeming approval of the approach. In particular he seems unaware that Zellig Harris proposed and illustrated almost exactly the same technique in "Simultaneous components in phonology" (1944), even including a general discussion of environmental conditioning of phonetic manifestations of one component by another. The earliest work Johns refers to is Halle 1959; other authors listed are Chomsky, Kiparsky, Postal, and Stampe. Thus the circle is ironically closed by another unwitting omission of a reference to Harris' place in the history of the *writer/rider* case.

In summing up the case of *writer* and *rider,* we can say that subsequent discussions have only obscured the outlines presented so clearly by Joos (1942). The descriptive problem stems from the disagreement between the phonological representations taken for granted, in which the first syllabics are the same and the medial consonants are different, and the actual pronunciations of the forms in the great majority of American dialects, in which the first syllabics are different and the medial consonants are the same.

A review of the sources shows that, first, the phonetic facts are not as Chomsky and Halle have represented them, at least not for most speakers, so that the obvious solution of the given data appears strange as a description of English; second, that the difference between the length contrast they allege and the attested height contrast is in fact highly significant within descriptive phonology; third, contrary to their claim, the transcription they regard as intuitively correct but inadmissible within taxonomic theory does *not* violate the principle of linearity as formulated by Chomsky; and fourth, in any case, linearity in this sense was both implicitly and explicitly *rejected* from phonological theory by Bernard Bloch, Zellig Harris, and Charles Hockett, the descriptivists whose phonological writings are cited by Chomsky as exemplary of the 'taxonomic' approach.

We seem to have come full circle in following the transformationalists' critiques of the descriptivist phoneme. The criticisms are wide of the mark, yet the rejection is steadfast and complete. Linearity, a spurious issue, has been used from the outset to condemn the phoneme for failing to accomplish descriptive tasks which its users reserved for other tools. Over and over again, we read that invariance, biuniqueness, linearity, and local determinacy are 'too strong' to be acceptable constraints on phonological representations. Too strong for what? For the representation of certain types of conditioned alternation by constant, unvarying phonological symbols. In brief, the phoneme has been condemned for not being the morphophoneme. This attitude is very close to the surface in some passages of Chomksy's early work, like this one (1957c:238):

The Jakobson-Halle neglect of distributional considerations, and more generally, of considerations of patterning and simplicity, however, leads to certain difficulties. Although this position is never explicitly stated, it seems clear that in their view there is a very direct, in fact, order-preserving relation between a phonemic representation and the associated sequence of speech segments. That is, speech is taken to be literally constituted of a sequence of phonemes, each with its distinctive and redundant features; accordingly, the phonetic value of a sequence of phonemes is the sequence of phonetic values of these phonemes.

One must ask what is wrong with this conception of phonological structure, which is stated generally enough to be as true of Bloch's views as it is of Jakobson's and Halle's at that time. The trouble, from a Chomskyian point of view, is with the directness of the relation between phonemes and phones. It is not possible to achieve certain morphophonemic levelings within those constraints. In addition, there was thought to be a conflict between the sequential ordering of phonological rules for maximum simplicity and generality and the use of the phoneme as an intermediate level of representation. Accordingly, there was an early and continuing tendency to relax the constraints which assured the directness of phoneme-to-phone relations, and to exploit rule-ordering to the full. The distinction between classificatory features, with no phonetic content, and phonological features with concrete phonetic significance, for instance, is a part of this movement toward greater flexibility and complexity in the relationship between Chomsky's 'phonemes' and the phone sequences which represent them.

This development did not take place without confusion, however. In the next section, we will show how profound the confusion became in at least one influential work.

In two works written at about the same time, but published two years apart, Paul Postal argued that 'taxonomic' phonology requires that all occurrences of a given form must be transcribed in the same way (1966:172):

It is necessary within taxonomic phonemics that utterances which are free variants be given the same phonemic representations. Hence all instances of *intentional* must be represented alike, and similarly for *employment, accelerate,* and the many other words of this type.*

* Even though in some instances each word is pronounced, not with ititial [I], [ɛ], or [æ], respectively, but with initial [ə]. That is, each of the first three vowels is in variation with the fourth (shwa).

Postal saw a contradiction in this, since such representations imply that any two elements in free variation with some third element are necessarily also in free variation with each other. He illustrated the consequences as follows (1966:172):

If the initial vowels of the different [free variant] forms are not represented distinctly it is impossible to state where [I], [ɛ] and [æ] will appear, i.e., this would amount to the false claim that these strong vowels are in free variation in unstressed word initial position. If, however, the initial vowels of these words are represented distinctly then the vowel shwa is assigned to different phonemes under the same phonetic circumstances. Hence complete overlapping. If, on the other hand, all instances of freely varying vowel quality are not given the same phonemic representation, free variation is not segregated from contrast. There is simply no way out of this dilemma within taxonomic phonemics which is thereby shown to be false.

Substantially the same argument is developed more fully in Postal (1968:216–28), where it is called the 'nontransitivity of contrast' (1968:218):

What is crucial [about the claim that free variation is an equivalence relation—JGF] . . . is the claim which autonomous phonemics makes that free variation is a transitive relation. That is, what is crucial is the claim that it is necessarily the case that if a form A is in free variation with a form B, and B is in free variation with a form C, then A is in free variation with C.

For Postal, since forms with variant pronunciations are to be given invariant representations, the nontransitivity of free variation (and contrast) is the same as phonemic intersection (1968:225):

Nontransitivity of free variation/contrast can be stated in other, perhaps more familiar, terms as 'complete overlapping' (Bloch 1941:280). Complete overlapping or intersection is normally defined as the assignment of the same phonetic segment to different phonemes in the 'same' phonetic contexts. All the cases of nontransitivity are simply cases of complete overlapping.

Postal seems to suggest here that complete intersection would eliminate the problem he has posed, but he does not investigate the reasons for its rejection or the alternative solutions to the 'dilemma' he constructed.

He seems to have based his argument on his reconstruction (by the use of four principles) rather than on a fresh examination of structuralist practice. Here are his four principles (1968:8):

(1.1) Given two identical phonological representations, the utterances they represent, that is, the phonetic representations they are associated with, may or may not be *identical* but are necessarily not *distinct*. That is, the associated phonetic forms must be free variants or repetitions.
(1.2) Given two phonetic representations which are not free variants (repetitions), and are hence necessarily not identical, their phonological representations are necessarily distinct.
(1.3) Given two phonetic representations which are free variants, their phonological representations are necessarily identical.
(1.4) Given two distinct phonological representations, the phonetic representations they are associated with are necessarily distinct.

It will be easier to discuss Postal's four propositions and to compare them with Chomsky's principle (10) discussed above (p. 1097) if all are presented in a normalized form. All refer to *identical* or *nonidentical* phonological representations (I or Ī) and to *equivalent* or *nonequivalent* phonetic representations (E or Ē), these last based on contrast. Postal's principles can then be cast in the form of categorical propositions as follows:

1.1   All I are E.
1.2   All Ē are Ī.
1.3   All E are I.
1.4   All Ī are Ē.

Chomsky's principle (10) stated that if X contrasts with Y (i.e. if X is phonetically nonequivalent to Y), then the phonemic representation of X differs from the phonemic representation of Y. This is evidently the source of Postal's proposition 1.2.

Three of these propositions are equivalent as a matter of immediate inference: (1.2), Chomsky's (10), is the contrapositive of (1.1), and (1.4) is the obverse of (1.1). Proposition (1.3) is not logically equivalent to the others, however, as it would be if it were the converse of (1.1). Some E are I. This is indeed where the difficulty, both logical and factual, is to be found, as we will show.

Having presented his four statements, however, Postal dismissed the possibility of significant differences within descriptive linguistics on these points, and the need for a more careful reading of the sources (1968:8–9):

Conditions (1.1) through (1.4) as a whole seem to me to be an absolutely uncontroversial reconstruction of assumptions which lie behind modern autonomous phonemics, so much so that I will not attempt to justify them textually here by quoting instances of them from the literature. But cf. the quotes from Lamb, Lounsbury, and Hockett in this and the following two chapters.

Nevertheless, there is no system of structural phonology known to us which conforms to Postal's principle 1.3 in the sense he gave to it.

Two crucial distinctions must be examined in evaluating Postal's reconstruction of phonemics: the difference between alternations of *forms* and of *segments*, and the difference between *free variation* and *free alternation*.

Postal does not distinguish representations of pairs of single segments, segment sequences, morphemes, or whole utterances. In the passage cited above, for example (1966:172), he referred first to utterances, then cited some words as examples, and then, in the next passage, discussed individual segments. It makes a vital difference, however, whether forms or segments are involved in the equivalence relation Postal called 'free variation'. If two *forms* are equivalent (that is, freely substitutable for each other), their alternating segments may nevertheless be phonemically distinct (e.g. [ɛmploimint] and [imploimint]), as warranted by a contrast, here between /e/ and /i/, in other forms (e.g. [džɛst] and [džist])). If two *segments* are equivalent in all environments, on the other hand, they never contrast, and so are phonemically identical, as are, for instance, plain and velarized allophones of American /r/. Postal failed, then, to distinguish between the *alternation* of phonetically and phonemically distinct segments (in equivalent forms) and the *variation* of phonetically but not phonemically distinct segments. Indeed, although he was aware of these terms, he explicitly rejected any valid distinction between the two types of phenomena. 'Some linguists might wish to claim a distinction between 'free variation' and 'free alternation', he wrote (1966:185), but

. . . these terminological distinctions have no force here since no one has ever presented any evidence whatever showing any difference between the two (or three in Hockett's case) cases other than the defining ones of reference to the different kinds of environments. What is at issue, however, is whether there is any empirical significance to the distinction just referred to.

It should be clear now that whatever its empirical significance, this distinction has logical significance within descriptive phonology. Postal referred to this passage from Hockett 1942 (in Joos 1957:102):

There is sometimes, in some definable position in utterances, a *free alternation* between phones that must be assigned to different phonemes. In some dialects of Spanish, for instance, there is free alternation between /d/ and /r/ before a stressed vowel as in *pedir* 'ask' and *preparar* 'prepare'. This is different, of course, from free variation between phones of different homeophones but the same allophone.

It is worth noting in passing that Postal himself advocated a distinction between two sources and thus two kinds of free variation, which he called trivial and nontrivial (1968:14–5):

There are then two different sources for free variation. Trivially it arises through the generation in any way whatever of identical phonetic representations. Nontrivially it arises through the operation of optional rules or their equivalent which associate *n* (n ≥ 2) phonetic representations with a single systematic representation.

This distinction, of course, parallels very closely that between subphonemic free variation and the free alternation of phonemes which he rejected in structural phonology.

Obviously, more than a nicety of phonemic terminology is involved in this controversy. Hockett has reviewed some of the history of the issues from a descriptivist point of view in two papers (1961, 1965) which Postal listed (1968) but apparently did not understand. In his earlier paper, Hockett introduced his discussion by presenting three propositions and showing that acceptance of any two implies the rejection of the third (1961:30):

(1) *Knife* and *knive-* are the same morpheme.
(2) *Knife* and *knive-* are phonemically different.
(3) A morpheme is composed of phonemes.

He explained that there are three positions which may be taken (*loc. cit.*):

If we (I) posit the first and third assertions as premises, the conclusion is that *knife* and *knive-* are phonemically identical. If we (II) posit the second and third as premises, the conclusion is that *knife* and *knive-* are not morphemically the same. If we wish (III) to posit the first and second as our premises, then we are forced to conclude that a morpheme is not composed of phonemes.

What Hockett then and later called the audibility principle is crucial to the resolution of the representation problem within descriptive phonology: '. . . two things are not phonemically different unless a native speaker can hear the difference' (1961:30). He added (1961:31) that

The principle [that phonemic differences are audible] . . . was recogized in the nineteen thirties, and the impossibility of the first 'solution' of the trilemma followed as a corollary.

This first solution is the one Postal took for granted.

Hockett returned to the audibility principle in a later paper, presenting it as one of five principles which he felt have 'played a part' in the history of phonemics from its beginnings. They are (Hockett 1965:195):

(1) *Audibility*.   The difference between any two distinct sentences of a language is audible to a native speaker in the absence of noise, even if there is no defining context.
(2) *Finiteness*.   Every sentence of a language consists of an arrangement of a finite number of occurrences of phonological units, and the total stock of units for all sentences is finite.
(3) *Patterning*.   Some arrangements of units occur more frequently than others, and some combinatorially possible arrangements do not occur at all.
(4) *Linearity*.   The arrangements in which units occur in sentences is exclusively linear (that is, one after another, with no simultaneity or overlapping).
(5) *Constancy*.   Recurrences of the same form (e.g. the same 'morpheme') are recurrences of the same phonological units in the same arrangement.

Hockett notes that linearity, 'inspired, of course, by the essentially linear nature of most writing systems', is superfluous, and he continues (1965:196):

The two mutually incompatible assumptions are those of audibility and of constancy. As I argued this point at length a few years ago, a single example should serve here. *Wives* rimes with *hives,* and *wife* with *fife,* but not *fife* and *hive* and not *fifes* and *hives.* We can insist on audibility, in which case *wife* and *fife* are phonologically alike at the end, and similarly *wives* and *hives,* but this means that the morpheme *wife* appears in two phonologically distinct shapes, violating constancy. Or we can insist on constancy, in which case *wife* and *fife* do not end the same way phonologically even though they are an exact rime, thus violating audibility. But we cannot maintain both principles at once. This was realized very early, and much of the history of phonological theory has been that of a search for a motivated (rather than arbitrary) compromise.

It makes no difference for Postal's argument whether the alternations between distinct phonological representations are conditioned or free; the result is the same in either case. One can see this easily if one of Postal's examples of 'free variation' is substituted for the conditioned alternation used by Hockett:

(1') [æksɛlərejt] and [iksɛlərejt] are the same morpheme.
(2') [æksɛlərejt] and [iksɛlərejt] are phonemically different.
(3) Morphemes are composed of phonemes.

In structuralist terms, then, Postal has singlehandedly discovered morphophonemics: the alternation, either conditioned or free, of two or more phonological forms of a morpheme. Incredibly, Postal was not only confident of the 'uncontroversial' accuracy of his principles as a reconstruction of phonemics, but he was also puzzled (or exultant) that '. . . the nontransitivity of contrast has not been, to my knowledge, explicitly noted or taken account of for more than a quarter of a century' except in passing by Lees in 1957 (Postal 1968:221–2). The magnitude of this scholarly blunder can only be appreciated when it is realized that Postal referred to Hockett 1961 and 1965 in connection with the status of the morphophonemic and allomorphic modes of structural description; much of that paper is devoted to a summary of the history and theoretical status of the points that Postal missed. Hockett even refers to Chomsky, Halle, and Lukoff 1956 and to Lees 1957 as efforts to justify the 'logically distinct' element arrived at by suspending the audibility principle.

It may be unfair to put all the responsibility for his somewhat belated discovery on Postal alone, however. The absence of a thorough and understanding discussion of the place of morphophonemics in relation both to the systematic phoneme and the descriptivist phoneme is one of the most glaring omissions in the transformationalist critique of descriptive phonology. Hutchinson (1972) covers this area rather well, discussing Schane (1971) and a few others. There is not much on this subject for him to review.

In the works examined in this section, we have seen much use of sets of principles as an expository or polemical device. Of course, the earlier descriptivist tradition so abounded in works written in this way that it has been criticized, not altogether fairly, for an obsessive concern with procedures. And still earlier, the Neogrammarians often presented their work in much the same way (as witness Paul's *Prinzipien der Sprachwissenschaft*). Indeed, this style of exposition is a natural one for the purposes of scholarly communication and debate.

Transformationalists have adapted it to polemical use, however, and certain characteristic features of it in this application need to be pointed out. First, we observe that although the number, wording, and sense of the principles themselves may change in the course of time, the examples are used again and again, sometimes to illustrate one principle, and sometimes another. With time, the origin of even the most important examples becomes more and more obscure, until each takes on a life of its own, being cited in its latest form rather than its earliest. A

similar process of attenuation can be seen in the relationship of the principles themselves to the works they are said to epitomize. Early in the process, one finds actual
references to specific works, if rarely to specific pages. Later, the names of a few
linguists are mentioned, perhaps in a footnote; which of their works is at stake,
and how they may differ from other linguists, is no longer clear. Still later, even the
names are dropped, and criticisms are directed against a 'school of thought'.

7.   TOWARD HISTORICAL ADEQUACY

Let us conclude by mentioning some topics which particularly require research, if
an adequate history of structural linguistics in the United States is to be written.
Lines of research that contribute to descriptive adequacy (7.1, 7.2) lead into questions of underlying relations (7.3, 7.4), questions that may be seen as involving
explanatory adequacy. With regard to the latter, we advance a hypothesis as to the
continuity and dynamic of our subject (7.3), and then consider periodization again
(cf. 1.3.1), an issue which links the preceding topics and puts our subject within
the context of the history of linguistics as a whole.

7.1   *Neglected Topics (1): Forms of Expression*

It is obvious that much fundamental work needs to be done in every aspect of the
history of structural linguistics: rescue and preservation of evidence, editing of
published and unpublished work, biographical studies, studies of the history of
technical terms, arguments and problems. The subject is poorly mapped. We have
earlier stressed the need for study of institutional contexts. Let us here call attention to a further dimension. The cognitive content of the subject will doubtless
continue to attract study; the social context is likely to receive attention from
sociologists and historians of science. A further dimension is that of the forms of
expression of linguistic work. Although these may appear more properly the domain of literary scholars, it is essential for linguists to participate, for they have the
native speaker judgments, so to speak, necessary to notice and weigh many of the
phenomena.

The point to be made about study of forms of expression is simply that they
matter. They express identifications and affiliations, of course; they enter as well
into the constraints on what can be expressed, and hence on what is likely to be
conceived. Our point is not a naive 'Whorfianism' (though it is unfair to Whorf to
associate his name with a naive position). The point is one that seems to us incon-
testable: forms of available expression condition what is expressed.

One might ultimately envisage a 'grammar', 'rhetoric', and 'poetics' of forms of
expression in linguistics, along the lines envisaged by Burke for study of the re-

sources of linguistic expression in general.[56] Here we shall only mention three pertinent foci of study: genres, styles, and terminology.

7.1.1 Genres

Linguistic discussion, like other cultural uses of language, falls into a variety of genres. Some attention has been given to this with regard to Bloomfieldian work in (5.1) above. One would like to have careful definitions of genre (emulating the example of Burke 1951) — it can be worthwhile to try to capture the essentials of even an isolated form of presentation. Beyond this, the sources, development, popularity, and persistence of genres are revealing aspects of the subject. By and large, a person entering the field does not invent the ways in which communication, and evidence of his or her status as a participant, will be attempted. If we consider genre to comprise not only work at the level of books, monographs, and types of article, but also modes of handling quite specific pieces of work, including such detail as conventions of transcription and statement of relationships, then there is much of interest, indeed a wealth of material. Note that genres are not to be equated with only a given scholar, school or period of time, along the lines of a mainstream model of successive paradigms. They may persist marginally or covertly in tradition, as it were. The Boasian typologically oriented overview of grammatical categories attenuated in his own life time, cf. Ferguson (1964). The genre of the set of postulates, identified with Bloomfield and Bloomfieldian work (Bloomfield 1926, Bloch 1948 (and unpublished materials), Hill 1967) is marked for recasting in sociolinguistic terms to honor the fiftieth birthday of Bloomfield's initial set.

Obvious topics for careful study, with attention to overall form and specific features, are modes of grammatical presentation: the Boasian analytic grammar; the Sapirian grammar (Takelma, Southern Paiute, Tonkawa, Yokuts, Eskimo, Nootka, Tunica, Chitimacha); the morpheme index and positional classes mode of presentation, having antecedent in Boas' work (cf. Stocking 1974b:181), but developed notably by Voegelin and by Pike; the typical phonemic article, the typical morphological statement, the text with analysis, the syntactic argument article, the abolition-of-a-level-by-finding-of-a-generalization-the-level-prevents-capture-of (reminiscent of the reputed Boasian argumentation against evolutionary cultural levels

[56] In Burke's sense, these three projects would be concerned, first, with universal dimensions of reasoning and argument inherent in the subject, and with their interrelations. These would be studied as they shape specific works and frames of reference, both through selective emphasis, and through suppression, ambiguity, and other forms of unavoidable wrestling (unavoidable, because the dimensions are indeed universally inherent in the general subject). That would be the 'grammar'. The 'rhetoric' would attend to the ways in which works and frames of reference are shaped by expression, persuasion, and identification, by, in short, relations between linguist and audience. The 'grammar' and 'rhetoric' might be thought of as a logic and a sociology of linguists' forms of expression, or as answering to cognitive and socio-expressive motives. With just these two, however, understanding would be incomplete. There would be also a 'poetics' that considered exploration, elaboration, and completion of formal possibilities for their own sake. Burke's conception of language as symbolic action emphasizes symbolicity as a motive in its own right.

and generalizations, through the citing of an ethnographic exception, in adhering to an all-or-nothing principle). The 'textbook on the American pattern, with problem-sets for each chapter and a glossary of technical terms' (Sampson 1970: 267) deserves placement as well.

7.1.2 Styles

Only one or two observations can be made here. Obviously one can deploy the concept of style, and the resources of stylistics, at any level, from that of a comparison of texts to those of comparison of scholars, schools, periods. The Bloomfieldian period appears strongly impersonal in dominant style, the Chomskyan period much more self-expressive, and yet it is impossible to miss the personal note in the writing of men such as Hockett and Joos, or indeed, Bloch and Bloomfield. Any style, as selective use of means, will have its resources for personal expression, even if the personal element is a mode of use of ostensibly impersonal means. Conversely, the most informal or personal style will contain some appeal to the authority of the science or of others, if only through the dropping of a reference or the casting of a rule format before one's audience.

One point of interest among many is the recourse to informal presentation in work that assumes formal justificiation to be available in principle — the 'meaning shortcut' of some Bloomfieldians, and the use of phonemic representation in work that theoretically rejects the phoneme, or the use of 'something like' to indicate a syntactic structure not itself worked out, are examples. From one point of view, the latter two usages seem to be professional instances of what Bernstein calls a 'restricted code' — a pointing that takes for granted common values and understandings, such that explicitness is not required. From another point of view, the use of inexplicit presentation on behalf of a theoretical position calling for complete explicitness in any work that is to be taken seriously (cf. Chomsky 1964:951, n. 40) poses the problem of contradiction between style and content.

7.1.3 Terminology

The shifting relationship between concepts and terms is important, yet difficult, to map. Clearly the relationship is not one to one. A given term maps onto more than one, or parts of more than one, concept, and a given concept finds expression, directly or partly, in more than one term. As with other sectors of culture, terms may proliferate because of focus of interest in a particular domain — disparities of this sort are of obvious interest to an understanding of the culture of linguists. Instrumental or cognitive interest of course is not the only kind — some proliferation of terminology may be due to socio-expressive motives, such as desire to have one's own nomenclature, to express one's own outlook, or to maintain a boundary (cognitive and socio-expressive motives are commonly intertwined). Again, felt need for a term, whether cognitive or socio-expressive, may be met by invention, extension, borrowing — the gamut of possibilities recognized in studies of lexical borrowing and acculturation generally. The 'ethnolinguistics of linguistics' is an open field.

In addition to questions of origin and proliferation, questions of the career of terms are of great interest, and again, the mode of study is one familiar to linguists from study of terms not their own. Obvious topics of great centrality are the career of '*phonème*' to 'phoneme', the subsequent decline of the latter (beginning perhaps with Hockett 1955:163 and Joos 1957:108, 228), but with some persistence and now tentative revival; the career of '*morphème*' to 'morpheme', and the relation of the latter to 'formative' (cf. Matthews 1972); the interrelations over time of 'phonology', 'morphophonemics', and 'systematic phonemics'; the earlier use of 'speech act', especially in the form 'act of speech', in the sense of the physical occurrence of speech, vis-à-vis the later use of 'speech act' in the sense of a social action, and the effort to replace the earlier use of 'speech event' in the sense of physical occurrence by a use in the sense of socially organized activity. Many other topics await study.

Analysis of course requires a standpoint from which one can calibrate differences and similarities in definition and usage, but the first requirement, of course, is close reading, contextual reading, to establish the usage of the specific text, author, and time. Later analysis may find essential unity where participants found a difference worth worrying about, and conversely. Thus in the 1940s and 1950s a number of linguists in the United States felt there to be something at issue (some of the time at least) as between 'descriptive' and 'structural' linguistics; Chomskyan linguists have felt transformational generative grammar to be wholly different from both, joined together as 'structural': and we have advanced reasons for interpreting 'structural linguistics' as encompassing all of these. Conversely, the perceived identity of position as to distributional analysis, non-semantic basis of analysis, concern with explicit procedures, item-and-arrangement model, as between Trager and Smith, and Harris, has seemed to us in retrospect to conceal a difference in weighting and orientation of enormous ultimate consequences. While both approaches had much in common, much that characterized the period of work (in virtue of their own efforts in large part), we have seen the one as summing up the lesson of past experience, the other as setting a lesson for the future. Such 'dynamic synchrony' (to adapt Jakobson's term for states of language) in a state of linguistics inevitably affects one's reading of a term in authors so perceived; perhaps close reading would find purely textual support for differentiation given by historical outcome.

In this regard as in others, the great problem is not to project current understandings into earlier uses of terms; not to assume that sameness of terminology means sameness of meaning, and equally, not to assume that difference of terminology precludes sameness of meaning.

Studies of clusters of terms in specific works, authors, and periods, as they shift through a text, a career, and a time, would be invaluable (Joos 1958b is the one insightful commentary on this process that we know). Perhaps there are cycles of popularity and shift that answer to some of the same factors as motivate lexical change in nonprofessional sectors, such as slang — factors of generational replacement, of sheer overuse, of new sources of prestige — all these being more than merely factors of cognitive need. Very likely preferred terms carry conscious or unconscious metaphors; thus Matthews (1972:114, n. 7) says of the use of 'shapes' — 'a common and revealing metaphor'. The inductive orientation of Bloomfieldians is clearly expressed in such a comment as that of Hockett, objecting to a way Nida had put something (Hockett 1944:253):

> Linguists know perfectly well what 'selection' means; we know perfectly well that a 'form-class' is a list of forms which the analyst puts down because of some common feature of behavior. But unless the 'selection' and 'form-class' terminology is handled with care, a newcomer to the field is all too apt to decide that a certain word acts in a certain way BECAUSE [sic] it belongs to a certain form-class, which is certainly putting the causality in the wrong place.

The orientation of the Chomskyan approach is clearly reflected in its use of 'language acquisition' instead of the standard 'language learning'. The 'deep' 'surface' (or 'superficial') terminology carries a metaphor that has implications quite different from Whorf's 'covert': 'overt'. The introduction of the terms 'competence', 'performance', and 'creative aspect' of language use has been criticized as promising more (because of the ordinary language senses of the terms) than delivered, claiming the name of a whole for study of a part. And so on. Despite some hopes for a truly neutral metalanguage, and despite the widespread use of a particular terminology as a lingua franca, socio-expressive and theoretical connotations, if not implications, appear throughout the history of our subject.

In sum, the written work that provides documentation for history needs to be studied as situated, expressive, and addressed — as being functionally complex, just as discourse of other kinds. (The point holds even more for oral data — tape recordings of conversations, talks, and lectures, such as we hope will figure increasingly in historiography, so much of recent linguistics having been orally mediated — a point stressed to us by Neustupný.) As structural linguistics in the United States acquires serious historians, many and varied features of forms of expression will emerge as important for tracing and explanation — terms, metaphors, topoi, conventions, formats, usages, styles routines, genres of many kinds, of varied persistence, prevalence, and weight. But let us turn now to neglected topics within the language of historiography itself.

7.2   Neglected Topics (2): Terms for Patterns

We are far from having an adequate understanding of the terminology required within the historiography of linguistics. Of the various aspects of *metalanguage*, let us deal here with terms that have to do with selecting and grouping aspects of the history into schools, periods, and the like. Such terms have considerable currency and are of special importance. Any attempt at explanation of the history is dependent on the description of patterning that it accepts.

Pattern terms are not much discussed, and we know no attempt to establish an adequate set of them. One can observe that 'school' is often unpopular, that 'paradigm' is quite popular, and that the period or periods covered by this study are designated and defined in quite various ways. Let us consider the problem posed by the term 'school', as a way of entering into issues that lead us to propose a term not ordinarily used in historiography of linguistics, and to relate it to terms such as 'circle', 'tradition', and 'paradigm'.

7.2.1 *'School'*

This term is familiar in such collocations as 'Prague School', 'Yale School', and, less often in the United States, 'Harvard School' (Ivić 1965, Leroy 1967). It is eschewed or disliked by many linguists. Akhmanova and Mikael'an (1969:22) write:

It should be emphasized in this connection, that the divisions adopted in the present book are not based on 'schools' or groups of persons brought together by common territories or allegiances. The main purpose here is to explain the different approaches, the different points of view as such.

They support their point with statements from putative representatives of three 'schools': Fischer-Jørgensen on the 'Copenhagen School', Vachek on the Prague School', and, especially pertinent here, Fries, beginning an article on "The Bloomfield 'School' " (1961:196):

Bloomfield ... despised 'schools', insisting that the usual attitude of the adherents of a 'school' strikes at the very foundations of all sound science. ... To Bloomfield one of the most important outcomes of the first 21 years of the Linguistic Society of America was that it had saved us from the blight of the odium theologicum and the postulation of 'schools'.

(Cf. Hall 1969:223, quoting Bloomfield 1946b:1–3.) Bloomfield was thinking especially of the 'school' that is the extension of a single scholar's views (and prejudices), lengthened into a shadow and dogma.

Schools, as groups with party lines, may indeed be destructive of certain intellectual values, as Bloomfield held. Certainly the superficial use of the concept can easily obscure the history of the subject. Lounsbury (1962:284–285) has put the point well with regard to the term 'the American school of linguistics':

The label, it must be noted, is inevitably misleading, since not all American linguists belong equally to the 'school' or subscribe to all of these tenets. Some accept more of them than others; and all, in fact, have varied more or less in their own practice, adhering more often in word (programmatic statements, 'theory') than in deed (applied linguistics). And some, it should be added, place themselves quite outside this tradition. With all respect to the facts of diversity, and the claims of individuality, significant synchronic groups of scholars have existed, and do exist. One needs to designate them. If it is misleading to impute uniformity to the members by a label, it is absurd to suggest that all linguists are equidistant from one another in intellectual space. There obviously have been teachers who have shaped the work of their students; groups self-consciously asserting common views against others; many acts of personal inclusion and exclusion.

The answer to the problem may appear in the kinds of terms that are in fact used commonly and without great objection. On the one hand, modifiers in the name of a leading scholar do not meet with much objection.[57] Even Fries consented to write of the 'Bloomfield 'school' ', though immediately pointing out that Bloomfield would have disliked the label; and the varying forms, 'Bloomfieldian', 'post-Bloomfieldian', and 'neo-Bloomfieldian' have been widely used, as has also 'Chomskyan'; both meet an obvious need for designation of relatively coherent, self-conscious groups central to the development of structural linguistics. On the other hand, modifiers designating an approach are common parlance: tagmemic, stratificational, 'extended standard theory', generative semantics. Such terms suggest that the term 'school' itself is offensive, especially when combined with a geographical label; 'school' is taken to imply identity of view, and the geographical label to imply that all linguists who fall within its scope geographically belong there by affiliation as well. The term 'circle' does not attract such objections.

For the linguist affected by such labels, the main consideration appears to be misattribution of an intellectual position on the grounds of a common teacher or common location. Terms involving personal names are acceptable, apparently, insofar as affiliation is felt to be voluntary (Fischer-Jørgensen probably would have granted the existence of a 'Hjelmslev school', though she very much doubted the existence of a 'Copenhagen school'). Terms involving a model of grammar, or approach, are acceptable, apparently, insofar as affiliation is felt to be voluntary, and insofar as the label can be taken to imply the sharing of a frame of reference, but not necessarily adherence to a line defined by others. 'Circle' is acceptable because it is interpreted primarily as a designation of common location and, beyond that, a frame of reference at most.

For the historiographer of linguistics, the misattribution of an intellectual position on grounds of common teacher, common location, or common time of work, is a serious problem too. Inaccurate overgeneralization concerns both practicing linguist and historiographer. The latter's problem, however, has additional dimensions. On the one hand, there are in fact groups of linguists who exhibit the characteristics of 'schools', and that fact must be registered, whether or not the participants would have accepted the categorization (often enough differences loom larger

---

[57]   Though compare Halliday's response to the term 'neo-Firthian' (Halliday 1966:110, n. 1). The difficulty seems to be twofold: there are different, rather opposed views subsumed under the term, and in Halliday's case, the sense of continuity with Firth has to do with quite general orientation and stimulation, not with specific views.

within a group than they do from without). On the other hand, the issue is not limited to one of positions held. It extends to what holders of positions do about them, especially when action takes the form of concerted advocacy. While individuals rightly reject the implication of concerted advocacy, when mistakenly attributed to them, the historiographer must recognize such advocacy as a central force. A term other than 'school' can be used, a term that is perhaps more appropriate, though it may attract similar objections. Let us explore the situation further with regard to periods of time as a whole. It is the relation between dominant groups ('schools' or the like) and the periods they dominate, or to which they prove a central force, that the problem of term, and concept, arises most importantly.

First, as to overextended attribution of common position: the designation of a period of time as a whole as 'Bloomfieldian' or 'structural linguistics' (in the Chomskyan usage), for example, as against 'Chomskyan' or 'transformational generative grammar' may be intended only to signal the major force for change in a period. Nevertheless, the usage invites interpretation of the term as equivalent to all that is at work in the period. The common 'mainstream' model of thinking invites one to equate the 'mainstream' with the 'whole stream'. The difficulty extends to participants in the 'mainstream' itself; V. Makkai (1972:vii) puts it:

It is all too easy to think of a theory as set and fixed, and to regard all the articles written within a particular theoretical framework as reflecting the same basic assumptions. Nothing could be further from the truth . . . .

Second, as to the actual existence of 'school'-like groups, recall that Hockett (1968:9) refers to a consensus reached about 1950, and that Wells (1963) recognizes a common frame of reference and specific set of assumptions as flourishing over a period from approximately 1933 to 1957. Both are participants in the work that they characterize. Although the term 'school' might itself be rejected, the existence of concerted effort is taken for granted.

Third, as to the inadequacy of intellectual positions alone to characterize the relation between dominant groups and periods: let us compare the specific characterizations given by Hockett and Wells. To do so is unfair in one respect: the two aim at different levels of characterization. If this fact is borne in mind, a useful point can be made. Hockett refers to a consensus reached about 1950 (1968:9). Specifically, he speaks of a reasonable working consensus with regard to (1) the confluence of the historical-comparative, and the philosophical-descriptive, traditions (the practical descriptivism of missionaries and anthropologists entering as an important tributary); (2) serious efforts to integrate the findings of these traditions into a single discipline and even more to establish that discipline as a respectable branch of science with proper autonomy; (3) discovery and development of the phonemic principle; (4) attempts (particularly in the 1940s) to put the rest of grammar on as good a footing as had been thought to be achieved for phonemics. At this very general level, amounting in the circumstances of the time almost to a description of the ingredients of a commitment to linguistics as such, Hockett is quite apt. Specific positions within linguistics, however, enter into the picture at this point only in two ways, as technical details, and neglected issues (1968:9):

Most of our arguments were about technical details. Certain issues, however, had been not so much settled as swept under the rug.

Hockett discusses three of these issues: the relation between language structure and language change, the design of grammar (language minus phonology), and the relation of grammar to meaning. These issues come close to defining the central concerns of theory within structural linguistics!

Where Hockett may seem to find too little specific agreement to explain the coherence of a group, Wells may seem to impute too much. He states eight ideals as characteristic of DL (descriptive linguistics); (1) that the basis of linguistic work should be purely descriptive (not interpretive, historical-comparative, explanatory, or evaluative); (2) idioglottal (in terms of itself rather than another language); (3) 'asemic' (without appeal to meaning); (4) static and nonfictive (i.e., in terms of items and arrangements, rather than processes); (5) agglutinatively oriented (using juxta-position as the chief grammatical relation); (6) procedural rigor (i.e., include evidence of the procedures by which arrived at); (7) economy ('simplicity'); and (8) grammar reducing (i.e., impute the least necessary grammar). Of these traits, or ideals, the first two had their origins a generation or two before the period in question in the work of Boas; the third and fourth were not true of the work of the 1930s by Sapir and his students, and not strictly true of the work of Bloom-field himself (nor of the work of Hockett later); the fifth and sixth traits again pertain really to the 1940s and the Bloomfieldians, not to Sapir or to Sapir himself (cf. Fries 1961:222–223 on Bloomfield's diffidence with regard to procedures and techniques of analysis); the seventh is shared with the following period, and the eighth is particular to the work of one scholar, Harris (as is the fifth also, when contrasted to immediate constituent analysis).

These ideals, as Wells considers them, are neither technical details nor issues swept under the rug. Nor are they distinctively characteristic of the whole of the work intended to be described in terms of them. The first and second are general, but inherited; the fifth and eighth (agglutinative, grammar-reducing) are specific to one major figure's approach; the third ('asemic') would divide major figures, as perhaps would the seventh (economy) if given specific implementation (a point Wells implicitly recognizes). The static-nonfictive, and procedural rigor, goals do characterize the main thrust of most work in the period of the Bloomfieldians proper (the 1949s).

Our purpose is not to single out Wells for criticism. It would be difficult for anyone to devise a list of any extent of features universally shared by work of the period in question, if the features are to be defined in terms of methodological positions. Recall that acceptable group terms appear to imply voluntary affiliation, and sharing of a frame of reference. The crucial thing for historical description appears to be sharing of a frame of reference, together with commitment to a common purpose. Wells' first two ideals refer in large measure to such a shared frame of reference, and the rest to positions as to the way in which to implement the purpose implied by the frame of reference.

In short, the coherence and cohesion of the central groups in the history of structural linguistics in the United States appears to depend in essential part upon the sharing of common purpose. It is the common difficulty of historiography to attempt to treat the unity of such a group in terms of specific positions.

To say this is not to deny the element of truth in attempts to characerize explicitly what has lain implicit in the work of a group of scholars. Such reconstruction is necessary for historiography of genuine depth; but the criterion is understanding of the work in its actual complexity, not reduction of it, or replacement of it by an imposed model (cf. Voegelin and Voegelin 1963:22, and the analysis of Marx's historical method in Öllman 1971:66–67). A logical reconstruction, devised for the purpose of playing a part in later work and debate, has its place, but the place is like that of a recreation of a poem in a second language. The reconstruction, like the recreation, may be meaningful, but neither is to be confused with its original.

The true center of unity of leading groups in structural linguistics in the United States in any case is not found in texts alone. Such groups show the kind of covert unity that Cassirer ([1942] 1961:139–140 — cf. [1927] 1964:viii–ix) found in the philosophy of the Renaissance:

What we are trying to give expression to here is a unity of *direction*, not a unity of *actualization*. The particular individuals *belong together*, not because they are alike or resemble each other, but because they are *cooperating in a common task* . . . .

7.2.2 *Movements and traditions*

The kind of unity in context described by Cassirer can be designated in a variety of ways. If 'school' suggests too great a sameness of positions, where unity in problems addressed is meant, 'circle' may suggest too limited a unity, not going beyond contiguity and interaction. *Movement* seems an apt term. The history of structural linguistics in the United States can be readily interpreted in terms of three successive (and overlapping) movements:

(1) the movement for autonomous study of language, i.e., for a profession of linguistics;

(2) the movement for autonomous study of linguistic structure;

(3) the movement for autonomous study of grammar (syntactic structure).

In each case the movement for autonomy was also a move to make the subject of concern central to general concern with language: first, linguistics itself, as distinct from other disciplines concerned with language; then, synchronic structure, as distinct from history (and culture); and finally, syntactic relations, and covert structure, as distinct from phonology and overt structure.

One can see each movement as incorporating the leading motive, cooperative common task, of its predecessor. The Bloomfieldian movement was committed to a profession of linguistics, of course, and indeed made synchronic structure the key justification. The Chomskyan movement deepens the autonomy of linguistic structure and the centrality of an autonomous linguistics. (Chomsky's classification of linguistics as a branch of cognitive psychology, like Hockett's classification of linguistics as a branch of cultural anthropology, does not imply any less of autonomy (cf. Hockett 1968:9, n. 1).)

The notion of *movements* does not suffice to explain the broad history of structural linguistics, but it has the virtue that it clearly does not suffice. It may signify a mainstream, but clearly not the whole.

7.2.3 *Movements, paradigms, and traditions*

The notion of *movements* answers to an important aspect of the notion of *paradigm*, as explicated usefully by Wallace (1972). One essential qualification is necessary, if the latter notion is to be applied to structural linguistics, however; Kuhn's original notion of paradigm treats the history of a science as a succession of paradigms in such a way as to invite identification of paradigm and period. Wallace's notion allows, and the facts of the history of linguistics require, restriction of the notion of paradigm to just a central thrust of change within a period.

Participants in the dominant thrust of a period do appropriate the general name, 'linguistics', for what they do. Perhaps this criterion of central change and dominance, such as to succeed in becoming the unmarked exemplar of the general term, would satisfy Kuhn's notion. Certainly the intellectual demography of the actual discipline of linguistics does not satisfy a simple equation between paradigm and profession, as appears when rights and obligations have to be honored in selection of papers for meetings and congresses, of representatives and officers, and other actions on behalf of the professional constituency as a whole.

We will accept use of 'paradigm' in the sense indicated above, as equivalent to a movement that is the central focus and force for change in a period of time. This usage fits with some current usage, wherein 'paradigm' is used hopefully to suggest that a particular line of work may become the next central focus and force for change, but where it can not seriously be intended that the line of work is or will become mutually unintelligible with others (genuine, successive paradigmatic differences in Kuhn's theory are not mutually intelligible). The debates and interchanges (e.g., among 'extended standard theory', 'generative semantics', and 'variation theory' show considerable mutual intelligibility). Let us set aside the merely prestige-claiming sense of the term, which can be translated as equivalent to 'cynosure' (cf. Hymes 1974).

There is another possible interpretation of the present state of affairs in terms of Kuhn's notion of paradigm. In what he calls 'an outrageous suggestion' Bursill-Hall (1970b:240) writes:

The present state of linguistics is typical of what may be called pre-paradigmatic insecurity and we have been passing through a period of unprecedented theoretical activity which Kuhn has characterized as typical of the last stage prior to the universal paradigm.

The sense of approaching the emergence of a new paradigmatic integration may be accurately prophetic, but there does not seem much reason to expect any new paradigm to integrate linguistics as a whole. Past history and present circumstances suggest that the future will continue to show central, dominant trends, but not all-inclusive theory and modes of work. The study of language, even when one considers just that part of it conducted by linguists, appears to be irremediably diverse. There are differences in materials studied, and methods required for their study, as between phonetics, say, grammar proper, and comparative-historical linguistics, that do not permit other than artificial reduction to a common theory. There are partly different purposes and partly different traditions as well. Relations may be close, and there may be a considerable amount of integration, but that is less than identity of paradigm. Within the study of the organization of linguistic means in synchronic states, it may not be possible to unite formal analysis, directed to underlying universals; analysis of variability; and analysis of discourse and style, though again there may be considerable integration.

Comparative-historical linguistics is a telling case in point. When succeeded as central focus of development by synchronic, structural linguistics, it did not disappear, but continued (cf. Hockett 1968:18). It has been massively affected by structural linguistics, and a considerable amount of conceptual integration has sometimes been achieved. Yet irreducible differences, having to do in important part with the nature of the materials, and the tradition of work, remain (cf. Hockett 1968:18). At a more particular level, traditions of work stemming from involvement with the language of a certain family, or region, or from training with a certain group of scholars, or for a certain set of problems, persist through changes of cynosure and movement at the center of the attention of the discipline. Indeed, it is a difficult, but vital task of historiography to engage in 'stylistic' analysis, as it were, to trace the continuities and linkages in this regard, among persons, institutions, language families, etc.

So far as the history of linguistics reveals, then, any synchronic state of affairs is likely to be characterized by a relation between a central *movement* and a range of *traditions*. The interrelation may be complexly dialectic. Many departments of linguistics, and universities, will provide interesting evidence. The several traditions may themselves experience internal changes that answer to a sense of cynosure or generation-linked movement — only these changes will not capture the attention of the profession as a whole. One may wish to distinguish between *paradigm*, then, and *movement*, at the center of a profession as a whole, and *sub-paradigms*, and *peripheral movements*. (*Tradition* might then be reserved for more individual styles of work and orientation, as in the 'Boas tradition', the 'Sapir tradition'.)

The analysis of the paradigmatic process by Wallace (1972) is flexible enough to fit location of the process at different levels of scope. The analysis has the decisive virtue of insisting on the factor of social interest and change, as against purely intellectual change. Wallace specifies five essential components: innovation, paradigmatic core development, exploitation, functional consequences, and rationalization (1972:476). The model applies only to change sequences in which paradigmatic core development occurs, not to all sequences of innovation and consequence. The point is that the paradigm-forming innovation need not be a complete and adequate theory or model, but it opens up a new line of development, and has a symbolic and charismatic quality. Core development is the continuous elaboration of the ideas of the original paradigm by members of a community, a self-conscious reference group. Wallace stresses the peculiar arbitrariness of the process: it is often remarkably independent in its direction, once launched, from surrounding events, as though, once defined, it must develop according to an inner law of its own, working to realize latent implications. (In this respect, one infers, a long-continued paradigmatic development may settle into a character easily describable as that of a tradition of thought or work.)

By exploitation Wallace means recognition and embracing of the paradigm at some stage in its evolution by an organization (we would add, or group) which sees an opportunity for protection or advancement of its own interests. So far, one sees an exact application in terms of the successive movements in linguistics in the United States, from students of language wishing freedom for their study to a younger generation entering the profession. Wallace goes on to distinguish *between* the paradigmatic and the exploiting communities; the application of this distinction is less clear, especially since Wallace regards it as rare for the paradigmatic community to be the exploiter of its own paradigm. Within a discipline such as linguistics it would seem that considerations of generational displacement, personal advancement, intellectual opportunity, would suffice to explain the essential identity of community as regards both development and exploitation (the situation may be rather different in a discipline such as physics). The relations between linguistics and various institutions, however, may contain something of this distinction.

By functional consequences Wallace simply means that the core development process creates advantages and disadvantages both, solves problems and creates new ones. Finally, rationalization concerns the ethical, philosophical, religious, and political justifications which members of the paradigmatic community offer for the participation in the core development process, and which general community members offer for their relationship to the paradigm. In linguistics this sphere would encompass features of world view, aspirations of various kinds, associations with various extrinsic positions, not themselves indispensable to the technical development within the paradigm. There is an important distinction between rationalizations in response to paradigms, and motivations which may inform its initiation. We have noted that Bloomfield's adoption of behaviorism seems to have been secondary to views long held; and as we have seen, the full panoply of theoretical significance for transformational grammar, as of the early 1960s, was not apparent in Chomsky's initial work of the mid-1950s. In each case, however, there is continuity with the initial motivation, and the later ideas are not so much rationalizations in the usual sense as they are amplifications — further connections and associations which it is hoped or believed that central process of development will support. Still, these larger ideas do sometimes serve as rationalization for work remote from them.

The union of the paradigmatic core development process and exploitation appears to characterize closely what can be seen as movements within the history of structural linguistics. In the case of the first movement, the innovation was the idea of an autonomous linguistic *science*, the paradigmatic core development was accomplished by the founders and sustainers of the LSA, who shared in exploitation as well; functional consequences are poorly known, and, by Wallace's model, would have to be traced in other disciplines and in aspects of institutions outside linguistics itself; rationalization would also have relevance to the context of the new development as well as to its participants. Clearly the goal of a science was central for members of the paradigmatic community itself.

In the case of the second movement, one can see the innovation as the development of phonology (phonemics) as an autonomous sector of study, independent of particular languages, and requiring general, abstract, explicit models. The core development was accomplished particularly by students of Sapir and Bloomfield (the latter through the Linguistic Institute and the language work of the Second World War), who also became the exploiting community in the development of an academic discipline of linguistics with its own departments in the years after the Second World War. Functional consequences of this development, within linguistics and outside it, are little studied; rationalization would preeminently remain that of constituting a science, but also that of contributing practically through foreign language teaching and teaching of English.

In the case of the third movement the innovation is of course transformational generative grammar, 'an event which solves a limited problem' in the hands of its initiator Harris perhaps, but which 'does so in a way which opens up a whole new line of development' in the hands of Chomsky (quoting again from Wallace 1972: 409). The paradigmatic core community and exploiting community is far larger in number, and attracted from within the now extant profession a swell as from without. Functional consequences and rationalization are matters of current debate, and outside our scope here.

Notice that the series of three movements do not include reference to Boas. One can, and indeed must, speak of a tradition of analytic concern stemming from Boas, and can point to a specific body of work, especially the grammars in the *Handbook of American Indian languages*, and the theoretical position of Boas' "Introduction" to the first volume of that series (1911). At the time of its accomplishment, however, the Boasian grammatical work appears to have been essentially the reflection of the conception and dedication of the one man, rather than concerted advocacy on the part of a group. In terms of apparently self-generated enthusiasm on the part of a group, the notable instance in the period is the intensive concern with new genetic relationships among American Indian languages from about 1910 to 1919 (cf. Hymes 1964:693). That involved anthropologists rather than students of language generally. The theses of analytic, idioglottic study of linguistic form were clearly laid down by Boas (1911) and given pungent expression and rich demonstration by Sapir (1921), but the climate of a movement does not appear until Sapir has taught a few years at Chicago and moves to Yale (i.e., circa 1930). There is something amounting to a movement at Columbia, reflecting the influence of Boas, in the 1920s, but it has cultural anthropology as its scope. Sapir is attached to it, and some of its members do linguistic work on American Indian languages, sponsored by Boas, but general concepts of pattern, configuration, and the like are its central concern, not specifically linguistic pattern. Or so it now seems, lacking close study of these years.

The problem of the position of the work of Boas underlines the difference between movements, as paradigmatic communities, and the intellectual development of the subject overall. Even if our tentative conclusion (separating Boasian work off as 'pre-movement', so far as structural linguistics is concerned) should be sustained, it will still be necessary to include Boas in a general analysis of the range and development of intellectual positions. A comparison and contrast of leading scholars on such dimensions as position toward mentalism, universals, processes, grammatical (semantic) categories, expressive function, social meaning, homogeneity of speech community, field work, and the like, would be essential, both to place individual scholars fairly, and to be able to trace the actual course of ideas and work with regard to each such dimension. Again, Boasian grammar must be included in a general study of frames of reference, comparing and contrasting groups of scholars, and modes of work, as to characteristic data base or source, sector of structure of primary concern, conception of analytic statement, and conception of interpretation and explanation. One virtue of comparative study over such a range of work and time will be the more adequate base for empirically justifying the dimensions found essential for adequate description of the history of linguistic description in the United States. A comparative study, and descriptive theory, limited to Chomsky and his most explicit immediate rivals in the 1950s is desperately foreshortened.

7.2.4   Drift

Although it is common for participants in one movement, or paradigmatic community, to feel a drastic gap between themselves and immediate predecessors, a longer view often discloses substantial continuities between the two. We shall say a little about this question of self-consciousness in the next section. Let us conclude the present section by introducing one further concept, derived from linguistics, that may prove useful as a complement to that of movements. In brief, insofar as there is a deeper patterning to the development of linguistic science than successive revolutions, some cumulative or perduring direction, then one may adopt *drift* as the name for it. We suggest this, conscious of the parallel (mutatis mutandi) to Sapir's use of the term for an aspect of language history (1921, ch. 7). The relative autonomy of linguistics in this century in the United States, as a discipline in which a certain direction may persist over generations, and across conscious paradigms, can be expressed by substituting the disciplinary name in Sapir's well known statement (1921:60): '[Linguistics] moves down time in a current of its own making. It has a drift.' When we consider how vast a variety of activities and researches are engaged in by the multitude of scholars involved in linguistics, and yet how small or selective a portion are considered the 'news' of the discipline as a whole, we may find applicable another of Sapir's statements (1921:155):

The linguistic drift has direction. In other words, only those individual variations embody it or carry it which move in a certain direction, just as only certain wave movements in the bay outline the tide.

The identification and explanation of such drift is easy enough from the standpoint of a single movement, or paradigmatic community. We shall hazard a hypothesis from the standpoint of the three movements of the century together. But first let us consider further the periodization presupposed by our hypothesis.

7.3 Underlying Relations (1): The 'Red Thread'

In section (1) it was noted that periodization cannot be separated from valuative premises. For many participants in transformational generative grammar, the major periodization in linguistics may appear as a three-fold division, into the 'Cartesian linguistics' of the seventeenth and eighteenth centuries, the neglect of such questions, under the reign of historicism and empiricism, until about 1960, and the return of such questions in recent years. This view is a very strong form of the *interregnum* perspective. It is a very common perspective in Western cultures (and perhaps others), and has been given memorable form by Hegel, Marx, Morgan, McLuhan, and others, in terms of the return (at a higher stage) of an earlier, valued characteristic.

The sense of ancestors as remote, if existent, that goes with such a perspective is fed by the characteristic 'eclipsing' stance of participants in major new developments in the history of linguistics in the United States. Boas himself did not much mention predecessors in anthropology and linguistics, sometimes refuting men such as Daniel Garrison Brinton merely anonymously. His students commonly formed an image of their work and their profession as having begun with him, as against the mistaken evolutionism of preceding generations; and professionally at least, they were right (on continuities and discontinuities in this regard, see Darnell 1969). Bloomfield conveyed a sense of being at the beginning of adequate study of language (e.g., 1933:3, 21) and imparted it to others, as to some extent apparently did Sapir. Linguists such as Hoijer, Voegelin, and Hockett have occasionally expressed a revealing sense of a decisive break through their attitude toward work done prior to, and without benefit of, the phonemic principle. Hockett still dismisses such work (personal communication with regard to Kroeber's Yokuts vocabularies). The stance of Chomsky, Postal, and some others is familiar.

The stance of rejecting a preceding dominant approach, or frame of reference, in as thoroughgoing, indeed as inverse as possible a way, may be a necessary ingredient of a successful movement. It would be difficult to argue that it is a necessary ingredient of scientific advance, unless one found that movements themselves were necessary. Such a conclusion would imply that scientific work tends not to be self-correcting, insofar as frames of reference are concerned, on the part of those who have come to identify the frame of reference with the science. The conclusion would imply that an ambitious new generation is a necessary force. Or, one would infer that such a generation is a necessary force, or perhaps merely an inevitable force, given the sociocultural structure that supports science in the United States. We can not judge these alternatives now, but it is clear that study of them is essential to explanation.

There does seem to be persuasive evidence that the rejecting stance has been linked with the efforts of a young generation in the case of each of the three movements. When the LSA was founded in 1924, Bloomfield, who played a major part, was 37, and Sapir 40. Their books of 1914 and 1921, in which the theme of the autonomy of linguistic science and linguistic form play such a major part, were published when they were 27 and 37, respectively. Sapir's thought on the relation of language to culture seems to run strongly in the direction of autonomy from his first post-doctoral years until the mid-1920s (i.e., from about age 25 to 40), and then to develop in the direction of integration of linguistics with a larger context of study (cf. Hymes 1970a). The generational character of the surge associated with the 'first Yale school', Sapir's students Hoijer, Swadesh, Newman, Whorf, Haas, Emeneau, Li, Dyk, and (informally) Trager and Voegelin is evident, as is the second wave of this surge, involving many of the same people, plus Hockett, Harris, and others, at the time of the last pre-war Linguistic Institutes and the work for the Army during the Second World War. The generational dimension of the surge associated with Chomsky's version of transformational generative grammar is familiar.

New generations, or groupings within a generation, and attitudes of transcending or rejecting received approaches, are probably always available. So perhaps are ideas, methods, techniques felt to be novel and deserving attention by the profession at large. The additional ingredient that appears essential to the success of a potential movement appears to be this: access to a sector of language previously inadequately treated or explored. It is the sense, the justified sense, of opening up a new horizon, and of doing so in terms of a principle, a methodology, of general scope, that is essential both to the conviction of participants in the movement and the convincing of others.

In sum, a successful movement appears to have three ingredients: in form, rejection of a preceding dominant approach; in content, development of a new sector of language; in context, formation of a generational consciousness.

To summarize these ingredients is short of full explanation. One needs close studies of the conditions that support the ingredients, and of the balance among them — cultural climate of opinion, institutional demography, originality of mind, personal style, take different forms and have different force. But given the acceptance of scientific advance as an overriding value, then it would appear to be the development of a new sector of language that is fundamental to the continuity to be perceived in the development of structural linguistics in this century in the United States. It is this ingredient that appears basic to unifying of a movement, its separation from other lines of activity, its prestige in its own eyes and the eyes of others, and the development of an effective frame of reference; together with the attitudes of loyalty, pride and awareness of a norm that accompany it. (We take up again here the Prague School delineation of features of a standard language.)

The first movement can be seen as opening up the sector of language itself as sector of study independent of others; Boasian analytic grammar would have cleared the way, by its critique of received general linguistics, showing the need for expanded empirical work, and Sapirian and Bloomfieldian emphasis on the autonomy and regularity of the development of language would have justified its separation from other historically-oriented disciplines of the time. The LSA and the journal *Language* gave professional focus and support. The independent study of phonology was already in view in the 1920s, but acquired adherents and the force of a movement in the 1930s. As noted, phonology was the weak link in the intellectual chain of existing study of language, and became the central claim of the new discipline to recognition as an autonomous, basic science. Morphology developed in the 1940s under the same auspices, and within its continuing frame of reference, but with the sharp emergence of a more doctrinaire tenor and a novel strength of commitment to the development of explicit formal models independent of any particular language family, or structure. It is in the 1940s that phonology and morphology (i.e., linguistic models, linguistic theory) are established as basic, general subjects. In these terms, the development of transformational grammar is a development in depth, not in goal. Bloomfieldian work had been an incomplete model of language (as Hockett, Joos, and others readily enough admitted) in regard to syntax. Chomskyan work focused on this weak link in the Bloomfieldian chain.

The sense of dramatic conflict between philosophies of science, between extreme inductivism and extreme rationalism, while real and affecting enough for participants, does not seem the fundamental feature of the historical development. We have indicated various ways in which there is continuity, or mirror imaging, between the two movements. We suggest that the crucial factor in the success of the Chomskyan movement was general recognition that it did indeed open up a new sector of relationships in language and did so with a methodology that promised solutions to problems. (And, one should add, it has been expansion into further sectors (semantics, pragmatics) through pursuit of the Chomskyan methodology that has brought about something of a secondary movement in recent years ('generative semantics').) The conception of transformations as relating sentences to a deeper (covert) level, rather than as relating sentences at the same level (overt, as in Harris' work), can be seen as the decisive step. (The effectiveness of the step in attracting adherents, and its elaborations, of course have depended on many other factors as well.) But, to put the point another way, Chomsky did not succeed in convincing linguists generally of his own solutions, premises, and prejudices; he did succeed in convincing linguists generally of the existence, the central existence, of the problems to which he proposed solutions.

Whereas Harris' analysis of transformations made of syntax a summarizing, 'grammar-reducing' activity (cf. Wells (1963), cited above in 7.2), Chomsky's analysis of transformations made of a syntax an area both rich and formally penetrable. Concern with productivity, process, and formal models of syntax had been present already, as we have indicated; but it was with Chomsky's work that syntax became a central, accessible area of data.

As we have said in earlier chapters, it does not seem that such positions as mentalism have been crucial. Many structural linguists were mentalists, and many of the specific positions adopted or developed by Chomskyan grammar can be traced to structuralist origins. The field as a whole did not become ready for concerted activity in syntax on mathematical foundations until the 1950s; Chomsky took leadership of this activity, and integrated many features of preceding structuralism on the new basis (there were indeed notions of deep structure as well in Whorf's cryptotypes and Hockett's 1958 textbook). Nor does such a difference as 'data' vs. 'theory' orientation appear fundamental. To be sure there is a partial truth, in that there is change of dominant attitude. Bloomfieldian adherents developed formal theory, but their concern for validity of data, and objectivity, and toward the empirical basis of generalization carried with it considerable caution toward substantive claims. Chomskyan adherents attend to empirical data, and indeed to a greater range of empirical data, but their concern for universals, and introspective insight, carries with it an attitude toward substantive claims and generalizations that strikes many as quite incautious. From the one attitude, the disarray and the rapid tumbling one after another of theoretical and substantive claims will seem justification for 'old-fashioned' caution. From the other attitude, such caution will seem condemned never to reach important questions of theory at all. From one attitude, the cost of current focus on theory will appear high, as measured in inattention to languages that may disappear unrecorded and materials that languish unanalyzed, though their human as well as scholarly interest may be great. Concern with theory, mediated by introspection in one's own language, will seem to have reinforced a naive ethnocentrism. From the other attitude, focus on theory will be seen as providing more effective tools for insight into any language, and a frame of reference within which attention to particular languages may take on new significance. All of this is vital to an understanding of the dynamics and consequences of the movements concerned, but our general point is that such conflict of attitudes, however important, is secondary to expansion of the scope of data that is handled in normal practice.

In other words, the equation between transformational generative models and philosophical rationalism, and between descriptivist models (of various kinds) and empiricism, is a secondary factor. It is not intrinsic, but like the social valuation of 'Brooklyn' pronunciations of 'bird' in New York City. What is stigmatized there (and spelled as 'boid') is the prestige form in Charlestown, Virginia. The equation between pronunciation and status is not intrinsic, but secondary, depending on situation. So too with equations between models of linguistic structure and philosophical preferences generally. To the participants in movements the establishment of a general position may be inseparable from the development of the particular model, but a larger view will see the discipline as a whole developing its attention to a new set of problems, and doing so in terms of a variety of personal outlooks and philosophical commitments. So it was with the development of phonology — as we observed earlier in this study — nearly every possible philosophical position was brought to bear on the interpretation of phonology at some point or another. So it has been with the development of syntactic relations.

The greatest significance of the rationalist appeal may prove to have been in its association with belief in the sufficiency of formalism and introspection, attracting young students and faculty to what others could not but regard as a lazy man's linguistics. ('Be the first in your class to discover a new deep structure', as one put it, appalled at first-year students being invited to think of themselves as contributing to the frontier of a science.) The net result, as of the time at which we write, appears to be a view among the leaders of the younger generation in the transformational generative school that just the one language, English, is very poorly known. The sense is of a vast richness of data, opened up by the approach, but of very little certainty as to its analysis.

In a recent book by a scholar considered a brilliant leader in the school, one finds (Postal 1974:xiii):

... there is another point of view, one which would criticize a work like this, not for its depth, but for its superficiality. For, despite the fact that this work hardly suffers from brevity, few of the matters dealt with have really been adequately treated, and the empirical ramifications of claim after claim have in general been only superficially investigated, if at all. This is, I think, due more to the vast extent of English grammar, the incredible number of interactions between diverse grammatical proprties, and the fact that even in 1972 most of English grammar remains uncharted than to research defects.

An important related point is that among the many limitations of current grammatical description and theory, even for an extensively studied language like English, there appear to be few, if any, really solidly supported analyses. . . . The whole system is so little understood that every part of any proposed structure is somewhat shaky.

From the point of view of the historian of linguistics, then, one can adapt the remarks of Engels to Starkenburg (25 January 1894) (Marx and Engels 1942: 517–518):

Linguists make their history themselves, only in given surroundings which condition it and on the basis of actual relations already existing, among which the empirical relations, however much they may be influenced by the other political and ideological ones, are still ultimately the decisive ones, forming the red thread which runs through them and alone leads to understanding.

The notion of the 'red thread' in relation to the form of movements of change is given fuller content in another letter (Engels to J. Bloch, 21 September 1890; Marx and Engels 1942:475, replacing 'economic' by 'empirical'):

The empirical situation is the basis, but the various elements of the superstructure . . . and then even the reflexes of all these actual struggles in the brains of the combatants: political, legal, philosophical theories, religious ideas and their further development into systems of dogma — also exercise their influence upon the course of the historical struggles and in many cases preponderate in determining their *form* [sic]. There is an interaction of all these elements, in which, amid all the endless *host* of accidents (i.e., of things and events whose inner connection is so remote or so impossible to prove that we regard it as absent and can neglect it), the empirical movement finally asserts itself as necessary.

If one considers 'productive forces' equivalent to the means of analysis available in linguistics, and substitutes 'linguist' for 'man' in general, and 'history of study of language' for 'history of humanity' in general, then the following early letter of Marx can be used to bring out the point as to continuity (Marx to P. V. Annenkov (28 December 1846) (Marx and Engels 1942:7):

Because of this simple fact that every succeeding generation finds itself in possession of the productive forces won by the previous generation which serve it as the raw material for new production, a connection arises in human history, a history of humanity takes shape which has become all the more a history of humanity since the productive forces of man and therefore his social relations have been extended.

(By 'social relations' in the linguistic interpretation can be understood the linkages of linguistic work with work in other fields.)

The slow growth of empirical adequacy in the analysis of linguistic structure, and of theory adequate to such structure, has a history far antedating the period of our subject. The fact is well known, though the content of the history is far too little studied. It does seem that it is in the emergence of a distinct profession of linguistics, and of the general focus of concern with linguistic structure, that the scope of empirical adequacy becomes central, and shows such connectedness over time, that it is the 'red thread' running through the development of the field as a whole. In the nineteenth century, clearly, the comparable thread is adequacy in the analysis of linguistic change. Let us conclude by considering briefly how our conception of continuity in structural linguistics in the United States in the twentieth century fits with the views of other linguists as to the long-range periodization of their subject's history.

7.4   Underlying Relations (2): Periodization

Periodization involves both demarcation and weighting. Most writers on the recent history of linguistics have tended to treat the period of 'American structuralism' as extending from some date in the 1920s or 1930s to some date in the late 1950s. Our analysis has indicated that such a periodization treats the life history of work under the influence of Sapir and Bloomfield from early inception to full flowering, and that a closer study of the situation within the discipline at the time reveals that structural linguistics did not become central until about the time of the Second World War. From the standpoint, then, of movements at the center of the field, the years before Chomsky show a far more restricted, concentrated development of 'Bloomfieldian' linguistics — essentially, 1940–1960 in two phases. Further, we have included transformational generative grammar as developed by Chomsky within the scope of 'American structuralism'. Let us compare this demarcation, and weighting, to the two principal recent discussions of the periodization of linguistics as a whole.

Hockett (1965) divides the history of linguistics in terms of four salient breakthroughs, two in the nineteenth century [within historical linguistics], and two in the twentieth century [within structural (synchronic) linguistics]. This division is consistent with our analysis, inasmuch as the movement to form the Linguistic Society can be seen as primarily organizational, its technically intellectual concomitants being already in place within other organized contexts. No one could deny the importance of the four points of reference singled out by Hockett (cf. Stephenson (1969)). We would group them, however, treating the second member of each century, and pair, as a major change of orientation within a general conception. In the nineteenth century the neo-grammarians considered themselves to have a superior way of dealing with an object of study shared with predecessors, namely, language change. Just so Chomsky and his associates consider themselves to have a superior way of dealing with an object of study shared with predecessors (language structure). The break of highest rank occurs when the primary object of study itself is challenged and changed, that is, when synchronic, structural linguistics replaces diachronic, historical linguistics as center of concern.

To recognize relative orders of magnitude is to raise a problem for such a concept as 'paradigm'. Kuhn himself is not much help here. Since he associates 'paradigm' with 'the self-consciousness of a scientific community', and with change in respect to anomalies within a persisting set of problems, it seems appropriate to associate the term with the second change in each pair, and so, by implication with the level at which four 'paradigms' are to be distinguished. In consequence, one finds that the concept of 'paradigm' is not itself sufficient for explanation. One needs a term for the common features, and continuities, that link neo-grammarian historical linguistics and its predecessors in the nineteenth century, on the one hand, and that link Chomskyan grammar and its predecessors in the twentieth century. In other words, if neo-grammarian, Bloomfieldian, and Chomskyan are names of paradigms, then 'comparative-historical linguistics' and 'structural linguistics', as names for central foci, are at a higher level of contrast, a level itself without common designation.

One might want to modify 'paradigm' to adapt it to this situation, speaking of 'paradigmatic field', say, at the higher level of contrast. 'Comparative-historical linguistics' and 'structural linguistics' would be names of *fields* within which specific paradigms develop. Such a usage corresponds to a fairly common way of discussing comparative-historical linguistics, and structural linguistics, within programs of training in linguistic departments, i.e., as distinct 'fields'. With the name of the discipline itself as basic term, then, one would trace the history of linguistics in terms of the successive centrality, first of (paradigmatic) fields, and second, of paradigms within those fields.

Although one must accept Hockett's four divisions, his location of the first major change with Sir William Jones is questionable, even though traditional. Jones' claims have been cogently disputed by Hoenigswald (1963:2–3). A strong case can be made for the effective beginning of comparative-historical linguistics ('comparative philology') in Prussia and the other German states early in the nineteenth century, so far as an organized, concerted advocacy with continuous history is concerned. This is not to overlook the strong continuities and precedents in eighteenth century and earlier work, nor the reasons for locating a decisive methodological step in the later work of August Schleicher (Hoenigswald 1963, 1974).

Koerner (1972b) places the major change also in the work of Schleicher, although it is disingenuous to cite a forthcoming paper by Hoenigswald (1974) as appearing to share his (Koerner's) view, when Hoenigswald had argued the point almost a decade earlier (1963:5–8). In any case, Koerner's periodization of the history of linguistics into three successive paradigms, associated with the names of Schleicher, de Saussure, and Chomsky, is not one we can accept. Koerner is right to stress continuity between earlier and later work in the nineteenth century (259), citing evidence of direct dependence of ideas of the grammarians of the 1870s on their predecessor, Schleicher (259, 263). And Koerner rightly stresses that the historian must not be misled by arguments and accounts of participants, as against the evidence of actual practice. But he is not thoroughgoing enough with regard to the nineteenth century, and inconsistent with regard to the twentieth.

As to the nineteenth century: Kiparsky (1974) shows that the overt conflict in the 1870s between the Young Turk neo-grammarians and their contemporaries obscures a shift in underlying orientation that was common to both. The leading goal of historical linguistics, the kind of question one wanted most to answer, shifted from reconstruction of proto-language to explanation of the forms of descendant languages. Scholars on both sides of the famous neo-grammarian controversy, as to the exceptionlessness of sound laws — the principle commonly cited as their 'breakthrough' (e.g., Hockett 1965) — contributed to solutions of the new kind of problem. Beneath public controversy there was unstated common agreement. The agreement, encompassing the parties to the public dispute, is the general trait that defines the period. The participants were not wrong in sensing a 'paradigmatic' shift, but wrong in what they (and most subsequent scholars) took the shift to be.

As to the twentieth century: the principle of looking beyond the arguments and accounts of participants applies to the 1960s as well as to the 1870s. The shift in underlying orientation of the nineteenth century is paralleled in the twentieth: the kind of question most asked has shifted from inference of general pattern, starting with observable forms, to one of the rules necessary to explain observable forms, starting from underlying structure.

Koerner does not cite much evidence for consideration of Chomsky's work as a revolution comparable in weight to that of the origin of structural linguistics itself (265). He cites Bierwisch in support of this view (n. 61), but the quotation says the opposite: 'eine neue Entwicklungstufe der strukturellen Sprachwissenschaft' (that is a new stage, but a new stage *of* structural linguistics; Bierwisch's view is precisely ours). Chomsky is said to have developed certain Saussurean notions — no revolution there, and also to have introduced a rigorously formalized manner of stating facts and explaining operations; to have revived a general theory orientation; to have departed from inductive discovery procedures in favor of deductive procedures aiming at explanatory adequacy. In chapter 5, and earlier in this chapter, we have given our reasons for not considering such claims as evidence of basic revolutionary change. Let us add another consideration here, one that will lead into some final remarks.

Chomsky's development of a distinctive frame of reference has been explained by Hockett (1968a:35ff.) in terms of a particular student-mentor relationship. Hockett does not wish to underestimate Chomsky's originality, nor his debt to predecessors other than Zellig Harris, but he states:

No one as intelligent as Chomsky could fail to be stimulated by Harris' methodological inventiveness; no one as serious-minded as Chomsky could long rest content with Harris' theoretical nihilism (35).

Hockett suggests that Harris' consistent refusal to draw deeper inferences from analytical investigations led to Chomsky's opinion that heuristics has little or nothing to contribute to linguistic theory, and forced Chomsky back on his own resources and taste, 'towards the abstract fields of logic, mathematics, and philosophy, rather than to science' (36).

There is an important truth in Hockett's suggestion, but its terms must be recast. Harris himself distinguished between theory and heuristics, and could hardly be said not to be concerned with linguistic theory in the sense of explicit models of the general structural properties of language. Chomsky later incorporated a variety of things into his linguistic theory, such as Jakobsonian phonology in an untranslated form (recall that Harris translated it), but his basic difference from Harris, at the level of concern with theory, was not to broaden the scope of theory, but to broaden the scope of its perceived relevance. In other words, when all might be said and done, Harris' theory of linguistic structure would be just that, a theory of linguistic structure. Chomsky began to suggest that a theory of linguistic structure was also a theory of mind.

Hockett himself draws his contrast between 'methodology' (Harris) and 'theory' (Chomsky) in terms that do not in fact separate Harris and Chomsky much. Hockett writes (1968a:35):

It is fair to say, I believe, that Harris has been a superb *methodologist,* but never at any time a *theorist* of language. A theoretical concern with language must try to deal not only with techniques of analysis, but also with what language is to its users, and with how it performs its role in human life. [Emphases in original]

Now, for Chomsky, what language is to its users, and how it performs its role in human life, are held to depend, so far as linguistic theory is concerned, exactly on what linguists are concerned with in any case: linguistic structure. Enlarged terms, such as 'competence', and appeal to the image of language-acquiring children, do not in fact represent any enlargement of linguistics itself. Linguistics may be defined as a branch of cognitive psychology, but cognitive psychology is not allowed to affect it. Linguistics may stimulate new developments in psycholinguistics, but linguistic theory is not to be changed as a result of psychological experiment. Linguistics remains entirely autonomous, a challenge to psychology, but able to pursue its theoretical goals on the basis of logic and introspection, independent of research of other kinds.

In short, what Chomsky has done is to retain the scope of linguistic theory established by the Bloomfieldians and particularly in his case by Harris — formal linguistic structure — and, while deepening the conception of structure itself, *invest* theory of such scope with utmost significance. Put in other, and quite appropriate terms, the relation between methodological form and substantive content in Chomsky's work is consistently *interpretive*. His view of the relation between syntactic form and semantic content has been interpretive, the latter interpreted in terms of the former. So also for his view of the relation between the structure of language as a whole and the human mind, or human life.

In sum, Koerner's account of the nineteenth century is critical of its self-conceptions. His account of the 20th century adopts the standpoint of one party to its debates. Chomsky did not so much add theory to methodology, as find theory *in* methodology.

What would be required for a change to rank as of the same magnitude as the initiation of comparative-historical linguistics, or of structural linguistics, as central to the discipline? It is difficult to say, beyond the observation that it would have to constitute a whole paradigmatic field. On the basis of current stirrings, one can suggest that to the previous fields of change and structure might come to be added a field of use. If so, one's sense of periodization may change. It is entirely possible, however, that future change will not depend upon movements of the sort identified here, insofar as such movements involve self-conscious rejection of preceding work, and so a distorted view of the history of linguistics. Perhaps future major change can be integrative, not need to be self-consciously revolutionary. Perhaps study of the history of linguistics can contribute to change of that kind.

There seems to us some evidence of this prospect. The casting back to the seventeenth and eighteenth centuries for a usable past on the part of Chomskyan grammar suggests awareness that the revolutionary, eclipsing stance would be difficult to maintain in the light of adequate knowledge of the recent past of linguistics in the United States. The central topic here would seem to be Sapir. His phonological approach has received acceptance; his term, 'sound pattern', been taken up; and work by himself and his students seems a preferred hunting ground for structural restatement. Yet he is seen as remote and isolated, it seems, rather than as continuing to be active in the development of linguistic theory to the late 1930s, and to have been taken as significant predecessor by Harris. It is particularly notable that Sapir's concern with semantic structure, with universals, with native speaker intuitions, is not stressed, together with Whorf' work on 'cryptotypes', as close, almost immediate precedent close to home for current theory. Perhaps it is that recognition of such precedent would show that such concerns are not inextricably dependent on Chomsky's interest in rationalistic philosophy. Perhaps it is because Sapir's views are tied up with a view of theory as extending to the historically shaped, concrete manifestations of patterning in particular languages and cultures, and as implicating social life.

Chomsky's bisection of W. von Humboldt into an acceptable continuation of eighteenth century general linguistics, on the one hand, and a disregarded father of nineteenth century general linguistics (his true historical role), on the other, seems revealing in this regard. (Cf. Bloomfield 1914, ch. 10, and 1933:18).

Chomsky states (1966:86, n. 36):

Considered against the background that we are surveying here, it seems to mark the terminal point of the development of Cartesian linguistics (Humboldt's treatise Ueber die Verschiedenheit des Menschlichen Sprachbaues) rather than the beginning of a new era of linguistic thought.

But it was precisely that.

Humboldt's orientation continued, indeed, through the work of Boas and Sapir. Without minimizing the intercontinental factors in the development of linguistics within the United States, one can further observe that there is fundamental continuity from Boas and Sapir to the present. There is some evidence that this continuity is coming to be appreciated more widely. Students of linguistics are coming to realize more widely that theory did not begin in 1957, and that not to know of work outside an immediate moment is a deprivation. A clean slate and a fresh start, such as many felt to have occurred, can lead not only to progress, but also to travel in circles. Whereas history may have seemed a deadening irrelevancy, it may now be felt as a source of liberation.

We are conscious of the many mistakes of fact and interpretation that must appear in this study. We hope to have found enough that is true and relevant to demonstrate the worth of getting the history right. What we have said seems to us correct to the best of our present knowledge, but we are conscious of how different things may appear when history can be written on the basis of a full range of supporting studies. Let us hope they are soon forthcoming.

8.   EPILOGUE, 1979

8.1   *Overview*

In the five years or so since the first version of this monograph was completed, we have seen no major changes within the historiography of American structuralism. Overall, however, we find an increase in the number and quality of works dealing with the history of linguistics in general, and with American structuralism as a part of it. Alongside works, usually surveys, which continue a traditional and largely erroneous view of 'post-Bloomfieldian' linguistics, others, often with more sharply focused topics, show more awareness of diversity and nuances within the works of this period.[1]

The history of linguistics has apparently come to be cultivated as a primary or second-

---

[1]   Newmeyer, in his review of the LSA symposium (1978) perhaps unwittingly points up the continuing diversity of American linguistics when he notes that Pike's contribution will be inaccessible to anyone not well versed in tagmemic theory. He appears to take it for granted that readers will find Chomsky's views more accessible, although many not already well versed in Chomskyan theory, including many of Pike's followers, might be inclined to turn Newmeyer's remark end for end.

Tagmemics, though associated especially with Kenneth Pike, is really a family of closely related approaches. It should command respect for the number of linguists actively at work who rely on it, and for the volume of descriptive, comparative, and typological material on languages all over the world formulated in one or another version of it. There have been a number of surveys of tagmemics, bibliographies, and a history by a participant in its development (Waterhouse 1974). The reasons for its relative lack of prestige and influence within the academic branch of the linguistic profession suggest there is a need for a sociological study of it as well.

ary research specialty by a growing number of scholars, including some trained in the disciplines of the history and sociology of science, as well as some from the ranks of linguistics itself. Some of the recently published work by linguists acting as historians is as thorough and precise as any member of either discipline could wish, and deals besides with topics of continuing interest to linguists. A noteworthy example of this high standard of scholarship is Percival's review (1977) of Koerner's monograph on the Saussurean tradition (1973a), Percival carefully separates Koerner's historiographical theories, which figure prominently in the monograph, from his motives as a convinced Saussurean. Percival shows how these impulses work against each other, leading much of the time into confusion or contradication. For example, in commenting on Koerner's call for guidelines for the history of linguistics, Percival summarizes the detailed commentary to come (1977:386):

What he actually offers us is a pair of notions which have been discussed in the literature for some time – the idea of a paradigm, as proposed by Kuhn in 1962 (revised, 1970), and another notion to which Koerner gives various names but finally calls 'climate of opinion', a term which he has borrowed from Becker 1932. Regardless of the fact that neither idea is novel, one can ask of each of them, taken separately, how applicable it is to the history of linguistics; then whether, taken together, they form a logically compatible pair; and finally, whether an adequate methodology for the history of linguistics can be erected on these foundations.

Percival answers each of his questions in the negative. He finds the more general notion of 'climate of opinion' to be incompatible, as a major explanatory force in the history of linguistics, with the restricted notion of a 'disciplinary matrix' (Kuhn 1970) within a particular scientific community, let alone with the still more restricted notion of 'exemplars' or model problem solutions used in the initiation of members into such communities – a distinction Koerner (1973:221, cited by Percival) admits he does not understand. Percival's review is a helpful demonstration of historiographical technique and criticism.

Kuhn's view of the history of science, an important element in the works just noted, continues to attract the attention of others involved in the historiography of linguistics. Much of this work ends with unfavorable judgements of it. Pearson (1977) reviews the subject, emphasizing the continuity with earlier paradigms that can be seen through each of the major 'revolutions' Pearson delineates in the history of linguistics. Not surprisingly, the shift to diachronic studies in the nineteenth century is presented as one of these, but Pearson sees the neogrammarians as a consolidation and refinement of then-current methodology, rather than as amounting to a revolution in themselves. In this context, Pearson compares 'evolutionary' and 'revolutionary' models, and finds that for the history of linguistics, neither is satisfactory by itself, since as he sees it, revolutions in linguistics have not resulted in abrupt loss of continuity with past paradigms. A similar view is expressed in Percival (1976a). For the twentieth century, Pearson sees a similar pattern, with transformational grammar playing the same role of consolidation and refinement of structuralism that the neogrammarians played in their day. Our monograph is not cited in support of this view, making the coincidence another example of independent convergence.

Percival too has written an important paper on Kuhn's model. 'Since linguistics has never been characterized by the uniform assent which Kuhn sees as the distinctive attribute of the hard sciences,' he writes (1976a:292), 'an unhealthy situation might arise if linguists began to look upon all theoretical disagreements within their profession as conflicts between rival paradigms, i.e., incommensurable viewpoints, and used this as an excuse not to observe the ground rules of rational discussion.' Another danger Percival warns of in the same passage is the bandwagon effect, with linguists prematurely boarding each novel theory which seems destined for popularity, so as not to be left clinging to an outdated 'paradigm.' In this way, he notes, Kuhn's theory 'could lead to a lowering rather than a raising of standards in linguistics.'

Kuhn's model, often in a deceptively simplified second-hand version, nevertheless continues to appeal to enough writers to keep it in the current literature, despite the generally unfavorable view of it taken by most commentators.

In much the same way, but for a longer period of time, Whorf's name has been associated with a simplified version of his actual views (cf. Alford (1978) on this point), and a kind of linguistic determinism identified with him retains popular appeal and remains current in the scholarly literature. Fishman (1977), reviewing the 'Whorfian hypothesis' in one of the numerous recent survey/retrospective/prospective collections on current linguistics, continues to find it of very limited validity, but of seemingly inexhaustible appeal to newcomers. It has influenced the development of language-and-culture studies for decades, and despite his bleak view of the hypothesis itself, Fishman finds some benefits in its influence (1977:55):

There have been mistaken scientific and *Weltanschauungen* that have embroiled generations of scholars and students in conflicts to no greater end than to discredit thoroughly the views advanced. The Whorfian hypothesis, or, more accurately, efforts to test, refine, or revise the Whorfian hypothesis, have done much more than that for the language sciences. It has left us at least three very vibrant legacies in the form of productive research traditions and topical concentrations that we might not have otherwise come by.

These are, he believes, language universals, ethnolinguistics, and studies of the transmission of social structure through language. Of course, these all have very long histories before Whorf, as for that matter do some of the varieties of determinism that have come to be coupled with his name.

In some recent papers, in fact, there seems to be little of Whorf but his name. The price of such fame can be high. Some of the recent work on the 'Whorf hypothesis' and its place in the history of American linguistics is astonishingly bad. Thus, Levic Jessel (1978:85) blames him for ignoring ethnicity (we think):

Linguistic science donned its universalistic blinders—and deprived itself of a rational basis by the simple exclusion of its ethnic foundations. The natural history of group existence had no place in the study of language, the phenomenon of nationalism, its modern expression, was tantamount to original sin.

Jessel's own originality is in associating Whorf, who sought to explicate the distinctive interdependence of Hopi language and culture as an historically derived 'design for living', with blind universalism. Richard Ogle, on the other hand, offers what might be called a 'neocartesian' critique of Whorf, taxing him with failure to take due account of universals (1973). More usefully and far more cogently, Darnell (1974), in her reply to Ogle, considers the intellectual context of the Sapir–Benedict generation in which Whorf worked, and explicates the rationalist and universalist aspects of his thought in their contemporary setting.

Whorf will no doubt long continue to serve as a convenient symbolic token in the debate over determinism, creating a comparably durable need for more exact statements of his role in the history of this subject. There is every sign that Kuhn's role as a stimulus within the history of linguistics will be similar.

Alongside the individual contributions, there are tokens of institutional interest in the history of linguistics. In 1974, the Linguistic Society of America marked its Golden Anniversary with a series of three symposia: in Amherst, on the current state of American linguistics; in Berkeley, on the role of American Indian linguistics in its development; and in New York, on its European background. The proceedings of these symposia have now been published (Austerlitz, ed. 1975, Chafe, ed. 1976, and Hoenigswald, ed. 1979). We will discuss some of the individual papers below. Another institutional commitment deserving notice was a pair of conferences in 1979 at the University of North Carolina at Charlotte, making a start toward the establishment of a national archive on the history of American linguistics.

8.1.1 *Perceptions of Crisis and Climax*

Related to this growing interest in the history of linguistics, but explaining it only in part, is the widespread perception of a foundational crisis in the discipline, of a "curious wave of unrest and uncertainty, a softening of oppositions, a greater readiness to listen to one another on the part of 'schools' formerly exclusive . . ." (Haas 1978:293). Equally prominent in the stream of scholarly publication are signs of a sense of completion, of the end of a movement or historical period, of what we might call a climax, in the ecological sense. These signs, of course, may take either affirmative or negative form: some of the denials betray the sense of unrest mentioned above by Haas.

Within American linguistics, the crisis is affirmed or denied especially in connection with 'linguistics', that is, transformational grammar (cf. Fidelholtz 1978, Pullum 1978). It does not seem to have touched sociolinguistics, historical linguistics, or any other subfields. Pullum, for instance, comments on what seems to him an exaggerated concern with foundational questions with perceptions of crisis, in the past few years. "In general," he writes (1978:399), "the linguists who have the most to say about the supposedly impending methodological catastrophe seem to be precisely those who do the least linguistics." Of course, a refusal to engage in 'linguistics' in this sense may be a considered response to perceived crisis, rather than the other way around. Shorn of its tendentiousness, however,

Pullum's remark has its point: willingness to declare a crisis, and in particular, the end of an interregnum, varies with the distance between the writer and the school whose termination he is announcing. Thus Chomsky begins his contribution to a collection entitled *Current Issues in Linguistic Theory* as follows (Cole, ed. 1977:3) "In this discussion, I will assume without supporting argument a general framework that I have outlined and discussed elsewhere, and I will review some recent ideas on grammatical theory within this framework." The discussion that follows, like the opening lines, gives no evidence of a crisis within linguistics as Chomsky views it.

In this regard, however, the collection which his paper begins is a significant one, consisting as it does of the invited lectures delivered at the 1975 Linguistic Institute sponsored by the LSA. Even allowing for the bias of the organizers, we find the amount of space within it and the emphasis given to semantics, pragmatics, and sociolinguistics to be quite striking. What is more, among its contributors are several figures whose reputations were well established before the interregnum, and who might perhaps not have been invited to contribute to a collection on 'current issues' a few years ago. A comparison of the scope of this collection with the long paper by Chomsky of the same title (1964b), although manifestly unfair in some ways, does have symbolic value as an indicator of the change in climate in the intervening years.

A substantial part of that earlier paper was devoted to phonology. In October 1977, a conference was held at Indiana University to discuss competing phonological theories, most of which have arisen since the appearance of Chomsky and Halle 1968. Both the conference itself as it unfolded and the call to it seemed, to JF, who attended, to be in part a response to the sense of crisis we have been outlining. The recent theoretical positions taken by the invited participants were perceived as needing reconciliation; beyond that, it was a time for taking stock.

In general, even those views presented at the conference by Anderson and Schane, for example, representing a position closest to the 'standard theory' of *The Sound Pattern of English* (1968), had broken with that position in highly significant ways, on the abstractness of underlying representations and on rule ordering, for instance. There was no adherent of the 'standard' position on those issues who spoke at the conference, either from the podium or the floor.

More independent positions taken by other participants (e.g. by Hooper and Stampe) represented returns to some of the fundamental insights of structuralist phonemics and morphophonemics, though important theoretical and terminological differences remain, at least for the present. Still others, through their work, provided even more transparent instances of re-establishment of connections with the "pre-theoretical" past. In Goldsmith's presentation, Bloch and Harris were cited approvingly (and appropriately) in connection with his "autosegmental" approach, which indeed owes much to the partly componential, partly segmental models of Bloch and Harris.

To us, the sense of closure and the anxiety about centrifugal tendencies were quite noticeable among the participants in this conference who had come into the field during the period of development centered upon the Chomsky-Halle approach. It is worth noting that the conference was organized and held at Indiana University, whose linguistics department for its entire history can be described without prejudice as eclectic in its theoretical orientation. This again brings up complex issues of disciplinary politics which play an important but poorly documented role in the development of the field, and introduce serious complications into every judgement about schools and periods.

A sense of closure is signalled by the very title of a review by the British linguist, Geoffrey Sampson. Sampson focusses on differences between the famous published program of goals for linguistic theory, *Syntactic Structures* (1957), and the long unpublished attempt to provide a precise hypothesis as to a transformational grammar, and a new substantive theory of language, the work he is reviewing, Chomsky's *The logical structure of linguistic theory* (henceforth, LSLT). He stresses the remarkable situation symbolized by the book. For most of two decades, the central focus of linguistic research has been syntax, and the leading idea in syntactic theory has been Chomsky's claim that phrase structure grammar should be superseded by transformational grammar. Students are commonly taught that sequence as history of the discipline. Yet for the details of the body of theory on which transformational grammar was based, one was referred to a manuscript written in 1955-6, but not published (until 1975). In other words, states Sampson,

During the heyday of Transformational Grammar its hundreds or thousands of advocates in the universities of the world not only did not but *could* not really know what they were talking about (1979:356).

Sampson comments somewhat at a distance, perhaps, considering the development of the Chomskian movement only in terms of what was available in public print, and not considering the flow of influence and ideas through papers and personal communication at linguistic meetings and elsewhere. Certainly some definitive sense of orthodox practice and problem-solving was established rather early, and recognized by opponents as well as adherents, even if, as Sampson states, published work actually left quite uncertain just what could and could not count as a transformational rule. Nevertheless, Sampson is right to emphasize that the book which came to symbolize the "revolution", *Syntactic Structures*, was regarded by its author and others as a short, publishable sketch, and that the work not published until 1975 was regarded as the definitive support.

Sampson finds that the recent history of linguistics must be reconsidered in the light of LSLT. On the one hand, the impression that Chomsky only gradually came to think of linguistics as intuition-based, rather than observation-based, seems confuted by LSLT, where intuition is given as central a role as in any of the later writings (371). Perhaps the true history is one of a certain inconsistency (recall the comparison of writings in the late 1950s by Chomsky and Hockett given earlier in this monograph). And on the other hand, Sampson suggests, the actual history of linguistics would have been different, had LSLT been published when written. He finds the 1957 sketch a much more attractive approach than what appear to have been Chomsky's actual views, as set forth in the presumably definitive LSLT.

This review article contains interesting comments on received version of recent linguistic history; the circulation of important work, such as LSLT, in mimeograph and microfilm; pre-Chomskian recognition of syntactic phenomena requiring process descriptions; and the Chomskian definition of the analytical practice of predecessors as a Procrustean distortion. Sampson concludes that the success of transformational grammar must be explained partly in sociological terms. Many of his points coincide with points we have made in this monograph, and were arrived at independently of it (as Sampson has noted in a letter).

This aspect of the history of linguistics, probably as decisive for its course as any technical innovations, calls for the attention of historians and sociologists of science, as Stocking (1974c:518) has noted, but not only from them.

Even casual thought about the potential of a careful mapping of the movements of linguistics from school to school and of the sources and chronology of innovations in linguistics and their diffusion through the discipline at once calls to mind the techniques and models of dialect geography — settlement history, the wave theory, relic areas, and the rest. Linguists, then, might after all have a special contribution to make to the history and sociology of science — a kind of intellectual dialectology whose dangers, if applied to linguistics itself, promise to be at least as thrilling as its rewards.

The sixties and early seventies are also covered in the collection of 'underground' papers edited by McCawley (1976) and reviewed appreciatively by Fidelholtz (1978), who has something similar to Pullum's view of the scope of linguistics in mind when he writes (1978:931) that "the articles are all of interest for their influence on the development of linguistics in the last decade." What is more, he seems to take it for granted that linguists entering the discipline since these papers were sent around will need to be helped to extend their historical perspective back that far, or at least to get access to the papers (cf. op. cit. 930). Doubtless without ironic intent, he speaks of "the historical perspective [the collection] provides for linguists who have entered the field since many of these papers were first circulated."

This perspective is a double one, given both by the papers themselves and by the notes written for the volume by McCawley, offering the reader a kind of vicarious participation in the golden years from 1960 to 1970. "McC is in an excellent position to edit such a book, having been at MIT in the early 60's, and close to the top of the distribution list for most peoples' [sic] 'underground' papers (usually, in principle, prepublication versions) . . . " (loc. cit.).

Fidelholtz here artlessly raises the issues surrounding 'semipublication', distribution lists, and ranking on them — topics more often spoken of than written about. Semipublication, through the direct mailing of duplicated versions of typescripts, had (and has) several advantages: a faint odor of persecution clings to it (as to other *samizdat* networks), and one is spared the rigors of editorial review, while at the same time keeping a measure of control over access to the papers. What is more, large-scale reliance on this mode of communication produces an impression of ferment, of rapid progress outstripping the pace of regular scholarly publication, that is only partly illusory. Fidelholtz quotes McCawley on the reasons for such reliance on semipublication, with striking candor:

McC (pp. 3–4) makes two points about these papers: (i) they were not previously published, in most cases, because of the authors' 'sloth'; and (ii) they present important and original points which have either shaped research in the last decade or so, or are still relevant to issues under discussion in the literature — or they present suggestions which have never been pursued but should have been. A contributing factor to the 'sloth' of the authors may have been the in-group, rather elitist attitude of so many transformationalists in the 1960's (p. 2) (1978:931).

Householder, reviewing the first volume of conference papers published by the Linguistic Association of Canada and the United States, also speaks of an in-group during this period, of disgruntlement and bitterness (though not, he says, on his part), and of the existence and steady growth of LACUS as itself a sign of restlessness within the discipline (1978).

Another issue related to semipublication, though not mentioned by Fidelholtz or McCawley, is its use as a means of circumventing gatekeepers. Chomsky, for one, has at times referred to the difficulty of getting his early work published in the face of incomprehension if not hostility from the establishment of linguistics. In a very important forthcoming paper, Murray examines the facts surrounding this question very carefully, exhuming editorial correspondence and checking thoroughly on the relevant chronology. He finds that one article of Chomsky's was rejected, by André Martinet as editor of *Word*, hardly, as Murray observes, a "mainstream Bloomfieldian" journal. On the other hand, articles and reviews were solicited and published in *Language* and elsewhere by Bloch and Hill, as well as Jakobson and others. This particular image of rejection of the revolutionary new viewpoint by establishment gatekeepers, then, appears to be mythologizing.

8.2 Haas and Uhlenbeck

Two recent retrospective surveys of American linguistics by Europeans (Haas 1978, Uhlenbeck 1979) are quite similar in their views, and cover almost the same period of years (1920-1980 and 1924-1974 respectively).

Both rely on a 'mainstream' model, one explicitly (Haas 1978:295). Both point to the familiar list of practitioners (Bloomfield and Sapir; Bloch, Trager, Hockett, Hill, Harris); Uhlenbeck (1979:130) also speaks of Boas with Sapir, and identifies Newman, (Mary) Haas, Hoijer, and Pike as continuing their approach, which he sees as distinct from that of the Bloomfieldians.

Both of these surveys offer a list of traits characteristic of the post-Bloomfieldian approach: lack of a 'theory', emphasis on 'mechanical discovery procedures', rejection of meaning in favor of distribution as a criterion of analysis, and use of the phoneme as a model in the extension of structuralist description to other levels of analysis. Both devote most of their attention to Chomsky and his school, which they see as continuing the post-Bloomfieldian trajectory, but as having reached a culmination. Indeed, both see the now-ending period of transformationalist syntax dominated by Chomsky's thought as an interregnum, as an interruption of an approach to syntax which had only begun to show promise, and to which we may now presumably return,

to establish a theoretically coherent discipline of analytic operations, a discipline that would revise inadequate 'surface structures' rather than try to cure them by addition. It was the development of just such a discipline that had been interrupted in its progress by the rise of generative-transformational grammar. Analytic (operational) linguistics came to be discouraged, long before it had attained its objectives (Haas 1978:304).

Similarly, Uhlenbeck writes that "with Willy Haas I am convinced that in this way through the reliance of TG on immediate constituent analysis the syntactic investigation of the relational structure of the sentence was arrested (Haas 1973:107-10), and to this very day there are in America few signs of progress in this area since Longacre's article on 'String constituent analysis' (1960)" (1979:138).[2]

It will surely seem odd to many linguists actively working in syntax to call into question the principle of IC analysis, since the impression is widespread that this technique comes to us straight from traditional grammar, heavily encrusted with fully satisfied intuitions. Alternatively, some believe it is different in some not very important ways from the mode of syntactic analysis carried on by traditional grammar, but that IC analysis is a more precise formulation of the older approach, capturing what is 'correct' about it (cf. Langendoen 1979).

Percival (1976b) has however shown very clearly, in one of the 'underground' papers reprinted by McCawley, that traditional syntactic theory and IC analysis are not only not the same, but are logically incompatible and that the main features of IC analysis, binary splitting and the resulting single hierarchy of word-groups, were developed by Wundt, apparently in the 1870's, and popularized among American linguists especially by Bloomfield, in both his 1914 and 1933 books. It is interesting that this is one of the few technical features of his approach to language (another being the comparative method) to be carried over intact through the period of his conversion to behavioral psychology. Bloomfield, as both Percival and McCawley have noted, seemed to be aware of the novelty of IC analysis, compared to traditional syntax, and himself attributed it to Wundt in the 1914 book. Incidentally, Percival suggests, it seems likely that dependency theory offers a better formalization of the traditional model of syntactic relationships than does IC analysis, a view that accords fully with the outlook of Uhlenbeck and Haas.

Finally, to return to their papers, both look to the study of language in the speech community as the proper future center of linguistics. It scarcely needs to be said that we agree with this view, but since neither author cites any of our work to this effect, we take

---

[2]   Haas has sounded this theme before; the references are gathered in his 1973 review of Lyons 1972.

this additional opportunity to hail, somewhat hoarsely by now, another independent affirmation of it.

Both Haas and Uhlenbeck single out structuralist phonology for special mention: Haas briefly, as an example of achievement within narrow limits (1978:295), and Uhlenbeck at greater length, as a major focus of theoretical activity. His views of the role played by phonology in the development of American structuralism are no doubt not fully revealed by his remarks in this article, but to us he seems to impute more homogeneity to phonology than we find in it. It would be interesting to compare the diversity of a selection of papers from twenty, thirty, and forty years ago with those of the recent Indiana conference on phonology, for example, or of some other collection. Even an informal comparison might be revealing, and the effort to construct a more explicit measure of diversity might be quite rewarding.

Langendoen served as discussant of Malkiel's and Uhlenbeck's papers at the last LSA symposium; his comments elicited a reply from Uhlenbeck, and in turn a surrebuttal from Langendoen. The issues raised in this exchange vary widely in importance. In some respects this exchange is similar to the series of papers by Householder and by Chomsky and Halle in 1965 on phonology. In both, there are sharp disagreements over facts and interpretations; many arguments and counterarguments seem to glance off each other or pass wide of the mark rather than meeting squarely. Neither side appears at its best, though in this more recent exchange, a higher level of civility is maintained. And like the earlier exchange, this one may be useful as a source not only of technical linguistic issues, but of more general questions of scholarly practice. We will therefore take up some of these issues, in what we feel is a decreasing order of importance for linguistics and its historiography, but of roughly equal weight as specimens of scholarship.

Uhlenbeck and Langendoen disagree about the role of a 'dynamic' mode of linguistic description, or conception of linguistic structure (this distinction is consistently drawn by neither author) in the development of Bloomfieldian and Post-Bloomfieldian American linguistics. Briefly, Langendoen disputes Uhlenbeck's ascription to Bloomfield of a static descriptive model, and correctly so, we feel. He ascribes such a view to Saussure, and maintains, for obvious reasons, but again, we feel, correctly, that both Sapir and Bloomfield themselves were deft users of a dynamic approach to description. In this connection, however, Langendoen makes a commonly asserted but unjustifiable equation between Wells'. 'dynamic' formulation of automatic morphophonemic alteration and Hockett's 'item and process' model of description, and another between Wells' 'static' formulation and Hockett's 'item and arrangement' model. Langendoen is certainly correct in asserting that Wells (1949b) is less influential than it deserves to be. In thirty years, nothing has surpassed it as a compendium of problems and a guide toward coping with them. It is, however, very exacting reading. For those used to dealing with such phenomena in terms of the ordering relations among rules for generating them, the consistent but now unfamiliar treatment by Wells in terms of relations between basic and derived forms (or segments of forms) may be hard to follow.

At issue is the automaticity (that is, the strictly phonological conditioning) of the alternation of Latin participles such as *pat + tus = passus*, or the comparable Sanskrit case of *rabh + ta = rabdha*. In his discussion of the alternative treatments of such alternations, Wells does make it clear that except for the 'static' formulation, the alternatives amount to different orderings of the rules (1949b:109-10):

> Using the metaphor of change, we might describe the change of *rabh + ta* to *rabdha* in any of three ways: (i) in one step: *rabh* and *ta* change simultaneously. This is the pure dynamic conception. (ii) In two steps: first *rabh + ta* becomes *rabh + dha*; then *rabh + dha* becomes *rab + dha*. (iii) Again in two steps: first *rabh + ta* becomes *rab + ta*; then *rab + ta* becomes *rab + dha*. In (ii) *ta* changes before *rabh*; in (iii) after it; and in (i) simultaneously with it.

The discussion of *passus* (1949b:110-1), however, which is said to be automatic under the dynamic conception but not under the static conception of alternation, can also be fully translated into terms of rule ordering, as follows, where the first three alternatives follow the same order as in the discussion of the Sanskrit example above, and the last is the static conception. In each case, the ordering and environments within which the rule applies are different:

$$\text{Dynamic} \qquad t \longrightarrow s / \left\{ \begin{array}{l} \check{V}\_ + tV \\ \check{V}t + \_V \end{array} \right\}$$

$$\text{Compromise 1} \qquad t \longrightarrow s / \left\{ \begin{array}{l} \check{V}t + \_V \\ \check{V}\_ + sV \end{array} \right\}$$

$$\text{Compromise 2} \qquad t \longrightarrow s / \left\{ \begin{array}{l} \check{V}\_ + tV \\ \check{V}s + \_V \end{array} \right\}$$

$$\text{Static} \qquad t \longrightarrow s / \left\{ \begin{array}{l} \check{V}\_ + sV \\ \check{V}s + \_V \end{array} \right\}$$

Given the stated basic and derived forms, then, each of the four different formulations requires two applications of the rule changing *t* to *s* (or stating the alternation of the two sounds). They differ in the ordering of these applications, and in the environments in which the rule applies each time. The dynamic formulation corresponds to simultaneous application, and both apply to the basic environment. The compromises correspond to two different sequential applications, and for each, one environment is basic, the other derived. In the static formulation, the order of application is indifferent, and both environments are derived. What is required for the static formulation to work is an initiator —some device or convention which calls the rules into play, since without one, given the derived environments, nothing at all will happen. This is the major difference between the 'dynamic' and 'static' formulations as presented by Wells, as he himself was careful to explain: the environment is stated in terms of derived alternants in the static formulation.

There is, then, nothing in the *basic* forms alone which will trigger the alternation, as there is in the other formulations.

Normally, in grammars employing some version of the static descriptive mode, this initiator is in effect mention of the particular form or forms, or class of forms, to which the alternation applies. One might expect to find the section dealing with this particular Latin alternation in the chapter on past participles. The static technique, as Hockett makes quite plain in his 1961 paper, is not especially well suited to dealing with automatic alternations. Instead, this technique, often but not necessarily cast in terms of selectional restrictions on allomorphs, treats all alternations as if they were nonautomatic, that is, conditioned by the morphological environment wholly or at least in part. But nothing in any of this carries with it an obligatory commitment to a morphophonemic or allomorphic type of description, nor necessarily to an arrangement or process mode. Those choices are logically distinct from the choice of conventions for ordering the applications of rules. Any of the four pairs of rules, that is, can be construed as either '/ t / alternates with / s / at allomorph boundaries as stated' or 'morphophoneme t is replaced by phoneme / s / at morpheme boundaries as stated'; still other hybrid formulations are possible (cf. 5.2.5 above).

There is a persistent tendency, however, to couple a 'dynamic' label with the 'process' and 'morphophoneme' styles, and a 'static' label with the 'arrangement' and 'allomorph' styles, as both Uhlenbeck and Langendoen do, disagreeing only about which linguists' names to place under each heading. The history of this tendency would make an essay in its own right. Presumably the appeal of dynamism plays a part, and presumably also the adoption of a process formulation by the Chomsky camp does also.[3]

Langendoen's discussion of the principle of complementary distribution, like so many others, deals with it in isolation. In the practice of structuralists, however, it was used in conjunction with a principle of phonetic similarity (cf. 6. above). When so used, as we have pointed out, the number of alternative solutions, of which Langendoen complains, is sharply reduced. Haugen and Twaddell (1942), whom Langendoen cites as condemning the principle of complementary distribution in their important joint paper 'Facts and phonemics', were actually objecting not to that but to liberties taken with phonetic facts, and to a critical use of an appeal to one's own solution as evidence which used to be called (and advocated as) the principle of pattern congruity.

---

[3] Flier (1978:923) evidences a different perception of the orthodoxy of American structuralist morphophonemics in this period when he writes, in reviewing Kilbury 1976 (which we have not seen), that 'With the ascendence of abstract generative phonology in the 1960's, morphophonemics was displaced from the pre-eminent position it had occupied in America in the preceding two decades, and was largely subsumed under phonology proper – usually in the form of high-level rewrite rules which commonly operated under highly abstract, non-grammatical conditions.' We can make no sense of this passage, since both the Chomskyan and 'Yale-School' writings on the issue agree that during the period in question, the morphophoneme was stigmatized by association with a process model, rightly so in the Yale-School view, and wrongly so in the Chomskyan. Moreover, to characterize the conditions of high-level rules as non-grammatical is at least to leap entirely over the 'standard theory' period and land full in the middle of 'natural generative phonology'.

Instances could be multiplied where one or the other, but more often here Langendoen, gets a fact wrong or misinterprets a position. To mention a last and most trivial example, in his surrejoinder, Langendoen seeks to clinch a point in an argument by stating that Bloch's Japanese phonemics article (1950) was the last major phonemics paper to appear in *Language*, marked the apogee of the genre, and was followed by a decline of interest in such questions as it dealt with. But Haugen's (1958b) paper on Icelandic phonemics appeared in *Language*, was a major paper, and was intended to illustrate an approach to phonemic description different from, and in many ways more conservative (e.g. fully segmental) than Bloch's paper. In the context of its time and place (and here one of us speaks from personal experience) it was to be seen as a powerful centrist statement on issues regarded as very much alive and important. Nor, if we take a not-very-liberal view of what to include in this genre, was Haugen's paper the last. Paul Friedrich's superb 1971 article on Tarascan should count also as a dual descriptive-theoretical statement.

It would be unfair, and it is certainly not our intention, to pick on Langendoen (or Uhlenbeck) as the unfortunate and no doubt unwilling representatives of a rather large group of linguists, by suggesting that they simply do not care about simple matters of scholarly accuracy, such as the date of the last representative of a genre and the inferences thereby supported. Rather, we suspect that a powerful and sinister force may be at work, in the form of a *fable convenu* so compelling that mere facts must bend to its service. This *fable* is the accepted history of American linguistics, according to which a 'mainstream' flowed for a time in the direction of Bloomfieldian, antimentalist, pretheoretical, asemic, distributionalist, flat-footed taxonomic descriptivism, and then dramatically changed course, to flow toward Chomskyan, rationalist, neocartesian, theoretical, elegant generative transformationalism.

We return, then, in concluding this monograph, to the inadequacies of the mainstream model, whose vitality seems undiminished in the past five years, and that is a disappointment to us which we hope the greater circulation of our work in its present form may do something to lighten. The many errors of fact and interpretation committed in the name of the mainstream model, one might almost say *induced* by it, are important not only because they distort the past, but also, and even more unfortunately, because they promise to distort the future as well.

8.3   REFERENCES TO THE EPILOGUE

ALFORD, D. 1978. The demise of the Whorf hypothesis. (A major revision in the history of linguistics). In Jaeger et al, eds, (1978), 485–499.

AUSTERLITZ, R. A., ed. 1975. The scope of American linguistics: The first golden anniversary symposium of the Linguistic Society of America, held at the University of Massachusetts, Amherst, on July 24 and 25, 1974. Lisse, Netherlands, Peter de Ridder Press.

BECKER, C. L. 1932. The heavenly city of the eighteenth-century philosophers. New Haven, Yale University Press.

CHAFE, W. L., ed. 1976. American Indian languages and American linguistics: Proceedings of the second golden anniversary symposium of the Linguistic Society of America. Lisse, Netherlands, Peter de Ridder Press.

CHOMSKY, N. A. 1975. The logical structure of linguistic theory. New York, Plenum Press.

——. 1977. Conditions on rules of grammar. In Coles, ed. (1977), 3-50.

COLE, R. W., ed. 1977. Current issues in linguistic theory. Bloomington, Indiana University Press.

DARNELL, R. 1974. Rationalist aspects of the Whorf hypothesis. Papers in linguistics 7(1-2):41-50.

FIDELHOLTZ, J. L. 1978. Review of Notes from the linguistic underground, ed. by J. D. McCawley (Syntax and semantics, vol. 7). Lg. 54:929-33.

FISHMAN, J. A. 1977. The sociology of language: Yesterday, today, and tomorrow. In Coles, ed. (1977), 51-75.

FLIER, M. S. 1978. Review of The development of morphophonemic theory, by James Kilbury. Lg. 54:922-5.

FRIEDRICH, P. 1971. Distinctive features and functional groups in Tarascan phonology. Lg. 47:849-65.

FULLUM, G. K. 1978. Review of Assessing linguistic arguments, ed. by J. R. Wirth. Lg. 54:399-402.

HAAS, W. 1973. Review of Introduction to theoretical linguistics, by John Lyons. JL 9: 71-113.

——. 1978. Linguistics 1930-1980. JL 14:293-308.

HAUGEN. E. 1958b. The phonemics of modern Icelandic. Lg. 39:55-88.

HAUGEN, E., and W. F. TWADDELL. 1942. Facts and phonemics. Lg. 18:228-37. (Reprinted in Makkai (1972), 91-8).

HOENIGSWALD, H. M., ed. 1979. The European background of American linguistics. Papers of the third golden anniversary symposium of the Linguistic Society of America. Dordrecht: Foris Publications.

HOUSEHOLDER, F. W. 1978. Review of The first LACUS forum (1974), ed. by A. Makkai and V. Becker-Makkai. Lg. 54:170-6.

JAEGER, J. J. et al., eds. 1978. Proceedings of the fourth annual meeting of the Berkeley Linguistic Society, February 18-20, 1978. Berkeley, California, University of California.

JESSEL, L. 1978. Whorf: the differentiation of language. International journal of the sociology of language 18:83-110.

LANGENDOEN, D. T. 1979. Discussion of the papers by Yakov Malkiel and by E. M. Uhlenbeck. In Hoenigswald, ed. (1979), 145-51, and 157-9.

LONGACRE, R. 1960. String constituent analysis. Lg. 36:63-88.

LYONS, J. 1972. Introduction to theoretical linguistics. Cambridge, Cambridge University Press.

McCAWLEY, J. D., ed. 1976. Notes from the linguistic underground. Syntax and semantics, vol. 7. New York, Academic Press.

MURRAY, S. O. 1980. Gatekeepers and the "Chomskian revolution." Journal of the History of the Behavioral Sciences 16(1):73-88.

NEWMEYER, F. J. 1978. Review of The scope of American linguistics, ed. by R. Austerlitz. Lg. 54:395-9.

OGLE, R. 1973. Aspects of a rationalist critique of the Whorf hypothesis. Papers in linguistics 6(3-4):317-50.

PEARSON, B. L. 1977. Paradigms and revolutions in linguistics. In The fourth LACUS forum, ed. by M. Paradis, 384-90. Columbia, S. C., Hornbeam Press.

PERCIVAL, W. K. 1976a. The applicability of Kuhn's paradigms to the history of linguistics. Lg. 52:285-94.

——. 1976b. On the historical source of immediate constituent analysis. In McCawley, ed. (1976), 229-42.

——. 1977. Review of Koerner 1973a. Lg. 53:383-405.

FULLUM, G. K. 1978. Review of Assessing linguistic arguments, ed. by J. R. Wirth. Lg. 54:399-402.

SAMPSON, G. 1979. What was transformational grammar? A review of Noam Chomsky, the logical structure of linguistic theory. Lingua 48:355-78.

STOCKING, G. W. Jr. 1974c. Some comments on history as a moral discipline: "Transcending 'textbook' chronicles and apologetics." In D. H. Hymes, ed. (1974c), 511-19.

UHLENBECK, E. M. 1979. Linguistics in America 1924-1974: A detached view. In Hoenigswald (1979), 121-44, and 153-7.

WATERHOUSE, V. G. 1974. The history and development of tagmemics. Janua linguarum, series critica, 16. The Hague, Mouton.

WELLS, R. S. 1949. Automatic alternation. Lg. 25:99-116.

REFERENCES

AARSLEFF, H. 1970. The history of linguistics and Professor Chomsky. Lg 46.570–585.
——. 1971. 'Cartesian linguistics': History or fantasy? LS 17.1–12.
——. 1973. A word on Koerner's historiography of linguistics. AnL 15(3).148–150.
AKHMANOVA, O., and G. MIKAEL'AN. 1969. The theory of syntax in modern linguistics. Janua Linguarum, series minor, 68. The Hague, Mouton.
ALKON, P. L. 1959. Behaviorism and linguistics: A historical note. L&S 2.37–51.
ALLEN, R. J. 1970. The work and thought of Edward Sapir in anthropology: An analysis. Honors paper in anthropology. Lancaster, Pa., Franklin and Marshall College.
ANDREWS, S., Jr. and J. WHATMOUGH. 1961. Comparative historical linguistics in America 1930–1960. In Mohrmann et al. (1961), 58–81.
APRESJAN, JU. D. 1966. From the history of structural linguistics. In Idei i metodi sovremennoj strukturnoy lingvistiki: Kratkij ocherk, 7–78. Moscow, Izd. "Prosveshchenie". [Translated as Principles and methods of contemporary structural linguistics, by D. B. Crockett (1973). The Hague, Mouton.]
ARENS, H., ed. 1955. Sprachwissenschaft: Der Gang ihrer Entwicklung von der Antike bis zur Gegenwart. Freiburg and Munich, Alber.
——. ed. 1969. Sprachwissenschaft: Der Gang ihrer Entwicklung von der Antike bis zur Gegenwart. 2nd ed., revised and much enlarged. Freiburg and Munich, Alber.
ARUTJUNOVA, N. D. et al. 1964. American structuralism. In Guxman and Guxman (1964), 177–306.
AUSTERLITZ, R. 1972. Review of Portraits of linguists, by T. A. Sebeok (1966). IJAL 38.212–218.
BAR-HILLEL, Y. 1954. Logical syntax and semantics. Lg 30.230–237.
BARRACLOUGH, G. 1972. A new view of German history: Part III. New York Review of Books 19(8).25–31.
BASILIUS, H. 1952. Neo-Humboldtian ethnolinguistics. Word 8.95–105.
BELYI, V. V. 1967. Some facts about Weiss' influence on Bloomfield. Zeitschrift für Anglistik und Amerikanistik 15.409–412.
BENDER, E., and Z. S. HARRIS. 1946. The phonemes of North Carolina Cherokee. IJAL 12.13–21.
BENEDICT, R. 1939. Edward Sapir. AA 41.465–477.

BENVENISTE, E. [n.d.] A brief survey of the development of linguistics. Reprinted in Problèmes de linguistique générale, by E. Benveniste (1966), 18–31. Paris, Gallimard.

———. 1954. Tendances récentes en linguistique générale. Journal de psychologie (Jan.-June) 139ff. Paris, P.U.F. (Reprinted in Problèmes de linguistique générale, by E. Benveniste (1966), 3–17. Paris, Gallimard. Translated in General linguistics, by M. E. Meek (1971), 3–15. Coral Gables, University of Miami Press.)

———. 1966. Problèmes de linguistique générale. Bibliothèque des sciences humaines. Paris, Gallimard.

———. 1971. Problems in general linguistics, trans. by M. E. Meek. Miami Linguistics Series, 8. Coral Gables, University of Miami Press.

BEVER, T. G. 1963. Theoretical implications of Bloomfield's 'Menomini morphophonemics'. Quarterly Progress Report of the Research Laboratory of Electronics, M.I.T., 68.197–203.

———. 1967. Leonard Bloomfield and the phonology of the Menomini language. Unpublished dissertation, Cambridge, M.I.T.

BIDNEY, D. 1953. Theoretical anthropology. New York, Columbia University Press.

BIERWISCH, M. 1966. Strukturalismus: Geschichte, Probleme und Methoden. Kursbuch 5.77–152. Frankfurt am Main.

———. 1971. American linguistics. Modern linguistics: Its development, methods, and problems, Ch. 6., 39–44. The Hague, Mouton.

BLACK, MAX. 1949. Language and philosophy: Studies in method. Ithaca, Cornell University Press.

BLOCH, B. 1941. Phonemic overlapping. AS 16.278–284. (Reprinted in Joos (1957), 93–96; and in Makkai (1972), 66–70.)

———. 1948. A set of postulates for phonemic analysis. Lg 24.3–46. (Reprinted in Makkai (1972), 167–199.)

———. 1949. Leonard Bloomfield. Lg 25.87–98.

———. 1950. Studies in colloquial Japanese, IV: Phonemics. Lg 26.86–125. (Reprinted in Joos (1957), 329–348.)

———. 1953a. Contrast. Lg 29.59–61. (Reprinted in Makkai (1972), 224–225.)

———. 1953b. Linguistic structure and linguistic analysis. In report of the Fourth Annual Round Table Meeting on Linguistics and Language Teaching, ed. by A. A. Hill (MSLL 4), 40–44. Washington, D.C., Georgetown University Press.

———. 1956. Remarks. Proceedings of the Seventh International Congress of Linguists (London, 1952), ed. by F. Norman, 394–396. London.

BLOCH, B., and G. L. TRAGER. 1942. Outline of linguistic analysis. Special publication of the Linguistic Society of America. Baltimore.

*BLOOMFIELD, L. 1914. An introduction to the study of language. New York, Holt.

———. 1919. Fifty years of comparative philology in America. Transactions and Proceedings of the American Philosophical Society 50.62–83.

* For most Bloomfield papers, see Hockett (1970).

———. 1924. Review of Cours de linguistique générale, by F. de Saussure. MLJ 8.317–319.

———. 1925a. Why a linguistic society? Lg 1.1–5.

———. 1925b. Call for the organization meeting. Lg 1.6–7.

———. 1926. A set of postulates for the science of language. Lg 2.153–164. (Reprinted in Joos (1957) 26–31.)

———. 1927. On recent work in general linguistics. Modern Philology 25.211–230.

———. 1933. Language. New York, Holt.

———. 1939. Review of Foundations of language, by L. H. Gray. Modern Language Forum 24.198–199.

———. 1942. Outline guide for the practical study of foreign languages. Baltimore, Linguistic Society of America.

———. 1943a. Meaning. Monatshefte für deutschen Unterricht 35.101–116.

———. 1943b. Franz Boas. Lg 19.198.

———. 1944. Secondary and tertiary response to language. Lg 20.45–55.

———. 1945a. About foreign language teaching. The Yale Review 34.625–641.

———. 1945b. On describing inflection. Monatshefte für deutschen Unterricht 37.8–13.

———. 1946a. Preface. In Linguistic structures of native America, by H. Hoijer et al. (Viking Fund Publications in Anthropology, 6.), 5. New York, Wenner-Gren Foundation. Later reissued by Johnson Reprint Corporation.)

———. 1946b. Algonquian. In Linguistics structures of native America, by H. Hoijer et al. (Viking Fund Publications in Anthropology, 6.), 85–129. New York, Wenner-Gren Foundation. (Later reissued by Johnson Reprint Corporation.)

——— 1946c. Twenty-one years of the Linguistic Society. Lg 22.1–3.

———. 1949. A set of postulates for the science of language. IJAL 15.195–207 (reprinted as obituary).

———. 1972. The original preface to Linguistic structure of native America. IJAL 38.265–266.

BLUMENTHAL, A. L. 1970. Language and psychology: Historical aspects oi psycholinguistics. New York, Wiley.

BOAS, F. 1908. Anthropology. In Lectures on Science, philosophy, and art, 1907–1908 (by several authors), 5–28. New York, Columbia University Press.

———. 1911. Introduction. In Handbook of American Indian languages, ed. by F. Boas (Bureau of American Ethnology, Bulletin 40, Pt. 1.), 1–83. Washington, D.C.

———. 1911, 1922, 1934. Handbook of American Indian languages, Parts 1, 2, 3. Bureau of American Ethnology, Bulletin 40. Washington, D.C.

———. 1938. Language. In General Anthropology, ed. F. Boas, 124–145. New York, Heath.

———. 1939. Edward Sapir. IJAL 10.58–63.

BOAS, F., P. E. GODDARD, E. SAPIR, and A. L. KROEBER. 1916. Phonetic transcription of Indian languages: Report of Committee of American Anthropological Association. Smithsonian Miscellaneous Collections, 6(6). Washington, D.C.

BOLELLI, T. 1965. Per una storia della ricerca linguistica: Testi e note introduttive. Naples, Mirana.

BOLINGER, D. L. 1968. Aspects of language. New York, Harcourt, Brace.

BOTHA, R. P. (with W. K. WINCKLER). 1973. The justification of linguistic hypotheses. A study of nondemonstrative inference in transformational grammar. The Hague, Mouton.

BROWN, R. G. 1958. Words and things. Glencoe, The Free Press.

BROWN, R. L. 1967. Wilhelm von Humboldt's conception of linguistic relativity. The Hague, Mouton.

BURKE, K. 1951. Three definitions. Kenyon Review 13.173–192.

——. 1968. Language as symbolic action. Berkeley, University of California Press. (Reviewed, Lg 44.664–669 (1968).)

BURSILL-HALL, G. L. 1970a. The history of linguistics. CJL 15.143–150.

——. 1970b. Review of A short history of linguistics, by R. H. Robins; Les grandes courants de la linguistique moderne, by M. Leroy; Trends in linguistics, by M. Ivić. Glossa 4(2).229–244.

CAMPBELL, B. 1967. Linguistic meaning. Linguistics 33.3–24.

CANCIAN, F. M. 1974. What are norms? A study of beliefs and action in a Maya community. New York, Cambridge University Press.

CARROLL, J. B. 1953. The study of language: A survey of linguistics and related disciplines. Cambridge, Harvard University Press.

——. 1956. Language, thought, and reality: Selected writings of Benjamin Lee Whorf. Cambridge, M.I.T. Press.

CASSIRER, E. 1927. Individuum und Kosmos in der Philosophie der Renaissance. Studien der Bibliothek Warburg, X. Leipzig, B. G. Teubner. (Translated with introduction as The Individual and the Cosmos in Renaissance Philosophy, by M. Domandi. New York, Harper and Row. Harper Torchbook, TB1097 (1964).)

——. 1942. Zur Logik des Kulturwissenschaften. Göteborg. (Translated as The Logic of the Humanities, by C. S. Howe. New Haven, Yale University Press (1961).)

——. 1945. Structuralism in modern linguistics. Word 1.99–120.

CHAO, Y. R. 1934. The non-uniqueness of phonemic solutions of phonetic systems. Academia Sinica (Bulletin of the Institute of History and Philology) 4(4).363–397. (Reprinted in Joos (1957), 38–54.)

——. 1968. Language and symbolic systems. Cambridge, University Press.

CHATTERJI, S. K. 1964. Discussion [of Les niveaux de l'analyse linguistique, by E. Benveniste]. Proceedings of the Ninth International Congress of Linguists (Cambridge, 1962), ed. by H. Lunt, 283–293. The Hague, Mouton.

CHOMSKY, N. 1955. Logical syntax and semantics. Lg 31.36–45.

——. 1957a. Syntactic structures. Janua linguarum, series minor, 4. The Hague, Mouton.

——. 1957b. Review of A manual of phonology, by C. F. Hockett. IJAL 23. 223–234.

——. 1957c. Review of Fundamentals of language, by R. Jakobson and M. Halle. IJAL 23.234–241. (Reprinted in Makkai (1972), 343–350.)

——. 1959. Review of Essays in linguistics, by J. H. Greenberg. Word 15.202–218.

——. 1962. A transformational approach to syntax. Proceedings of the Third Texas Conference in Problems of Linguistic Analysis in English, 1958, ed. by A. A. Hill, 124–158. Austin, Texas. In The structure of language, ed. by J. A. Fodor and J. J. Katz (1964), 211–245. Englewood Cliffs, New Jersey, Prentice-Hall.

——. 1964a. The logical basis of linguistic theory. Proceedings of the Ninth International Congress of Linguists (Cambridge, 1962), ed. by H. Lunt, 914–978. (Discussion, 978–1008.) The Hague, Mouton.

——. 1964b. Current issues in linguistic theory. In The structure of language, ed. by J. A. Fodor and J. J. Katz, 50–118. Englewood Cliffs, N. J., Prentice-Hall. (Revised from 1964a.)

——. 1964c. A transformational approach to syntax. In The structure of language, ed. by J. A. Fodor and J. J. Katz, 211–245. Englewood Cliffs, N. J., Prentice-Hall. (Reprinted from Proceedings of the Third Texas Conference on Problems of Linguistic Analysis in English, 1958, ed. by A. A. Hill, (1962), 124–158. Austin, Texas, The University of Texas Press.)

——. 1965. Aspects of the theory of syntax. Cambridge, M.I.T. Press.

——. 1966a. Cartesian linguistics: A chapter in the history of rationalist thought. New York, Harper and Row.

——. 1966b. Topics in the theory of generative grammar. In Current trends in linguistics, ed. T. A. Sebeok, 3.1–60. The Hague, Mouton. (Also issued separately under the same title (Janua Linguarum, series minor, 56.) The Hague, Mouton.)

CHOMSKY, N., and M. HALLE. 1965. Some controversial questions in phonological theory. JL 1.97–138. (Reprinted in Makkai (1972), 457–485.)

——. 1968. The sound pattern of English. New York, Harper and Row.

CHOMSKY, N., M. HALLE, and F. LUKOFF. 1956. On accent and juncture in English. In For Roman Jakobson: Essays on the occasion of his sixtieth birthday, 65–80. The Hague, Mouton.

CHOMSKY, N., and G. MILLER. 1963. Introduction to the formal analysis of natural languages. In Handbook of mathematical psychology, Vol. II, ed. by R. Luce, R. Bush, and E. Galanter, 269–321. New York, Wiley.

CHRISTMANN, H. H. 1958/1959. Strukturelle Sprachwissenschaft: Grundlagen und Entwicklung. RJb 9.17–40.

——. 1967. Beiträge zur Geschichte der These vom Weltbild der Sprache. Wiesbaden, Steiner.

COLLINGWOOD, R. G. 1939. An autobiography. Oxford, University Press.

COLLINSON, W. E. 1948. Some recent trends in linguistic theory with special reference to syntactics. Lingua 1.306–332.

CURRIE, H. C. and E. G. C. 1973. Sociolinguistics and the two American linguistic orthodoxies. Austin, Texas, Regional Research Associates, 1811 Alameda Drive.

DARNELL, R. 1967. Daniel Garrison Brinton: An intellectual biography. Unpublished M. A. dissertation, Philadelphia, University of Pennsylvania, Department of Anthropology.

——. 1969. The development of American anthropology 1879–1920: From the Bureau of American Ethnology to Franz Boas. Unpublished dissertation, Philadelphia, University of Pennsylvania, Department of Anthropology.

DAVIS, P. W. 1973. Modern theories of language. Englewood Cliffs, N.J., Prentice-Hall.

DE SAUSSURE, F. 1916. Cours de linguistique générale. Paris, Payot.

DERWING, B. L. 1973. Transformational grammar as a theory of language acquisition: A study in the empirical, conceptual and methodological foundations of contemporary linguistic theory. Cambridge Studies in Lingustics, 10. Cambridge, University Press.

DINGWALL, W. O. 1963. Transformational grammar: Form and theory: A contribution to the history of linguistics. Lingua 12.233–275.

——. 1966. Recent developments in transformational-generative grammar. Lingua 16.292–316.

——. 1971a. Linguistics as psychology: A definition and some initial tasks. In A survey of linguistic science, ed. by W. O. Dingwall, 759–802. College Park, Maryland, Linguistics Program, University of Maryland.

——., ed. 1971b. A survey of linguistic science. College Park, Maryland, Linguistics Program, University of Maryland.

DINNEEN, F. P. 1967a. An introduction to general linguistics. New York, Holt, Rinehart and Winston.

——. 1968. Review of A short history of linguistics, by R. H. Robins. GL 8(2).97–101.

——. 1971. Review of A survey of structural linguistics, by G. C. Lepschy. JL 7(2).287–291.

DIXON, R. M. W. 1965. What *is* language? A new approach to linguistic description. London, Longmans.

ECHOLS, J. M. 1949. Review of Morphology, by E. A. Nida. JEGP 48.377–379.

EDGERTON, F. 1939. Edward Sapir (1884–1939). Yearbook of the American

Philosophical Society 460–464. Philadelphia.

EMENEAU, M. B. 1943. Franz Boas as a linguist. In Franz Boas, 1858–1942, by A. L. Kroeber et al., 35–38 (Memoirs of the American Anthropological Association, 61; AA 45(3), part 2.). (Reprinted in Portraits of linguists, ed. by T. A. Sebeok (1966), 2.122–127. Bloomington, Indiana University Press.)

——. 1953. Edgar Howard Sturtevant (1875–1952). The American Philosophical Society Yearbook 1952, 339–343. (Reprinted in Portraits of Linguists, ed. by T. A. Sebeok (1966), 2.365–369. Bloomington, Indiana University Press.)

ESPER, E. A. 1964. A history of psychology. Philadelphia and London, W. B. Saunder.

——. 1968. Mentalism and objectivism in linguistics: The sources of Leonard Bloomfield's psychology of language. New York, American Elsevier.

——. 1971. Review of Language and psychology: Historical aspects of psycholinguistics, by A. L. Blumenthal. Lg 47.979–984.

——. In press. Analogy and associationism in linguistics and psychology. Atlanta, University Georgia Press.

FEKETE, J. 1973. McLuhanacy: Counterrevolution in cultural theory. Telos 15.75–123.

FERGUSON, C. A. 1964. The basic grammatical categories of Bengali. In Proceedings of the Ninth International Congress of Linguists (Cambridge, 1962), ed. by H. G. Lunt, 888–190. The Hague, Mouton.

FERGUSON, T. 1973. The political economy of knowledge and the changing politics of philosophy of science. Telos 15.124–137.

FIRTH, J. R. 1949. Atlantic linguistics. Archivum Linguisticum 1(2).95–116. (Reprinted in Papers in Linguistics 1934–1951 (1957), 156–172. London, Oxford University Press.)

——. 1955. Structural linguistics. TPhS 83–103. (Reprinted in Selected Papers of J. R. Firth 1952–1959, ed. by F. R. Palmer (1968), 35–52. Bloomington, Indiana University Press.)

FOUGHT, J. 1973. On the adequacy of recent phonological theories and practices. Annual Review of Anthropology, ed. by Bernard J. Siegel, Vol. 2.

FOWLER, M. B. 1952. Review of Methods in structural linguistics, by Z. S. Harris. Lg 28.504–509.

FREEMAN, J. E. (compiler) and M. D. SMITH (consultant). 1966. A guide to the manuscripts relating to the American Indian in the Library of the American Philosophical Society. APS, Memoir 65. Philadelphia, APS.

FRIEDRICH, P. 1971. Anthropological linguistics: Recent research and immediate progress. Report of the 22nd Annual Round table Meeting on linguistics and language studies; Developments of the sixties — Viewpoints for the seventies, ed. by R. J. O'Brien, 167–184. MSLL 24. Washington, D.C., Georgetown University Press.)

——. Forthcoming. The lexical symbol and its non-arbitrariness. (To appear in the Voegelin festschrift, ed. by D. Kinkade, in press.)

FRIES, C. C. 1954. Meaning and linguistic analysis. Lg 30.57–68.

——. 1955. American linguistics and the teaching of English. Language Learning 6(1–2).1–22.

——. 1961. The Bloomfield 'school'. In Mohrmann, et al. (1961) 196–224.

——. 1963. Linguistics: The study of language. Linguistics and reading, Ch. 2, 35–92 (and 223–232). [Published separately, New York, Holt, Rinehart and Winston (1965).]

GARVIN, P. L. 1948. Kutenai, I: Phonemics. IJAL 14.37–42.

——. 1950. Wichita, I: Phonemics. IJAL 16: 179–184.

——. 1951. Review of Recherches structurales 1949. IJAL 17.252–255.

——. 1954. Review of Prolegomena to a theory of language, by L. Hjelmslev. Lg 30.69–96.

——. 1958. A descriptive technique for the treatment of meaning. Lg 34.1–32.

——. 1967. American Indian languages: A laboratory for linguistic methodology. FL 3.257–260.

GILBERT, G. ms. Review of Area linguistics, by H. Kurath.

GIPPER, H. 1972. Gibt es ein sprachliches Relativitätsprinzip? Untersuchungen zur Sapir-Whorf-Hypothese. Frankfurt am Main, S. Fischer.

GLEASON, H. A., JR. 1955. An introduction to descriptive linguistics. New York, Holt, Rinehart and Winston.

——. 1961a. An introduction to descriptive linguistics. Rev. ed. New York, Holt, Rinehart and Winston.

——. 1961b. A file for a technical dictionary. Report of the 16th annual round table meeting on linguistics and language studies, ed. by M. Zarenchak and A. Guss, 115–122. MSLL 14. Washington, D.C., Georgetown University Press.

——. 1965. The origins of modern linguistics. In Linguistics and English grammar, Ch. 2, 28–47. New York, Holt, Rinehart and Winston.

GODDARD, I., C. F. HOCKETT, and K. V. TEETER. 1972. Some errata in Bloomfield's Menomini. IJAL 38.1–5.

GODDARD, P. E. 1914. The present condition of our knowledge of North American languages. AA 16.555–601.

GODEL, R. 1966. F. de Saussure's theory of language. In Current trends in linguistics, ed. by T. A. Sebeok, 3.479–494. The Hague, Mouton.

GOLDENWEISER, A. 1941. Recent trends in American anthropology. AA 43.151–163.

GOODENOUGH, W. H. 1956. Componential analysis and the study of meaning. Lg 32. 195–216.

GRAUR, A. and L. WALD. 1961. Scurtă istorie a lingvisticii. Bucharest, Editura Ştiinţifică (2nd ed., 1965.)

GRAY, B. 1974. Toward a semi-revolution in grammar. LS 29.1–12.

GRAY, L. H. 1939. Foundations of language. New York, Macmillan.
——. 1945–1949. Mécanisme et mentalisme. AL 5.65–72.
GREENBERG, J. H. 1968. Anthropological linguistics: An introduction. New York, Random House.
GRINDER, J. T., and S. H. ELGIN. 1973. Guide to transformational grammar: History, theory, practice. Waltham, Xerox.
GUXMAN, M. M. 1954. Ė. Sepir i ètnografičeskaya lingvistika. VJa 3(1).110–127.
——. 1964. The historical and methodological foundations of structuralism. In Guxman and Guxman (1964), 5–45.
GUXMAN, M. M., and V. N. GUXMAN, eds. 1964 Osnovnye napravlenija strukturalizma. Moscow, Izd. "Nauka".
HAAS, M. R. 1935. A grammar of the Tunica language. Unpublished Ph. D. dissertation, New Haven, Yale University.
——. 1941. Tunica. (Extract from Handbook of American Indian languages, vol. IV.) New York, J. J. Augustin.
——. 1953a. Sapir and the training of anthropological linguists. AA 55.447–449.
——. 1953b. The application of linguistics to language teaching. In Anthropology today, by A. L. Kroeber et al., 807–818. Chicago, University of Chicago Press.
——. Forthcoming. Edward Sapir. New York, Columbia University Press.
HAHN, E. A. 1952. Edgar Howard Sturtevant. Lg 28.417–434. (Reprinted in Portraits of linguists, ed. by T. A. Sebeok (1966), 2.369–384. Bloomington, Indiana University Press.)
HALE, K. 1965. On the use of informants in fieldwork. CJL 10.108–119.
HALL, R. A., JR. 1946. The state of linguistics. Crisis or reaction? Italica 23.30–34.
——. 1950a. Review of Kwakiutl grammar with a glossary of the suffixes, by F. Boas. IJAL 16.101–102.
——. 1950b. Leonard Bloomfield. Lingua 2.117–123.
——. 1951–1952. American linguistics, 1925–50. ArchL 6.101–125; 4.1–16.
——. 1965. American linguistics, 1950–1960. Annali, Cozione Linguistica, Istituto Orientale di Napoli 6.241–260.
——. 1969a. Some recent developments in American linguistics. Neuphilologische Mitteilungen 70.192–227.
——. 1969b. Sapir and Croce on language. AA 71.498–500.
HALLE, M. 1958. Questions of linguistics. Il Nuovo Cimento 13.494–517. (Reprinted in revised form as On the bases of phonology. In The structure of language, ed. by J. A. Fodor and J. J. Katz (1964), 324–333. Englewood Cliffs, New Jersey, Prentice-Hall.)
——. 1959. The sound pattern of Russian: A linguistic and acoustical investigation. With an excursus on the contextual variants of the Russian vowels by Lawrence G. Jones. The Hague, Mouton.
——. 1962. Phonology in generative grammar. Word 18.54–72. (Reprinted in

The structure of language, ed. by J. A. Fodor and J. J. Katz (1964), 334–352. Englewood Cliffs, New Jersey: Prentice-Hall; and in Makkai (1972), 380–392.)

HALLIDAY, M. A. K. 1966. The concept of rank: A reply. JL 2.110–118.

HAMMEL, E. A. 1965. Introduction. In Formal semantic analysis, ed. by E. A. Hammel, 1–8. Washington, D.C., American Anthropological Association.

HAMP, E. P. 1957. A glossary of American technical linguistic usage, 1925–1950. Permanent International Committee of Linguists; Publication of the Committee for terminology. Utrecht/Antwerp, Spectrum.

———. 1961. General linguistics: The United States in the fifties. In Mohrmann et al., 165–194.

HAMP, E., F. W. HOUSEHOLDER, JR., and R. AUSTERLITZ. 1966. Readings in linguistics, II. Chicago, University of Chicago Press.

HANSON, N. R. 1958. Patterns of discovery. Cambridge, University Press.

HARMAN, G., ed. Fortcoming.

HARRINGTON, J. P. 1945. Boas on the science of language. IJAL 11.97–99.

HARRIS, Z. S. 1940. Review of Foundations of language, by L. H. Gray. Lg 16.216–223.

———. 1941a. Review of Grundzüge der Phonologie, by N. S. Trubetzkoy. Lg 17.345–349. (Reprinted in Makkai (1972), 301–304.)

———. 1941b. Linguistic structure of Hebrew. JAOS 61.148–154.

———. 1942a. The phonemes of Moroccan Arabic. JAOS 62.309–318.

———. 1942b. Morpheme alternants in linguistic analysis. Lg 18.169–180. (Reprinted in Joos (1957), 109–115.)

———. 1944a. Yokuts structure and Newman's grammar. IJAL 10.196–211.

———. 1944b. Simultaneous components in phonology. Lg 20.181–205. (Reprinted in Joos (1957), 124–138; and in Makkai (1972), 115–133.)

———. 1945. Navaho phonology and Hoijer's analysis. IJAL 11.239–246.

———. 1946a. American Indian linguistic work and the Boas collection. Yearbook of the American Philosophical Society (1945) 96–100.

———. 1946b. From morpheme to utterance. Lg 22.161–183. (Reprinted in Joos (1957), 142–153.)

———. 1947. Developments in American Indian linguistics. APS Library Bulletin (1946) 84–97.

———. 1951a. Methods in structural linguistics. Chicago, University of Chicago Press. (Later reissued in paperback under the title, Structural linguistics.)

———. 1951b. Review of Selected writings of Edward Sapir in language, culture, and personality, ed. by D. G. Mandelbaum. Lg 27.288–333.

———. 1952a. Discourse analysis. Lg 28.1–30.

———. 1952b. Discourse analysis: A sample test. Lg 28.474–494.

———. 1952c. Culture and style in extended discourse. In Indian tribes of Aboriginal America, ed. by S. Tax, 210–215. Chicago, University of Chicago

Press. (Selected papers of the 29th International Congress of Americanists, 1949.)
———. 1954a. Transfer grammar. IJAL 20.259–270.
———. 1954b. Distributional structure. Word 10.146–162.
———. 1959. The transformational model of language structure. AL 1(1).27–30.
———. 1965. Transformational theory. Lg 41.363–401.
———. 1973. Review of A Leonard Bloomfield anthology, ed. by C. F. Hockett. IJAL 39.252–255.
HARRIS, Z. S., and C. F. VOEGELIN. 1953. Eliciting in linguistics. Southwestern Journal of Anthropology 9.59–75.
HAUGEN, E. 1938. Notes on 'voiced t' in American English. Dialect Notes 6.627–634.
———. 1951. Directions in modern linguistics. Lg 27.211–222. (Reprinted in Joos (1957), 357–363.)
———. 1958. Review of Papers in Linguistics 1934–1951, by J. R. Firth. Lg 34.498–502.
———. 1972. La linguistique américaine. BSL 66(1).45–58.
HELBIG, G. 1970. Geschichte der neueren Sprachwissenschaft, unter dem besonderen Aspekt der Grammatik-theorie. Leipzig, VEB Bibliographisches Institut; Munich, Hueber.
HEMPEL, C. G. 1952. Fundamentals of concept formation. International Encyclopedia of Unified Science, II, 7. Chicago, University of Chicago Press.
HENSON, H. 1974. British social anthropologists and language: A history of separate development. Oxford Monographs on Social Anthropology. Oxford, Clarendon Press.
HERZOG, G., S. NEWMAN, E. SAPIR, M. HASS SWADESH, M. SWADESH, and C. VOEGELIN. 1934. Some orthographic recommendations. AA 36.629–631.
HILL, A. A. 1952. A note on primitive languages. IJAL 18.172–177. Abridged in Language in culture and society, ed. by D. Hymes (1964), 86–88. New York, Harper and Row.)
———. 1955. Linguistics since Bloomfield, Quarterly Journal of Speech 41. 253–260.
———. 1958. Introduction to linguistic structures. New York.
———. 1962. A postulate for linguistics in the sixties. Lg 38.345–351.
———. 1964. History of the Linguistic Institute. ACLS Newsletter 15(3).1–12.
———. 1967. The current relevance of Bloch's 'Postulates'. Lg 43.102–128. (Reprinted in Makkai (1972), 241–246.)
HJELMSLEV, L. 1939. Nekrolog auf Edward Sapir. Acta Linguistica 1.76–77.
———. 1945–1949. Introduction. Acta Linguistica 5.i–xi.
HOCKETT, C. F. 1942. A system of descriptive phonology. Lg 18.3–21. (Reprinted in Joos (1957), 97–108; and in Makkai (1972), 99–112.)
———. 1944. Review of Linguistic interludes; Morphology, the descriptive analysis of words, by E. A. Nida. Lg 20.252–255.

——. 1947a. Peiping phonology. JAOS 67.253–267. (Reprinted in Joos (1957), 217–288.)

——. 1947b. Componential analysis of Sierra Popoluca. IJAL 13.259–267.

——. 1947c. Review of Morphology, the descriptive analysis of words, by E. A. Nida. Lg 23.272–285.

——. 1947d.   Problems of morphemic analysis. Lg 23.321–343. (Reprinted in Joos (1957), 229–242.)

——. 1948a. Implications of Bloomfield's Algonquian studies. Lg 24.117–131. (Reprinted in Language in culture and society, ed. by D. Hymes (1964), 599–609. New York, Harper and Row; and in A Leonard Bloomfield anthology, ed. by C. F. Hockett (1970), 495–511. Bloomington, Indiana University Press.)

——. 1948b. Review of Linguistic structures of native America, by H. Hoijer et al. (1946). Lg 24.183–188.

——. 1948c. A note on 'structure'. IJAL 14.269–271. (Reprinted in Joos (1957), 279–280.)

——. 1949.   Two fundamental problems in phonemics. Studies in Linguistics 7.29–51. (Reprinted in Makkai (1972), 200–210.)

——. 1950a. Which approach in linguistics is 'scientific'? Studies in Linguistics 8.53–57.

——. 1950b. Language 'and' culture: A protest. AA 52.113.

——. 1951. Review of Phonology as functional phonetics, by A. Martinet. Lg 27.333–342. (Reprinted in Makkai (1972), 310–317.)

——. 1952a. Review of Methods in structural linguistics, by Z. S. Harris. AS 27.117–121.

——. 1952b. Review of Recherches structurales 1949. IJAL 18.86–99.

——. 1958. A course in modern linguistics. New York, Macmillan.

——. 1959. Animal 'languages' and human languages. In The evolution of man's capacity for culture, ed. by J. N. Spuhler, 32–39. Detroit, Wayne University Press.

——. 1961. Linguistic elements and their relations. Lg 37.29–53.

——. 1965. Sound change. Lg 41.185–205.

——. 1966. What Algonquian is really like. IJAL 32.59–73.

——. 1968a. The background. In The state of the art, Ch. 1, 9–37. Janua Linguarum, series minor, 73. The Hague, Mouton.

——. 1968b. Review of Outline of stratificational grammar, by S. Lamb. IJAL 34.145–153.

——. 1968c. Bloomfield, Leonard. International Encyclopedia of the Social Sciences 2.95–99.

——. ed. 1970. A Leonard Bloomfield anthology. Bloomington, Indiana University Press.

——. 1973. Yokuts as testing ground for linguistic methods. IJAL 39.63–79.

HODGE, C. F. 1963. The influences of linguistics on language teaching. AnL 5(1).50–58.

HOENIGSWALD, H. M. 1960. Language change and linguistic reconstruction. Chicago, University of Chicago Press.

———. 1963. On the history of the comparative method. AnL 5(1).1–11.

———. 1973. Linguistics. In Dictionary of the history of ideas, ed. by P. Wiener, 3.61–73.

———. 1974. Fallacies in the history of linguistics and the appraisal of the early nineteenth century. In: Studies in the history of linguistics, ed. by D. Hymes, 346–358. Bloomington, Indiana University Press.

HOIJER, H. 1933. Tonkawa, an Indian language of Texas. In Handbook of American Indian languages, ed. by F. Boas, Part 3, 1–148. New York, J. J. Augustin.

———. 1945a. Review of Word. Acta Americana 3.243–245.

———. 1945b. Review of IJAL. Acta Americana 3.245–247.

———. 1945c. Review of IJAL. California Folklore Quarterly 4.438–441.

———. 1951a. Review of Selected writings of Edward Sapir in language, culture and personality, ed. by D. Mandelbaum. RomPh 4.311–315.

———. 1951b. Cultural implications of some Navaho linguistic categories. Lg 27.111–120. (Reprinted in Language in culture and society, ed. by D. Hymes (1964), 142–148. New York, Harper and Row.)

———. 1953. The relation of language to culture. In Anthropology today, by A. L. Kroeber et al., 554–573. Chicago, University of Chicago Press.

———. 1954a. The Sapir-Whorf hypothesis. In Language in culture, ed. by H. Hoijer, 92–105. Chicago, University of Chicago Press.

———. ed. 1954b. Language in culture. Chicago, University of Chicago Press.

———. 1958. Native reaction as a criterion in linguistic analysis. In Proceedings of the Eighth International Congress of Linguists, ed. by E. Sivertsen, 573–583. Oslo.

———. 1961. Anthropological linguistics. In Mohrmann et al., 110–127.

———. 1968. Review of Portraits of linguistics, ed. by T. A. Sebeok. Lg 44.96–98.

HOIJER, H., et al. 1946. Linguistic structures of native America. Viking Fund Publications in Anthropology, 6. New York, Wenner-Gren Foundation.

HOIJER, H., and E. P. DOZIER. 1949. The phonemes of Tewa, Santa Clara dialect. IJAL 15.139–144.

HOLMES, U. T., JR. 1940. Review of Mélanges de linguistique offerts à Charles Bally. Lg 16.237–240.

HOUSEHOLDER, F. W., JR. 1951. Review of Methods in structural linguistics, by Z. S. Harris. IJAL 18.260–268.

———. 1952. Review of The phoneme, by D. Jones. IJAL 18.99–105.

———. 1963. Review of Trends in European and American linguistics 1930–1960, ed. by C. Mohrmann, A. Sommerfelt, and J. Whatmough. Lg 39.78–87.

——. 1965. On some recent claims in phonological theory. JL 1.13–34. (Reprinted in Makkai (1972), 442–456.)

——. 1969. Review of Language and its structure, by R. W. Langacker. Lg 45.886–897.

——. 1970. Review of The state of the art, by C. F. Hockett. JL 6.129–134.

——. 1971. Linguistic speculations. Cambridge, University Press.

HUDDLESTON, R. 1972. The development of a non-process model in American structural linguistics. Lingua 30.333–384.

HUGHES, J. P. 1962. A brief history of the study of language. The science of language: An introduction to linguistics, 34–72. New York, Random House.

HUTCHINSON, L. G. 1972. Mr. Chomsky on the phoneme. Indiana University Linguistics Club.

HYMES, D. 1958. Review of Readings in Linguistics, ed. by M. Joos. AA 60. 416–418.

——. 1959. Field work in linguistics and anthropology. Studies in Linguistics 14.82–91.

——. 1961a. Alfred Louis Kroeber. Lg 37.1–28. (Reprinted in Language in culture and society, ed. by D. Hymes (1964), 697–707. New York, Harper and Row, and in Portraits of linguists, ed. by T. A. Sebeok (1966), 2.400–437. Bloomington, Indiana University Press.)

——. 1961b. Review of The anthropology of Franz Boas, ed. by W. Goldschmidt. Journal of American Folklore 74.87–90.

——. 1961c. On typology of cognitive styles in language. AnL 3(1).22–54.

——. 1963. Notes toward a history of linguistic anthropology. AnL 5(1).59–103.

——. 1964a. Introduction, Part I; Introduction, Part X, Toward historical perspective. In Language in culture and society, ed. by D. Hymes, 3–14, 667–669. New York, Harper and Row.

——. 1964b. History of linguistics and linguistic work in anthropology. (Bibliography with prefatory note.) In Language in culture and society, ed. by D. Hymes, 708–710. New York, Harper and Row.

——. 1964c. Language in culture and society. New York, Harper and Row.

——. 1964d. Directions in (ethno)linguistic theory. Transcultural studies in cognition, ed. by A. K. Romney and R. G. D'Andrade, 6–56. Washington, D.C., American Anthropology Association. (Issued as American Anthropologist 66(3), pt. 2.)

——. 1965. Review of Perspectives on linguistics, by J. T. Waterman. IJAL 31.270–274.

——. 1966a. Review of Trends in linguistics, by M. Ivić. AA 86.1309–1311.

——. 1966b. On 'anthropological linguistics' and congeners. AA 68.143–153.

——. 1966c. Two types of linguistic relativity. In Sociolinguistics, ed. by W. Bright, 114–158. The Hague, Mouton.

——. 1967. The anthropology of communication. In Human communication theory, ed. by F. Dance, 1–39. New York, Holt, Rinehart and Winston.

——. 1968a. Value of the Radin papers for linguistics. The American Indian: A conference in the American Philosophical Society Library, 35–45. Philadelphia.

——. 1968b. Linguistics: The field. International Encyclopedia of the Social Sciences 9.351–371.

——. 1969a. Review of Language in relation to a unified theory of the structure of human behavior, by K. L. Pike. AA 71.361–363.

——. 1969b. Modjeska on Sapir and Croce: A comment. AA 71.500.

——. 1970a. Linguistic method in ethnography. In Method and theory in linguistics, ed. by P. L. Garvin, 249–311. The Hague, Mouton.

——. 1970b. Linguistic aspects of comparative political research. In The methodology of comparative research, ed. by R. Holt and J. Turner, 295–341. New York, The Free Press.

——. 1970c. Bilingual education: Linguistic vs. sociolinguistic bases. Report of the 21st annual round table meeting on linguistic and language study, ed. by J. E. Alatis, 69–76. MSLL 23. Washington, D.C., Georgetown University Press.

——. 1971a. Foreword; Morris Swadesh: From the first Yale school to world prehistory. In The origin and diversification of language, by M. Swadesh, ed. by J. F. Sherzer, v–x; 228–270. Chicago, Aldine.

——. 1971b. Sociolinguistics and the ethnography of speaking. In Social anthropology and language, ed. by E. Ardener (ASA monographs, 10.), 47–93. London, Tavistock Press.

——. 1972a. Review of Noam Chomsky, by J. Lyons. Lg 48.416–427.

——. 1972b. The scope of sociolinguistics. Report of the 23rd annual round table meeting on linguistics and language studies; Sociolinguistics: Current trends and prospects, ed. by R. W. Shuy (MSLL 25.), 313–333. Washington, D.C., Georgetown University Press.

——. 1973. The use of anthropology: Critical, political, personal. In Reinventing anthropology, ed. by D. Hymes, 3–79. New York, Pantheon.

——. 1974a. Ways of speaking. In Explorations in the ethnography of speaking, ed. by R. Bauman and J. F. Sherzer, 433–451. Cambridge, University Press.

——. 1974b. Introduction. In Studies in the history of linguistics, ed. by D. Hymes, 1–28.

——. 1974c. Studies in the history of linguistics: Traditions and paradigms. Bloomington, Indiana University Press.

——. ms. (1970) The pre-war Prague School and post-war American anthropological linguistics.

IVIĆ, M. 1965. Trends in linguistics. Janua Linguarum, series minor, 42. The Hague, Mouton.

JAKOBSON, R. 1942. Kindersprache, Aphasie, und allgemeine Lautgesetze. Uppsala. (Reprinted in his Selected writings (1962), 1.328–340. The Hague, Mouton.)

——. 1944. Franz Boas' approach to language. IJAL 10.188–195. (Reprinted in his Selected writings (1971), 2.477–488. The Hague, Mouton.)

——. 1953. Chapter Two. Results of the conference of anthropologists and linguists, ed. by C. Lévi-Strauss, R. Jakobson, C. F. Voegelin, and T. A. Sebeok. IJAL, Memoir 8. Bloomington. (Reprinted in his Selected writings (1971), 2.554–567. The Hague, Mouton.)

——. 1958. Typological studies and their contribution to historical comparative linguistics. In Proceedings of the Eighth International Congress of Linguists (Oslo, 1957), 17–35. Oslo. (Reprinted in his Selected writings (1962), 1. 523–531. The Hague, Mouton.)

——. 1959. Boas' view of grammatical meaning. In The anthropology of Franz Boas: Essay on the centennial of his birth, ed. by W. Goldschmidt (American Anthropological Association, Memoir 89.), 139–145. Menasha, Wisconsin, American Anthropological Association. (Issued also in San Francisco, Chandler, 1959.) (Reprinted in his Selected writings (1971), 2.489–496. The Hague, Mouton.)

——. 1962. Retrospect. In Selected Writings, I: Phonological Studies, 631–658. The Hague, Mouton.

——. 1964. Results of the Congress. In Proceedings of the Ninth International Congress of Linguists, ed. by H. Lunt, 1135–1142. The Hague, Mouton. (Reprinted in his Selected writings (1971), 2.593–602. The Hague, Mouton.

——. 1971a. The world response to Whitney's principles of linguistics science. In Whitney on language: Selected writings of William Dwight Whitney, ed. by M. Silverstein, xxv–xlv. Cambridge, M.I.T. Press.

——. 1971b. Selected writings, II: Word and language. The Hague, Mouton.

——. 1971c. Retrospect. In Selected writings, II: Word and language, 711–724. The Hague, Mouton.

JAKOBSON, R., and M. HALLE. 1956. Fundamentals of language. The Hague, Mouton.

JANKOWSKY, K. R. 1968. The neogrammarians: A re-evaluation of their place in the development of linguistic science. Washington, D.C., Georgetown University. (Pre-publication edition.)

JOHNS, D. A. 1969. Phonemics and generative phonology. In Papers from the Fifth Regional Meeting of the Chicago Linguistic Society, 374–381. (Reprinted in Makkai (1972), 549–553.)

JOOS, MARTIN. 1942. A phonological dilemma in Canadian English. Lg 18. 141–144.

——, ed. 1957. Readings in linguistics: The development of descriptive linguistics in America since 1925. Washington, D.C., American Council for Learned Societies. (Reissued as Readings in Linguistics, Vol. 1, 4th ed.

(1966). Chicago, University of Chicago Press.)

———. 1958a. Semiology: A linguistic theory of meaning. Studies in linguistics 13.53–70.

———. 1958b. Review of A glossary of American technical linguistic usage, 1925–1950, by E. P. Hamp. Lg 34.279–288.

———. 1961. Linguistic prospects in the United States. In Mohrmann et al., 11–20.

———. 1967. Bernard Bloch. Lg 43.3–19.

KATZ, J. J. 1964. Mentalism in linguistics. Lg 40.124–137.

KELLY, L. G. 1969. 25 centuries of language teaching. Rowley, Massachusetts, Newbury House.

KENT, R. G., and E. H. STURTEVANT. 1926. Survey of linguistic studies: Opportunities for advanced work in the United States. LSA Bulletin No. 1. Baltimore.

KING, J., and J. TONDRÍAN. 1950. La linguistique aux U.S.A. et au Canada. Aevum 24.384–403.

KIPARSKY, P. 1974. From paleo-grammarians to neogrammarians. In Studies in the history of linguistics, ed. by D. Hymes, 331–345. Bloomington, Indiana University Press.

KLEIN, W. 1971. Einleitung. In Aspekte der Soziolinguistik, ed. by W. Klein and D. Wunderlich, 7–13. Frankfurt am Main, Athenäum.

KOERNER, E. F. K. 1970a. Bloomfieldian linguistics and the problems of 'meaning': A chapter in the history of the theory and study of language. Jahrbuch für Amerikastudien 15.162–183.

———. 1970b. Review of On language: Plato to von Humboldt, ed. by P. H. Salus. Lingua 25.419–431.

———. 1971. Review of 1969 MLA bibliography of books and articles on the modern languages and literatures, vol. III: Linguistics, compiled by H. T. Messerole, W. R. Schmalstieg, et al. (= General Linguistics 10(4)). Lg 47(4).915–918.

———. 1972a. Review of Sprachwissenschaft: Der Gang uhrer Entwicklung von der Antike bis zur Gegenwart, ed. by H. Arens. Lg 48.428–445.

———. 1972b. Towards a historiography of linguistics: 19th and 20th century paradigms. AnL 14(7).255–280.

———. 1972c. Glossaries of linguistic terminology 1951–1971: An overview. Linguistische Berichte 18.30–38.

———. 1973a. Ferdinand de Saussure: Origin and development of his linguistic theory in Western studies of language: A contribution to the history and theory of linguistics. Schriften zur Linguistik, ed. by P. Hartmann, 7. Braunschweig, F. Vieweg; Elmsford, N. Y., Pergamon Press.

———. 1973b. Review of Les grandes courants de la linguistique moderne, by M. Leroy. GL 13(1).54–56. (In German.)

———. 1973c. Review of Linguistic variability and intellectual development, by

W. von Humboldt. Lg 49.682–685.

——. 1973d. Review of Pāṇini to Postal, by P. H. Salus. FL 10.589–594.

——. 1974. An annotated chronological bibliography of Western histories of linguistic thought, 1822–1972. Part I: 1822–1915; Part II: 1916–1961; Part III: 1962–1972. Historiographia Linguistica 1(1).81–94; 1(2).105–202; 1(3). 351–384.

KOLAKOWSKI, L. 1968. The alienation of reason: A history of positivist thought. Translated from the Polish by N. Guterman. Garden City, New York, Doubleday. (Anchor Books, 1969; Polish original, 1966.)

KROEBER, A. L. 1939. An outline of American Indian linguistics. American Council of Learned Societies Bulletin 29.116–120.

KUČERA, H. 1967. Distinctive features, simplicity, and descriptive adequacy. To Honor Roman Jakobson, 1114–1126, The Hague, Mouton. Reprinted in V. Becker Makkai (ed.) Phonological Theory: Evolution and current practice. 491–499. N.Y.: Holt, Rinehart & Winston.

KUHN, T. S. 1962. The structure of scientific revolutions. Chicago, University of Chicago Press. (2nd. ed., 1970.)

KURATH, H. 1945. Review of Outline of linguistic analysis, by B. Bloch and G. L. Trager. AJPh 66.206–210.

——. 1972. Area linguistics. Bloomington, Indiana University Press.

KURATH, H., and R. I. McDAVID, JR. 1961. The pronunciation of English in the Atlantic States. Ann Arbor, University of Michigan Press.

LABOV, W. 1970. The study of linguistics in its social context. Studium Generale 20.30–87. (Reprinted in Sociolinguistic patterns, by W. Labov, Ch. 8. Philadelphia, University of Pennsylvania Press.)

LAKATOS, J., and A. MUSGRAVE, eds. 1970. Criticism and the growth of knowledge. Cambridge, University Press.

LAKOFF, G. 1971. On generative semantics. In Semantics: An interdisciplinary reader in philosophy, linguistics, and psychology, ed. by D. D. Steinberg and L. A. Jakobovits, 232–296. Cambridge, University Press.

LAMB, S. M. 1966. Prolegomena to a theory of phonology. Lg 42.536–573. (Reprinted in Makkai (1972), 606–633.)

——. 1971. The crooked path of progress in cognitive linguistics. In Report of the 22nd Annual Round Table Meeting: Developments of the Sixties — Viewpoints for the Seventies, ed. by R. J. O'Brien, 99–123. MSLL 24. Washington, D.C., Georgetown University Press. (Reprinted in Readings in stratificational linguistics, ed. by A. Makkai and D. G. Lockwood (1973), 12–33. University, Alabama, University of Alabama Press.)

LANDAR, H. 1974. Native North America. In Current trends in linguistics, ed. by T. A. Sebeok, 13: Historiography of linguistics. The Hague, Mouton.

LANGDON, M. 1969. Review of Perspectives in linguistics, by J. T. Waterman. RomPh 22(4).566–572.

LANE, G. S. 1945. Changes of emphasis in linguistics with particular reference to Paul and Bloomfield. Studies in Philology 47.465–487.

——. 1949. On the recent state of Indo-European linguistics. Lg 25.333–342.

LANGENDOEN, D. T. 1969. Review of In memory of J. R. Firth, ed. by C. E. Bazell, J. C. Catford, M. A. K. Halliday, and R. H. Robins. FL 5.391–408.

LEES, R. B. 1957. Review of Syntactic structures, by N. Chomsky. Lg 33.375–408.

LEPSCHY, G. C. 1970. A survey of structural linguistics. London, Faber and Faber. (Revised from La linguistica strutturale. Turin, 1966.)

——. 1973. Review of A Leonard Bloomfield anthology, by C. F. Hockett. Linguistics 108.120–127.

LEROY, M. 1963. Les grands courants de la linguistique moderne. Université Libre de Bruxelles, Travaux de la Faculté de Philosophie et Lettres, 24 Brussels, Presses Universitaires de Bruxelles; Paris, Presses Universitaires de France. (Translated as Main trends in modern linguistics (1967). Berkeley, University of California Press; Oxford, Basil Blackwell.) (2nd French ed., 1971.)

LESSER, A. 1968. Boas, Franz. International Encyclopedia of the Social Sciences 2.99–110.

LÉVI-STRAUSS, C. 1958. Anthropologie structurale. Paris, Plon.

LÉVI-STRAUSS, C., R. JAKOBSON, C. F. VOEGELIN, and T. A. SEBEOK. 1953. Results of the conference of anthropologists and linguists. IUPAL: Memoirs of IJAL, 8. Bloomington.

LEVICH, M. 1962. Disagreement and controversy in history. History and theory 2(1).41–51. (Reprinted in Studies in the philosophy of history, ed. by G. H. Nadel, 35–45. New York, Harper Torchbooks, TB 1208.)

LEVIN, S. R. 1965. Langue and parole in American linguistics. FL 1.83–94.

LICHTHEIM, G. 1961. Marxism: An historical and critical study. London, Routledge and Kegan Paul.

LIGHTNER, T. 1968. Review of Readings in Linguistics, ed. by M. Joos (4th ed., 1966). GL 8(1).44–61.

Linguistic bibliography for the years 1939–1947. 2 vols. Utrecht and Antwerp, Spectrum, for the Permanent International Committee of Linguists. (Each subsequent year with supplement for previous years.)

LLORENTE MALDINADO DE GUEVARA, A. 1967. Teoría de la lengua e historia de la lingüística. Madrid, Ed. Alcalá.

LOJA, J. V. 1961. Valodniecības vēsture. Riga, Latvijas Valsts Izd.

——. 1968. Istorija lingvističeskix učenij: Materialy k kursu lekcij. Moscow, Vysšaja Škola.

LOUNSBURY, F. G. 1956. Semantic analysis of the Pawnee kinship usage. Lg 32.158–194.

——. 1960. Language. In Biennial review of anthropology 1959, ed. by B. J. Siegal, 185–209. Stanford, University Press.

——. 1962. Language. In Biennial review of anthropology 1961, ed. by B. J. Siegal, 279–322. Stanford, University Press.

——. 1968. One hundred years of anthropological linguistics. In One hundred years of anthropology, ed. by J. O. Brew, 153–225. Cambridge, Harvard University Press.

LOWIE, R. H. 1965. Letters from Edward Sapir to Robert H. Lowie. With an introduction and notes. Berkeley, privately printed.

LYONS, J. 1962. Phonemic and non-phonemic phonology: Some typological reflections. IJAL 28.127–134. (Reprinted in Makkai (1972), 275–281.)

——. 1965. Review of Trends in European and American linguistics 1930–1960, ed. by C. Mohrmann, A. Sommerfelt, and J. Whatmough. JL 1.87–92.

——. 1968. Introduction to theoretical linguistics. Cambridge, University Press.

——. 1969. Review of Les grands courants de la linguistique moderne, by M. Leroy (1967 ed.). Lg 45.105–108.

——. 1970. Noam Chomsky. New York, Viking Press.

MCCAWLEY, J. D. 1967. Sapir's phonological representation. IJAL 33.106–111.

MCDAVID, R. I., JR. 1951a. American dialect studies since 1939. Philologica 4.43–48.

——. 1951b. Two decades of the linguistic Atlas. JEGP 50.101–111.

——. 1953. Review of Outline of English structure, by G. L. Trager and H. L. Smith, Jr. JEGP 52.387–391.

——. 1958. (Chapter on dialect study.) In The structure of American English, by W. Nelson Francis. New York, Ronald.

——. 1960. Hans Kurath. Orbis 9.597–610.

MCQUOWN, N. A. 1952. Review of Methods in structural linguistics, by Z. S. Harris. Lg 28.495–504.

——. 1968. Morris Swadesh 1909–1967. AA 70.755–756.

MAHER, J. P. 1973. Review of Linguistic change and generative theory, ed. by R. P. Stockwell and R. K. S. Macaulay. LS 25.47–52.

MAKKAI, A. 1972. Idiom structure in English. The Hague, Mouton.

MAKKAI, A., and D. G. LOCKWOOD, eds. 1973. Readings in stratificational linguistics. University, Alabama, University of Alabama Press.

MAKKAI, V. B., ed. 1972. Phonological theory: Evolution and current practice. New York, Holt, Rinehart and Winston.

MALÉCOT, A., and P. LLOYD. 1968. The /t/:/d/ distinction in American alveolar flaps. Lingua 19.264–272.

MALKIEL, Y. 1959. Review of Language, thought, and culture, ed. by P. Henle. IJAL 25.122–133.

——. 1962–1963. Leonard Bloomfield in retrospect. RomPh 16.83–91. (Reprinted in Essays on linguistic theories, by Y. Malkiel (1968), 165–174. Oxford, University Press.) (A review essay on Bloomfield and C. L. Barnhart, Let's read: A linguistic approach (1961).)

——. 1964a. Distinctive features of Romance linguistics. In Language in culture and society, ed. by D. Hymes, 671–688. New York, Harper and Row.

——. 1964b. Bibliographic notes: History of linguistics. RomPh 17(4).823–828.

——. 1967. Uriel Weinreich. Lg 43.605–611.

——. 1968. Leonard Bloomfield in retrospect. In Essays on linguistic themes, 165–174. Oxford, University Press.

——. 1970. Linguistics (including its history) and the humanist: Two new approaches to a fluid relationship. RomPh 23.223–235.

——. 1972. Linguistics and philology in Spanish America: A survey (1925–1970). (Janua Linguarum, series minor, 97.) The Hague, Mouton.

MALKIEL, Y., and M. LANGDON. 1969. History and histories of linguistics. RomPh 22(4).530–573. (Malkiel, parts I–III, 532–566, Langdon, part IV, 566–572.)

MALMBERG, B. 1959. Nya vägar inom språkforskningen: En orientering i modern lingvistik. Stockholm, Svenska Bokförlaget. (2nd ed., 1962; 3rd ed., 1966.)

——. 1964. New trends in linguistics: An orientation. Stockholm and Lund. (Translation of Malmberg, 1959.)

MANDELBAUM, D. G., ed. 1949. Selected writings of Edward Sapir in language, culture, and personality. Berkeley, University of California Press.

MANNING, C. 1957. A history of Slavic studies in the United States. Milwaukee.

MARCKWARDT, A. H. 1962. Opportunity and obligation. Lg 38(3), pt. 2; Supplementary Bulletin 35.

——. 1968. C. C. Fries. Lg 44.205–208.

MARSHALL, J. C. 1970. Review of Mentalism and objectivism in linguistics, by E. A. Esper. Semiotica 3.277–294.

MARTIN, S. E. 1951. Korean phonemics. Lg 27.519–533. (Reprinted in Joos (1957), 364–371.)

MARTINET, A. 1949. About structural sketches. Word 5.13–35.

——. 1950. Review of Morphology, by E. A. Nida. Word 6.84–87.

——. 1953. Structural linguistics. In Anthropology today, by A. L. Kroeber et al., 574–586. Chicago, University of Chicago Press.

——. 1955. Économie des changements phonétiques. Berne, Francke.

MARX, K., and F. ENGELS. 1942. Selected correspondence, 1846–1895. Translated by Dona Torr. New York, International Publishers.

MATTHEWS, P. H. 1972. Inflectional morphology: A theoretical study based on aspects of Latin verb conjugation. Cambridge Series in Linguistics, 6. Cambridge, University Press.

MEAD, M. 1952. Review of Methods in structural linguistics, by Z. S. Harris. IJAL 18.257–260.

——. 1959. An anthropologist at work: Writings of Ruth Benedict. Boston, Houghton, Mifflin.

MEAD, M. 1974. Ruth Benedict. New York, Columbia University Press.

MEHTA, V. 1971. John is easy to please: Encounters with the written and spoken word. New York, Farrar, Straus and Giroux.

MESSING, G. H. 1951. Structuralism and literary tradition. Lg 27.1–12.

MILLER, J. 1973. A note on so-called 'discovery procedures'. FL 10.123–139.

MILLER, R. A. 1970. Bernard Bloch on Japanese. Ed. with an introduction and analytic index, by R. A. Miller. New Haven and London, Yale University Press.

MOHRMANN, C., A. SOMMERFELT, and J. WHATMOUGH, eds. 1961. Trends in European and American linguistics 1930–1960. Utrecht, Spectrum.

MOULTON, W. G. 1961. Linguistics and language teaching in the United States. In Mohrmann et al., 82–109.

———. 1966. (The Linguistic Society of America, 1924 through 1966.) Lg 42. 855–856.

———. 1967. Leonard Bloomfield as Germanist. In A Leonard Bloomfield anthology, ed. by C. F. Hockett, 512–523. Bloomington, Indiana University Press.

———. 1969. The nature and history of linguistics. In Linguistics today, ed. by A. A. Hill, Ch. 1. New York, Basic Books.

MOUNIN, G. 1967. Histoire de la linguistique: Des origines au XXe siècle. (= Le Linguiste, 4.) Paris, Presses Univ. de France.

———. 1972. La linguistique du XXe siècle. (= Le Linguiste, 13.) Paris, Presses Univ. de France.

MUNDELL, G. H. 1973. A history of American dialectology. Ph. D. dissertation, University of Rochester. Ann Arbor, University Microfilms, 73–25, 838.

———. ms. (1973). A history of American dialectology.

MUNZ, J. 1972. Reflections on the development of transformational theories. In Transformational analysis: The transformational theory of Zellig Harris and its development, ed. by S. Plötz, 251–274. Frankfurt/Main, Athenäum Verlag.

NEHRING, A. 1962. Strukturalismus und Sprachgeschichte. Innsbrucker Beiträge zur Kulturwissenschaft 15.21–30.

NEUSTUPNÝ, J. 1975. E. Haugen and the history of sociolinguistics. (Review of The Ecology of language, by E. Haugen.) Lg 51.236–242. (Preprint in Linguistic Communications 11.74–88 (1973). Clayton, Victoria, Monash University.)

NEWMAN, S. S. 1932a. The Yawelmani dialect of Yokuts. IJAL 7.85–89.

———. 1932b. A grammar of Yokuts, an American Indian language of California. Unpublished Ph.D. dissertation, New Haven, Yale University.

———. 1944. Yokuts language of California. Viking Fund Publications in Anthropology, 2. New York, Viking Fund.

———. 1947. Bella Coola, I: Phonology. IJAL 13.129–134.

———. 1950. Review of Kwakiutl grammar with a glossary of the suffixes, by Franz Boas. IJAL 16.99–101.

———. 1951. Review of Selected writings of Edward Sapir in language, culture,

and personality, ed. by D. Mandelbaum. IJAL 17.180–186.
——. 1952. Review of Methods in structural linguistics, by Z. S. Harris. AA 54.404–405.
——. 1954a. Review of Anthropology today, by A. L. Kroeber et al. IJAL 20. 154–160.
——. 1954b. Semantic problems in grammatical systems and lexemes: A search for method. In Hoijer (ed.) (1954), 82–91.
——. 1967. Morris Swadesh. Lg 48.948–957.
NIDA, E. A. 1944. Morphology, the descriptive analysis of words. 2 vols. Glendale, California, Summer Institute of Linguistics.
——. 1946. Morphology, the descriptive analysis of words. University of Michigan Publications, Linguistics II. Ann Arbor, University of Michigan Press.
——. 1948. The identification of morphemes. Lg 24.414–441.
——. 1949. Morphology: The descriptive analysis of words. Second and completely new edition, based on actual-language materials. University of Michigan Publications, Linguistics II. Ann Arbor, University of Michigan Press. (1st ed., 1946.)
O'BRIEN, R. J., ed. 1971. Report of the 22nd Annual Round Table Meeting: Developments of the Sixties — Viewpoints for the Seventies. MSLL 24. Washington, D.C., Georgetown University Press.
OLLER, J. W., JR., and B. D. SALES. 1969. Conceptual restrictions on English: A psycholinguistic study. Lingua 23.209-232.
ÖLLMAN, B. 1971. Alienation: Marx's conception of man in capitalist society. Cambridge, University Press.
OLMSTED, D. L. 1970. Review of Mentalism and objectivism in linguistics: The sources of Leonard Bloomfield's psychology of language, by E. A. Esper. Lg 46.131–140.
PANDIT, P. B. 1970. Review of Selected papers of J. R. Firth 1952–1959, ed. by F. R. Palmer. JL 6.280–284.
PAUL, H. 1920. Prinzipien der Sprachgeschichte. 5th ed. Halle.
PEI, M. 1944. The state of linguistics: Reply to a mechanist. Italica 23.237–240.
PERCIVAL, W. K. 1968 (ms.). On the historical source of immediate constitutent analysis.
——. 1970. Review of On language: Plato to von Humboldt, ed. by P. H. Salus. GL 10.51–56.
PIKE, K. L. 1947a. Phonemics: A technique for reducing languages to writing. University of Michigan Publications, Linguistics 3. Ann Arbor, University of Michigan Press.
——. 1947b. Grammatical prerequisites to phonemic analysis. Word 3.155–172. (Reprinted in Makkai (1972), 153–165).
——. 1947c. On the phonemic status of English dipthongs. Lg 23.151–159. (Reprinted in Makkai (1972), 145–151.)

——. 1966. A guide to publications related to tagmemic theory. In Current trends in linguistics 3, ed. by T. A. Sebeok, 365–394. The Hague, Mouton.

——. 1967. Language in relation to a unified theory of the structure of human behavior. The Hague, Mouton. (First issued Santa Ana, California, Summer Institute of Linguistics, 1954, 1955, 1960, in 3 parts; slightly revised.)

PIKE, K. L., and E. V. PIKE. 1960–1967. Live issues in descriptive linguistics. Santa Ana, California, Summer Institute of Linguistics.

POSNER, R. 1970. Supplement: Thirty years on. In Iorgu Iordan and John Orr, An introduction to Romance linguistics, its schools and scholars, 395–579. Oxford, Basil Blackwell. 2nd ed.

POSTAL, P. M. 1964a. Constituent structure: A study of contemporary models of syntactic description. IJAL 30(1), part III. Indiana University Research Center in Anthropology, Folklore, and Linguistics, Publication 30.

——. 1964b. Boas and the development of phonology: Some comments based on Iroquoian. IJAL 30.269–280.

——. 1966. Review of Elements of general linguistics, by A. Martinet. FL 2.151–186.

——. 1968. Aspects of phonological theory. New York, Harper and Row.

——. 1969. Review of Patterns of language, by A. McIntosh and M. A. K. Halliday. FL 5.409–426.

——. 1974. On raising: One rule of English grammar and its theoretical implications. Cambridge, Mass., M.I.T. Press.

POUND, L. 1952. The American dialect society: an historical sketch. PAPhilosS 17.3–28.

PRESTON, R. J. 1966. Edward Sapir's anthropology: Style, structure, and method. AA 68.1105–1128.

PRESTON, W. D. 1948. Review of Morphology: The descriptive analysis of words, by E. A. Nida. IJAL 14.56–57.

PULLUM, G. K. 1973. Yokuts bibliography: An addendum. IJAL 39.269–271.

(Recherches structurales.) 1949. Recherches structurales 1949. Interventions dans le débat glossématique. Publiées à l'occasion du cinquantenaire de M. Louis Hjelmslev. Travaux du Cercle linguistique de Copenhague, 5. Copenhagen, Nordisk Sprog- og Kulturforlag.

REID, T. B. 1956. Linguistics, structuralism and philology. ArchL 8.28–37.

——. 1960. Historical philology and linguistic science: An inaugural lecture. Oxford, Clarendon Press.

ROBINS, R. H. 1964. General linguistics: An introductory survey. London, Longmans.

——. 1967. A short history of linguistics. London, Longmans, Green. (Bloomington, Indiana University Press, 1968.)

——. 1973. Review of Les grandes courants de la linguistique moderne, by M. Leroy (1967 ed.). AA 75.1085–1086.

ROLLINS, P. C. 1971. Benjamin Lee Whorf: Transcendental linguist. Unpublished Ph. D. dissertation, Cambridge, Harvard University.

RUTHERFORD, P. R. 1966. Linguistic research in American universities: Dissertations and influences from 1900 to 1964. Commerce, Texas, East Texas State University.

SALUS, P. H., ed. 1969. On language: Plato to von Humboldt. New York, Holt, Rinehart and Winston.

——. 1971. Pāṇini to Postal: A bibliography in the history of linguistics. Linguistic bibliography Series 2. Edmunton, Linguistic Research Inc.

SAMPSON, G. 1970. Review of The study of syntax, by D. T. Langendoen. JL 6.267–277.

SAPIR, E. 1916. Time perspective in aboriginal American culture: A study in method. Canada Department of Mines, Geological Survey, Memoir 90; Anthropological Series, 13. Ottawa. (Reprinted in Mandelbaum (1949), 389–462.)

——. 1917. Linguistic publications of the Bureau of American Ethnology: A general review. IJAL 1.76–81.

——. 1921. Language. New York, Harcourt, Brace.

——. 1922. Takelma. Handbook of American Indian languages, ed. by F. Boas, 3–296. Bureau of American Ethnology, Bulletin 40, part 2. Washington, D.C.

——. 1925. Sound patterns in language. Lg 1.37–51. (Reprinted in Mandelbaum (1949), 33–45; in Joos (1957), 19–25; and in Makkai (1972), 13–21.)

——. 1930. Totality. Language Monographs, 6. Baltimore, Linguistic Society of America.

——. 1931. The concept of phonetic law as tested in primitive languages by Leonard Bloomfield. In Methods in social science: A case book, ed. by S. A. Rice, 297–306. Chicago. (Reprinted in Mandelbaum (1949), 73–82.)

——. 1933a. Language. Encyclopedia of Social Science 9.155–169. (Reprinted in Mandelbaum (1949), 7–32.)

——. 1933b. La réalité psychologique des phonèmes. Journal de Psychologie Normale et Pathologique 30.247–265. (Reprinted in Mandelbaum (1949), 46–60; and in Makkai (1972), 22–31.)

——. 1944. Grading: A study in semantics. Philosophy of Science 11.93–116. (Reprinted in Mandelbaum (1949), 122–149.)

——. 1947. The relation of American Indian linguistics to general linguistics. Southwestern Journal of Anthropology 3.1–4.

SAPIR, E., and M. SWADESH. 1932. The expression of the ending-point relation in English, French and German. Ed. by Alice V. Morris. Language Monographs, 10. Baltimore, Linguistic Society of America.

SCHANE, S. A. 1971. The phoneme revisited. Lg. 47.503–521.

SCHLAUCH, M. 1946. Early behaviorist psychology and contemporary linguistics. Word 2.25–36.

——. 1947. Mechanism and historical materialism in semantic studies. Science and Society 11.144–167.

SCHNELLE, H. 1969. Review of Kursbuch, Vol. 5, ed. by H. M. Enzensberger. FL 5.449–453.

SCHOLTE, BOB. 1973. Toward a reflextive and critical anthropology. In Reinventing anthropology, ed. by D. Hymes, 430–457. New York, Pantheon.

SEARLE, J. 1972. Chomsky's revolution in linguistics. New York Review of Books 18(12).16–25.

SEBEOK, T. A., ed. 1966. Portraits of linguists: A biographical source book for the history of Western linguistics, 1746–1963. 2 vols. Bloomington, Indiana University Press.

SILVERSTEIN, M. 1972. Linguistic theory: Syntax, semantics, pragmatics. Annual Review of Anthropology 1.349–382.

——. ms. (1973). 'Distinctive features' in Leonard Bloomfield's phonology. (To appear in a volume honoring Clarence Edward Parmenter.)

SLEDD, J. 1955. Review of An outline of English structure, by G. L. Trager and H. L. Smith, Jr. Lg 31.312–335.

SPERBER, H. 1960. Linguistics in a strait-jacket. MLN 75.239–252.

SPIER, L., A. I. HALLOWELL, S. S. NEWMAN, eds. 1941. Language, culture, and personality: Essays in memory of Edward Sapir. Menasha, Wisc., Banta. (Reprinted 1960. Salt Lake City, University of Utah Press.)

SPITZER, L. 1946. The state of linguistics: Crisis or reaction? MLN 71.497–502.

STANKIEWICZ, E. 1966. Slavic morphophonemics in its typological and diachronic aspect. In Current trends in linguistics, ed. by T. A. Sebeok, 3.495–520. The Hague, Mouton.

STARK, B. R. 1972. The Bloomfieldian model. Lingua 30.385–421.

STARKE, P. A. 1972. On characterizing contrast. LS 22.17–20.

STEPHENSON, E. A. 1969. Schools of modern linguistics: Is a rapprochement possible? Emory University Quarterly 23(4).222–261, 261–2 (discussion).

STOCKING, G. W. 1968a. Race, culture, and evolution: Essays on the history of anthropology. New York, Free Press.

——. 1968b. Franz Boas collection. The American Indian: A conference in the American Philosophical Society Library, 1–19. Philadelphia.

——, ed. 1974a. The shaping of American anthropology, 1833–1911. A Franz Boas reader. New York, Basic Books.

——. 1974b. The Boas plan for American Indian languages: A preliminary historical examination. In Studies in the history of linguistics, ed. by D. Hymes, 454–484. Bloomington, Indiana University Press.

STUART, C. I. J. M. n.d. Foreword. Introduction to the Handbook of American Indian Languages, by Franz Boas, vii–xiv. Washington, D.C., Georgetown University Press.

STURTEVANT, E. H. 1940. Report of the special committee on the Linguistic Institute. Linguistic Society of America, Bulletin 13: 83–101.

———. 1947. An introduction to linguistic science. New Haven, Yale University Press.

———. 1950. Leonard Bloomfield. Yearbook of the American Philosophical Society (1949), 302–305.

SWADESH, M. 1933. The internal economy of the Nootka word: A semantic study of word structure in a polysynthetic language. Unpublished Ph.D. dissertation, New Haven, Yale University.

———. 1934. The phonemic principle. Lg 10.117–129. (Reprinted in Joos (1957), 32–37; and in Makkai (1972), 32–39.)

———. 1939a. Edward Sapir. Lg 15.132–135.

———. 1939b. Nootka internal syntax. IJAL 9.77–192.

———. 1948a. On linguistic mechanism. Science and Society 12.254–259.

———. 1948b. Review of Kwakiutl grammar with a glossary of the suffixes, by F. Boas. Word 4.58–63.

TAGLIAVINI, C. 1970. Panorama di storia della linguistica. 3rd rev. ed. Bologna, R. Patròn.

TAX, S., L. C. EISELEY, I. ROUSE, and C. F. VOEGELIN, eds. 1953. An appraisal of anthropology today. Chicago, University of Chicago Press.

TEETER, K. V. 1964a. Descriptive linguistics in America: Triviality vs. irrelevance. Word 20.197–206.

———. 1964b. Anthropological linguistics and linguistic anthropology. AA 66. 878–880.

———. 1965. Review of Perspectives on linguistics, by J. T. Waterman. Lg 41. 512–518.

———. 1966. The history of linguistics: New lamps for old. Report of the 17th annual round table meeting on linguistics and language studies: Problems in semantics, history of linguistics, linguistics and English, ed. by F. P. Dinneen, 83–95. MSLL 19. Washington, D.C., Georgetown University Press.

———. 1969. Leonard Bloomfield's linguistics. LS 7.1–6.

———. 1970a. Review of The Menomini language, by L. Bloomfield. Lg 46.524–533.

———. 1970b. Review of The Menomini language, by L. Bloomfield. IJAL 36. 235–239.

THORNE, J. P. 1965. Review of Constituent structure: A study of contemporary models of syntactic description, by P. Postal. JL 1.73–76.

TIMPANARO, S. 1970. Sul materialismo. Saggi di varia umanità, 12. Pisa, Nistri-Lischi.

TOGEBY, K. 1953. Review of Methods in structural linguistics, by Z. S. Harris. MLN 68.190–194.

TRAGER, F. H. 1972. Review of Method and theory in linguistics, ed. by P. L. Garvin. AA 74.95–96.

TRAGER, G. L. 1940. Review of Phonologie: Een hoofdstuk uit de structurele taalwetenschap, by N. van Wijk. Lg 16.247–251.

——. 1941. Review of La catégorie des cas, by L. Hjelmslev. Lg 17.172–174.

——. 1942. The phoneme 't': A study in theory and method. AS 17.144–148.

——. 1945. Analysis of a Kechuan text. IJAL 11.86–96.

——. 1946. Changes of emphasis in linguistics: A comment. Studies in Philology 48.461–464.

——. 1948a. Review of Lingua. IJAL 14.207–209.

——. 1948b. Taos, I: A language revisited. IJAL 14.155–160.

——. 1950a. Review of Recherches structurales 1949. Studies in Linguistics 8.99.

——. 1950b. Review of Phonemics: A technique for reducing languages to writing, by K. L. Pike. Lg 26.152–158.

——. 1951. Review of Morphology: The descriptive analysis of words, by E. A. Nida. IJAL 17.126–131.

——. 1953. Review of Oneida verb morphology, by F. G. Lounsbury. Studies in Linguistics 11.93–96.

——. 1955. French morphology: Verb inflection. Lg 31.511–529.

——. 1959. Review of A course in modern linguistics, by C. F. Hockett. Studies in Linguistics 14.77–81.

——. 1968a. Review of The state of the art, by C. F. Hockett. Studies in Linguistics 20.77–84.

——. 1968b. Whorf, Benjamin L. International Encyclopedia of the Social Sciences 16.536–538.

——. 1970. Language and languages. San Francisco, Chandler.

TRAGER, G. L., and B. BLOCH. 1941. The syllabic phonemes of English. Lg 17.223–246. (Reprinted in Makkai (1972), 72–89.)

TRAGER, G. L., and H. A. SMITH, JR. 1951. An outline of English structure. Studies in linguistics, Occasional papers, 3. Norman, Oklahoma, University of Oklahoma Press. (Reprinted, Washington, D.C., ACLS, 1956.)

TWADDELL, W. F. 1935. On defining the phoneme. Language Monograph, 16. Baltimore, Linguistic Society of America. (Reprinted in Joos (1957), 55–80.)

URMSON, J. O. 1956. Philosophical analysis: Its development between the two world wars. Oxford, Clarendon Press.

VACHEK, J. 1949. Yaleska škola a strukturalistická fonologie. Slovo a Slovenost 11.36–44.

——. 1967. Review of Osnovnye napravlenija strukturalizma, ed. by M. M. Guxman and V. N. Guxman. Linguistics 37.117–125.

VALESIO, P. 1967. Aspetti della tradizione linguistica negli Stati Uniti. Verri 24.35–74.

VERBURG, P. A. 1974. Vicissitudes of paradigms. In Studies in the history of linguistics, ed. by D. Hymes, 191–230. Bloomington, Indiana University Press.

VOEGELIN, C. F. 1940. Review of Etudes phonologiques dédiées à la mémoire de M. Le Prince N. S. Trubetzkoy. Lg 16.251–257.

——. 1942. Sapir: Insight and rigor. AA 44.322–324.

——. 1948a. A sample of technical terms in linguistics. IJAL 14.115–130.

——. 1948b. Distinctive features and meaning equivalence. Lg 24.132–135.

——. 1949a. Review of Morphology: The descriptive analysis of words, by E. A. Nida. IJAL 15.75–85.

——. 1949b. Linguistics without meaning and culture without words. Word 5.36–42.

——. 1949c. A decade of American Indian linguistic studies. PAPhilosS 93(2).137–140.

——. 1951. Culture, language and the human organism. Southwestern Journal of Anthropology 7.357–373.

——. 1952a. The Boas plan for the presentation of American Indian languages. PAPhilosS 96.439–451.

——. 1952b. Edward Sapir. Word Study 27.1–3. (Reprinted in Portraits of linguists, ed. by T. A. Sebeok (1966), 2.489–492. Bloomington, Indiana University Press.)

——. 1952c. Review of Methods in structural linguistics, by Z. S. Harris. JAOS 72.113–114.

——. 1952d. Linguistically marked distinctions in meaning. In Indian tribes of aboriginal North America, ed. by Sol Tax, 222–233. Chicago, University of Chicago Press.

——. 1958a. Meaning correlations and selections in morphology-syntax paradigms. BIHPAS 29.91–111.

——. 1958b. Review of Joos 1957. IJAL 24.86.

——. 1958c. Review of Syntactic structures, by N. Chomsky. IJAL 24.229–230.

——. 1959a. Review of Eastern Ojibwa, by L. Bloomfield. Lg 35.109–125.

——. 1959b. The notion of arbitrariness in structural statement and restatement, I: Eliciting. IJAL 25.207–220.

——. 1965. Sociolinguistics, ethnolinguistics and anthropological linguistics. AA 76.484–485.

——. 1974. Review of A Leonard Bloomfield anthology, ed. by C. F. Hockett; Mentalism and objectivism in linguistics: The sources of Leonard Bloomfield's psychology of language, by E. A. Esper; and Review of A Leonard Bloomfield anthology, by Z. S. Harris. Ms.

VOEGELIN, C. F., and Z. S. HARRIS. 1945a. The scope of linguistics. AA 49. 588–600.

——. 1945b. Index to the Franz Boas collection of materials for American linguistics. Language Monographs, 22. Baltimore, Linguistic Society of America.

VOEGELIN, C. F., and D. HYMES. 1953. A sample of North American Indian dictionaries with reference to acculturation. PAPhilosS 97.634–644.

VOEGELIN, C. F., and J. E. PIERCE. 1953. Review of The nature of culture, by A. L. Kroeber; Culture, a critical review of concepts and definitions, by A. L.

Kroeber and C. Kluckhohn. IJAL 19.237–242.

VOEGELIN, C. F., and F. M. VOEGELIN. 1957. Hopi domains: A lexical approach to the problem of selection. IUPAL Memoirs of IJAL, 14. Bloomington.

——. 1963. On the history of structuralizing in 20th century America. AnL 5(1).12–35.

WALLACE, A. F. C. 1972. Paradigmatic processes in culture change. AA 74. 467–478.

WATERMAN, J. T. 1957. Benjamin Lee Whorf and linguistic field theory. Southwestern Journal of Anthropology 13.201–211.

——. 1963. Perspectives in linguistics: An account of the background of modern linguistics. Chicago, University of Chicago Press.

——. 1970. Perspectives in linguistics: An account of the background of modern linguistics. 2nd rev. ed. Chicago, University of Chicago Press.

WEINREICH, U. 1959. Mid-century linguistics: Attainments and frustrations. Review of A course in modern linguistics, by C. F. Hockett. RomPh 13.320–341.

WELLS, R. S. 1947a. De Saussure's system of linguistics. Word 3.1–31. (Reprinted in Joos (1957), 1–18).

——. 1947b. Immediate constituents. Lg 23.321–343. (Reprinted in Joos (1957), 229–242.)

——. 1949. Review of Human knowledge by B. Russell and The philosophy of E. Cassirer, ed. by P. Schilpp. Lg 25.322–325.

——. 1951. Review of Recherches structurales 1949. Lg 27.554–570.

——. 1954. Meaning and use. Word 10.235–250.

——. 1958. To what extent can meaning be said to be structured? In proceedings of the Eighth International Congress of Linguists (Oslo, 1957), ed. by E. Sivertsen, 655–666. Oslo.

——. 1963. Some neglected opportunities in descriptive linguistics. AnL 5(1). 38–49.

——. 1971. Distinctively human semiotic. In Essays in semiotics/Essais de sémiotique, ed. by J. Kristeva, J. Rey-Debove, and D. J. Umiker, 95–119. The Hague, Mouton. (First published in Information sur les sciences sociales 6 (1967)/7 (1968). The Hague, Mouton, for Unesco.)

——. 1974. Phonetics in the Nineteenth Century, 1876–1900. In Studies in the history of linguistics, ed. by D. Hymes, 434–453. Bloomington, Indiana University Press. (Presented to Conference on the history of anthropology, Social Science Research Council, 1962, as "Phonemics in the nineteenth century, 1876–1900".)

——. ms. (ca. 1948). History of the phoneme concept. (Cited in A set of postulates for phonemic analysis, by B. Bloch (1948) 9, n. 14, who adopts a term from it.)

WHEATLEY, J. 1964. Meaning and meaningfulness in Fries. CJL 9.83–97.

WHITEHALL, H. 1944. Some languages are better than others. Review of The loom of language, by F. Bodmer. Kenyon Review 6(4).672–676.

WHITMAN, R. H. 1973. Review of Selected writings I, II, by Roman Jakobson, and Roman Jakobson: A bibliography of his writings, with a foreword by C. H. van Schooneveld. Lg 49.679–682.

WHORF, B. L. 1938. Some verbal categories of Hopi. Lg 14.275–286.

——. 1941. Linguistics as an exact science. Technology Review (M.I.T.) 43. 61–63, 80–83. (Reprinted in Language, thought, and reality: Selected writings of Benjamin Lee Whorf, ed. by J. B. Carroll (1956), 220–232. Cambridge, M.I.T. Press.)

——. 1943. Phonemic analysis of the English of eastern Massachusetts. Studies in linguistics 2.21–40. (Written in 1940.)

——. 1945. Grammatical categories. Lg 21.1–11. (Written in 1937.)

——. 1950. Four articles on metalinguistics. Washington, D.C., Foreign Service Institute, Department of State.

——. 1956. A linguistic consideration of thinking in primitive communities. In Language in culture and society, ed. by D. Hymes (1964), 129–140. (Written ca. 1936.)

WILLIAMS, R. 1965. The long revolution. London, Pelican Books.

WOLFF, H. 1952. Osage, I: Phonemes and historical phonology. IJAL 18.63–68.

WONDERLY, W. L. 1951. Zoque, II: Phonemes and morphophonemes. IJAL 17.105–123.

WONDERLY, W. L., and E. A. NIDA. 1963. Linguistics and Christian missions. AnL 5(1).104–144.

WOOLFSON, A. P. 1970. An examination of Sapir's concept of language in the light of ethological theory and Piagetian developmental psychology. LS 11.8–10.

ZVEGINCEV, V. A. 1956. Khrestomatija po istorii jazykoznanija XIX–XX vekov. Moscow.

——. 1960. Istorija jazykoznanija XIX i XX vekov v očerkax i izvlečenijax. 2 vols. Moscow. (Revised ed., 1964–1965.)

INDEX TO PERIODICALS MENTIONED

INDEX TO ORGANIZATIONS